The Mystery

Are you satisfied with your life? Do yo
ahead and new things to look forwarc
unfulfilled expectations? Have you come to terms with who you
are and what life is about?

For over ten years, Ron Goldschlager has been exploring the idea of happiness and questioning what living and life are all about, searching for meaning and value. He challenges the superficiality of mundane and material existence, devoid of spiritual dimension and plays with the concept of rules, restrictions and limitations in societies and communities.

Ron wants to help people to improve their lives by exciting their imaginations to experience new, positive and creative growth as well as personal satisfaction.

In *The Mystery of You* many important issues are explored:

> What is happening to humanity?

> What kind of individuals and communities are we producing?

> What have morality and ethics got to do with everyday living?

> What is life about and how can we solve many of our deep, personal dilemmas to improve the quality of our lives?

the Mystery of You

A journey through the paradoxes of life

Ron Goldschlager and Adin Steinsaltz

HYBRID
PUBLISHERS

Published by Hybrid Publishers

Melbourne Victoria Australia

© Ron Goldschlager, Adin Steinsaltz 2010

PO Box 52, Ormond VIC 3204, Australia.
www.hybridpublishers.com.au

First published 2010

National Library of Australia Cataloguing-in-Publication data:
Author: Goldschlager, Ronald.
Title: The mystery of you : living life /
Ronald Goldschlager, Adin Steinsaltz.

ISBN: 9781876462987 (hbk.)

Subjects: Ethics. Jewish philosophy.
Other Authors/Contributors: Steinsaltz, Adin.
Dewey Number: 170

Cover design: © Dynamic Creations

All paintings in this book and on the cover by © Victor Majzner
Photo of Rabbi Steinsaltz on last page by © Emmanuel Santos
www.mysteryofyou.com

Contents

⚘

Life is like a roller coaster
Pulling us along
Driving us at rapid pace
No song, no face, just race!

Perceptions do become the rule
No time to dig, just run
The superficiality – routine becomes reality
Daily normality – no fun.

A break, a rest, some time to jest
To sleep, to breathe at best.
To search for depth, to keep, to make
Life full of what to take?

We work and play, we move and stay
Each day another challenge –
We live, we search, we hope, we find, we hold –

The truth be told

We trust, we grow, we mellow.

Ron Goldschlager

Introduction

How young are you? Are you satisfied with your life? Do you have fresh challenges ahead and new things to look forward to? Are you suffering from unfulfilled expectations? Have you come to terms with who you are and what life is about?

I am already closer to sixty years *young* rather than fifty years *old*. Sounds like a contradiction? I don't think so.

I have been writing these thoughts for well over ten years now; a bit here and some more there. It has been challenging as well as fun. My thoughts rush through my mind, but move from pen to paper ever so slowly. I print each word in bold characters, letter by letter. No clear plan initially, just a flow of ideas and experiences. My left hand struggles to keep up and smudges over the inked lines written on the sheets of paper as it steers my pen.

Although I have a very busy life with no spare time, I always have the impulse to write: a bit in airplanes, some more during vacations, occasionally taking an hour off on the run or late at night. Even a few minutes in the car, in between the normal rush, but always moving forward, finding just little snippets of time to write, then to write a bit more and to write in between everything else.

Thomas Nisell is more like a brother than a friend. Affectionately called *Schwedi* (Swede, in Hebrew), he made *aliyah* (immigration; literally – "ascent") to Israel from his native Sweden. We have much more than salmon, herrings and fine whisky in common. Thomas is blessed to be the personal assistant of Rabbi Adin Even Yisrael Steinsaltz. I am indeed fortunate to have Thomas as a brother and the Rabbi as a soul mate.

The Rabbi read these chapters in draft form. We had an amazing time together at the Vatican in Rome over six years ago at an interfaith dialogue; we stayed there for nearly a week and made time to work on this book. I will never forget one particular session one afternoon. We were sitting by an old wooden table in the old kitchen of the old gatehouse in the beautiful garden of the old Piccolomini Estate, next to St Peter's. We became silent and just looked at each other. We felt exhausted.

I noticed the time. It was starting to get darker outside. We had been discussing and thinking and talking intensely for over three and a half hours in that session, yet it seemed like no time at all. We had battled about the nature of the *yetzer ha-ra* (evil inclination) as against the *yetzer ha-tov* (the good inclination). It was a formidable battle. I felt weightless. I was just floating around the room feeling totally exhausted. It was difficult to keep my eyes open. I felt like drifting off to sleep.

It was time for *Mincha* (the afternoon prayer). The Rabbi just looked at me with those incredible eyes of his – eyes that can see what others do not see, eyes filled with caring, love and compassion, eyes which were tearing, eyes revealing a depth of human understanding beyond our normal experience.

I met Yehudit Shabta in Jerusalem only about four years ago. She was recommended to me by my friend Thomas Nisell. Yehudit had spent many years working in the Steinsaltz institutions. She is a translator and editor with much practical experience, which includes working on many of the Rabbi's books. Prior to my visit, we sent her a draft copy of my writings for preliminary evaluation.

It was *motzei Shabbat* (Saturday night, after the Sabbath is over). We had arranged to meet in the lobby of my hotel – a public place, yet somewhere where we could talk. Somehow, we seemed to recognise each other and sat down at a table. We ordered weak black teas and started talking. We seemed to feel comfortable. I showed her photos of my family. When we got to the subject of this book, Yehudit was very polite. Without wishing to cause any offence, she softly tried to explain that she didn't think she could do the job. We agreed to meet at the Rabbi's office the next morning.

I arrived first and had a coffee with Schwedi. "*Nu?*" he asked me. "How did it go?" I explained our discussions and said that I didn't think Yehudit would be able to edit this book.

"Why?"

Because her world was too far away from my world and she really was not my primary audience, I heard myself respond. I am not a writer and my work is not presented in any conventional, logical manner.

Then Yehudit arrived. Same questions. She looked at me.

"Please, Yehudit," I said, "please, just tell it the way you see it and the way you feel." The Rabbi called us into his study and we sat down. He was puffing at his pipe in his characteristically Steinsaltz fashion. He was surrounded by piles of books and manuscripts. We were all multilingual and very comfortable together, but decided to speak in Hebrew because I thought that this would be the most natural for Yehudit on this occasion.

Same questions, this time from the Rabbi. Yehudit looked at me. I encouraged her just to tell him the way it was.

Yehudit looked at the Rabbi, then at me and back at the Rabbi.

"*Ze lo mesudar.*" (Literally: it is not orderly; meaning: it's a mess and I really can't do this.)

The Rabbi looked at her with those eyes of his. It was as if he could read inside her mind. He said to her, "I think this will be good for you to do."

"I don't understand," she meekly responded.

"I think that this will be a very good thing for you to do," he repeated.

"But, I don't understand,", she offered. "*Ze lo mesudar.*"

The Rabbi smiled and asked her in his soft, very human voice. "Have you ever seen a Japanese garden?"

"Actually, yes, I have," Yehudit replied with some surprise in her voice.

"What did you see?" he asked.

"I don't understand,", she repeated.

Then we all heard what only Rabbi Steinsaltz could say. "You see, there are all kinds of gardens. For example, consider a French or an English garden: what do you see? Everything is perfectly put in place. Every leaf is manicured. It is very beautiful to some people and is *mesudar* (in order).

"Now you walk past a Japanese garden. It is not for everyone. You might not stop to look in. But if you do go in, what do you see? A rock over there. A tree over here. Maybe even some water. Maybe you find a seat. If you look closer you might imagine a picture – some kind of colours and patterns and textures. It is a bit like some forms of modern art where you see a bright yellow ear over here and a red shape of a leg, upside down, over there and a blue hand sticking out of a distorted green body. That is what you have here. Sometimes there is a deeper beauty, even though on the surface it appears *lo mesudar*," he said. "It is not for every person, but some people like it. I think this will be good for you." Yehudit sat silently, deep in thought.

Thus began our working relationship. It has only grown and become much deeper and open, full of mutual respect. It has also been lots of fun. You can just imagine the "in jokes" about me.

Why is the book not *mesudar*? Because real life is not *mesudar* and most people think and live in a non-*mesudar* way.

Few people have had the opportunity and privilege to be able to be truly inspired intellectually. Many people have become "turned off" by bad experiences, mainly perpetrated by bad examples. Consider the schoolroom: how many people feel excited to re-enter a classroom? Most of us lack motivation and inspiration to even give it a try!

If my book does anything positive to help people to improve their lives by exciting their imaginations to experience new, positive and creative experiences, then I am a very happy and fulfilled person.

I hope to offer some kind of a glimmer of light which shines or sparkles out through the small window of such an apparently empty classroom – out onto the street. I hope to attract some curiosity for a passer-by, who probably would not have given this simple, plain classroom even a first look, let alone a second.

If I succeed in this, if I make the passer-by pause and think and notice the window, then, maybe this person might feel like coming a bit closer and taking a little time to peep inside the window. And if this casual peep of initial curiosity yields an attractive picture, then perhaps these people might wish to step inside to gain a closer look. This is where they will personally meet my very dear friend, Rabbi Steinsaltz. Then a new panorama of life will open up for them, a new dimension, a new relationship.

I explore the idea of happiness in life and try to build it into a framework of freedom and liberation. Liberation from what? From the mundane, the physical and the material that are devoid of the spiritual.

I play with the whole concept of rules, regulations, restrictions and limitations ("fences") in societies and in communities. We do need fences; fences define who we are and, even more importantly, who we will become.

Who makes the fences? Who defines the rights and the wrongs? What have morality and ethics got to do with everyday living? Why? Who is inside the fence and who is on the outside? Who is sitting on the fence?

The true fence lies inside each person. We can think, imagine, dream and experience life within the fence, which is healthy – or risk exposing ourselves to dangers by allowing, or even enticing and then encouraging our minds to venture outside the boundaries imposed by the fence.

This is about human behaviour.

In this book I float through water, life and numbers. An apparently strange combination? I venture out on a voyage of discovery to explore the differences and similarities between science and belief in G-d. Science? Religion? Are they mutually exclusive? Or can they coexist in harmony and equilibrium?

I question what life is and the process of living and ageing: birth and death and what lies in-between. Beginnings and endings. The forces of good and of evil. Why? What is this all about? This is the unique journey which every person experiences through living life.

I have become so enriched, personally, by applying my mind to such issues and by putting pen to paper. I have discovered the joy and the privilege of growing and of understanding, the pleasure of fulfilment, the peace and serenity of being.

Living through ageing is the voyage of our body and mind, as they encounter the very essence of their being. It is the confrontation of one's *yetzer ha-ra* and the coming to terms with one's "fence".

I challenge how one's personal belief can engage with communal bureaucracy and then I confront the issue of continuity: continuity of what?

At this point it is appropriate for me to express my heartfelt gratitude to one of this world's very special people, my secretary and personal assistant, Maree Thompson. Maree has devoted over thirty years of her life to my family. Not only does she work tirelessly and aim always for perfection – a big call for a mortal human being – but, even more importantly, she is a *Mensch* (Yiddish: a very positive and decent sort of human being), with a capital "M". Maree organises my life and our group of companies. She is the very efficient behind-the-scenes quiet achiever. On top of everything else in our hectic week, Maree gets dumped with all of my papers and bits and pieces. These include my *lo mesudar* writings, with never a comment or complaint.

Maree typed it onto the computer, fixed up my spelling mistakes and added in her own little notations for me to look at after she had finished with a batch of work. She is always encouraging and enthusiastic; a very positive person. So, a big, special thank you to my Maree.

There are three other very special people in this world who have also greatly impacted upon me and my life. These are our "proof readers", in alphabetical order – Timmy Rubin, Orlee Schneeweiss and Vivienne Wenig. Thank you, thank you, thank you. You have injected much more than your language skills. You have given of the heart and touched the soul. Your advice, encouragement and positive feedback is inspirational and this has nurtured me beyond words. I express my heartfelt appreciation for who you are.

Victor Majzner – we have known each other even before we met. Your artistic expression is inspirational. Your work sings and dances – it is passionate and alive – it talks! The colours, shapes and harmony of balance resonate into the soul; *Kabbalah, Midrash* and Torah – Israel, Australia, humanity, nature and the Divine – all connected together. Thank you, Victor.

Thank you to Leor Broh for assistance in translations and interpretations; and Rabbi Eli Gutnick for his creative hand-written illustration [*fig. 1*].

I also wish to thank my family and to acknowledge their advice and support over all of this time. Dina is the matriarch of our family. She grew up in Israel under very difficult conditions, arriving there as a one-year old, Italian-speaking immigrant. She was raised without a father and her late mother had to work hard to support the family. At fifteen she moved to Sydney, Australia, where she had to learn English while completing her high school education.

Today we are blessed with four children, all of them married to wonderful partners in life who are also like our own children. They are all university-educated and have good careers. Most importantly, all are fine, decent, honest and caring people. We are blessed with ten beautiful grandchildren whom we see a lot of and enjoy immensely. We are all very close and share an intimate, loving and caring relationship.

Over the years Dina, Tony and Sharon, Sharonne and Michael, Tammy and Joel, and Dalia and Adam have encouraged me and have also been variously critical of my work. All in all, my gratitude and unqualified love goes out to each and every one of you. Without you, I could not have achieved this work.

I am a lucky person to feel loved by so many.

There are many kinds of love and one can love many people at the same time. There are also many colours and dimensions of love. Each love contains overlapping feelings, devotions, passions and loyalties; but despite the overwhelmingly similar qualities, there are also differences.

It is good to love and to feel loved. In fact, life is terribly empty when it is devoid of love. People search for perceived love in so many ways and, sadly, so often the search proves to be futile. Perceived love is not true love. Love is inside a person. It can be opened up and nurtured or it can be suppressed and denied.

It is healthy to tune into the warmth and the love which is all around. This is what life has to offer as its most sparkling treasure.

There are some wonderful people who have devoted quality time to reading the early drafts of the chapters contained in this book. You know who you are and your encouragement, support and assistance to me have been invaluable. Thank you.

These people include a wide range of different human beings: young and less young, religiously observant and non-observant, intellectuals and everyday people, passionate and passive people from many walks of life and of different nationalities. Some became deeply involved. Many encouraged me with their patient feedback. Some were even inspired by what they read.

From my own, personal point of view, I have gained and grown immeasurably from all of your truly amazing feedback to me. You gave my writings literary credibility, spiritual personality and human value. Moreover, you helped bring all of the various parts together for me and breathed life into it so that it became a complete book, a work of integrity.

We were finally ready for publishing, but Thomas (Schwedi) cautioned me as he shared his experiences. This initiated a new search over another year – may I say, a most worthwhile search, after many meetings, thanks to Ze'ev of Sunflower Bookshop in Melbourne. We could not have worked with finer publishers than Hybrid Publishers. Thank you Louis de Vries for your warm, personal, professional commitment and thank you, Anna Rosner Blay, artist, creative writer and talented editor-in-chief.

Thank you, my friends. This book is for you all.

I pray that Rabbi Adin Even Yisrael Steinsaltz should be healthy in long life, to continue to share all of his wisdom, together with his humility and humanity and thus to help improve the world.

Thank you for sharing my thoughts and my journey. *Nesi'ah Tovah – bon voyage* – with yours.

Enjoy the journey more than the destination. The joys of life are in all of the little things along the way.

Ron Goldschlager
Melbourne, Australia 2010

1: Ageing

Everybody wants to feel loved and valued for who and what they are. This need to feel wanted and worthwhile plays a major role in our decision-making, moods and wellbeing.

To a great extent, life revolves around these feelings and the perceived fulfilment of this need. This need is driven by expectations which, in themselves, reflect our perceptions of life. Experiences fuel and modify these expectations.

Ageing is the life journey of the body and the mind. Body and mind may progress together, synchronised by realities – or move along two very different, largely unrelated routes, as a result of misperceptions that cannot be fulfilled.

There it was at the top of the gentle rise, just a few hundred metres ahead: the Emmy Monash Home for the Aged. I was startled by a clang followed by a clacking noise. It was only a green and yellow tram moving along its tracks in the middle of Hawthorn Road. I looked over to my left as I continued walking up the hill and observed happy faces peering out at me from the tram windows and a few cars driving along the road behind the tram. Things to do. Places to go. People to see.

I came to the traffic lights at the intersection, turned right and found myself at the entrance. I looked around. Pretty flowering shrubs were growing out of the garden beds on both sides. I was enchanted by the sweet fragrance and watched a few large bees buzzing around the flowers as I heard a distinctive click and saw the door in front of me slide open.

Inside I went. The smell was quite different, as was the atmosphere. There was some noise. I looked around me: a small office just ahead; a lounge to my left. The noise attracted my attention. I walked over to the corner where two people sat in animated conversation, or was it conflict? Both were talking loudly at the same time. No one was listening. Did they hear each other, in order to be able to respond? Was this a discussion I was observing? It seemed almost comical: two discourses going on at once – at times interweaving, sometimes at odds with each other, sometimes indifferent to each other.

The more I listened, the more fascinated I was. I approached – I felt drawn in and was becoming involved with them.

"Hello," said one of them. "What's your name?"

"Ron," I replied.

"What did you say?" was shot back at me loudly.

"Ronny," I responded.

"Speak up!" was shouted back into my face. "Why don't you speak up, you're so quiet. No one can hear you! Can't you talk so we can understand you!"

That was the beginning of my encounter with the Emmy Monash Home for the Aged.

I began visiting regularly, always smiling at the residents who were either sitting around or moving about. I dropped a kind word here, a polite response there. Mostly, conversation topics were routine and superficial; but were they, really? I don't think so. To me they definitely seemed so, initially, but to the residents of Emmy Monash, they were most definitely not so. For them, my visits were an important distraction from their customary daily routines; a breath of fresh air, a stimulating diversion.

Interesting! Different people were experiencing the same thing, at the same time, in very different ways. Those people were projecting strong images with theatrical personalities. There was the always-angry one; there was the sweet, serene one; the sleepy one; the fidgety one; the funny one; the inquisitive one; the worried one; the frightened one; the searching one; the old one, the younger one and the other one.

People with thoughts, feelings, needs, memories; people who had once been children and then had parented their own children. People with names given to them by their parents – names filled with hopes and dreams and people with labels tacked onto them by other people. People living and people dying.

I could not resist attaching labels to the first two people I encountered that very first time at Emmy Monash: the "agro one" became *alter zisser* and the "softer one" became *zisser alter*. In Yiddish[1], the word *alter* means "old one" and the word *zisser* means "sweet one". So there was the old sweet one and the sweet old one; or was it really "not so sweet" and "sweetie"? Which one was which and why were they so different? Were they really so different? Why did this matter?

We so often put name tags on people superficially, based on our first impressions. First impressions do count for something and are important as relationships start to develop. Some first impressions can be accurate but others can be quite misleading and deceptive, especially when created out of context.

Some time later – I cannot now remember when this transition occurred – I renamed them: the nicer one became *chaviv ve-zaken*, whereas, the unpleasant one was most definitely *zaken velo chaviv* (*Zaken* in Hebrew means "old" and *chaviv* means pleasant, likeable). So there was the sweet and elderly one, who was always pleasant to be with and the old and unpleasant one, who was mostly hard work.

A famous Shakespeare line from *Romeo and Juliet* says: "A rose by any other name would smell as sweet". Flowers can be labelled – this is surely true for roses (although today, many of the perfumed roses have been replaced by scentless ones) – but it's not true for people. Labelling a person is dehumanising, because it ignores the complexities and sensitivities of the personality, its abstract and delicate spiritual essence – all those things that are integral parts of the non-mundane essence of humanity.

---

[1]   A Jewish-German jargon, spoken by Ashkenazic Jews from Central and Eastern Europe.

We are born and we begin to develop. We grow, we experience and we remember. Our memories then influence our destinies by "programming" our reactions to the events we encounter and impacting our impressions of random occurrences, by interpreting them through our own unique patterns of thought and behaviour.

While our bodies age, intellectually we are ageless. We continue to experience an egocentric, individual reality for as long as our memories allow us to function. These two dimensions operate in parallel. The physical world has a beginning and an end; its existence is purely a function of time. The spiritual world, in contradistinction, is timeless. Biologically, as we age, more and more of our cells cease to function, but psychologically, we remain much the same – only with more memories and experiences ... and fewer and fewer people who are older than us.

Thinking back to that particular day, it was so different from most other days at Emmy Monash: there was a lot of noise. People sounded frustrated and angry.

"Can't you see I don't want to talk with you?"

"Help me!"

"You can't sit here!"

"Help me, Nurse, help me!"

"I love you."

"Can I have a cup of tea?"

"Speak up, I can't hear you!"

"I want to talk with someone. People here are old. Look! They're sleeping."

Two people were arguing passionately about nothing. They were talking about different things; each of them was arguing with an imaginary person and neither was listening to the other. Unfinished business, I thought to myself. One was complaining about all sorts of things, reminiscing over various disappointments he felt he had suffered in his life. He felt so cheated and hard done by. The other one was bemoaning apparent lost opportunities; more disappointments; bad luck; things he should have said and things he should have done. Two people living the sunset days of their lives, unhappy with their memories.

"Excuse me," I heard suddenly. "Excuse me please!" Looking across the room, I spotted the person who was calling to me and walked over. "Do you have a few minutes' time to push me out into the garden? The nurses are too busy and I want to sit away from these people." I released the two handbrakes of the wheelchair and pushed it along the corridor and out into the garden. "Thank you," I heard. "What's your name?"

That was the start of another deeply informative chat about life and life's experiences.

All of the Emmy Monash residents had started their lives, physically at least, in a very similar way: as tiny, dependent babies. But, equally obviously, their life circumstances and environmental dynamics had been so different, as were their feelings and memories, their perceptions and, even more importantly, their misperceptions; their experiences of giving and of taking, of loving and of feeling loved; feelings of security and insecurity, expectation and disappointment; the psychological programming of fulfilment and achievement with the associated positive experiences of enjoyment and contentment; or else of frustration and failure and the accompanying negative experiences of sadness and lack of contentment; facing up to problems and dealing with issues, or running away from problems and avoiding issues.

All these great forces act on people's personalities and behaviours: actions and reactions; giving and taking; expectation and reality; happiness and sadness; needing and wanting; hunger and thirst; equilibrium and serenity; touching and being touched.

Ageing is about coming to terms with ourselves and with life; it's about reconciling the many internal conflicts which life throws out at us; it's meeting our *yetzers* – *yetzer ha-tov* (the good inclination) and *yetzer ha-ra* (the evil inclination) face to face.

The lucky ones among us have come to terms with their *yetzer ha-ra* by suppressing or distracting it as often as needed, even if they have not been able to fully overcome this potent force within each of us; and they have also been able to nurture their *yetzer ha-tov*. These are the saintly ones, a small minority of people who accept their lives as they are and feel an overall serenity, contentment, fulfilment and enlightenment. They are content with their material existence and do not experience material dissatisfaction. There is spirituality, hope and continuity in their lives and no sense of real finality. This spirituality is ageless and timeless. Therefore, they age peacefully and leave this world with serenity, having reconciled themselves with life and with themselves.

Traditional Judaism is the ultimate example of this approach to life and of living. Adjusting our everyday life routines according to the Jewish daily, weekly, monthly and yearly cycles gives us a wonderful opportunity to balance our material and spiritual existences and to progress and grow as human beings. Unfortunately, however, too many among us emphasise only the material aspects of life, while denying or suppressing the non-material. Too many people choose the short-sighted approach of remaining static. Selectively, they heavily dilute their Jewish spritual or non-material living by modifying their Judaism (beliefs) to comply with their current "feel-goods"; but rather than helping them maintain their overall situation, this tends to cause a decline.

One of the most basic phenomena of human existence, which very strongly influences human behaviour, relationships and self-esteem, is a rather hidden, subconscious element that "programs" our perceptions/misperceptions and responses. Let me illustrate through an example:

Person A grows up experiencing active responses and focused participation in dialogue. *Person B* grows up experiencing the opposite – namely, passive listening, with little active dialogue – unless something specific comes up, along with an ability to tune in and out of various activities simultaneously. Now put these two people together and try to visualise their interaction. Most likely *Person B* will naturally listen to *Person A*, observing and absorbing. Person A, however, will feel awkward: it's not the kind of dialogue they are used to and *Person A* will soon feel that *Person B* is not participating or listening because of a lack of interest.

With time, empathy, care and awareness, both *A* and *B* can learn from each other and adapt to each other. But in most cases, the opposite is much more likely to occur, because of individual programming, experiences, expectations and reactions, comfort zones, familiarity, exposure to new situations and to different people.

That visit to Emmy Monash had a great impact on me. On my way back to my car, I was lost in thought and then was day-dreaming as I drove home. Something very profound flashed into my mind. Very shortly before having walked into the aged care home, I had been startled by the noise of a tram. Those happy young faces that had peered out at me then were peering into me now. My imagination was vivid: young people, busy and buzzing with so many things to do and people to see and places to go. The faces that looked out at me at Emmy, on the other hand, were old faces – though also filled with dreams, memories and expectations. There were two dramatically different time-frames operating simultaneously: the young and the old. For the old, time is much more limited; it takes them so much longer to do things that not so long ago had taken so much less time. For the young, time is much less of an issue.

Life is full of expectations. Our emotions are powerfully driven by our own perceptions of events. But, our perceptions can often be confused with the misperceptions of other people who are interacting with us – or are our misperceptions the perceptions of others? Life is full of these conflicting impressions. How often do our superficial views become the notions that drive our emotions?

I believe that maturing is very much about finding out about ourselves. It is a life-long process of resolving issues and conflicts, of handling insecurities and unknowns and searching for our own unique truths. Surely, a large chunk of our lives is spent providing for our basic needs – food, shelter, safety –

by grappling with our perceived insecurities. But over and above these mundane, yet essential, drivers are our fundamental psychological and spiritual needs. Yet so many people get this wrong and try to fulfil their non-material needs through material pursuits.

This brings me back to the first two characters I met at Emmy. For me, they illustrated the ageing process. I have met so very few people who radiate serenity and have a quiet, saintly aura about them and so many more people who are cranky, dissatisfied, unhappy, or outright angry with life and with the people around them.

Life offers us ample opportunities to resolve our inner and outer conflicts. The saintly people take that opportunity while the others, the majority, carry with them a lot of "unfinished business" – namely, unresolved issues. Therefore, they are not likely to ever find peace of mind. Most unfinished business is blamed upon others, rather than being perceived as our own responsibility. But at the end of the day, each one of us is responsible for our own inner truths and has the ability to find our own, unique inner peace.

This capacity enables us to meet our real "self" and feel comfortable about who we are. Only after we do that can we feel comfortable with the people with whom we interact. Our memories can either help or hinder us. Much depends upon the balance between our inward and outward focus.

Another vivid memory surfaces: a gift I have recently received from a very close business partner. Terry is a self-made man with very strong ethical and moral principles: a truth-seeker, constantly looking for the inner meaning of life and living. He is a man on a journey to the beginning of creation, a journey into the universe and beyond it – and at the same time, a down-to-earth family man looking to do good deeds in the here-and-now. Although Terry and I come from very different backgrounds and have travelled very different paths, we share similar thoughts about so many things.

Terry's gift was a surprise. It was a small paperback book which he told me was out of print, written by a Catholic priest named Henri Nouwen, an academic reputed to be one of the greatest spiritual thinkers and writers of the twentieth century, who lived and worked within the Western secular culture. His major commitment in life was his work with the mentally handicapped in the L'Arche Daybreak Community in Toronto, Canada.

This small paperback contains two very deep and moving pieces about living and dying. Nouwen attributes value and deep meaning to every life. His analysis about living is from a viewpoint of becoming aware of feeling beloved. He develops the principle of being the beloved into becoming, and living as, the beloved. For him, life's greatest gift is our acceptance of life, as it is reflected in what we do with it – namely, our ability to care, share and experience – or, in other words, to rise above the superficial and the material. He speaks about the beauty, the meaning, the value and the memories of giving and of receiving and about the positive impact we leave upon others. The warmth and love he finds in mentally handicapped people and the immense values he attributes to every small, day-to-day thing, impact on the very essence of life itself. This is a strongly reciprocal and interactive relationship, in which every participant can both give and receive.

This is so relevant to the whole issue of ageing and what living is all about.

At least two miracles occur in every human being's life:

Birth – from a humble beginning of two cells joining together there evolves a highly complex body and personality. The moment of birth is the point at which the tiny baby child emerges out of its mother's womb into this world. Out it goes from a small, secure, fluid and dark place into a huge space full of light and noises. Almost instantaneously, the baby "switches on" and starts to operate independently. This is surely a miracle.

Death – the point at which a living human being ceases to live. Life departs, even though certain physical processes continue for a while. The body lies there, seemingly the same, but it has changed and will quickly continue to change without the life force. This too is a miracle.

Life is how we live between these two miracles. Every day, hour and minute of life shortens the amount of available time, until the end of this phase of existence. Most people do not know how much time they actually have; but the main difference between the baby and the old man is that for the child, time feels never-ending whereas for the old person it feels very limited.

We humans have a spiritual dimension, which is closely connected with our consciences. We constantly experience forces acting on us in different ways. Our "goodness" *(yetzer ha-tov)*, creates "feel-goods" that are not physically or materially based and are also not connected with any immediate reward. For instance, we have a desire to help others, to relieve pain and suffering, to improve someone else's lot. In a Jewish context it is called performing *mitzvoth* (commandments). Even though we are promised a reward in the world to come, our motivation to follow our *yetzer ha-tov* is often pure and selfless. We have this drive to do what is good, proper and right. This goodness of humankind is our G-dliness, the "Divine spark" within us.

However, to varying degrees we also are the victims of the *yetzer ha-ra*, which is a very potent negative and destructive force. This force has been called "the devil in us". The Hebrew word for it is *lehastin*, which can be translated as to beguile, to tempt, or to mislead or lead astray – it is an active word which is used as a verb. The word "Satan" is derived from this root, (STN). But however we choose to brand this force, it too plays on our "feel-goods" – in a different way: it attacks our mind and tries to lure us to imagine all sorts of material gain and instant gratification of our natural desires. We are susceptible to it, especially when we are vulnerable; it tempts us, takes advantage of us and plays on our minds and emotions by evoking images and stirring our imaginations.

However, we have the power to stifle these thoughts and quench these images; this power is called "freedom of choice". We are free to consciously substitute those thoughts and images with others, out of our memory banks. Needless to say, the earlier we choose to activate these counter-measures, the easier the job; and the more we delay to counteract our *yetzer ha-ra*, the more difficult will the task become and the longer it will take for us to succeed. The more we allow ourselves to become influenced by the *yetzer ha-ra*, the more will this evil force be enabled to take hold of us and assume control over us. The very first such instance is the story of Adam and Eve, in which we are told that Eve "saw that the fruit was a delight to perceive".

One rather simple way of testing ourselves is to ask ourselves honestly: will this "proposition" of our *yetzer ha-ra* stand up to public scrutiny? Or, in other words: could we honestly do such a deed openly, with pride and dignity? If the answer is "yes", think it through rationally; if the answer is "no", forget about it.

From a Jewish point of view, it is much easier to cross-check such "propositions", because we do it against an absolute system of rights and wrongs.

Interestingly, the Jewish daily prayer book contains strong statements about protecting us from this evil influence, both in the Morning Prayer: ("Rescue me today and every day ... from the destructive Satan") and in the Evening Prayer: ("Remove Satan from before us and behind us").

The good inclination and the evil one are the two most basic forces in human nature. Every human being must get to know these two forces during their lifetimes and, even more importantly, take control over them. We must learn to perceive and understand how the *yetzer ha-ra* tries to act upon our minds and develop the ability to overpower this negative, destructive force. At the same time we must also be able to understand our individual *yetzer ha-tov* and feel not only comfortable, but also in companionship with it.

Goodness leads to serenity and satisfaction with life, because it brings us in touch with the essence of living. Evil, on the other hand, leads to dissatisfaction because it becomes insatiable. When allowed to operate uncontrolled, it leads to emptiness, loneliness and ultimate destruction.

This is the journey of ageing, as we live our lives.

The lucky ones find this out early in life. How sad it is, however, for a person to simply become older in age (i.e. to realise that life has become almost entirely spent) without experiencing personal growth. What a profoundly shocking experience it is to feel hard done by and cheated, when reflecting back on the memories of their past experiences.

There is nothing wrong with the material, the physical and the many pleasures and enjoyments which life has to offer. But – everything in its time and in relative proportion to everything and everyone else. Never "me" at the expense of "you"; it's "me" together with "us".

This, to me, is the secret of living life.

The *Midrash* (homilies of our Sages on the Scriptures) brings a very interesting illustration of the material way of life, compared with the spiritual way of life.

Our patriarch Isaac fathered twin sons: Esau and Jacob. Esau was the earthy, material brother, while Jacob was the more esoteric, spiritual one. Later in life, Jacob was renamed Israel (literally: "He who strives with G-d") – a name which reflects this characteristic.

Much later on in history, the Romans destroyed the Holy Temple in Jerusalem and expelled most of the Jews from the Land of Israel. Some were brought to Rome and began living in Italy.

Italy is one of the most beautiful countries in the world: the landscapes, the seascapes, the art, the architecture, the food and the wine all are exceptionally beautiful. Its people are friendly and courteous and its music happy and often dramatic. Yet all of this is merely superficial beauty and majesty, lacking in spirituality. Italy has been likened to Esau.

Our mystics say that one must first descend to the lowest depths before being able to rise to new heights. So, too, the Jewish people were exiled to Rome and had to remain in exile for nearly two thousand years before being able to return to their homeland in Israel.

The physical world on its own is devoid of meaning. Its beauty is apparent one day, but may wane and disappear with time. The spiritual world, however, is timeless and ageless. Life that is devoid of spirituality is lifeless. Its physical attraction is like a fleeting ray of sun that, after it goes away, leaves us with nothing at all.

This image reflects the passing of life. What happens when we age? The material comes and goes, leaving memories of the past and expectations for the future, whereas the spiritual remains with us, in the present, bridging our past into our future.

Most people go through life seeking their parents' approval. Some people never experienced any lack of parental approval. How lucky for them! (Or is it? In some cases this may be detrimental to their psychological development.) Older generation parents were often unable to express open approval and love for the children and ended up communicating mostly instructions, discipline and corrections. On the other hand, many modern-day parents are instructed to voice love and approval of their children, but neglect their parenting responsibilities, which include setting and maintaining consistent and fair standards along with clear limits and boundaries.

I'm trying here to explain how many people's mindsets affect their behaviour throughout life. You see, ageing is such an interesting phenomenon that affects every single human being on a daily basis, both in how people internalise it and how they externalise it. Biologically speaking, our bodies age: with time, our organs deteriorate and our bodily functions wear down. Our inner self, however, as it is stored in our experiential memory, does not really age. We may forget things, but memory has an amazing capacity to retrieve images and relive experiences. Thus, even though the physical cells deteriorate, die off and regenerate, the "persona" lives on as long as life itself persists. Our soul is ageless. It is not subject to the metamorphoses of time; it lives within its own unique framework of existence. Thus, even when the body is very old and decrepit and "can't anymore", the soul "can" and is as fresh and young as ever.

That is why even though time marches on, we feel inside much the same as we have always felt.

As life goes on, there seem to be fewer people to look up to, people who are older than us, and more and more people who are younger than us and whom we do not know and have not interacted with. As life goes on, most of us encounter new people whom we never encountered before. New experiences, new ideas, new challenges – and still, we don't really feel very different inside ourselves. Both consciously and subconsciously, we keep seeking approval for what we are and how we feel.

Generally, we shun not only disapproval, but even indifference. This, I believe, is one of the strongest forces we encounter within us throughout our lives. It is also one of the most dominant and potent forces that constantly influence our perceptions, reactions, relationships and behaviour. The reality of our physical survival is driven by our emotional control system.

An important part of ageing is "finding ourselves" and resolving issues. Ageing should involve reconciliation of our unresolved issues and coming to terms with ourselves.

Not too many people actually achieve this during their lifetimes – so few of us do really become serene within and saintly towards those around us. Most people simply continue to go through the motions of living – merely existing, without developing or growing as human beings. Most people also fail to realise their true potential, or understand the forces that help or hinder true growth.

Some people even have vivid memories of having crossed that mysterious boundary between life and death and having returned to being alive again.

The decision when it is time to "cut the silver thread" (see Ecclesiastes 12:6) is not made in the physical realm. Death is the discontinuation of bodily life as we experience it here on earth. But for the soul there is no death, since it is connected with the eternity of spiritual existence.

Each living person knows when they have completed their earthly existence and it is time for their soul to be freed to continue in another realm of existence. There is final peace and acceptance.

For those who are close to the departed and are "left behind", there are questions, uncertainties, longing and, often, much sadness and feelings of emptiness. And there's also guilt: did we really do everything we could? Did the departed suffer, or did they make their peace?

Being given time to prepare for death is a blessing and a most precious gift, since it enables us to leave no "unfinished business" and no "unreconciled issues". Even in life, we all need time and space to bid our farewells. Belief in the hereafter offers great comfort and many advantages in confronting death; but even for those lacking this dimension of belief, a final opportunity for reconciliation is most important.

Too many people are full of regrets and uncertainties. An unfulfilled need for parental approval often develops into a general need for approval. We are governed by our perceptions and even more often – by our misperceptions, which so strongly influence our externalised behaviour. Our behaviour, in turn, influences the behaviour, reaction and responses of third parties.

Ageing is a fact of life. It is inevitable. It is simultaneously positive and negative. Life is not only about living: it is about *how* we live and *how* we age. We grow older, but our persona does not feel older.

The main question is, do we confront ourselves? And if so – how? Even more importantly: have we found ourselves in a true sense, by overcoming our own deep personal issues and resolving our inner conflicts?

This is ageing.

This is death and this is life.

Something stirred me. I was dozing; or was I dreaming? No, it felt as if I were floating, weightless. I must have been asleep. The sensation was unbelievable. Never before had I felt like this.

I looked around me. There was a strange kind of light glowing all around me. It wasn't bright, but it wasn't dark either. It felt serene. Somehow, I felt secure. I was floating weightlessly and could sense familiar sounds drifting softly around me.

As I looked around I saw a kind of a silvery thread, or was it some kind of a cord? I didn't know. This was all so new. Where was I? There was a sense of familiarity and comfort, but this floating, dreamy sensation was unfamiliar.

The silvery, string-like thread was also very gently and very softly drifting about. I was watching it. It seemed to be floating upwards towards me. It was joined to me. As I focused more on this silvery string I started to notice people.

I looked. I could feel. I could sense and comprehend. These people were familiar to me, but there was this strange kind of a haze between us. I looked closer. What was happening to these people?

They were crying and whispering and holding onto each other. They laughed and then were quiet. They looked and they closed their eyes. There were tears. It was sad but it was also happy.

There was someone else there with them. I couldn't see. Who was this? They were close to this other person and it was all so blurred.

I continued to feel myself floating. I was floating very close to these people.

My silvery string was attached to me, but there were two "me". There was a "me" there together with the people and there was "me", myself, floating around "me and my people".

The silvery string floated. I felt weightless. I didn't need to look or listen: I could perceive. I was somehow connected to their feelings and thoughts. It all felt so effortless and natural, so strange yet so comforting and whole.

I kept on floating weightlessly above them and was able to float closer and further away at the same time. There were others floating close to my space; I could sense them. There was serenity and familiarity.

My silver string was thinning, but still perceivable. There was no space or time. I existed, but did not have any form or substance.

Two worlds – two separate dimensions in space/time – two energies: the infinite coexisting with the finite, each with its own unique dimensions within one continuous existence.

I remember so well that first night after my first *minyan* (prayer quorum) as a mourner.[2] We had buried my late Mother a few short hours before and I found myself sitting *shiva* [3] for the first time in my life.

I have helped many people bury their loved ones and I have attended and

---

[2]   A Jew who lost a member of his/her immediate family (parent, spouse, sibling or descendant) is commanded to "sit *shiva*" – namely, stay at home for a week, usually the home of the departed and observe certain customs. Wherever possible, all their daily prayers are conducted in a minimum quorum of ten at the house of mourning.

[3]   *Shiva* – literally, "seven", in Hebrew. To "sit *shiva*" is to observe the Jewish law of the first seven days of intense mourning after the death of a close relative: parent, spouse, brother, sister or child.

1: Me

(acrylic on canvas 76 x 56 cm) 2008

You can view/download the paintings in original full colour, free of charge at:

www.mysteryofyou.com

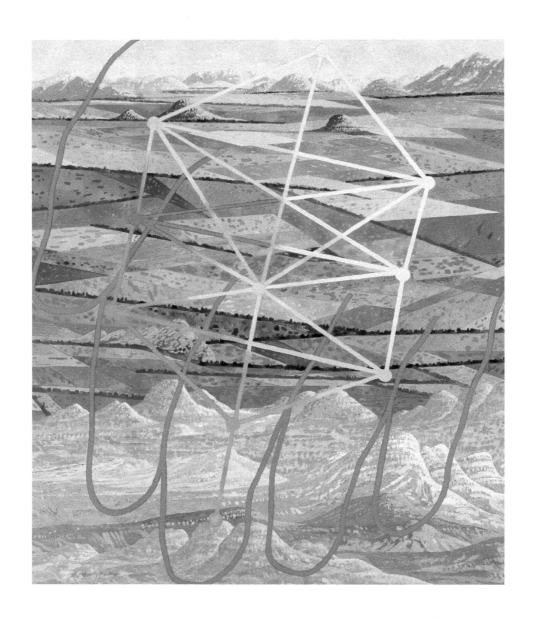

2: (G-d's) Open hand

(watercolour 57 x 51 cm) 2008

You can view/download the paintings in original full colour, free of charge at:

www.mysteryofyou.com

3: Bereishit – In The Beginning

(watercolour 57 x 51 cm) 2008

You can view/download the paintings in original full colour, free of charge at:

www.mysteryofyou.com

4: Fences

(acrylic on canvas 56 x 81.5 cm) 2008

You can view/download the paintings in original full colour, free of charge at:

www.mysteryofyou.com

participated in many *minyanim*. Each was familiar to me; each had its own uniqueness.

This was different.

It was around 9:30 at night in early winter. Hundreds of people had come to pay their respects. Their warmth and well-wishing were a tremendous source of comfort.

Now there was a strange kind of loneliness: a bit intimidating, a bit frightening, a bit overwhelming, a bit comforting.

My mobile phone had been switched off for most of the day. There was someone who I knew was in crisis and would need my advice. This image came into my mind as I sat in the darkness of our lounge room on the low mourners' chair, in my socks,[4] alone for the first time that day, thinking thousands of thoughts and only now becoming aware of the moonlight softly seeping into the room through the window.

I switched on my phone, intending to make that call, when my message bank started to beep out counting message after message, startling me out of my daze. Then my cell phone rang.

I really didn't feel like talking to anyone. I looked down and the screen did not display any familiar caller; it just flashed and rang dogmatically.

Should I – or should I not? I wanted my privacy; I also really had to make my call, before it got too late.

Of course I should answer! How inconsiderate of me!

I pressed the green button and heard a very warm familiar voice: my Israeli friend Thomas (Schwedi). "Hello Ronny, we heard your sad news and wanted to *menachem ovel* you (to comfort a mourner). We called you from New York on the way to the airport and then again from the airport and just before we boarded our flight to Israel. We called as soon as we landed at Ben Gurion and then as we walked through the airport on arrival and on the way up to Jerusalem and just now as we arrived. How is everyone – you, your father, Dina, your children, brother and family? Just a minute please – here is someone who wants to speak with you."

---

4   Mourners are prohibited from wearing leather shoes.

I couldn't believe it. Rabbi Steinsaltz was on the line! Adin Even Yisrael – my soul mate – with his beautiful, soft, warm and so humane voice, with his closeness, deep understanding and heartfelt concern. Only a few weeks earlier I had been overseas myself and had heard the sad news that the Rabbi had lost his ageing mother-in-law in Paris. I had phoned him to express my love and our condolences.

Life is so strange, so full of surprises. Later that night, after I had called my friend in crisis, I retrieved all seven voice mail messages that these two amazing friends had left.

So there I was, walking around the dark room in deep conversation with one of the very few people in this world I feel so close to, as if there are no boundaries between us. We talked for nearly half an hour, but time flashed by as if it were a second. We talked about life and about parenting. We shared our feelings about losing loved ones.

This conversation – its timing, its participants, its deep, heartfelt emotions – was the most meaningful experience for me at that point. I shall never forget what the Rabbi told me then. He said that no one can ever repay a parent; the only thing that we can do is to try to be better parents to our children than our parents were to us.

Isn't this the main message in life? Each and every one of us is given a unique opportunity to live life as a better person than we might otherwise have become. We have a special human quality called *chesed* (kindness) – compassion for others. We have the unique capacity – which no other living being shares – to improve the world and, by so doing, help save it.

That Divine spark within each of us enables us to activate our *chesed* by finding it within us, connecting with it and remaining true to it. It is not far away from us; our *chesed* is not in the heavens. It is very close to us as it is within each of us (see Deuteronomy 30:12).

In the Hallel[5] King David first praises G-d as being all powerful, by comparing Him with man-made idols which he describes as follows (Psalms 115:5-7):

---

[5]   Psalms 113-118, recited as a prayer of adulation on the Jewish festivals, the new moon and a few other occasions in the yearly cycle.

They have a mouth, but cannot speak, they have eyes, but cannot see.
They have ears, but cannot hear; they have a nose, but cannot smell.
Their hands – they cannot feel; their feet – they cannot walk;
they cannot utter a sound from their throat.

This is almost like stating the obvious. We have five senses: smell, touch, sight, hearing and taste, which enable our bodies to experience and identify external phenomena. Our brain then processes, interprets and stimulates our actions. We can choose to pay attention to the messages we receive, ignore them, or even suppress and override them.

Our freedom of choice enables us to make informed choices within a framework of absolutes. The Jewish concept of *emet* (truth) is Torah truth. Choosing "truth" turns our short-term decisions into long-term ones. It defines our path in life as well as our consistency – and, paradoxically, allows for much flexibility and spontaneity, adventure and contentment.

What is the alternative? The alternative is allowing ourselves to become blinded by short term "feel-goods" or instant gratification, at the expense of an absolute framework of good and evil.

What happened between Cain and Abel?

The Biblical text is very sparse. We are told that G-d forewarned Cain about the consequences of his *yetzer ha-ra*; but what was Cain's real issue? And what about Abel?

The *Midrash* fills in the blanks. It tells us that Cain suffered from enormous jealousy, whereas Abel was full of lust. Both of these negative forces involve envy and both, in the extreme, become addictive.

Cain was obsessed with the desire to possess every material thing around him, whereas Abel had an obsessive desire to enjoy everything he perceived as his.

The difference is that Cain needed to possess externally, whereas Abel was possessed internally. Cain allowed his *yetzer ha-ra* to lead him to temptation and this made him unable to share anything with anyone else. Abel's *yetzer ha-ra* pushed him towards the exclusive enjoyment of everything he saw.

Both brothers were possessed and neither could share. Their extreme, exclusive desires came at the expense of everything else. Therefore, both were punished so that neither could enjoy life.

The Torah offers each of us the opportunity of living life to the fullest and enjoying it, but within a framework of *Torat Emet* – the Torah of Truth. Our challenge is to be better than our ancestors and do everything we can so that our descendants become better than we are.

How do we do this? How do we live? How do we age?

This is a call for everyone to journey, to delve and explore and, most importantly, to ask questions and search for answers.

Time can be conceived of as time intervals which include special highlights in life as well as living life itself. We age in the same way that we live. The choices we make reflect our awareness of the availability of choice.

Towards the end of Deuteronomy (chapter 30) Moses sums up some essential issues for humanity. Before he dies in the desert, he says:

> *There shall come a time when you shall experience all the words of blessing and curse that I have presented to you.* (verse 1)

> *This mandate that I am prescribing to you today is not too mysterious or remote from you. It is not in heaven so [that you should] say, "Who shall go up to heaven and bring it to us so that we can hear it and keep it." It is not over the sea so [that you should] say, "Who will cross the sea and get it for us, so that we will be able to hear it and keep it?" It is something that is very close to you. It is in your mouth and in your heart, so that you can keep it.* (verses 11-15)

> *See! Today I have set before you [a free choice] between life and good [on one side] and death and evil [on the other].* (verse 16)

> *I call heaven and earth as witnesses! Before you I have placed life and death, the blessing and the curse. You must choose life, so that you and your descendants will survive.* (verse 19)

The way we feel about ourselves and those around us reflects how we have aged. And how we are seen by those around reflects who or what we have become.

The spiritual or the physical?

Our thoughts, our deeds and our actions!

If I am not for myself, who am I? If I am for myself, what am I?

The body ages.

The memories live on.

Each life impacts upon so many other lives.

2: Belief and Bureaucracy

It is May 2007. Actually, it is Sivan, 5767. Some 4,000 years of difference – apparently – and yet, these two time-frames intersect. Maybe the difference is in civilisation, but that is a matter of perception and experience. Maybe there are differences in beliefs? Or could they be due to the impact of bureaucracy upon belief? The depths of personal belief or the lack of personal belief? The superficiality invading everyday living?

People – as individuals and as parts of groups.

It is *Shavuoth* (Pentecost) and I'm back at the *Kotel* (Western Wall) again. It is part of the remnant of the biblical Temple first built by King Solomon about three thousand years ago, then destroyed by the Assyrians and rebuilt again about a hundred years later, only to be destroyed again by the Romans just over two thousand years ago. It is my "*Kotel Shule*" (synagogue). Actually, it is the second day of *Shavuoth* for me, as well as for many others like me,[6] but an ordinary weekday for Israelis (and, of course, also for people who are not religiously observant). There are many people praying at the *Kotel* and others just visiting or passing by for a look or a photo experience.

---

[6] People living outside the Land of Israel celebrate two days instead of one, in each of the major festivals.

Every week, on Mondays and Thursdays, we take out a Torah scroll during the morning prayer (*Shacharit*) and read an excerpt of the weekly Torah portion (*parsha*). On *Shavuoth*, as on all festivals, we read from two Torah scrolls.

Shavuoth is one of the three "pilgrimage festivals" prescribed in our Torah. It has no specific date, unlike *Pesach* (Passover) and *Succoth* (Tabernacles) whose dates are specified; rather, it is celebrated on the 50th day after the start of *Pesach* (7 weeks x 7 days, plus 1). It is the time of the giving (and our receiving) of the Torah at Mount Sinai after the Exodus of the Children of Israel from Egypt, on their way to the Land of Israel.

During the First and Second Temple eras, many of the people of Israel did indeed make a foot pilgrimage to Jerusalem three times every year to celebrate our festivals. They brought along their offerings and were blessed by the priests.

So here I am, standing at the site of our Holy Temple, which is also Mount Moriah, the place where Abraham, Isaac and Jacob stood and so much of our history took place.

There is a beautiful hum all around me; not an intrusive kind of noise but the warm and happy sound of my people. There are a number of different *minyanim*[7] taking place all around me: Ultra-Orthodox, Modern-Orthodox, *Chassidim, Sephardim, Ashkenazim*, bar mitzvahs. I hear Moroccan, Yemenite, Eastern and Western European, British, French, American, Iraqi and Israeli accents and different prayer versions, each at a different stage of the Morning Prayer service – all in Hebrew, although some sound more Yiddish while others sound more oriental. It is easy to pick the Anglo-Saxon and American accents.

I look around and see a group of Ethiopian Jews next to some modern-looking people who are obviously not religiously observant; young and old

---

[7]   Prayer quorums – at least ten males above the age of 13. According to Jewish law, every male over 13 is supposed to pray three times a day: morning, afternoon and evening (*Shacharit, Mincha and Ma'ariv*), preferably within a *minyan*. Women are generally exempt from time-related laws due to their duties and routines, but are free to pray according to their own choices.

people, traditionally dressed people and very pious-looking people, a proud American grandfather arranging a small private space for a family celebration – each and every person with their own, unique expression. Some people are standing close to the wall, gripping the stones and crying. People with their eyes closed are asking for solutions to their problems. Some of the people are praying in unison, while others are praying by themselves. People dreaming; people in a haze; people with a gaze; people watching other people.

Beggars who collect charity give festival greetings to those people who, like myself, are unable to carry money because they celebrate an additional day, then move on to their next target.

I like to pray on my own; I become absorbed in prayer and am oblivious to my surroundings, yet I feel part of a wider group. I am part of a *minyan* – not only the *minyan* of those around me but also the *minyan* of my people – as I connect to our religious and cultural heritage. It is a historical combination with a spiritual bond.

A bar mitzvah procession of Indian Jews passes by me and I wish them a *mazal tov*. A Torah scroll is being carried and, as is the custom, I point the fringes of my prayer shawl (*tzitzit*) towards it and then kiss them.

I hear the high-pitched sounds of rejoicing from Oriental Jewish women on the other side of the partition (*mechitzah*) separating the men from the women, as another bar mitzvah boy completes his public Torah reading. I turn in their direction and smile. I am both tearful and happy seeing their joy. I hear *Kaddish*[8] recited nearby and I respond in the appropriate manner as I include myself among those who recite it, according to tradition.

Keddushah[9] is being recited next to me. I close my eyes and respond to these holy phrases. I am crying warm tears. As the Priestly Blessing is heard, I place my *tallith* (prayer shawl) over my head and close my eyes as I respond with my "*Amen – ken yehi ratzon*" (so may it be) to each of the three verses of this blessing. I feel my tears again. I feel serene and blessed. I breathe the sweet air

---

[8]   A liturgical prayer recited at specified points during each of the three daily services; also Mourner's *Kaddish* (sanctification) used during mourning.

[9]   A section of adulation in the daily prayer which is recited only in a *minyan*.

and feel alive and healthy. I feel clean in a spiritually holy kind of way.

My own morning prayer continues. I hear my voice singing these ageless and beautiful poetic phrases. I turn the pages of my prayer book. I am praying together with my people, in just the same way as our people have prayed for centuries upon centuries – to the One and only G-d – the G-d who created the world – my G-d – our G-d, King of our entire world.

5767 and 2007. Four thousand years of difference and four thousand years of similarity.

We have a tradition and a culture which has absorbed so much from the multicultural world around us throughout history – and yet we have retained our own unique collective identity.

This now brings me to an interesting kind of a tension: the individual and the group; praying as an individual and praying together with a *minyan*.

Obviously there can be many differing experiences. We are human; we are not supposed to be robotic. It can be difficult to feel one's spirituality during prayer or meditation when group dynamics are at play. Yet, our individual prayers, as part of a group, are preferred over our prayers in isolation.

It is the golden middle path, without compromising Jewish law but with compromise towards our fellow human beings. There is a time for solitude and personal meditation, just as there is a time for being an active participant in community.

This, then, is the free spirit of personal belief within a communal framework containing bureaucracy. Both dimensions form an important component of existence and of continuity.

People are much more strongly influenced by example than by words. People do or don't do what they experience others doing. It is the "do-what-I-do" rather than "do-as-I-say" syndrome. We have the ability to synthesise the two and to juggle with both according to the environment we happen to be experiencing at a particular time.

They are a mixed multitude – my people – the Jewish people. We have been continuously and repetitively oppressed, persecuted, exiled and dispersed into every corner of the world and yet, we remain alive, creative and productive and unified by our religion. Why?

Every group which is on a positive growth path increases in numbers and then becomes a community. Every community requires leadership and organisation as well as institutions which are designed to serve the community. By their very nature, these institutions and organisations require bureaucracies to manage their activities. With time, bureaucracies tend to grow and become more impersonal and detached from their original purpose. Rather than having a culture of service and a conscious drive to achieve appropriate results, bureaucracies often assume their own culture and dynamic of becoming inwardly focused and have little to no regard for the actual services or the outcomes they are supposed to deliver.

So too, regarding religious organisations. They often lose their identities and fall into self-serving spirals of inwardly-focused behaviour and cease to relate to the actual human beings. Thus, individual belief may find itself under attack from bureaucracies which are unsympathetic to individuality.

What can one do then: Fight? Rebel? Retreat? Withdraw? Disassociate?

Inappropriate bureaucracies cause tension and conflict within society. I don't believe that extremism is the correct or most effective approach. Obviously, we must remain true to our beliefs and to ourselves; but we must also be true to our community and to those around us.

Judaism is about *emet*, Truth. We are encouraged to be free thinkers, to challenge what we see and what we hear, to analyse, to be creative, to learn and to grow as individuals. At the same time, however, we are also encouraged to act with kindness and to participate in our actions with consistency.

For instance, a Jew is supposed to follow the dietary laws, to observe the Shabbat (Sabbath) and the festivals, to be charitable, to engage in the study of Judaism. Thus the character and personality of the individual Jew is formed as part and parcel of the Jewish people. It has a collective dimension.

This tension is a real and alive one, an active part of expression and living life, just like the tension between praying as an individual and praying as part of a minyan. The search for identity and for belonging is an integral part of the search for truth. It is one aspect of the fight between the good and bad inclinations, the *yetzer ha-ra* and the *yetzer ha-tov*.

Our Sages teach us that during the First and Second Temple eras of

Jewish history, there was never overcrowding when our people entered the limited space of the Temple. No matter how many people came to Jerusalem to celebrate the Jewish festivals, each person always found sufficient space. Moreover, one of the ten constant miracles on the Temple Mount was that when people stood erect, they felt crowded; but when they prostrated themselves, there was space between them. Indeed, there were many people at the *Kotel* when I was there, and I am a person who needs space. But I, too, did not feel crowded, distracted nor disturbed by those around me.

We are the "chosen people" and "the people of the book". Our mission is to be *"ohr laGoyim"*, i.e. "a light unto the nations". Surely, we feature in the world press in a high profile, much out of proportion to our actual numbers. There are less than 20 million Jews in the entire world, 6 million of them in Israel and probably less than 50 per cent are involved with Jewish tradition and some kind of religious observance. So many Jews are ignorant of their history, culture and religion.

What is this "light" then with which we are illuminating the world? Sadly, the way in which we are profiled in the media is an aberration of truth, often motivated by anti-Semitism; it is mass-marketed ignorance based on gross exaggeration of small issues. To be sure, we are not a perfect people, nor is democracy a perfect system; the only perfection in this world is G-d. We should not pretend to be perfect, or be apologetic about our imperfection; at the same time, though, we must aim towards perfection.

We must not try to justify our existence or our right to exist. We also should not need to buy acceptance. What we need is to understand who we are, where we came from and where we are going. We Jews cannot escape our destiny. We are, in a way, like the prophet Jonah, who tried to run away from his duty and deny his destiny, but with the intervention of a Divinely sent big fish, accepted his mission in life and acted accordingly.

Our mission in life is to live according to the laws that G-d gave to Moses. Our light will illuminate the world when we become a living example of a true and meaningful human existence. We are part of humanity – in fact, a very positive and important part. However frail and dispensable on an individual basis, we are indestructible on a collective basis. Indeed, our existence defies logic. And one of the reasons for our continuity is that our system of belief has remained true to its fundamental contents, which has generally continued to serve the needs of our people.

In our system, G-d is the One and only One, King of the Universe, the Creator of life, energy/matter and space/time. And it is G-d who makes the rules that man lives by. At the same time, however, like most Western people, we live in a democracy, not a theocracy. We respect our rabbis, rather than worship them.

Some Jews are more superstitious than others; some are more spiritual. But while we may ask righteous people, dead or alive – whom we feel are closer to G-d – to help bring our prayers to Him, we do not worship any human being. We learn about our patriarchs and matriarchs, prophets and kings and we try to emulate them, or at least some of their positive qualities.

We are the "people of the book". This "book" and "these people" live with the daily issues pertaining to both belief and bureaucracy, with their inherent conflicts. We have to confront possible contradictions and experience the consequent enrichment. We just live life one day at a time. Our "book" is well and alive in today's world. It is relevant. It is actually modern. It is applicable. Our "book" is consistent. It is about living life and continuity of life. It is real and we are part of it.

One Shabbat I was in Florence and attended the magnificent old Sinagoga in Via Farini. After the service, the community had a small *kiddush*[10] where Rabbi Levi spoke to us in Hebrew, English and Italian. It was the Shabbat of the Torah reading of the tabernacle with the well known verses we all sing every time we take out the Torah from the *Aron Ha Kodesh*[11] and again replace it after the reading. Rabbi Levi chuckled and said that many of us Jews feel that our Judaism has been achieved by just being Jews, i.e. "simply belonging to the club". But, he went on to explain that this was not an ending, but merely a beginning. All of us are on a journey. The journey is about learning

---

[10]   Blessing over wine, accompanied with some snacks.

[11]   A closet or chest in which are kept the Torah scrolls used in the public worship of the synagogue.

and understanding and growing as a human being. Our journey never ends until we leave this earth at the end of our life.

Let us consider some other kinds of spiritual "bureaucracy". There are many people who claim to believe in the One and only G-d, yet worship other things – mostly, the accumulation of wealth and power; and the general population, the "simple folk", are manipulated to serve the "common good". How does that happen? In non-democratic societies, people are "convinced" either by fear or by coercion, while in emancipated societies, this is achieved through rules and regulations, accepted standards of behaviour and the media; for conformity is so much easier and more comfortable than non-conformity.

The "bottom up" approach to communications and to influencing outcomes is to appeal to the intellectual side of individual people and to progress by appealing to their intrinsic logic and common sense. This is a very non-physical as well as a more creative and stimulating approach which works within societies where people have the capacity for free thought and free choice on an individual basis.

The "top down" approach to communications and to influencing outcomes is to create an environment of either euphoria (charisma) or of fear (despotism). This is a much more physical approach which has little need for intellect but may very well involve passion. This system is undemocratic and usually repressive. It requires the power of the masses and represses individual free thought as well as individual free choice. In fact, the individual citizen becomes generally unimportant to the mission.

Today, the "people of the book" are again under open and quite fashionable attack from "people of darkness".

When the early Jews arrived in Rome, some three centuries before the destruction of the second temple in Jerusalem, i.e. about 2,300 years ago, they observed a strange holiday celebration. It was a well established and popular pagan festival. Families gathered together and prepared lavish picnic lunches, which they brought to their cemeteries and shared with their deceased ancestors. There was a portion for each visitor present plus one especially for the deceased person. They clinked their glasses with the glass designated for the deceased person. They made a toast over their wine and poured the first drink through a hole in the sarcophagus near the nose. They toasted the dead. Then morsels of food were pushed through another hole in the sarcophagus, near the mouth. Then they all ate in merriment and enjoyed the occasion together with their deceased. This practice was also supposed to gain favour for the living among the ranks of the dead. This important holiday was a celebration together with the dead. It evolved into Halloween which occurs every year on 30 October.

The Jews were shocked by what they saw. It is said that our toast on wine – *"Le chaim"*, i.e. "to life", originated in contradistinction from that time and that our tradition of not clinking wine glasses also forms part of this.

In today's liberal western democracies, we value our freedoms. Our primary focus is upon celebrating life rather than death. Society places freedom of speech and freedom of the press as pinnacles of our democratic way of life. But, not all freedoms are equal.

The freedom of life, i.e. the sanctity of life over death is a far higher freedom than is the freedom of speech – every individual has the fundamental right to life; the right to feel and to be safe and secure. The individual right to free movement and to free thought are essential basic rights. Democracies must engage with these fundamental principles and confront their true priorities.

Freedom of speech under the protection of democratic law cannot be used to incite the killing of other human beings in an undemocratic and lawless manner. This is not a democratic freedom but a denial of the most basic democratic principle which the founders of democracy fought so hard for and died for. The fundamental right of life.

Life, liberty and fraternity. This is the correct order of principles.

The "people of the book" value life above all else. Jewish law is about life and how to live life. When a person dies, Jewish law covers the correct procedures, as do our customs and traditions.

The whole point behind the famous biblical story about Abraham and Isaac on Mount Moriah, when G-d tested them to make their sacrifice, is about life. G-d forbids us to kill a human being to prove our love and our belief in Him. Only G-d gives life and takes life. No servant of G-d has the right to kill in the name of G–d. G–d is the G–d of the living here on our earth.

We have the right of self-defence and this must only be applied very carefully. All such "rights" become relevant due to communities comprised of groups of individual human beings.

Belief is a personal dimension and experience of life. Bureaucracy, on the other hand, is a man-made necessity as well as expediency to help organise society. Bureaucracy should never dictate belief and belief should never become affected or compromised by bureaucracy.

Many people have negative experiences on some occasions when they visit a religious communal service. They quite likely may feel uncomfortable, unfamiliar, unwelcome; they could be distracted by others, not enjoy the experience, find it boring, or not wish to participate. There are many people who associate belief with what their negative experiences of particular bureaucracies may have been. It is interesting to note that the vast majority of people who go to restaurants, theatres, movies, sporting events etc., or who read books, do not simply avoid such activities due to particular bad experiences. They learn from the experiences and look for new and improved, often different ones.

Bureaucracies may not adequately reflect belief, but surely such situations should not challenge an individual's basic personal belief. True belief is above bureaucracies.

The individual and the group; a family or a club comprised of people who choose to belong; the prayer of an individual and the collective prayer of a specific group which considers itself an integral part of a larger, wider group – this tension can be resolved by being inclusive rather than being exclusive.

This is belief together with bureaucracy.

3: Continuity

What is continuity? Why should one want to continue? Continue what? And what about Jewish continuity?

First one has to define what is "Jewish". One is either born to a Jewish mother, or can convert *Halachically*[12] and thus join the Jewish people. Anyone can become Jewish.

What is "being Jewish"?

Obviously, being Jewish is deeper than eating chicken soup or listening to Jewish music. Jewish culture is very interesting and absorbing for some; but in which period of history and within which geographical location?

A Frenchman is French to the end, as is an Englishman; but what about their grandchildren who emigrate to Canada or to Sweden? What is the identity of a person living in Germany whose great-grandparent was born in Morocco, or of an Iranian family that moved to Argentina, Peru or Brazil a hundred years ago? And how would you define a South African immigrant to Australia whose family had originally lived in Holland or Russia for centuries? And what about the children of such a person?

There is no end to the possibilities: marriage between a Spaniard and an Italian; the offspring of a Yemenite father and an Indian mother; a third-generation Chinese living in the US, or a seventh generation Ugandan African working in the Congo ...

If this approach to identity were the true definition of "being Jewish", then

---

[12]   From *Halacha* – the collective body of Jewish religious law, including Biblical law
(the 613 *mitzvot*) and later Talmudic and rabbinic law, as well as customs and traditions.

Jewish continuity would have been gone long, long ago. All the world's great ancient civilisations have left behind some relics, but no readily identifiable descendants. We can visit the remains of ancient Rome, climb the Parthenon in Athens and enter the pyramids in Egypt. There are magnificent, exciting, enchanting and breathtaking ruins of great civilisations in Peru, Mexico, Guatemala, Cambodia and elsewhere – but where are the offspring of those who created them?

When we compare ourselves to every other people and civilisation, we find out that we Jews have defied every possible parameter of history and logic and all the standards of self-preservation.

But Jewish continuity is not about living in the past; rather, it is all about the future connecting with the past through the present. It is about caring, sharing and belief. It is about quality of life, spiritually and physically. Rather than ignoring or negating materialism, Judaism contains it – without worshipping it. Its truth and power are components of a lifestyle which does not allow them to be used for the mere exploitation of others. It contains justice and righteousness. It values the future even more than the present. Its focus is the priorities and commitment of the group, beyond individual self-interests; caring and sharing.

We all like to feel good about ourselves and some of us even like to feel good about others, but so what? We say that people should be "good people", but what does this mean?

Is this a modern-day phenomenon, "A Current Affair"? Not really! It has been alive and relevant in each and every generation throughout history. Even way back, in Biblical times, our ancestors were confronted by the same issues. Throughout the Book of Genesis, the "Jewish People" are called the "Children of Israel". They were then an extended family. In a certain sense, the Jewish people have always remained an extended family. By calling ourselves "the Children of Israel" we declare ourselves the descendants of the family of our patriarch Jacob (also named "Israel") – his "twelve tribes". Our patriarchs, Abraham, Isaac and Jacob, were real human beings. This was their continuity.

At the very end of *Bereishit* (Genesis), Joseph dies in Egypt. Joseph – one of Jacob's sons, brother of twelve and father of two of the "twelve tribes of Israel", the man who became the right hand of the great Pharaoh of Egypt and who was instrumental in saving Egypt from the great famine, thus making Egypt the mighty nation that it became – that wonderful, outstanding human being died.

The Second Book of the Bible, the Book of Exodus, opens with a short genealogy of the family of Jacob – all seventy members of this family, relating that they reproduced and prospered. Then a new Egyptian king, who became a tyrant, redefined "the people of the Children of Israel" as some kind of a mighty nation which was a terrible threat to Egypt:

> *... and he said to his people: Behold, the people of the children of Israel are more and mightier than we. Come, let us deal wisely with them; lest they multiply and it come to pass that, when any war should chance, they also join our enemies and fight against us ... therefore they set over them task masters to afflict them.* (Exodus 1:8-11)

Does Pharaoh's proposition sound familiar? That is because it resembles the ideas of so many dictators and despots throughout history and to this very day.

Moses, who led the People of Israel ("the congregation of the Children of Israel") out of Egypt and took them to the Land of Israel, was a descendant of Levi, another one of Jacob's sons. In the Book of Deuteronomy, Moses refers to his people collectively as "Israel". The entire basis for the existence of the people of Israel is recounted in terms of continuity. The concept of nationhood was introduced by Moses only after the Children of Israel had received the Torah and were about to enter the Land of Israel.

Who or what defines Jewish identity? Do we Jews define this for ourselves, or is it our enemies who define it for us?

For most people, the idea of identity is quite simple, at least superficially. If you don't have to think about it too deeply, you can easily believe that who you are and how you feel is pretty obvious, that it really isn't an issue.

But is that really so? And is it equally true for Jews?

We know that even our close friends, extended families and children have their own unique feelings and ideas about things, which are influenced by their own unique life experiences, personalities and other factors.

Let's see: at the outset, we were a family. The first man in history to define us as a nation was Pharaoh, but he did so in a very negative sense. Moses' positive definition of Jewish nationhood came only much later, towards the end of the forty years in the desert.

During those forty years of wandering in the desert we encountered other tribes, nations and kingdoms, some of whom were our blood relations. But despite that and in spite of our peaceful requests, we were refused safe passage through their territories and we were also ambushed, attacked and plotted against.

This phenomenon of demonising minority groups has recurred throughout history and is very much alive today; it has even become fashionable in our times.

Now Hamas is sending suicide bombers and launching missiles into civilian areas in modern-day Israel – and blames it on the "Zionist occupation". Whenever Israelis try to defend themselves, they are "the aggressor". When they send humanitarian aid to Hamas, they are "interfering". If they employ Palestinian workers, they are "exploiters". If they do not employ them, they are "racists" and guilty of creating "a humanitarian crisis".

Confusing, isn't it? Indeed, with this in the background and in the context of our modern, multicultural environment, it is small wonder that so many among us are indeed becoming confused about the definition of who and what we are.

There is no question that our enemies have played an important role in our Jewish continuity. By trying to define us as who we are not, they keep reminding us of who we are. They challenge us and force us to make "identity decisions". This is certainly true for Jews at the fringes, but it is also valid for Jews at the core, those with a strong Jewish identity; they too are provoked by this, at least to some extent.

Sometimes it happens that rather than provoking and attacking us, our enemies entice us. When that occurs, many of us are only too happy to run to them. There is nothing like being accepted. Hellenisation in olden times and open, tolerant democracies today, have made assimilation so easy. Paradoxically, oppressive societies that harass, cloister, murder or expel their minorities, often make us want to be more like ourselves.

Assimilation occurs when the "pull" or "push" factors are stronger than the ties to what was. Wanting to "feel good" about ourselves and even more than that – wanting others to "feel good" about us, does not help us with continuity. Because although we should feel good about our identity, our identity is not a "feel good". We must value our identity, knowing what it is, identifying with it, understanding and living what it really entails: its rights and its responsibilities, its past, future and present.

The way in which we live in the present affects our future. If our past influences our choices in the present, then our future becomes better defined.

This is what Jewish continuity is about.

All those who choose to belong to the family which is the People of Israel and are active participants in the life of this family, stand a good chance that our children, too, will be the Children of Israel.

Are you a link in the chain or a broken link? Was your grandmother Jewish? Will your grandchild also remain Jewish? How important is this to you? Why?

The two of us walked through the Jaffa Gate into the Old City of Jerusalem. It was late morning on a pleasant late February day, just five hours before my flight out of Israel.

Avi, a distant relative, had specially driven up to Jerusalem from Ramat Hasharon, a "yuppie" northern Tel Aviv suburb about an hour's drive away. It takes just one hour to cross Israel by car from west to east across its most densely populated part.

I felt happy and sad at the same time: happy to be in Israel and sad to be leaving. Avi had arranged to spend a few more hours with me during this visit and had kindly offered to drop me at the airport on his way home. I had already checked out of my hotel and my bags were safely stowed in the boot of Avi's car.

We walked and we talked.

We took the way through the Old City Souk, the traditional Arab market – a narrow, mainly undercover stone alley flanked on both sides by little shops, alive with colour, sounds and smells, and filled with all kinds of people. There were a few shoppers here and there, vastly outnumbered by shopkeepers vainly but persistently trying to attract attention to their wares. Then there were crowds of people trying to hurry through in both directions. It was a colourful experience.

After about fifteen minutes we came to a security checkpoint which we were checked through; and then, there it stood, just down below us across a beautiful stone-paved square: the *Kotel*. Generations of Jews have both mourned and dreamt of the *Kotel*, which attracts thousands of visitors every day of the year.

I excused myself from Avi for about ten minutes. I walked down, washed my hands in a ritual manner from the water fountain nearby, using a plastic cup, and approached. It was time for *Minchah* (the afternoon prayer, the second service out of the routine three daily prayers).

Before opening my prayer book, I found myself leaning towards the wall, resting my forehead onto one of its large stones, my eyes closed. An eternity of time passed, although my wristwatch showed the passage of but a few moments. Another kind of relativity of time.

Strong emotions stirred inside me. I felt tears welling up in my eyes. My mind was devoid of thoughts. Somehow I felt my spiritual being separated from the mundane. I prayed and I thanked G-d for all of His goodness and for everything in my life. *Minchah* followed.

This was a *Minchah*! I could hear and feel every word. My voice was singing these beautiful sentences and paragraphs. The Hebrew felt so deep and meaningful. There was nothing else but *Minchah*; no other thoughts, no other people. Just me by myself, but I was not alone. I felt fulfilled, enlightened, happy and sad, all at the same time.

When I was ready, I moved away from the *Kotel* and returned to the open plaza where Avi joined me. Avi said that he had been watching me. He saw me leaning with my head against the wall. He envies people who have faith, he said, but he himself does not.

As we walked back through the Souk to Avi's car we talked a lot about this.

I asked him what he thought this experience had meant to me. He said with some conviction and authority in his voice that that was my place. He explained that when I was in Australia, I was far away and missed being here. It was only here that I was somehow close. He continued to tell me that he himself didn't really feel anything much at all when he was there at the *Kotel*. In his opinion, a person is better off finding a partner in life with whom he can feel happy rather than a coreligionist who would make him unhappy. He said that all too often, religion causes unnecessary problems and divisions between people. It is much better to have a friend who brings happiness, he said, even if that friend is from another culture − although he conceded that a coreligionist can also bring happiness.

I thought that one thing had nothing to do with the other. Happiness comes and goes. A person can be extremely happy one day and feel most unhappy the next. Happiness is a "now thing". It also seems to me that a person is more likely to find long-term happiness, contentment and fulfilment with a partner of a similar background and culture than with someone very different, especially when children and family become involved in everyday life, or in the long term, as we age.

The longer term and the short term!

Now I asked Avi if he was interested to know what the *Kotel* really meant to me, as it was very different from what he had thought. He said yes. I explained that he had never seen me pray my daily *Shacharit* (morning service). To me, it is always fairly much the same, but special; of course, sometimes it may not be quite as deep and spiritual as at other times; but in any case, I never feel properly dressed in the morning without my *Shacharit*. My *Shacharit* is the same at home in Australia as it is in America, Europe, Israel or East Timor − it is the same anywhere and everywhere in the world. The *Kotel* does have a very deep and sentimental meaning which enhanced my experience; but, it is not its stones that created that enhancement.

I said to Avi that both of us were here as children of Holocaust survivors. We were both part of a continuity of a people that has survived for over two thousand years of exile and dispersion in many parts of the world. Our survival defied logic. Whether we agreed or disagreed with organised religion and whether or not we felt part of it was not the point. The point was that our children and their children, our grandchildren and our future generations, all form part of this continuity.

Avi replied that his identity was anchored in Israel; this was all that mattered to him. He did not need religion, he said, as he simply did not have any feelings for religion nor belief in G-d. When his children were young and asked him, their father, if G-d existed, he had answered that he could not really tell them yes or no.

I told him that there are many people in the world who think the same way as he does and that at least he and his children are lucky to be living in Israel, because there they generally mix with an Israeli Jewish society and thus have some kind of identity. Elsewhere this is more problematic.

For me the *Kotel* represents Jewish continuity and connects the present with the past as well as with the future. When I prayed at the *Kotel* I felt a close togetherness with my people; in my prayers, I was praying with them through history and eternity. I was not alone. I was an individual – and at the same time also a part of the Jewish nation. I felt part of Jewish continuity. I acutely experienced myself as being closely intertwined with a congregation of Jewish souls; I felt this on a spiritual level, very far from any physical experiences.

We then walked back to Avi's car and drove to Abu Ghosh, an Arab village, where one can get the best humus in all Israel, according to Avi. An hour later I sat in the King David lounge at Ben Gurion airport, as my flight was delayed due to demonstrations in Frankfurt, where President Bush was visiting ...

I sat in the lounge, sipping on a glass of red wine. I was reminiscing. I closed my eyes and thought about Avi and Abu Ghosh. I dozed. I was back at the *Kotel*. I felt as if I were at home on Shabbat.

Over the years we have enjoyed the company of many people in our home as well as when we are away, or invited out. You see, Shabbat is Shabbat everywhere we are and everywhere we go.

It is never important to us how people arrive or leave, except that they are safe and as comfortable and as happy as we can make them feel. Shabbat is not exclusively ours. Shabbat is for everyone to enjoy and so many people have remarked about how they had never known what Shabbat feels like; until they came to us, they experienced Shabbat as just another day of the week. But when they came to our home ...

Both psychologically and practically, the Sabbath is the focal point; our weeks revolve around it, rather than it getting in the way of the rest of the week.

Our self-imposed restrictions, synchronised with Torah law, dictate that each week, Shabbat starts no later than a fixed time (sunset on late Friday afternoon) and ends at another fixed time (when three medium-sized stars are visible in the sky on Saturday night). This provides about twenty-five hours of serenity, spirituality and family togetherness each and every week, wherever we may be around the globe: no phones, no television, no cars, no switching lights on and off, no cooking, no working, no anything involved with the other six days of the week.

This story has been repeating itself every week of my life since I started keeping the Sabbath. It is not just a case of "Monday is pizza night, Thursday is sushi night and Friday is Shabbat night"; no, at least not for me. Shabbat is special, very special and very different. We sit around the table – all together: family, young and old, friends and visitors. How many people in today's world make time to sit around a table for a meal together any time during their week?

As Shabbat begins, the world of the rest of the week fades away. We have time for each other – to talk together, sing a few songs, sometimes play a game. It is happy and informal. There is a feeling of warmth, love, friendship and hospitality. The food is always great, too – but the truth is that my wife Dina does wonders in everything that she does. When we are a large group, people sometimes wander off into smaller groups – casually, relaxed, naturally.

Thank G-d for Shabbat.

Over the years we have enjoyed the company of many people in our home and also when we've been away, or invited out. You see, Shabbat is Shabbat everywhere we are and everywhere we go.

Here are some stories about very special and unique Shabbats I have experienced.

Shabbat in Casablanca, Morocco

It was late morning in January 1994. We were floating weightlessly among the clouds; I was drifting in and out of sleep, having slept only very little the night before. A voice jolted me back into consciousness. "Fasten your seatbelts. Secure your seats upright and prepare for landing."

Our last night in Rome together with our family had been so much fun. The togetherness, the pasta, the *vino* (wine), the *pesce* (fish), the caring and sharing and telling and listening; the closeness of family, where so often language and culture are of little consequence. But although all of that had taken place only a few hours before, it seemed like ages ago.

The five of us – my wife, two of our daughters (14 and 8), a niece (15) and myself – were about to enter Casablanca, Morocco. One man and four young women on a short vacation, before returning from the European winter to our Australian summer; five Aussies landing in Casablanca on a bleak Thursday in January.

We disembarked, feeling happy and excited about our arrival at such an exotic place. "Here's looking at you, Babe," we imagined Humphrey Bogart saying to Ingrid Bergman. But as we entered the terminal we were surrounded by armed uniformed paramilitary troops.

"Passports," we heard.

I handed over our five passports.

On our way to the baggage hall, we were forced to show our passports no fewer than eleven times to various armed bureaucrats. What a wonderful and hospitable place, I thought. What a stupid mistake to choose this as our holiday resort. We should have gone to Sicily or stayed in Rome or gone to Florence and enjoyed the warmth of the people, despite the wintry weather and snow.

We found our baggage and exited the airport building after showing our passports another two times, once "scrutinised" upside down. Maybe these people were multilingual and possessed reading skills unknown to us?

We approached a taxi and asked the driver his fare to the Sheraton Hotel, which was quoted at about ten times the rate we had been briefed it should be. We tried to negotiate, but the driver simply walked away.

I walked over to another taxi. Same story. Had all these taxi drivers seen the same movie?

It was getting cold and there were no other tourists standing outside the main terminal building of the capital city of Morocco. In fact, it didn't look much like an urban centre at all.

There were no taxis.

And there were five of us cold Aussies.

A few hours later, we somehow managed to get to the Sheraton Hotel in downtown Casablanca.

My brother-in-law, Isaac, had an ex-Moroccan friend in Sydney whose family – the Ifergans – still lived in Casablanca. Isaac had asked us to phone this family to give them his best regards. It was Friday afternoon when we got around to phoning them and we tried our best to pass on the regards and to wish them all the best for Shabbat; but communication was difficult, as they spoke Arabic and French and we spoke English, German and Italian.

Shortly afterwards we received a phone call from the desk advising us that there was someone downstairs to see us.

Her name was Edith and she was the youngest daughter of the Ifergans. She spoke some English. She was on her way home from the dentist, where she had just been operated on for two abscesses under her teeth. She was a bit pale, but insisted that she would wait for us and walk us to the synagogue, about twenty minutes away; she explained that it was not safe for us to try to walk to the Old City by ourselves, especially as it was getting close to dusk and she was on her way home anyway.

Soon we were all walking together.

We were fascinated by the sights, the sounds and the smells of the Old City. It was very close to sunset, maybe fifteen or twenty minutes to go. The red of the low western sky was magnified and distorted by the pollution in the air. We could hear muezzin voices chanting out of loudspeakers in minarets. People were milling around buying and selling their last goods before the end of the day.

It was the end of Friday, the end of Islam's holy day of the week and the beginning of the Jewish holy day of the week.

Edith stopped at a wooden door in a narrow alleyway. She knocked and the door opened. We followed her inside.

"*Shalom Aleichem* (welcome!)" we heard. "*Shabbat Shalom*." We conversed in English and in Hebrew and a smattering of other languages.

The synagogue was nice. It felt so much like home.

The service and prayer book were very similar to ours. The tunes, however, sounded different. And there was no prayer leader; instead, one of the elders pointed to various congregants, each of whom, in turn, chanted a paragraph; other parts of the prayer were chanted by all in unison.

The sound of the Hebrew was beautiful; the tunes, however, sounded more Arabic to our ears. But the conviction, the respect, the participation and the profound familiarity of the congregants with all the parts of the prayer were truly something to be experienced.

This was the beginning of Shabbat.

Many people were dressed casually, some young people even in jeans and open-necked shirts; others were more formally dressed. Everyone treated everyone else with respect, warmth and caring dignity. We felt a very special feeling of Jewishness, that Friday evening. We also felt part of this community.

After the service, Edith insisted that we join her parents at their home for Shabbat dinner. We felt embarrassed that we were imposing on them; we did not even have anything to bring to them. But she wouldn't take no for an answer; rather, she insisted that her parents were expecting us.

We walked a short distance through a few more twisted alleyways until we came to a gate in the wall. Edith took some keys out of her pocket, unlocked the gate, opened it and beckoned us through. She closed it after us, locking it securely and told us to proceed up some stone stairs to a wooden door, where she knocked.

We heard the distinct sound of a number of locks being unlocked and sliding bolts being slid open. After what seemed to us to be some time, the door was opened and we were warmly welcomed in by an elderly gentleman with whom we instantly felt comfortable. "*Shabbat Shalom – Shabbat Shalom u-mevorach* (A Shabbat of peace and blessing)". His loud, husky voice enveloped us. He then gestured in the direction of his wife, introducing us. Edith was not feeling well after her ordeal at the dentist. She tried her best to be hospitable, but after a short time reluctantly excused herself and went to her room.

We all sat down at the Shabbat table. We sang *Shalom Aleichem* and *Eshet Chayil*.[13] Mr Ifergan – Yaakov – proceeded with the *kiddush* in a loud and passionate way, full of emotion. We all washed our hands, made the blessing and returned to the table for the blessing over the bread.

Yaakov took the Shabbat cover off the two *challahs* (special bread for Sabbath), lifted them up high over the table and, in a loud voice full of dedication and faith, raising his eyes, he said (as is the Sephardi custom): "*pote'ach et yadechah umasbi'a lechol chai ratzon*" (You open Your hand and satisfy the desire of every living thing – Psalms 145:16), then made the blessing over the bread. He broke bread, tearing off small pieces by hand, gently tossing a piece to each of the people sitting around the table, after dipping it in some salt.

This warm and meaningful togetherness was, in many ways, just like being at home.

We ate and we talked. We sang and we enjoyed and then ate and we talked some more in a hodgepodge of languages and gestures, but with a strong bonding and all-encompassing enjoyment. Soon it was after 11:00 p.m. and it was time to call it a night.

Yaakov insisted on walking us the short distance to the nearest gate in the wall of the Old City and pointed out the way back to the Sheraton Hotel along a well-lit main road.

The next morning we walked back to the synagogue and after the service we were introduced to other members of the Ifergan family, as well as to other

---

[13]   Two prayers recited or sung before the *kiddush*, the blessing over the wine; the first is a welcome to the angels that accompany us from the synagogue to the home; the second is the latter part of chapter 31 in Proverbs, a hymn to the "woman of valour".

congregants. Again we were invited to Shabbat lunch; no refusals accepted.

The afternoon flew by and Saturday night was upon us. We experienced a richness of Jewish togetherness, religious belief and expression. We felt like parts of one extended family.

Since that Shabbat in Casablanca, I have adopted reciting the verse *Pote'ach et Yadechah* as the preamble before making the blessing over bread; and each time I feel a happy tear of sentimentality as I reconnect with Yaakov and with all of my people – past, present and future.

Shabbat in Santiago de Chile

The 1980s were particularly exciting and challenging times in Chile, especially the mid-eighties. Chile had been the only nation in the world to democratically elect a Communist government, back in 1970. Salvador Allende was its President for three years. The people suffered. The economy collapsed. The people suffered even more.

When the situation in the country reached an unbearably low point, a military junta was formed which led to a *coup d'état*, typical of many other violent changes in South American governments. The Communists and this new right-wing government imposed their control and leadership over Chile. General Augusto Pinochet Ugarte purged the country of its Communists and proceeded to manage a dramatic program of political and economic reform, reconstructing and rebuilding a failed economy, democratising and educating his country, empowering his people and lifting the standards of living with impressive success over a relatively short period – just over a decade.

How I became involved and how I met my Chilean business associates, who later became close and trusted friends, is not important here.

I started visiting Chile during that period and continued travelling there for a few years. During my first visit there was still shooting and bombing outside my hotel, in the heart of Santiago, the capital city, as well as in Concepción, Chile's second largest city.

Chile is a predominantly Catholic country with a warm, Latin flavour. Its people are kind and good, family-oriented people, diligent and capable workers with a good ethical approach to life and moderately nationalistic worldview.

Our plantation forest products trading was risky, but proved successful only due to the commitment and attention to detail of those involved.

One special fringe benefit of my regular trips to South America was that I flew in and out via Argentina, where my aunt, uncle and cousins live. I always spent my weekends with them, plus as many extra days as I could spare, working in Chile during the week. This has created a treasured and close personal bond for us all, to this day.

On one particular trip I had to be in Chile when there were no possible flights to Argentina in time for Shabbat, nor were there any flights after Shabbat that would bring me back to Chile on time. I was constrained to stay over in Santiago for the weekend for the first time ever. Normally, I would have either made inquiries beforehand regarding the Jewish community and synagogues, or simply made my own arrangements for a Shabbat by myself. On this occasion, however, something unexpected – and very nice – occurred.

My friend Akos, a Catholic Argentinean of Hungarian descent living in Chile, had already taken matters into his own hands without even consulting with me. Akos had phoned and informed me that he had taken it upon himself to check out information for my Shabbat. There had been quite a strong Jewish community in Santiago before all the trouble began, he said, but most of the people had left for other countries. He had located a "temple" but thought that this was not for me. He had also found a newer organisation called "Jabad" (the South American spelling for Chabad, a *Chassidic* movement) which was located in a nice residential area in a suburb called La Gloria, and there was a motel I could stay in only a few hundred metres away. This was the place where I was to spend my Shabbat in Santiago de Chile.

Note that Santiago is on the opposite side of the Pacific Ocean from Melbourne, Australia. The same sun sinking into the ocean in the port city of Vina del Mar, heralding the end of one day, is rising to illuminate the east Pacific coast of Australia, at the beginning of another day.

Before leaving Melbourne, I had looked up the telephone number of Chabad in Santiago and late one night I phoned. A young voice answered in Spanish. After checking out a few possible languages, we agreed to speak in

Hebrew. Young Rabbi Moishe immediately told me that they were very much looking forward to my visit and that I was invited to his house for Shabbat dinner on Friday night and by Rabbi Menashe for Shabbat lunch. I asked Rabbi Moishe if he could possibly check out the home situations first, to see if there was room and if my visit would not be inconvenient. His reply was instantaneous and warm: "Of course we're expecting you!"

My flight landed in Santiago and standing there, waiting for me, was the smiling Akos. It was late Friday morning. Santiago was fresh and the air crisp with the white, glistening, snow-capped Andes mountains majestically looking down at us. It felt so beautiful. It was winter time and Shabbat was due to come in early.

We chatted as Akos drove me to La Gloria, to the hotel he had arranged for me. On the way, Akos circled the green-treed suburban side streets and pointed out "Jabad" only a few blocks from the hotel. I checked in, quickly set up my room and just as quickly returned downstairs to Akos. We drove off for lunch and then visited his office, before he dropped me back to my hotel in the mid-afternoon to prepare for Shabbat. We made arrangements for going to a big soccer match on Sunday afternoon.

No wonder I enjoyed doing business in Chile and loved each of my visits. Such a beautiful country with such wonderful people!

I ran up to my room, showered, shaved and dressed for Shabbat. Everything was organised. I was feeling relaxed and happy and free. I walked to Chabad, carrying a few presents, my *tallith*, *siddur* (daily prayer book) and *Tanach* to the *shule*. As I entered Chabad I was warmly greeted by a young Chabadnik who turned out to be the Rabbi Moishe I had originally phoned. We sat around and chatted. It was still early. I helped him set up for the Shabbat services. A few people started to arrive. I was introduced to Rabbi Menashe, who reminded me about the invitation to his house the following day.

A few minutes before the afternoon prayers, Rabbi Menashe addressed the few congregants. It soon became evident that most of them were visitors and only a few families were locals. Rabbi Menashe asked who spoke what language and it was decided that our *lingua franca* for this occasion would be

Hebrew – the only common language of this group of Jewish people from all over the world, who made up this congregation in which we were to celebrate this Shabbat together as one warm extended family.

The prayers were uplifting. There was much singing.

After the evening prayer, I walked home with Rabbi Moishe together with the other invited guests. He lived in a tiny apartment with his young wife and little baby. What they superficially lacked in material possessions was much more than adequately compensated for in warmth, hospitality and spirituality. We all shared the food and drink. We all were interested in each other. We chatted and we sang *niggunim* (Shabbat songs) and talked about Jewish things and current Israeli news. Rabbi Moishe ended his share of hospitality by walking us back to the main road and pointing each of us in the direction of our hotels.

On Shabbat morning we all met up again in the synagogue. Again, the Shabbat services were most enjoyable. One of the local congregants had prepared a *kiddush*. We ate and drank and Rabbi Menashe gave a short talk derived from the scriptures. We all then went back inside the Synagogue for *Minchah* (afternoon service).

A few of us accompanied Rabbi Menashe for Shabbat lunch at his home. It was a very pleasant twenty-minute walk in the sun through a green, gardened residential area. We arrived happy and in good spirits.

Rabbi Menashe was a *Shaliach* (emissary) of the Lubavitcher Rebbe, whose task was to build a Jewish community. He had come to Santiago after a few years in Uruguay. He had seven children, two of them studying in distant yeshivas. His household, too, was frugal, but filled with warmth and hospitality.

We all enjoyed the long lunch at Rabbi Menashe's: interesting discussions, songs, tasty food, more discussions and songs.

Soon it was getting dark and it was time to go, to move back from this real world with its demands and deadlines into another real world with its demands and deadlines.

Rabbi Menashe, too, walked us back to the main road and pointed each of us towards our destinations. We parted with warm wishes for a happy new week. I walked back to my hotel, washed, shaved and changed from my suit and tie into my smart casual clothes, grabbed my leather jacket and some gifts I had brought with me for my Chilean friends, Jaime and Jesse, and their three children and hurried downstairs.

Jaime came to pick me up. We hugged and slapped each other on the back. It was so good to see each other again. Soon we drove into Jaime's estate in the mountains overlooking Santiago. The stone and wooden house had a crackling wood fire in the lounge. I greeted Jesse and then the *ninjas* (children). We toasted each other and each other's families over a pisco sour (a Chilean national drink made of lemon juice, a strong spirit base similar to vodka and some ice). There is nothing that feels nicer on a cold night than a pisco sour between friends next to a wood fire.

Jaime and I had met a few years before and had immediately built up a very strong brotherly bond based on integrity, mutual trust and commitment. We had established, then nurtured and shepherded forest-based trade between Chile and Australia and I had helped Jaime build up an exciting industry. Jaime and Jesse were the "new generation Chileans" – educated and cultured young, modern Catholics, passionate about rebuilding their country and improving living standards for their people. We felt as if we were related in a familial way.

Jesse had prepared a vegetarian dinner which she served on new dishes. We ate, drank and chatted. This was another memorable time.

Jaime drove me back to my hotel and arranged to pick me up again late on Sunday morning. We returned to his house. Jaime and Jesse had prepared a brunch barbecue with a few close friends. They even "went the extra mile" to have fish with scales and fins, with mine wrapped up in aluminium foil and cooked on the clean side of the fire using brand new tongs.

Later that afternoon we drove to the big soccer match, which was due to start at 4 p.m. This was a big event in Santiago. We had four great seats: for Jaime, Akos, me and one for a very close university friend of Jaime's (who worked in Chile's central bank, overseeing every investment-funded project in Chile which had been made under a special economic law designed to help eliminate Chile's substantial international debt, as its economy became reconstructed and modernised).

We had a fantastic afternoon together. The soccer was really exciting. We cheered and we yelled out against unfair moves. We drank some Chilean beer and reminisced. We talked a lot about Chile, its economy and people, important projects, laws, human rights. We shared experiences. We analysed scenarios and ventured to make predictions.

Close comradeship; intelligent intellectual conversation; an exciting sporting event to add; very interesting discussions – the few hours we enjoyed together flew by as if only a few seconds of time.

Soon it was time for me to return to my motel.

Another week packed with business meetings and another flight followed by more movements and move activities.

Life is full of friendships and good memories and even more things to do.

But Shabbat is Shabbat, the focal point of each week, where time moves in its own time frame as an integral part of living life.

Shabbat in East Timor

In February 2000 I was invited to visit East Timor by the East Timorese freedom fighter, its official leader and now President, Xanana Gusmao. I spent ten days there together with a few leaders of the CNRT (Council of National Resistance) – commanders who had survived nearly 25 years of armed resistance against the brutal Indonesian invasion. At that time, East Timor was nearly broken. UN forces, led by Australia, helped save this little nation from genocide and assisted in rebuilding the country, enabling East Timor to become the first independent new nation of the new millennium.

This was probably one of the crazier projects of my life. It has left me with a deeply enriching experience – but that is a different story. What I'd like to share with you now is about the Shabbat that occurred within those ten days.

It was very hot and humid along the entire coastal region. There were mosquitoes infected with malaria and dengue fever. The water was not drinkable. In stark contrast, in the mountainous inland region – with some peaks as high as 2,500-3,000 metres – the air was fresh and cool; there were no mosquitoes; there was lots of pure, chilly water from natural springs, tasty tropical rainforest fruits and plenty of fish, brought freshly caught from the pristine waters of the sea.

East Timor is a small island between Australia, New Guinea and Indonesia, only about 700 by 100 kilometres: a beautiful place inhabited by friendly, warm-hearted, decent people. Only about 700,000 of them have survived.

I felt myself highly sensitised to the plight of this people and motivated to assist. On the plane flights back home (there were four consecutive flights) I wrote a heartfelt poem before falling into a deep sleep. Although it is very personal I include it, to share my feelings and thoughts.

Lafaek[14] is Timor

24 February 2000

To Xanana and his people
With love and respect
From your new and loyal friend
Ron G. in Melbourne

The Philosopher and Poet cries
With the salty tears of the sea
For the thick red blood of his people
Which flooded his land as the
Heavy downpouring of the monsoonal rains

The enemy from without sought to
Obliterate his homeland of her life
To plunder and pillage and rape and destroy
To remove and replace for the greed of the few

And to pervert from within with poisoning the minds of the hungry,
the poor, the oppressed and confused.

---

[14] Lafaek (in Tetun, the common dialect of East Timor) is how they call their country, likened to a crocodile which became transformed into the island of Timor.

In a thoughtless attempt of genocide
Which was hidden from view in our world.

The people alone defended themselves
To try to survive and live on
In a very pure way without help from outside
They moved up through their steep mountainsides

Little by little, from day to day
Together they stood side by side
The thin subtle thread of the spirit of life
Was as thick and as strong as steel chain

One people as one from within
they strove, united by their own common cause
They struggled in death for their life to
Preserve, the soul of the people so pure

For twenty-five years at great sacrifice
And deprived and in personal pain
But enriched in a way so strange in our
Day, so simple, advanced all the same

Yet lost in our world which has blinded
Itself as it moves far away from true life
Our everyday thoughts are so filled with the
Fog ... trivially caused by ourselves

The Aussies arrived and everyone breathed a
Full breath of the cool mountain air
Which is filled with a rare and sweet fragrance of life
At a time we together all share

An explosion of life sprouted out of the earth
As the womb of the people produced
The coffee, the fruits and the corn and the rice
All smiled and the children, these children broke forth

A profusion of life reproduction abounds;
Baby buffalos, chickens and piglets and goats
Farm animals as well as home hounds

The trauma, the pain and the loss all so fresh
But their hearts and their minds find new peace

Their friends from outside were so kind to
Them all; these uniforms gentle and good

The children so pure with their smiles so sweet
"Hullo Misterr!" they call day and night
With a trust and a hope for a future naive
As they strive and they work in bare feet

These children, these faces, these thousands of faces –
The little sweet faces – the future of Timor
Its beautiful, beautiful faces.

A people united so morally
As they share and they plant and they eat
Such a strength which is bound with an ethical
View as clear and as clean as a pure mountain spring

Survival assured by our world round about
To the faces, these faces
These sweet pretty faces of children
All looking out

At their friends from outside who have
Come to help and to build and
To teach and to share

An innocent people who forgive and don't hate
No revenge only justice they seek
A trusting people with nothing but hope
But with everything meaningful dear

We from without must take control of ourselves
And look hard and think harder within from without
With respect and with care and a focused approach
As all givers, receivers must share

Our common bond which links all humankind,
Which maintains our humanity –
A sensitive balance of self-esteem
Within a culture so pure and unique

We must carefully view our well
Intentioned attempts,
Our motivation and the satisfaction it brings
For in the end, our dear friends from within
Have their own lives and dreams of fine futures ahead

The clear danger now
Again hidden from view
Exploitation from without of within,
This danger's most difficult to detect
As it's void of an enemy form
But subtle as clouds form to darken the skies
Blocking sunlight and every thing

We from without in our haste to give help
Need to help our dear friends from within
In their need in their time in their way
In their land as their culture should
Always stand

Lafaek is their land as the legend is told
Lafaek chose to turn to Timor
Lafaek is so strong in its culture so pure
Which within gives without as its lure

To rebuild we all start but to what we

Must care from grass roots and then up
From its strength we all share

Not imposed from the top from outside
But from where
The soul of the people is there.

I became closely associated with these kind, gentle and very poor people because I empathised with their silent suffering, identifying their traumatic experiences as being similar to those of my own people during the Holocaust.

Most East Timorese survivors did not openly talk about their past. However, I heard some terrifying stories and eyewitness accounts of how at least half of their population was murdered.

We lived very basically in East Timor. I had no problems maintaining my kosher diet. One night I even slept in an orphanage in Laga (a remote eastern village), run by Salesian Sisters; four "angels" mothered over one hundred children there, with meagre resources. During dinner, the Mother Superior said to me, "So you come from the land of the Father," – confusing Israel with Judaism and Australia.

There were only a few hours of electrical power each day and not even every day. Water was electrically pumped. They grew their own food and had a small truckload of rancid maize which had been delivered by the UN food aid program. They seemed to be happy with their lot in life.

I burst into tears when we drove into the orphanage in our four-wheel drive late on Thursday evening and saw the children. They were illuminated only by our headlights, sitting in their orphanage courtyard. We heard their sweet little voices singing some songs of welcome to us in beautiful harmony – pure, harmonious, melodious music from angels in the dark.

That night I slept on a broken old steel bunk bed with a mosquito net hanging all around me. There were my three CNRT[15] travelling companions sharing this little room, with frog and insect noises audible from a nearby bog.

---

[15] National Congress for the Reconstruction of East Timor.

But I slept like a baby that night. It was pitch dark until the early morning dawn arrived to beckon us into a new day.

I went for a few hours to Ailieu, a remote village hidden in the mountains which had served as the CNRT headquarters during the Indonesian military occupation and continued to function as such. I met General Cosgrove at a very moving ceremony in which roles were formally handed over and the East Timorese tribal leaders officially wore their tribal attire again and publicly followed their inherited customs for such formal occasions. After that amazing military ceremony I briefed the East Timorese leadership, as requested, regarding a socio-economic model to rebuild their country and then had lunch with their military commander, Matan Ruak, in his house.

So much activity in such a short time.

We drove through much of East Timor. We saw a lot. We did a lot. We worked hard. There was so much to do. And Shabbat was approaching fast.

I had asked my hosts to make sure that I would arrive at the place where we would be sleeping Friday night – wherever it might be – no less than two hours before sunset, so as to have enough time to prepare for Shabbat. I explained to them that from sunset on Friday evening until after dark on Saturday night, I could not drive, but had to rest in one place – my "home" for the Shabbat.

We drove to Baucau (East Timor's second largest city after its capital, Dili), a coastal town on the eastern side of the island, arriving mid-afternoon. There was an open fruit and vegetable market on both sides of the street in the centre of town. We came to a broken white house which had seen better days under the colonial Portuguese administration some decades ago.

This was to serve as my home for Shabbat. I was shown my room and unpacked my few things. The communal bathroom had a leaking faucet which dripped into an old bathtub which overflowed onto the stone tiled floor, running over the stone floor and out of a hole in the wall into the garden.

The water was very cold. I felt as if I was immersing myself in a traditional *mikveh* (ritual bath) and imagined myself in Jerusalem on a wintry afternoon two or three thousand years ago. My bathing was extremely brief. I dried myself, feeling frozen but refreshed. I dressed for Shabbat. A few minutes before sunset I lit the two Shabbat candles on a brick in my room and, with my *kippah* (skullcap) on my head, closed my eyes and made the Shabbat blessing over their flickering light, just as my wife does every Friday evening, as our mothers had done over the years. My blessing felt very deep and meaningful.

I prayed the *Kabbalat Shabbat* service; then I prayed the evening Shabbat service. I made *kiddush* over some kosher wine I had brought with me in a small flask. I sang a few *zemiroth* (songs) in the candlelight and then walked down to a small dining room in the house where my hosts were waiting. There was no electricity. A wood fire burned in the stone fireplace, illuminating the room. Outside, in the courtyard, a young East Timorese girl had cooked a whole fish for me over a small wood fire, by skewering it through with a wooden branch of a tree and turning it slowly over the glowing charcoal. She had also baked a few vegetables on the fire and made me some hot tea to drink. There were also fresh tropical fruits – very sweet and tasty.

This was my Shabbat meal. It was delicious.

During my singing of the grace after meals and again after my recitation of the *Shema*[16] before going to sleep, I thanked the Almighty for everything that He does and for protecting me. I thanked Him for giving us the Shabbat.

The next morning I washed my hands and face before putting on my *tallith* and reciting the Shabbat morning service. It felt so good and so rich. I sang every word and then took time to read the weekly portion of the Torah reading in English, just to enjoy it and to search for deeper meanings.

After this I made *kiddush* and indulged myself on a very tasty sweet bar I had brought with me. I sang a few songs, ate some fruit and drank some water.

Shabbat is such a special day. And that Shabbat was particularly special. I sat on a flat rock out in the courtyard under a beautiful tree in the warm tropical sun and read a book I had packed in my knapsack.

Later that morning my hosts took me for a walk around Baucau and we visited the United Nations command post where armed Thai troops were on guard.

Life is so strange at times. A handsome young man in his mid-twenties,

---

[16] A liturgical prayer consisting of three Scriptural passages recited twice daily by adult Jewish males to affirm their faith.

casually dressed in a sporty civilian outfit, strolled out of the UN office onto its front verandah. His thick, but unmistakably English-educated Arabic accent pricked the air. We chatted. After a few minutes I asked him where he was from. "From Palestine," he comfortably responded. Even as a well-travelled young Australian aged fifty, this caught me by surprise.

"Yes, but where in Palestine?" I heard myself ask.

"From Gaza,", he said.

"I've been in Gaza," I said. "You're a long way from home. Don't your people need educated young people like you to build your own country?"

The free scholarship to England and a high, tax-free UN salary appeared to offer a more attractive future to this young Palestinian.

This is the world we live in. "What is in it for me now" is the modus operandi and the culture of choice for so many westernised and privileged individuals. Makes it a bit hard for all the other people.

Thank G-d for Shabbat! It helps make the world an "us" place rather than a "me" place. The values, the ethics, the morality, the community, the continuity – all flow out of Shabbat.

Thank G-d for Shabbat.

My flight was being called. I woke up, rubbed my eyes and moved from the lounge to the plane.

As I fastened my seatbelt and my flight departed from Israel, I thought to myself: was a good humus in Abu Ghosh comparable to the *Kotel*? And was the *Kotel* comparable to my family in Melbourne?

Life is full of so many experiences.

Abu Ghosh is a friendly Arab Israeli village near Jerusalem, a nice place to visit. The *Kotel* represents the important historical foundations of Jewish existence and is a focal point of Jewish belief. It is also one of my favourite places: a very spiritual place.

My children and now also my grandchildren are the continuity of my people. We are alive and we are living a Jewish existence. To me, this is the ultimate which life has to offer.

Towards the end of the Pentateuch (Deuteronomy 29:9-14, 21; 30:19-20) we are told in no uncertain terms:

> *You are thus being brought into the covenant ... He is establishing you as His nation, so that He will be a G-d to you ... but, it is not with you alone that I am making this covenant ... I am making it both with those who are standing here with us today before G-d our Lord and with those who are not (yet) here with us today ... A future generation, consisting of your descendants, who rise up after you, along with the foreigner from a distant land ... (you must thus make the choice) to love G-d your Lord, to obey Him and to attach yourself to Him. This is your sole means of survival and long life when you dwell in the land that G-d swore to your fathers, Abraham, Isaac and Jacob, (promising) that He would give it to them.*

G-d has guaranteed us that the Jewish people will survive to the end of time.

Who defines our Jewish identity: is it we ourselves, or others? How does our individuality fit in with the group? How does our group relate to us? Which group? Who defines the identity of the group?

Continuity – of what?

What for?

What do you want to be a part of?

What do you think? What works for you?

4: Behaviour

If I am not for myself,
Who will be for me?
And if I am for myself,
What am I?
(*Pirkei Avot* [Wisdom of Our Fathers] Chapter 1, *Mishnah* 14)

This most profound statement was made by the very famous first century BCE (Before the Common Era) Sage, Hillel, and continues to be applicable for all time and for all people, on both the individual and the collective levels.

Me, myself, so what?

Karin was a well groomed young lady in her mid-twenties who worked at the Dan Carmel Hotel business centre lounge in Haifa, Israel. She had a certain presence about her, a caring efficiency and graceful intelligence. She helped solve a network communications problem I was experiencing with my Australian cellular telephone and we chatted for some time before the arrival of my next business appointment. Her Hebrew was very good, with a slight European accent; her English was even better. Karin had immigrated to Israel from the western Ukraine (in Russia) only four years previously. She had actually enjoyed a good standard of living in Russia, but had uprooted herself to become relocated into a new culture for a new beginning, which had offered a brighter and more secure future. Karynna Byalkanaya had become reborn as Karin Bat-Ami (*bat ami*; literally: "daughter of my nation").

As we chatted about life and I enquired into her experiences adapting to living in Israel, Karin told me the following story.

She had been born to Jewish parents, but communist Russia openly forbade religion and thus Karin and her friends actually knew close to nothing about Judaism and had experienced even less than that. I suppose that it was the mystical "Jewish spark" which had connected her to her people, with the help of the Jewish Agency that had hosted her *aliyah*. She and some of her Russian friends had found adjusting to Israeli culture difficult at first. The climate and the Middle Eastern attitudes were very different from those of her homeland. *Ulpan* (a crash course in Hebrew) had gone well and she had found a job which was an OK start. However, her work consumed six days of the week and there was little free time for leisure, or to explore the new country.

Finally, they saved up for something very precious: the first free time off work, which they had planned and coordinated for their first *tiyul* (excursion). It was so exciting. They had already lived in Haifa for nearly a year and had not yet had the opportunity to visit other places in Israel, or to personally experience things they had heard so much about. They were planning to visit Jerusalem, a two-hour drive southeast from Haifa. They happily rented a cheap car and were looking forward to being in Jerusalem for the first time in their lives. It was like a treasured dream about to come true.

It was a Friday afternoon when they finally set out on their way. They chatted lightly as they drove along with the traffic, exchanging recent work experiences, laughing, joking, singing songs and generally enjoying each other's company, merrily anticipating what was to come.

As they drove into Jerusalem, dusk was already falling and there was little traffic. The streets were narrow and winding and the street signs were hard to read. The road map they had was no great help either in the gathering dark and they were unsure about where they were. They stopped to get their bearings and to ask for directions.

People were walking around them. It felt strange.

Suddenly Karin heard a thud, followed by another sharp noise. She was startled. Their car started to rock and shake. There was the crash of metal against metal. She looked through the window and was instantly seized by fear.

People were milling outside the car. They appeared to be angry, shaking their fists in the air and shouting abuse. Karin heard some of their ugly words: "Filthy Russians", "Russian prostitutes", "Desecrating the Shabbat and polluting the land", "You should be stoned for driving on the Holy Sabbath" ...

Karin saw a young man running towards them waving a steel post in his hands; another young man threw a rock that landed on the roof of their car. Fists were banging onto their windows. She screamed and urged her friends: "Let's get away from here, quickly!"

There was a surge and a screeching noise. The car was skidding. Karin felt nauseous and found it difficult to breathe. She saw the blurred vision of people starting to disappear through the windows, as she sensed their car accelerating up the street. A few minutes later they were driving in a wide street that was well lit and quite deserted. They stopped and sat in silence, hearts still pounding, senses numb, a kind of exhaustion overcoming their breathlessly breathing weightlessness.

After some time, Karin mustered enough courage to wind down her window, sucking in a breath of cool, fresh air. She breathed and breathed. How good it felt to be alive!

Stop! Hold it! Rewind the video!
Sound, lights, action! Take two!

Karin and her friends arrive in Jerusalem at dusk. The time is about 4.30 p.m. on a cool winter's Friday evening. As they start driving through the narrow, winding streets they become disoriented and confused.

It is already dark. The street signs are difficult to read and the map is hard to follow in the darkness. They stop to get their bearings and to ask for directions. It is 5 p.m. and people are walking along the street all around them. Karin winds down her window to seek assistance.

"Excuse me please," she calls out to a passer-by, "Can you please help us?"

She hears a friendly greeting: "Good *Shabbos*, we are on our way home from the synagogue. What are you doing here, driving on a Friday night?" the Jerusalemite continues.

Karin responds, "We are visiting the Holy City of Jerusalem for the first time. We live in Haifa and this is our first ever excursion here in Israel. But we seem to have lost our way. Can you please direct us to the *Kotel*?

"The *Kotel* is only a half hour's walk from here," responds the man, "but it is Shabbat and you must be hungry, or at least a little thirsty! Would you like to join us for a Shabbat meal? It doesn't seem like you have any major commitments. Please come and be our guests at the Shabbat table. After dinner we'll walk with you to the *Kotel* and show you around our beautiful city."

Karin instantly feels warmth, a bond, some kind of inexplicable connection with her heritage and with her people. There is a trust there that seems to reach beyond cultural and geographic boundaries and extends deeper than the many masks of custom, clothing and cuisine (that seem to categorise so much of humanity). She senses a collectivity that transcends her individual consciousness.

She glances at her friends and notices their smiles. There is no need for words.

They park their car, get out and introduce themselves to their hosts.

Me, Myself, Who Am I?
Where am I going? Why? Who cares?

The Talmud (tractate *Avodah Zara* 17a) tells an interesting story about a man who had been very selfish and sinful throughout his life – mostly because he had overindulged in sex for his own insatiable enjoyment and pleasure. Until one day he realised his sinfulness and began asking for forgiveness for all his wrongdoings.[17] When this man passed away, the story continues, he found that not only had he been forgiven, but also that the angels regarded him

---

[17]   In his *Hilchot Teshuvah* (Laws of Repentance), Maimonides writes with great clarity about the principles and practice of repentance. He explains that a person must undergo a

as having a higher status than that of many other souls who had lived much purer lives on earth.

How is it possible? It seems like such a contradiction and so unfair! The Talmud answers: a person who is knowledgeable in Jewish law and who has accepted upon himself to live a moral and ethical life must be judged accordingly. For them, even small details and minor points are significant. In contrast, a person who has never had a proper sense of right and wrong is not likely to become self-motivated to genuinely repent; if such a person does repent it is such a major change, that even if it occurs only during the last few minutes of life, that person has actually achieved a much higher level of holiness than that achieved throughout an entire lifetime of an "ordinary" good person.

Why does this particular story come to my mind at the moment?

Thus far, in my own life, I have felt disturbed about the growing division between the observant and non-observant (or, should I say, the "outwardly observant and/or non-observant"). The "middle ground" is under attack from both sides and its legitimacy keeps shrinking, for no truly justifiable reasons. I observe this accelerating process, see the human psychology of how this is being driven and ponder the logic of this otherwise illogical transition.

Fundamentalism is a very unhealthy phenomenon. It is a condition of sickness with fatal ramifications; its symptoms badly affect the vast majority of innocent "middle-of-the-roaders", who generally are not even consciously aware of having become infected.

I am a religiously observant Jew but no extremist; by choice I refuse to wear any "uniform". I view myself as a human being who accepts the Torah,

---

three-phase genuine, heart-wrenching process in order to successfully effect change and gain repentance from sin. These three phases are:

(i)   identifying and admitting the fact that a sinful act had been committed and acknowledging all its details;

(ii) feeling and expressing remorse about having done that sinful act (in other words, taking responsibility for one's actions and feeling the pain of having done wrong);

(iii) taking upon oneself unequivocally not to repeat that particular sinful act, whatever future circumstances and temptations one may encounter.

5: The hidden Aleph = letter A of Hebrew alphabet

(watercolour 57 x 51 cm) 2008

You can view/download the paintings in original full colour, free of charge at:

www.mysteryofyou.com

6: The (hidden) Menorah of the Torah (Torah code)

(watercolour 57 x 51 cm) 2009

You can view/download the paintings in original full colour, free of charge at:

www.mysteryofyou.com

7a: Nisan – the idea of the two first months

(watercolour, 57 x 51 cm) 2009

You can view/download the paintings in original full colour, free of charge at:

www.mysteryofyou.com

7b: Tishrei – the idea of the two first months

(watercolour, 57 x 51 cm) 2009

You can view/download the paintings in original full colour, free of charge at:

www.mysteryofyou.com

believing that it was given to us on Mt Sinai over 3,300 years ago and is still alive and relevant today. I believe in G-d with all my heart and soul. I am one of His many servants. But I am not G-d's policeman. Nor am I His salesman, as He doesn't need to sell anything.

Strange? Perhaps; but I certainly don't feel strange or embarrassed. Neither am I an unstable person, nor in any way suffering from psychiatric abnormality.

Why do I feel compelled to say these things? And why here?

My analysis is non-partisan and it is based on many years of practical observation. Most problems that we encounter are the result of misperceptions, misunderstandings and misinterpretations born of partial truths, pre-assumptions, bias and suspicion; sometimes they are the result of premeditated manipulation. Whatever the cause, the victim is always the innocent majority.

Another fascinating Talmudic story (tractate *Bava Metzi'a* 59b) revolves around a passionate intellectual debate between the leading Talmudic giants of the day about some delicate points of Torah law. All of the rabbis ruled one way, except for one dissenting rabbi, Rabbi Eliezer, who argued most eloquently for the alternative. Then the Talmud relates an amazing series of events:

> "If the *Halachah* (law) agrees with me, let this carob tree prove it!" (says Rabbi Eliezer, the dissenting Sage). Thereupon the carob tree was torn a hundred cubits out of its place ...

> "No proof can be brought from a carob tree," they (the other rabbis) retorted. Again he said to them: "If the *Halachah* agrees with me, let the stream of water prove it!" Whereupon the stream of water flowed backwards.

> "No proof can be brought from a stream of water," they rejoined ... Again he said to them: "If the *Halachah* agrees with me, let it be proved from Heaven!"

> Whereupon a Heavenly voice cried out: "Why do you dispute with Rabbi Eliezer, seeing that in all matters the *Halachah* agrees with him?"

> But Rabbi Joshua arose and exclaimed: "It (the Torah) is not in heaven!" (Deuteronomy 30:12).

The point is that we were all created as equal human beings living real lives on earth, imbued with the power of thought and free will to make conscious as well as subconscious choices. We were not created as humanoid robots that can abrogate our responsibility for this Divinely-given freedom of choice, nor did we come into this world as artificial clones.

We are what we are and there is an incredible amount of ingenuity, individuality and beauty in what and who we all are. None of us human beings was created perfectly, nor does the Divine Creator ever expect us to function to perfection. More importantly, none of us should ever have the arrogance of even thinking that we, human beings, can ever be perfect. G-d made each and every one of us individually; He knows our weaknesses.

Many third-world societies have very highly developed social structures. People in these communities live and work together, helping and caring for each other. They are very moral and ethical groups of people; their members do not kill or injure each other, nor do they steal, rape or take advantage of each other. Their economy is honest, with no inequitable bartering or claims for goods or services of unfair quality or quantity. People listen to one another attentively, without raising their voices or interrupting each other. The elders and the leadership are not corrupt and are highly respected. There is natural harmony in such social structures which respond collectively to outside threats.

This takes me back to my story of Karin's first encounter with the Sabbath which, so unfortunately, is symptomatic of the fundamentalist division.

The *Mishnah* in *Pirkei Avot* (Ethics of the Fathers 1:1) instructs us to "make a fence around the Torah". The Talmud (tractate *Bava Metzi'a* 58b) decrees that embarrassing a person in public is akin to murdering them and should be punished accordingly. What could possibly be the connection between these two sayings?

The Talmud in tractate Shabbat laboriously and logically analyses the 39 forbidden kinds of work derived from the Torah and lists the commanded and recommended conduct for Jews during the Sabbath.

Karin's and her friends' experience is most probably very foreign to many readers. The actions of her aggressors were the actions committed by "holier than thou" people, people who set themselves up over everyone else, a perverted version of "G-d's Army".

It is bad enough when one human being sins and unduly harms another. But in my opinion, what is far worse is when a group collectively "flies its flag" in the name of whatever cause and acts aggressively towards other people, whose sole crime is that they happen to be different. And when this is done in the name of religion, it is a terrible offence against that religion. Worse still, it is a desecration of G-d's name (*Chillul Ha-Shem*, in Hebrew).

So then, what about the "fence" and the "making of the fence"?

A fence is most usually designed as a barrier. In farms, for example, it keeps animals in so that they should not stray, or else keeps other animals out so that they should not feed on crops within the fenced area. In public domains – such as in a park, a forest or a coastal foreshore – a fence defines a boundary. Fences are often erected between adjacent properties as a line of demarcation. And when someone adopts a neutral or non-committal position, we say that he or she is "sitting on the fence". In many societies, both past and present, there are societal fences based on class distinction, genetics, wealth, power and the like.

Jews are instructed to create a boundary between our Torah and everything which may lead us astray from a Torah way of life. On one hand this boundary, this metaphoric fence, is designed to protect our holy Torah from being changed, diluted or corrupted in any way over time – or, in other words, to remain unchanged and unchangeable. The interpretation of the law in every generation and its application to modernity is called the *Halachah* (literally – "the way"). In the *Halachah*, the majority rule applies, even though a dissenting minority opinion is recognised as such. The Torah was given to humankind on earth and survives in the earthly realm due to this fence (or stipulation).

On the other hand, this boundary, or fence, is designed to protect people from themselves, because when left to their own devices, humans can be extremely dangerous and destructive. Freedom of choice is based upon the concept of ethics and morality; it cannot and must not be a random choice of "today's personal feel-goods", but are Torah-specified absolutes. Thus, the creation of fences helps create a self-protection mechanism, designed to keep wrongdoing out (or at least subdue the temptation to do wrong) and to keep oneself within, so to speak.

From a group or communal point of view, collective boundaries are created and maintained by the leadership for the perceived benefit of their communities. Thus, the perpetuation of these fences is often intertwined with pressures to conform and caveats against non-conformity.

Think about any group, club or organisation: its very existence is based upon its constituency. There are collections of people who belong to this or that particular group. These people may have chosen to belong to the group, or may have been recruited, enticed or even forced to join it. Some groups – mostly older, more established ones – comprise only members who have been born into them and sometimes they have to find ways of attracting new membership. But in any case, the very existence of a group implies a code of ethics and conduct, sometimes also certain qualifications (paying financial dues also helps), commitment to the cause, or acceptance of certain beliefs and rituals.

There are, however, other kinds of clubs too. For example: joining the very special, international and exclusive "grandparents club" requires no skill, no effort and no application forms. It's a great "club" to be in for any person lucky enough to have attained this status. All you have to do is enjoy – and spend quality time, if you choose to.

Everyone needs to feel wanted. Everyone wants to feel secure, to give and to receive, to talk and to listen, to love and to feel loved. People need to be part of something – to belong. Even extreme non-conformists or hermits connect with their own realities and what they are seeking, and separate themselves from what they cannot identify with.

This is the great voyage of discovery in life upon which each individual embarks, to a greater or lesser extent. Personal frailties, restrictions and limitations affect both the outward and the innermost manifestations of this great journey from birth through to death. Birth and death are the only two certainties in life. The first one is simply inflicted upon the person, who then starts to grow and develop and tune in. The second one is certain yet unpredictable, time-wise. It is the in-between, with its many uncertainties, which is the life of every person.

Many psychologists point to three major shells (or defence mechanisms), that people create around their psyches. The outer shell reflects the persona, which is what we show to other people in general. This shell is fairly readily open to penetration in situations of friendship and trust. When penetrated, it reveals an intermediate shell containing values, feelings, fears and aspirations. Then comes the deepest shell, one that hides the innermost personal makeup of each individual and which remains unrevealed – often even to ourselves.

These shells are like fences – barriers established to protect the inside and also to demarcate it from the outside. They split into sub-shells, depending upon life experiences and environment. Moods, self-esteem and quality of life all have a share in influencing the overall balance.

What is the difference between a boundary and a fence, a fence and a wall, a wall and a fort? Surely it is only a matter of intensity.

Every group of people includes a large sub-group of middle-of-the-roaders and a smaller, more intense sub-group of both extremes. Whichever way we define the average, we will always have to accept a statistical spread falling on either side of the middle. In different groupings, one might find oneself either in the average, or above or below it – depending on the definitions.

Two obvious phenomena can be observed:

- Most people can readily associate with multiple groupings of people simultaneously;
- In any grouping, whether formal or informal, some people will fit in better than others and feel comfortable and accepted.

It is easy to picture how some people find it much easier than others to fit into a group and to feel comfortable and accepted. It is also easy to picture how some people would find it difficult to fit into a particular group and would feel uncomfortable and unaccepted.

These self-erected fences become automatically adjusted (or even tailored) to one's environmental circumstances. This phenomenon is usually ous defence mechanism, which turns into awareness only ⸀erson's comfort zone is being challenged. In such situations, ⸀stic behaviour may be triggered to compensate for the lack of comfort, ⸀familiarity of the environment or the insecurity.

Personal fences are very complex and also very variable in nature. When fences are created for the benefit or control of a group, all kinds of additional complex issues arise. Some fences are designed to cater for the perceived average of the group, while others need to cover "worst-case scenarios".

In a military system the rules must be clear, precise and readily applicable for the simplest foot soldier. The entire machine must be able to achieve specific objectives under stressful and dangerous conditions, in which individuals can be sacrificed expeditiously for the overall survival of the group.

Religions offer comfort, security and purpose in life not only in the here and now, but usually also in the hereafter. Participation is made easier by belonging and contributing, as well as by abstaining from certain things. Questions are often perceived as threatening – even though questioning is a positive activity which should be encouraged, as the answers can strengthen the entire fabric of the group – because they are perceived as threatening: they might shake one's belief, encourage putting an end to blind faith, or even present an open challenge to religious rulings or teachings. So often in our human existence there is a disparity between the practical and the theoretical. In many religious orders the leadership is unable to relate to the members; and worse still, it fails to set a living example.

People need mentors, role models they can respect and trust, look up to and emulate. As we all know, when there is a discrepancy between word and deed, children will behave according to what their parents do, not according to what they say.

Karin and her friends, who were frightened by the violence of their fundamentalist attackers, did not have the slightest idea what the problem was. As for the attackers, I do not believe that their aggressive behaviour was motivated by an evil intention; rather, I believe that in some distorted way they had a sense of Divine mission, accompanied by a misguided fear of witnessing the desecration of religious belief. I am also quite convinced that they had no idea about the possible consequences of their aggressive and frightening behaviour. Blind obedience and robotic observance are terribly dangerous, especially within a fundamentalist or cult framework.

I believe that a positive approach towards those perceived to be on the outside of the fence – where "can" is given priority over "don't" and where living examples of "what's nice/good" are deemed more important and valuable than behaving like self-appointed judges and executioners – will yield far better results than mere concern for the fence itself.

The old cliché of not being able to see the forest for the trees seems quite appropriate, especially since some trees also make good fence posts.

When you place yourself on the inside of something, you usually identify with it – at least to some extent – or wish to identify with it. Thus, the "don'ts" become easier to live with, if priority is given to learning about them alongside the "do's".

To me, the real problem was the fence.

A religiously observant Jew should be able to maintain some kind of reasonable fence around the observance of the Shabbat laws, yet that must be done within the overall context of Torah laws. Torah law does not allow the contravention of one law in preference to performing another law. A great deal of Torah law deals with priorities: in case of a clash between two values, what should take precedence? The most extreme example is the preservation of life itself. Saving a life is equated to saving the whole world and in order to save a life, a Jew is exempted even from the laws of *Yom Kippur* (the most awesome day of the year).

This strongly contradicts the actions of those who, in order to "defend" the sanctity of the Shabbat, do things that are hurtful and harmful to others. Their actions can be likened to a driver who focuses only on maintaining speed limits, while ignoring all other traffic laws. Such a driver could approach an intersection at maximum legal speed, anticipating that the green light remain green; but what if the totally unexpected happens and the light changes to red? That driver may well believe that he is strictly observing the law; but others who observe his behaviour would certainly call it dangerous driving.

It is quite obvious that observance of the law must go hand in hand with the spirit of the law. Undue emphasis on certain aspects only, without proper understanding of the bigger picture, creates a distortion of the original intention of the law, which is fundamentally offensive to the entire foundation of the entire system. In such situations confusion reigns and fences, originally designed to beautify and protect a domain, turn into fortresses that repel everything that lies without.

This is a primary responsibility of the leadership of any group. Living groups are dynamic by nature. Regular positive communication, effective education and consistent and constructive example are necessary to maintain the health and balance of the membership. This, in turn, helps to ensure the longevity of the group.

Here is an experience I had some years ago. I was walking to synagogue one Sabbath morning. I was dressed in my suit and was carrying my prayer book together with my prayer shawl bag under my arm. I was singing to myself as I strolled happily along the footpath, happy to be alive and just enjoying nature. Suddenly I was jolted harshly back into reality by the voices of two young boys calling out: *Muktzeh!*"

Muktzeh is a term that refers to a group of objects that are not to be used on the Sabbath and therefore should also not be moved or handled on that day – e.g. a pen or a hoe. At first, I was puzzled: what were those boys trying to say? Then it dawned on me that they found my carrying on Shabbat to be offensive. Carrying things in the public domain is forbidden (unless there is an *eruv*, as will be explained further on). The kids had a point, they were just using the wrong term; but more importantly, they approached the whole matter in the wrong way. In my mind, I had always been careful to differentiate the Sabbath and thus my actions during the Sabbath from the rest of the week. For example, I would never have taken a pen or a garden tool in my hands during the Sabbath, but my prayer book, to me, was totally appropriate (even though, as I understand it today, carrying things in the public domain on Shabbat without an *eruv* was wrong).

For in addition to the fences – the boundaries, the "do's" and the "don'ts" – there are also the "how's" and the "why's".

Our community had employed a new rabbi who was a controversial kind of personality. He decided to build an *eruv*.[18] In preparation, the rabbi gave a series of lectures on the subject. Sure enough, the community was seething with arguments. Some people supported this idea enthusiastically, claiming that it was high time for Melbourne, Australia, to take its place among so many of the world's major Jewish communities that already have an *eruv*. Others questioned the rabbi's qualifications for such a specialised and complex project. Others yet argued that if Melbourne had managed without an *eruv* for so many years, this matter would best be left alone. Another group voiced the fear that an *eruv* might encourage people to become too lax with their Sabbath observance, whereas another argued to the contrary: that an *eruv* would improve the quality of Sabbath observance (e.g. it would enable strictly observant mothers to push their prams on the streets and elderly people to ride in their wheelchairs or use their walking sticks outside their houses, etc.). Another opinion stated that an *eruv* would prevent many people from unknowingly desecrating some of the Sabbath laws ...

Opinions. Opinions. Opinions. People's comfort zones were being challenged. New fences were becoming established, while some of the old ones were facing attack. People were thinking. People were learning. People were arguing.

Some people were growing. Others were finding it very difficult to cope. Some really didn't care and others openly ridiculed those who did care.

For me, this was a real mind expander. I had never heard of an *eruv*, nor did I even realise that there was an entire Talmudic tractate named "*eruvin*" devoted to this topic. I found the whole thing very exciting.

---

[18]   On Shabbat, a person is allowed to carry appropriate objects (those which are not *Muktzeh*) inside one's private domain, but not between two private domains that are separated by a public domain (e.g., a street). This is as much of a prohibition as lighting fire, building, ploughing etc. The *Eruv* is a kind of a fence that makes it permissible to carry things from the house into the street and vice versa. This is a highly complex *Halachic* issue and many volumes have been written about it.

During my own journey of discovery I had already, somehow, in my own way, created a boundary between my acts and thoughts on Shabbat and those of the rest of the week. It was a kind of a personal *eruv* which, for me, enhanced the Shabbat, making it different and special and elevating it from the rest of the week by adding holiness to it.

As I was progressively becoming more religiously observant, one day my father spoke to me about all the things I was missing out on due to my Sabbath observance. Funny, that! His was the same world I had grown up and lived in. But now, I and my family had something very special – a quality of life and relationship that the Shabbat provided, which was over and above the mundane, everyday life. We were gaining a very beautiful quality of life rather than losing anything at all.

In fact, when my parents visited our home and joined us at the Shabbat table on Friday nights, they always enjoyed our times together and often commented how nice it felt for them to share these times with us.

Every Saturday night, before returning to the mundane, we all meet up in the kitchen and recite the *Havdalah* – a short ritual (involving a cup of wine, a multi-wick candle and some sweet fragrant spices, accompanied by the recitation of some beautiful prayers), whereby we thank G-d for separating the Sabbath from the rest of the week. Then we all kiss each other and wish each other a good new week.

Within a few seconds the phone starts ringing, the TV is on, there's hustle and bustle ... A new week begins.

So what is this fence? Is it a beautiful, loving and warm fence, an invitation to people (friends, family and visitors) to come inside and feel part of the Sabbath? Or is it designed to keep people out? How high or low is it? And where are the entry and exit points? Is it rigid and predictable – or does it fluctuate and change? How different is one fence from another? Are there any common parameters? How similar or dissimilar are communal fences within one community or culture? What differences are there across various nationalities, customs, climates and languages?

One beautiful feature in Judaism is the unique combination of consistency and commonality on the one hand, with differences and individuality on the other.

In many ways, this defies logic. On one hand we are encouraged to practise our individual free choice. On the other hand, we have gone through many centuries during which we have developed separately in so many different villages, towns, cities and countries, often facing persecution and economic hardship; often forced to dislocate and always challenged by the lure of assimilation.

It is the fences that have helped us keep together for thousands of years and survive as a people. What do we have in common? We are the Children of Israel who believe in the one G-d, the same G-d that Abraham, Isaac and Jacob believed in; the same G-d who revealed Himself to Moses and orchestrated our exodus from Egypt. Whether we are the descendants of many generations who have been living comfortably in England, Holland, Morocco, Iraq or Yemen, or whether we are seventh-generation Australians, Americans, Poles, Russian, French or Israelis, our many differences pale before our similarities.

As a fascinated observer of people, I have come to the conclusion that implementation is so often more important than what was originally designed to be achieved. In other words, the how's and why's and the impact of what is being done weigh much more than what was intended to be done.

Let me return to the "*Muktzeh* boys".

One of their grandparents did not live within walking distance of their house. This created a problem for the parents of those boys, since religiously-observant Jews should not drive on Shabbat or festivals. The parents, who did not want to be a cause for desecrating the Shabbat, banned people from driving to their home at all such times. I am no judge, nor do I wish to impose my value system onto this family. They have surely built their fence very strictly.

But on *Yom Kippur* (the Day of Atonement), the most awesome day of the year, every Jew has the opportunity to do penance and thereby become absolved of sins. One very powerful prayer which is repeated many times during that day, the *Al Het*, is a confession of all the sins we may have committed. Among other things there, we confess whatever we may have committed "knowingly and unknowingly".

In our home, we have often invited people to join us on Shabbats and festivals. We don't tell them how to come to us or how to dress; we ask them to join us if it is convenient for them and we welcome them to our home if and when they visit. Over the years we have enjoyed the company of many people who might otherwise have sat at home, lonely, watching TV, or may have gone out to the movies, a restaurant, a disco or a party. When an elderly person visits us, we prefer to help them to their car, if that's how they have chosen to return home, rather that risking them to fall if left to their own devices.

Moreover, imagine the inner conflicts of one who has to choose whether or not to point out to someone else that this or that action is sinful. A person who knows the law and cares about it is likely to appreciate such advice and even expect it and be grateful for it. But if the would-be "sinner" is not "tuned in to the game" – that is, if that person is ignorant of the law, or does not accept it or care for it – then the only outcome will be that instead of transgressing the law unknowingly, that person will now transgress the law knowingly, which is much worse. A difficult choice!

I feel sorry for the *Muktzeh* family. Grandparents should have gained the status and respect of their offspring to enjoy a meal and the companionship together with their younger generations. If, instead, they are excluded from the family because of religious reasons – or are they pretexts? – they surely must feel very lonely, unloved and rejected.

However, the "*Muktzeh* business" also has a very positive side to it – namely, the educational value of clear differentiation between right and wrong, yes and no. In today's "everything goes" world of western tolerance, children are so often confused as to where they stand regarding so many issues and, in particular, vis-à-vis conflicting values.

I remember one very humorous lecture I once attended at my children's school. The lecturer was a leading educational consultant who put on a vivid one-man show, walking up and down the hall, acting out various scenarios and mimicking different voices. One cute story he told was about a five-year-old boy who was angry with his parents and ran away from home. A friendly neighbour spotted little Johnny on the corner of their street, holding his teddy bear in one hand and his lunch box in the other. The neighbour approached the child and asked him if he needed any help or was lost. Little Johnny told him that he had run away from home because his parents had punished him for something. When the neighbour asked him why he was standing at the corner, Johnny replied with a very serious little face that Mummy and Daddy had always told him that he was not allowed to cross the road by himself.

Muktzeh! A clear exclusion, a distinctive boundary, a fence.

It is necessary to teach children about rights and wrongs, so as to enable them to feel natural about differentiating one from the other. It is, however, equally important for children to learn how to behave towards those who are different and how to handle live *Muktzeh* situations. This requires appropriate and consistent examples that the children will be able to observe and then emulate.

We all need to build and to maintain our fences: personal ones, family/friend ones and those that define different groups. Like the *eruv*, one's private domain can be extended into the public domain. The inside of the house can be connected with the backyard, a group of houses can be identified as part of a block and blocks can be grouped into suburbs, etc.

And yet, both the private and the public domain continue to exist as such. There is a big difference between a personal fence and a group fence, even where the individual has accepted and closely identifies with the group fence.

A fence defines boundaries between things. It can protect. It can injure. It can be effective or ineffective.

For an individual, a fence can protect from unwanted external influences. This makes it easier for an individual to stay inside the fence rather than stray outside of it. However, when the domain is not one's personal property, using the fence to exclude others or impose one's own personal standards upon others may be dangerous.

The purpose of "building a fence around the Torah" is to elevate the Torah, to reveal its essence – a beautiful treasure to behold, as well as a fountain of knowledge to aspire to. We protect the Torah in its original form for ourselves and for posterity. No Torah-committed Jew can ever claim exclusivity to the Torah, or exclude others from becoming attracted by the Torah, drawing close to it and being nurtured by Torah learning. Quite the opposite! The Torah is an all-inclusive gift to the Jewish people and to all humanity.

One of the strangest distortions of the fence I have observed occurred in a kosher restaurant.[19] I noticed a prominent member of a very orthodox congregation dining at a nearby table along with three obviously non-Jewish people. The atmosphere was relaxed and friendly; they were visibly enjoying each other's company. The waiter approached their table carrying a bottle of kosher wine and proceeded to ask the strictly orthodox host whether he wanted to open and pour the bottle of wine by himself, or preferred that the waiter do it for him. The host took the unopened bottle from the waiter, uncorked it and filled his own glass. Then he handed the bottle back to the waiter to "do the honours" for his three guests. (I had seen similar "wine business" once at some Jewish event where leading caterers and their experienced staff provided the hospitality service).

Why have I labelled this "a strange distortion"? To answer this question requires some explanation about the whole concept of kosher wine.

Basically, there should be no problem about wine, since it is made from grapes, which are neither dairy nor meat.[20] So what is "kosher wine"? There are three different reasons why the concept of "kosher wine" evolved.

1: Certain wines became disqualified for Jewish religious rituals because they were desecrated by pagans – namely, used for idolatrous purposes. Pasteurised ("cooked") wine, (*yayin mevushal*) however, cannot be thus "contaminated" and can therefore be drunk socially.

---

[19] Jewish people are commanded to eat kosher food – namely, to observe special dietary laws, where milk products and meat products are kept strictly separate and only specified animals, birds and fish may be consumed. In commercial premises, a qualified supervisor must be in attendance to ensure that the law is kept.

[20] Generally speaking, cutlery, crockery or utensils that were used for milk products and came in contact with meat products under certain conditions (and vice versa) become non-kosher and have either to be re-koshered, if possible, or thrown away.

2: Another reason for supervising the wine arose during the Middle Ages, when the Church poisoned wines intended for Jewish consumption.

3: A third reason was created in Jewish communities which enjoyed relative freedom from oppression. In such communities, there evolved a tendency to socialise and mix with the gentiles. Assimilation followed. In order to prevent this, the rabbis, in their wisdom, forbade Jews to drink wine together with non-Jews (generally in public places).

This now brings me back to the strange distortion I observed earlier. If the orthodox Jewish businessman felt comfortable entertaining his non-Jewish business associates in the kosher restaurant – nothing wrong with that – then why go through the whole wine-serving nonsense, which was originally designed to discourage fraternisation? Would it not have been better to accept that, on this occasion, there was a conscious choice intended to avoid conflict? The problem I see here is twofold:

The host was insensitive to his guests' feelings – to the point of *chillul Ha-Shem*, desecrating G-d's Name; he should have thought more about the impact of his behaviour on them.

Secondly, he seems to have misunderstood the whole point of "cooked wine". If the purpose of the occasion was hospitality (take a look at how our patriarch Abraham treated his guests!), he could have chosen to honour his guests by pouring their wine himself; or he could have allowed the waiter to do so and declined the wine; or he could have graciously permitted the waiter to serve all of them equally. By doing so he would have sanctified G-d's Name and Judaism and would have surely achieved so much more.

Fences are necessary and desirable in many situations, but they have to have gates in them. It is always essential to understand the purpose of the particular fence and where one is situated relative to it – namely, inside, outside or on top of it.

I am definitely not advocating diminution of standards or compromising observance of established traditions and ethics. I am also definitely not poking fun at the man in the restaurant. I do, however, wonder how he would have responded had any one of his guests asked him, innocently, about his unusual custom with the wine. Would he say that this was meant to "keep us apart"? Telling the truth in this way would surely be undiplomatic, insensitive and insulting. It would also seem untrue, because of the friendly atmosphere during the meal.

Fences which are intended to protect people, perpetuate moral and ethical standards and to preserve cultural and religious traditions for the overall benefit of a group, serve a constructive purpose. Along with effective education, one that provides a framework of understanding within a consistent context, such fences strengthen their constituencies without negatively impacting other groups of people who have other ways of life.

Unfortunately, all too often power corrupts and fences are created to the detriment of others: either to consciously exclude them or, worse yet, to deprive or even harm them.

One such example is the operation of the Inquisition of the Catholic Church throughout the Middle Ages. The Inquisition, whose philosophy called for the forceful conversion of the Jews or their elimination, caused tremendous suffering to many people, Jews and non-Jews alike. In today's "live and let live" Western democracies, where we find it easy to reconcile with, accept and respect others' views and beliefs, such a philosophy is difficult to comprehend. Today we can easily conceive of a world where Christians, Moslems, Jews (believers in monotheism) and non-believers can all live in harmony, without taking the elimination of everyone else as a prerequisite.

Some time ago the head of the Catholic Church in France, Cardinal Jean-Marie Lustiger, visited Australia. I attended one of his lectures in Melbourne. Cardinal Lustiger was one of the most serious candidates for the office of the Pope. He was Jewish-born and was saved by a Catholic family during the Holocaust of World War II. His Jewish heritage was not hidden from him, yet he chose to convert to Christianity. I found the synthesis of his Jewish connection with his freely chosen Catholicism fascinating: at times, they seemed to become confused, as he was not prepared to deny any of them, but seemed to wish to live both of them. To me it appeared like a fluid fence. It must be very difficult to be "both of an either/or". To be sure, a strong background in one camp or culture can serve to enrich other camps or cultures; and yet, there are clear differences that necessitate fences.

Another example of this phenomenon is the steep rise in Islamic fundamentalism. The Koran, which is about 650 years "younger" than the New Testament and some 3000 years the junior of our Torah, contains very many laws. For example: Moslems are supposed to value life and are not supposed to kill; they also have dietary laws, which are very similar to kashrut but less stringent. Nowadays, we can obviously witness how misinformation, corruption, abuse of education and suppression can very quickly breed generations of people who have no regard for any other point of view and, worse still, who fanatically believe that the lies which they have been pumped full of are the absolute truth. The fence they have built for themselves is one that requires extreme abuse of its own membership within and the annihilation of everything which lies without.

This is certainly not what their prophet Mohammed taught. It surely cannot provide any acceptable or sustainable future. G-d forbids killing, so how can wanton murdering be done in His name?

One contemporary example of this phenomenon and its logical process is Iran. Deposing of the Shah, about a quarter of a century ago, was followed by a period of fanatical repression, brutalisation and terror, which resulted in the isolation of Iran from the rest of the world and its moving backwards in time. Today, the younger generation is beginning to rebel: youths are demanding education, women ask and get more rights – it is not difficult to imagine a new Iran, a moderate Islamic state with a more democratic political leadership that respects its own population. The whole world is now confronting the consequences of the cruelty and extremism of the Taliban regime in Afghanistan – a fence that suffocated their people and smashed under the excessive strain.

The Hezbollah – a fundamentalist Islamic terrorist organisation – owns and operates the television station which, morning, noon and night, screens intensive hate propaganda. Showing the map of tiny Israel within the vast sea of Arabia, they call: "There are only five million Jews among fifty million of us Arabs – what are we waiting for? Let us unite to destroy them!" This is often followed by "educational" programs on bomb making, suicide bombing and the like.

How can anyone growing up in such an environment develop any concept of "live and let live", tolerance and compromise? What is their definition of peace? Can pluralism even be considered as an option by them?

Yasser Arafat, the terrorist leader of the PLO, publicly encouraged his followers to kill and to destroy and suppress any contrary points of view within his own people. He openly stated that the best Arab weapon was the Arab women's wombs and, as such, had complete disregard for how many of his own people lost their lives. The recipe for his struggle for liberation was a systematic killing of all Jews. As, historically, it took a few hundred years for Arabia to overcome the Crusaders, time is on Arabia's side to take over the world.

Sadly, this extremism has now been exported to many parts of the world in the form of different terror-based "liberation movements" which actively subvert, undermine and destroy. It is a very sad time in world history when a small group of crazy people, funded and encouraged by "respectable" oil-rich countries, succeed in murdering thousands of innocent people in New York and Washington in a well-synchronised terrorist attack, while also undermining the world's financial systems ("9/11"). They lurk in shadows and justify their actions by misguided, crippled religious ranting.

These are examples of fences gone very wrong. But in truth, fences can perpetuate tradition and define moral and ethical standards without terrorising anyone.

Will the world survive? Naturally! Once our complacency is shaken enough, values such as truth, justice and decency will be mobilised and light will ultimately prevail over darkness. For this is the war between "good" and "evil".

We are now in the latter part of the sixth millennium since Creation. Kabbalists say it is the beginning of the final era, because the world will only exist for a maximum of seven millennia. The seventh millennium will herald in the Messianic period – the final "Golden Age". World history has gone from the tribal systems to the dynastic kingdoms that flourished for various periods of time and then disappeared. We have lived through the times of the prophets, judges and kings. We have ruled and we have been ruled.

The world became smaller after the great periods of discovery. We survived great power struggles – first between church and state, then between the masses and the privileged classes. We endured military dictatorships and the Communist dictatorship of the people. We have experienced capitalism and democracy and now – globalisation. The world is flooded with new technology.

Today, in most western societies, racism has become unpopular, as many of the "old fears" have been subdued by education, together with non-confrontational positive personal experiences of numerous people. Marginalisation has been declared illegal and the workplace is increasingly free of discrimination of all kinds (sex, race, religion, culture, age, disability).

Socialisation is much more possible, especially among the more educated, where intermarriage is quite acceptable. Adoption of children from African, Asian and Hispanic origins by more affluent Europeans is also becoming common.

The overall trend, then, is to break down all those fences that are based on prejudice, hatred and fear.

Yet we, Jews, are supposed to be "the chosen people", "the people of the book" and "a light unto the world". What kind of a fence does this imply? One very common error is the notion that we are superior to non-Jews. This concept has aroused much anti-Semitism from without, along with a feeling of self-consciousness, or embarrassment, from within.

"The chosen people" is expected to accept a level of ethics and morality; to be a living example of good behaviour towards others, to assume a responsibility for the world, which would serve as a beacon. In short, we were chosen to be a living example to the world.

This defies logic.

Throughout history there were always less than twenty million Jews living in any given period (usually much fewer). We have been exiled and dispersed in so many different communities within so many different countries all over the globe. We have existed as a stateless people for more than three-quarters of our history. No other group of people in the world has ever even come close to this.

G-d created us with free choice. Whenever we chose to follow our natural instincts and neglected making the right choices, we were "hammered" and reminded who we are (see Leviticus 26:14-46; Deuteronomy 28:15-69 – "the curses"). Whenever we succeeded in making the right, yet difficult choices, which often conflicted with our natural instincts, we thrived (see Leviticus 26:3-13; Deuteronomy 28:1-14 – "the blessings"). The Bible is brutally clear when it sets out "the Blessings and the Curses", reminding us that all the choices we make have consequences.

The standards are very high; often they even seem too high. And the higher we reach, the more we see what needs to be achieved and the better we understand how far away we are from attaining the high goals we set for ourselves.

Most people take the path of least resistance and, by "not knowing", or choosing not to know, get through life without too much threat or effort. Some people even run away and try to hide – a bit like the prophet Jonah. But sooner or later, we all find ourselves confronted with our consciences.

This is the convergence of the infinite with the infinitesimal. The Divine spark within us stirs and creates an uncomfortable feeling deep within us, which interferes with the routine patterns of our behaviour.

The convergence of the infinite with the infinitesimal

Later on, we shall encounter the concept of a "singularity" in space/time. One illustrative example is the creation of the universe, where an extremely vast amount of energy/matter originated within an extremely minute part of space/time. There is no known mathematics that functions in these kinds of situations, as there is an immediate contradiction in the boundary conditions of the event. This is the apparent contradiction of the simultaneous occurrence of the infinitely large with the infinitesimally small.

I call this "the convergence of the infinite with the infinitesimal", because both the infinite and the infinitesimal are the limits of this kind of a convergence, which is far beyond the grasp of our intellectual imagination. However, when one contemplates the convergence process from a point in space/time which is only ever so slightly removed from the actual convergence condition, then one can readily visualise the very large and the very small coexisting at the same point within time/space.

We shall also very briefly encounter the mathematical concept of imaginary numbers, which are based on the notion of the square root of minus one. As we all know, the square root of minus one cannot exist in the real world, because a square root of any number, when multiplied by itself, must – by definition – equal that number; and two minuses, when multiplied by each other, make a plus.

Mathematicians label this concept "i" ($\sqrt{-1}$ = "i").

Although the "i" exists only in the imaginary world, it is very useful in solving many mathematical equations which are used in many everyday, real world situations, including electricity and electronics. Very often, solving the "real world equations" makes us enter into the "unreal or imaginary world" and then go back again to the real world. Sometimes we simply find that the imaginary numbers are eliminated in the course of the solution process, so that only real numbers remain. At other times we are left with both real and imaginary number solutions, and logic demands that we disregard the imaginary number solutions as unreal and accept only the real number solutions.

When I contemplated singularities, I concluded that from the viewpoint of an observer in a post-creation universe, anything that is "pre-creation" could only be imaginary, because for the observer, time = 0 when viewed all the way back to the original point of its creation.

This point of the singularity forms an impenetrable boundary. In other words, we simply cannot connect with "pre-creation" in a material or physical sense, because there is nothing that can connect us with what was outside of our universe before it came into existence. Since its creation, our universe has been expanding, which is observable from both within and without.

The spiritual is imaginary from our point of view, since it has no physical or material connection to the real world where we live – except for the point of singularity. (For some people, however, it is the exact opposite: the physical world seems ephemeral, while the spiritual world is the real world.)

Nevertheless G-d, the Creator, pre-existed our universe and He continues to connect to every living soul on our planet. Such a spiritual connection is not only continuously experienced by many humans throughout history: it is also conceivable philosophically. Our Torah is filled with such connections and each and every religiously observant person has their own conceptualisation of their relationships with G-d.

To me this is the convergence of the infinite with the infinitesimal; G-d is infinite. The vastness of our universe and – even more so – man, are both finite and infinitesimal by comparison. We are told that there is some G-dliness in all humankind and that G-d resides not only in the supernatural heavenly abode, but also in the earthly abode.

Even those who do not believe in the supernatural will readily admit to the human conscience – to ethics and morality, to right and wrong, to free choice and the struggles it creates within each of us. Some people, at different stages of their lives, feel that something is missing in their lives and yearn for something other than the mundane. The suppression of spirituality usually manifests itself in a state of dissatisfaction with life – a kind of loneliness and a terrible thirst for more and more of – what? It is an insatiable appetite that feeds upon itself and that cannot be satisfied with the physical or the material.

At such times, amazing opportunities are created for people to reconnect with their inner spark of spirituality. Like a very faint, smouldering ember, a tiny bit of awareness, when followed with attention and care, is like a small flame that re-ignites; with some fuel and air, it has the potential to grow into a burning bush or even into a real live fire. This fire, when balanced and controlled, can be of great comfort; only very rarely does it rage and get out of control, like a forest blaze.

Thus, like a person lost in the wilderness in a dark, ice-cold winter night, who yearns for some warmth, light and comfort, so too a soul that has been locked away from spirituality yearns to reconnect, because it cannot be nurtured by the mundane. Such a soul, deprived of its essence, becomes reduced almost to nothingness. But as long as there is life, it persists.

This then is the convergence point of the infinite (G-d) with the infinitesimal (man).

People who believe are readily aware of the need to nurture their individual spirituality. One way of doing so is by connecting with their Maker through a well-established heritage and tradition.

We are neither robots nor clones and therefore must not allow ourselves to fall into the trap of relegating our free choice to some third party. We must retain full responsibility and accountability for ourselves. Our lives are bound up with our spirituality; our spirituality impacts upon our entire attitude towards life and affects our actions in countless situations.

In many ways there is no difference between a believer and one who thinks that he doesn't believe, when both are connected with their own spiritual makeup. The consequences of their spiritual connections are manifested in their thoughts and actions and determine, in turn, the quality of their spirituality.

The advantage of having connected with G-d is the certainty that our spirituality is somehow linked to an absolute set of moral and ethical values. The resulting behaviour has real meaning and provides possibilities for finding out the truth, whereas there is this "warm and fuzzy" feeling that leads us to pick, choose and rationalise what should be on our "good" list and what should be placed on the "free choice menu", because of inconvenience. This is a random, subjective method of trying to achieve the same result, even when accompanied with the best of intentions. Working in a vacuum is very difficult, even close to impossible. Fulfilment can be achieved within a framework of absolutes, not through random choices.

In other words: most "normal" people understand that murder, rape and theft are bad and indeed, in most societies they are considered unacceptable. There were and still are certain milieus where such fundamental ethical and moral values do not exist; the accepted norm in such groups is what we would consider unacceptable conduct. But in truth, the choices of moral and ethical right and wrong are absolute, universal and timeless. Freedom of choice is individual and is a function of one's spirituality together with external circumstances at any given point in time. It is freedom of choice, then, rather than the categorisation of the choices that makes the difference. It's only that a person who is tuned in to G-d has an advantage in that he has a clear starting point.

This is not to imply that every religiously observant person is a spiritual person, connected with G-d; quite the contrary. We all know people who are in no way religiously observant and yet are very saintly. But of course, there are also saintly people who are true believers in G-d.

In every human being there is this Divine spark; it can be suppressed and remain hidden – or it can be nurtured to grow and affect life itself in a very positive way.

Today, the major confrontation is between fundamentalist extremists and everyone else. There is no escaping this threat; it has radically affected people at random and no one is immune to it. Turning a blind eye to what is liable to crush the complacency and routine of our everyday life is not the easy way out: it is a dead end. In order to safeguard our future security and comforts we need to confront and overcome this enemy of our freedom.

The Jewish way is eternal. It is the acceptance of a system of absolute moral and ethical values. Our Torah teaches us that there are 613 laws, all of which can be categorised within the Ten Commandments. But the world at large is required to observe only the seven Noachide laws.[21]

Jews need not fear education, because education is the foundation stone for the fulfilment of their destinies as good human beings. Finding out about and experiencing our rich cultural and religious heritage is no threat at all to the everyday quality of our lives. The real threat is darkness, because it makes us lose our way. Light illuminates us and thus we are enriched. We don't need to try to emulate anybody: not the Nepalese, not the Buddhists, not the Hindus; nor do we need to search for exotic sects or gurus.

Along with "build yourself a fence" we are advised to also "find for yourself

---

21   See Genesis 9:1-8.

a rabbi (or spiritual teacher)" (*Wisdom of Our Fathers* 1:6).

Today, of all times, technology provides us with such easy access to information in so many user-friendly forms. In today's free world, then, ignorance of the facts is pure laziness. We have a myriad of sources and a myriad of different approaches and connections. There is something for everyone within Judaism. The Talmud speaks about seventy different paths, or facets, of the Torah – which stresses individuality and legitimises freedoms of expression.

Many people are scared of finding out about Judaism, lest it hurt them by introducing lots of restrictions and negative changes into their lives. This is quite illogical, because knowledge of positive things results in the exact opposite.

In my own ongoing journey, my experience has been one of deep enrichment and vastly opened horizons. Knowledge provides a deeper understanding of life. It does not necessarily imply acceptance or change; for even if people undertake to explore their roots and heritage, it does not necessitate that they will dramatically change their ways. Change generally occurs differentially, when the timing is conducive for change. Dramatic changes usually occur at times of crisis.

Is the cup half full or half empty? This depends only upon how you wish to view it!

G-d asked Abraham to look up into the night sky and told him that his descendants would be like the stars. There is an implication there about our influence: how many of us are drawn by the illumination and vastness and beauty of the stars and how many are motivated to count them?

During my own journey I have encountered many synagogues, congregations and rabbis. Each had its own, unique flavour. Some I found to be more pleasant than others. Yet even when I experienced things not to my liking, my response was not to reject the whole (for this would include the great unknown) but rather to move forward and keep looking. Excuse the analogy, but will a poor meal stop us from eating?

Each of us is a *bona fide* human being with his or her own likes and dislikes. In my journey I keep going, looking and searching for my own harmony of existence. I have found that there is so much beauty and truth close at hand. The answers are not that deeply hidden, nor are they remote or obscure.

Looking back, it is now so obvious – the keys are in the everyday, because that is the very place where they are required.

We all live in a "myself" society (*moi*, in French; *anochi*, in Hebrew). However, as we are not hermits, we interact with other people and thus must open our awareness to those around us. As soon as we open ourselves up, move away from the material and connect with our spiritual makeup, we experience a closeness with that which is outside of ourselves. Thus begins our relationship with G-d, which will manifest itself in many ways in our relationships with others. For example, in the *Kol Nidre*, the prayer recited at the very beginning of *Yom Kippur* (the Day of Atonement), we are instructed that we cannot be at peace with G-d if we have not first made peace with our fellow humans.

Consider the beautiful verse sung by the congregation when the Torah scroll is placed back in the Ark after the completion of the Torah reading, as well as whenever we lift up the Torah scroll for the congregation to see:

> *Etz chayim hee la-makhazikim bah, ve-tomkeheiha meushar ...*
> *Derakheiha darkehi noam ve-khol netivoteiha shalom.*

("It is a tree of life for those who grasp it and its supporters are praiseworthy ... Its way are ways of pleasantness and its paths are peace." Proverbs 3:18, 17).

So simple – so true – so unintimidating, it is timeless and applies to everyone.

Similarly, every time an observant Jew eats a certain minimum quantity of bread, he washes his hands with water (in a certain ritual manner) and makes a blessing before eating the bread. Then, after having completed the meal, he will say Grace after Meals. Towards the end of the Grace after Meals there is another most beautiful sentence, which is often also sung: "*Oseh shalom bi-meromav hu ya'aseh shalom alienu ve-al kol Yisrael.*" (He who makes peace in His heights, may He make peace upon us and upon all Israel.)

Judaism is a religion of peace. We do not in any way look down on others, nor are we a missionary religion, actively trying to recruit membership through conversion. Non-Jews can convert to Judaism only after having undergone a supervised educational program and made a heartfelt commitment; it is only then that the conversion ritual can be held. It is a lengthy and difficult process. We do not encourage conversion openly, because we know how difficult it is to choose to be Jewish.

Funny, that! A child born to a Jewish mother is Jewish regardless of whether he is observant or not. A non-Jew cannot just become Jewish on a whim or for the sake of marriage, but must consciously accept the belief in the one G-d as well as the commitment to observance.

The convergence of the infinite with the infinitesimal occurs within the soul of every human being. So many people look up into the sky above when they speak of, or try to conceptualise G-d; even more so, we should connect with the unique Divine spark that is within us, the "G-dliness of human life".

Yetzer ha-tov and yetzer ha-ra – the good inclination and the evil inclination

The convergence of the infinite and the infinitesimal within each human being lies in the *yetzer ha-tov* (i.e. the good inclination or innate "goodness"). It is that dimension of the subconscious which attracts people towards the good and helps them resist their *yetzer ha-ra* (i.e. the evil inclinations, which will be further discussed later on).

It is so much easier to grow wholesomely when our search actually clicks and we experience this strange and wonderful spirituality driving our lives. Once we open ourselves to G-d's existence within each of us, we understand that there is no hiding from Him. Our souls and consciences become closely interconnected, while our freedom of choice becomes integrally bound up with a set of absolute standards, rather than random ones. Confusion, uncertainty and even fear of the future disappear and life becomes more serene, pleasant and enjoyable. While we may not have fewer problems or encounter fewer conflicts, we find more solutions with greater certainty.

This is the convergence of the infinitesimal with infinity: the synthesis of the spiritual and the material, the individual blueprint along each path through life.

Every individual is unique and is endowed with free choice. All of life is intertwined around the concept and process of free choice and its consequences. Our perception of reality is greatly influenced by our expectations, as well as by our morality and ethics, when confronted with temptation. Each person feels, at least to some degree, this individual freedom of choice within the externally imposed limitations of environment.

However, "no man is an island"; none of us wants to or can be "self-programmed from zero" according to our own whims, desires, experiences and needs. A time-proven framework exists which defines "good and bad", "right and wrong". The challenge is not to invent this framework but to discover it, investigate it and learn about it. This challenge exists for every individual, since all of us, or at least the luckier ones among us, are taught most of the basics at home and at school.

A conscious – or, more often, subconscious – acceptance of this framework and its rules, regulations and customs is then required. Any community (whether a family, tribe, society or successfully operating group of people or peoples) that wants long-term survival must ensure that the concept of "we" exists along with, or above, the concept of "self". Only then will a positively operating community have a chance to grow. Such a positively operating community has the ability to withstand challenges from without, which inevitably produce inner tensions, whereas a negatively operating community will destroy itself from within and collapse.

I deem it totally unnecessary to have to create the framework, because G-d provided us with the rules and regulations when He created the universe.

G-d's system works. It is up to us to choose to follow it. Acceptance of this unique system as the core value system, with free choice being only relative to it – that is what living life is all about.

This, then, is the foundation of "the fence".

One who has accepted the moral and ethical framework and has devoted time to comprehending it, is well equipped to properly build and maintain his fences. For such persons, there are no real contradictions between what the choices should be, only the degree and, often more importantly, the way forward. This impacts the behaviour of the person when challenged, which presents new choices and new challenges.

Thus the real issue confronting us is not the fact that there is a fence, but how we react to whatever calls upon us to defend our fences when they are under attack. All too often we react "naturally" – namely, by "gut feeling"; but why is it that what feels "natural" to one person feels so "unnatural" to another? It is because what feels natural to us is what has actually been acquired along the road throughout life.

This is the meeting point of randomness, individual free choice and the absolute. This convergence of real and perceived factors is an integral part of everyday life, which continually impacts humanity and produces the many situations and circumstances that each of us needs to contend with incessantly. Its outcome may be harmony, serenity, satisfaction and happiness – or disharmony, frustration, anger, dissatisfaction and unhappiness. Our individual ability to recognise and implement our power of free choice is what life is all about.

Does free choice allow room for differences? Is self-control the same as self-denial? Not in the least. Rather, free choice is about diversity; as mentioned above, it is the communication of the free choice, which manifests itself in our behaviour and in our responsibility for the consequences of our actions.

People respond to what they see, hear, feel and experience. Self-control can quite often become self-denial (usually vis-à-vis negative influences). However, denial for the sake of denial is unhealthy, because it bypasses the self-control system. Harshness and severity in isolation from this framework bring about a sad waste of the many things that life has to offer.

The core of Judaism is the belief in the one G-d. We are commanded to reaffirm this in our prayers three times a day: once early each morning as soon as possible after we awaken, during our morning prayers; once each evening, in our evening prayers; and the third time, right before we go to sleep. The following is a well known passage straight out of the Torah:

Shema Yisrael, Ha-Shem Elokeynu, Ha-Shem Echad (Deuteronomy 6:4)

(Hear, O Israel: *Ha-Shem* our G-d, *Ha-Shem* is one)

This statement is then followed by three key paragraphs (Deuteronomy 6:5-9; ibid., 11:13-21; Numbers 15:37-41). The first two paragraphs are also the ones handwritten on the small parchments which are placed inside the *mezuzoth* (the small containers fixed on the doorposts of every Jewish dwelling).

One very beautiful aspect of this highlight in our daily prayer book (*siddur*) is the crescendo build-up leading up to the *Shema*.

The immediately preceding paragraph is filled with love and adulation. It begins with: "*Ahavah rabba ahavtanu* (with great [abundant] love You have loved us)" and ends with "*Habocher be-ammo Yisrael be-Ahavah* (He who chooses His people Israel with love)".

This is followed by a paragraph that commences with the word *emet* (truth) and talks about the fairness, faithfulness, goodness and beauty of Jewish continuity.

It is very interesting to note the custom where the *tzitzit* (i.e. four tassels – the specially knotted threads tied to each corner of the prayer shawl) are held together and kissed each time they are mentioned in the third paragraph of the Shema and then again when they are released before the end of the subsequent paragraph.

The main topic of the third paragraph is the *tzitzit*. The key purpose of the *tzitzit* is described as follows:

> *That you may see it (the tzitzit) and remember all the commandments of the Lord and perform them; and not explore after your heart and after your eyes after which you stray ...*

This turns my mind back to the story of Creation. There, in Genesis 3:6, we are told:

> *... and when the woman saw that the tree was good for eating and that it was a delight to the eyes and that the tree was to be desired to make one wise, she took of the fruit thereof and did eat; and she gave also unto her husband with her and he did eat.*

This well-known story of Adam, Eve and the serpent is a basic lesson in human psychology. Let us examine the sequence of events: Eve had clearly been aroused and was being tempted. Intellectually, she was aware that a restriction had been imposed upon her; it was actually a restriction of "not eating" rather than one of "not touching". When she saw the tree she was acutely aware of her choices. She could have chosen to walk away from that singular tree, as there was the entire Garden of Eden for her to enjoy; but no: she stayed there, gazing, becoming ever more tempted and more aroused, until the temptation completely overrode her intellectual reasoning and overcame her free will to exercise self-control.

Now, that's what our *tzizit* is all about! *{Do] not explore after your own heart and after your own eyes after which you stray ...*

In other words, G-d created us with the will to "stray". It is part and parcel of each of us. We have the ability to nourish this will to such an extent that it becomes a mighty force to contend with. We have the ability to substitute certain thoughts or images with others, or to simply feed our imagination and encourage it to run wild. Sooner or later, our eyes connect with our imaginations and we find ourselves confronted with real, actual, powerful temptations.

This is the message concerning free choice. This is also the basis for building fences. However, every fence can be circumvented by going over, under, round or through it.

The sequence of events in the Garden of Eden story is both fascinating and instructive in this regard. These two dozen or so verses are filled with insights about us humans. Let us look into some of the discussions from the *Midrash* (homiletic exegesis) on this incident.

In Genesis 2:7 there is a description of how G-d creates man; immediately after that, in verse 8, we are told that G-d plants the Garden of Eden, where He places man. In verse 9, G-d makes every tree that is pleasant to the sight and good for food to grow out of the ground, including two special trees located in the midst of the Garden; the Tree of Life and the Tree of Knowledge of Good and Evil. In the next five verses G-d tells us about the river that waters the Garden and then divides into four different rivers. In verse 15, G-d takes man and puts him into the Garden of Eden to work in it and to look after it.

Now comes a most interesting point: G-d gives man an instruction made up of two parts, the first positive and the second negative. This commandment is given in one continuous sentence which is divided in the Torah into two verses (16-17); fascinatingly, each verse finishes with a "double verb".[22]

> *And the Lord G-d commanded the man, saying: "Of every tree of the Garden **you may freely eat** [akhol tokhel]; but, of the tree of knowledge of good and evil, you shall not eat from it; for in the day that you eat from it **you shall surely die** [mot tamut]."*

Chapter 2 ends with the creation of woman and the concepts of companionship, marriage and conception. Verse 24, the last verse of Chapter 2, "opens the scene":

> *And they were both naked, the man and his wife and they were not ashamed.*

Now, again, consider the sequence of events: G-d chooses the serpent to provoke the woman. The serpent's question is characterised by ambiguity and elusiveness:

> *"Did G-d really say that you should not eat of any [all] tree[s] of the Garden?"*

But the woman seems to accept it at face value and she answers it in greater detail. (Please note that according to the Torah, only Adam was commanded by G-d not to eat from a particular tree and later on, when the woman came into existence, he relayed this commandment to her.)

> *"We may eat of the fruit of the trees of the Garden, but G-d said that you [= we] should not eat of the fruit of the tree in the midst of the Garden. G-d did say that you [we] should not eat of it, nor touch it lest you [we] die."*

---

22 The "double verb" is a typically Hebrew form, whereby the same root appears in two forms: the infinitive and the future tense, for extra emphasis. It cannot be translated into English. In the text, the places where the "double verbs" appear in the Hebrew are in bold letters, followed by the transliteration of the Hebrew.

The serpent continues: he makes a contradictory statement and then tries to justify it.

"You shall not surely die ... G-d knows that as soon as you eat it, your eyes shall be opened and you will be like G-d, knowing good and evil."

It seems that the serpent did not get that information from Adam; it also seems that his intention to provoke Eve and try to deceive her was premeditated. Now, the woman gazes at the tree and starts to feel irresistibly drawn to its fruit – so much so that reason and self-control are clouded. Or, in the words of the Torah, the woman saw that tree was good for food:

– a delight to the eyes – desired to make one wise.

She took of the fruit, ate some of it and then gave some to her husband. Note: the serpent openly provoked the wife, but her husband appears to be a willing participant in eating the fruit, which G-d Himself directly forbade him to eat.

Now comes a mind-blowing statement (3:7):

And the eyes of both of them were opened and they knew that they were naked and they sewed fig leaves together and made themselves girdles.

This verse connects back to verse 25, at the end of Chapter 2:

And they were both naked, the man and his wife and they were not ashamed.

The word for "know" in Biblical Hebrew – *yada* – means both to know and to have sexual relations. But, as many people say, "been there, done that – so what?" So now comes an interesting twist to our story: suddenly Adam and Eve hear the voice of the Lord G-d in the Garden. And what do they do? They hide themselves from His presence. To G-d's calls *"Where are you?"* man replies:

"I heard your voice in the Garden and I was afraid because I was naked and I hid myself."

But man was not supposed to know that he was naked! So G-d asks:

"Who told you that you were naked? Have you eaten from the tree which I commanded you that you should not eat?"

Now listen to man's response:

"The woman who You gave to be with me she gave me of the tree and I did eat."

So G-d addresses the woman:

"What have you done?"

To which she now responds:

"The serpent beguiled me and I did eat."

After this G-d punishes all three with earthly sufferings for all future generations and expels man from the Garden of Eden. The lifespan of all living things on earth is limited. They are cursed with a variety of curses. Two of these are particularly well known:

For dust you are and unto dust shall you return; In the sweat of your brow you shall eat bread.

The human characteristic illustrated here so clearly is the tendency to apportion blame for one's errors to others, rather than to accept one's own shortcomings and take responsibility for them. In this case, at least, all three accept their punishments in silence, rather than arguing or making further excuses. None of them begs for forgiveness or asks for another chance, for mitigated punishment, or even for the opportunity to make good.

Another illustrative example of this blueprint of human psychology and behaviour comes out of the Cain and Abel story. Chapter 4 opens with the conception and birth of Cain and his younger brother Abel. Immediately, their order of importance is reversed. The Torah provides us little background information about these two boys, while the *Midrash* enables us to gain a better insight as to their characters and motivations.

Abel was a shepherd and Cain was a farmer. After some time, both of the brothers brought gift offerings to G-d. Cain just brought some of the fruit which he had grown; Abel carefully selected choice firstlings of his flock, as well as highly valued fat cuts.

G-d showed respect for Abel and his offering, but not for Cain's. Cain became very angry and dejected. Then G-d spoke to Cain:

"Why are you so angry and why is your countenance fallen?

If you do well, shall it [or: you] not be lifted up?"

And G-d continues:

"And if you do not do well [or: not do good], sin crouches at the door and unto you is its desire, but you may rule over it."

The whole concept of sin as the consequence of someone's actions is likened here to a hungry beast lying in wait for its prey, ready to barge in through whatever door it finds open.

(How many people throughout history have had the unique opportunity of receiving counselling directly from G-d Himself? Had you or I had such an amazing experience, what would our response be?)

Now Cain speaks to his brother Abel. The Torah does not specify what he said; the *Midrash*, however, makes a few suggestions. At any rate, when they are in the field, Cain attacks Abel and kills him. (Was this a premeditated murder or just the outcome of an impulsive, angry argument? We do not know and it is not the issue here.)

Now comes another very famous statement, preceded by what I think is a most fascinating interchange. G-d asks Cain:

"Where is Abel your brother?"

To which Cain replies:

"I don't know! Am I my brother's keeper?"

To this G-d responds:

"What have you done?!" (This is an exclamation, not an interrogation.)
"The voice of your brother's[23] blood is crying out to Me from the ground."

G-d then proceeds to inflict upon Cain various punishments that are to affect his future and turn him from a farmer into a fugitive and a wanderer.

Now, all of a sudden, Cain expresses remorse; but that remorse is for himself only. He says to G-d:

"My punishment [or: sin] is greater than I can bear!"

---

[23]   Please note that the word "brother" appears six times in verses 8-11.

Crime and punishment. Temptation and its consequences. Here we once again encounter the concept of *yetzer ha-ra*, the evil inclination ("Satan", "the tempter").

Kabbalistic works shed more light on the spiritual world of angels and other supernatural beings. All of us are aware, to varying degrees, of the different kinds of forces that act upon our innermost selves and how our consciences can play on us. Our subconscious has the propensity to lead us astray, usually with various images and temptations which are the subject matter of our illusions. The boundary between our conscious and subconscious is often a very, very fine line. Our freedom of choice gives us the ability to suppress the subconscious, especially when the *yetzer ha-ra* is playing on us and thus to override the beguiling thoughts with other, more positive ones. The earlier we opt for exercising our control, the easier it becomes. It also gets easier as we get more practice and experience. However, if those subconscious thoughts are fuelled, they quickly grow into images, which take on a reality within our conscious existence. This is how we become misled, deceived or seduced in real life situations.

This is my understanding of the mechanism and process of temptation, free choice and our ability to differentiate between good and evil.

On *Yom Kippur* we have the opportunity to reflect upon and analyse the whole concept of sin and how our behaviour relates to the blueprint of our world. "Knowingly and unknowingly." To me, the "unknowingly" is simply a matter of education, or lack of education. It is definitely not difficult to find out if a person is so motivated to inform themselves.

In fact, in the *Shema* itself we are commanded, "... *and you shall teach them* (= the words of the Torah) *thoroughly to your children*". Parents must ensure that their children receive a full and proper education. This commandment is further expanded upon: "*and speak of them while you sit in your home, while you walk on the way, when you retire (to sleep) and when you arise*".

Obviously, we humans require an active and ongoing education in order to positively feed our minds and turn our moral and ethical code into a framework to live by.

"Knowingly" is actually a question of the fence. Once people exercise their free choice to erect fences – hopefully, based upon correct fundamentals of ethics and morality – the quality of their life choices really boils down to their ability to confront their *yetzer ha-ra*. This becomes a lot easier when they learn to understand how the *yetzer ha-ra* mechanism works. (See article on p. 214.)

In this context of fences, the most important aspect of our behaviour is not a difficult issue to contend with. When our focus is the self, we tend to have little regard for others; but when our focus is the other – namely, other people's needs and feelings – then we tend to be much more considerate. The actual outcomes of our actions and their impact on others are much more important than the intention behind them. It is imperative that our behaviour be consistent with the values upon which our fence is built.

There is always tension within ourselves between the good and bad inclinations. This tension can be healthy or unhealthy. It is a healthy one when it is part of our inner lifelong struggle towards a higher and more meaningful existence. Then it has the potential of becoming a very positive, guiding force in our lives which can provide us with security and comfort. But when the good inclination is suppressed as the bad one is nurtured, the result is a negative, misguiding force that produces an unhealthy outcome.

Short-term sacrifices for the sake of long-term achievements are much more meaningful than instant gratification at the expense of long-term gain.

This struggle of good against evil is very much a matter of self-discipline, the main goal being ethical and moral behaviour. It is the self versus the others and it is reflected by our external behaviour, while our feelings remain concealed. Our personal attributes and character traits feature in the moulding of our behaviour patterns.[24] Our fences, then, are internally imposed but externally expressed.

Let me consider here two more relevant sources:

Ase lecha rav u-kneh lecha chaver (Appoint a teacher for yourself and acquire a friend for yourself) (Avot 1:6).

Ase lecha rav ve-histalek min ha-Safek (Appoint a teacher for yourself and remove yourself from uncertainty) (ibid., 1:16).

A teacher has two principal roles: to impart information and to be a role model. Our behaviour is very much influenced by the images, experiences and memories we acquire.

A good friend should also be a good and trusted counsel.

It is the combination of the fence and the behaviour that makes the human being.

Din (judgment) and *Rachamim* (clemency or compassion) must act together in a true, fair and well-balanced manner. *Emet* (truth), as defined by our Torah, and *Chesed* (loving kindness) define not only the boundaries of our fences but also the correct approach for applying them.

Reyshit chochmah yirat Ha-Shem (The beginning of wisdom is the fear of the Lord) (Psalms 111:10).

Al sheloshah devarim ha-olam omed: al ha-Torah, ve-al ha-avodah, ve-al gemilut Chassadim (The world stands on three things: on the Torah, on the service [of G-d] and on acts of loving kindness (*Avot* 1: 2).

These three pillars are the foundation stones of life on earth. Removing any one of them is like undermining the entire foundation. This is the beginning and end of all things.

Jacob (Israel) was the patriarch of the Twelve Tribes of Israel. They and their children were the seventy souls who went down to Egypt. There they were enslaved and yet also grew into a people which eventually was taken out of slavery and became the People of Israel. These seventy individuals who were bound together as a family stand against the seventy nations of the world and the seventy different paths for Torah study.

Now, why did our patriarch Jacob merit to be renamed "Israel"? Genesis 32:25-30 recounts the story of Jacob's ordeal and his wrestling with an angel for an entire night – and prevailing.

What is so special about this? All of us have struggles of conscience; some of

---

24 Interestingly, the Hebrew word for "character traits" is *middot*, which means, literally, "measures" or "quantities". The underlying idea is that no character trait is good or bad in and of itself, but rather that it is a matter of quantity and how this characteristic is used.

them continue throughout our lives. I believe that Jacob actually confronted his *yetzer ha-ra*, his evil inclination, head-on and was able to overcome it once and for all. In Hebrew, the name Israel – ישראל – can be split into two words: ישר אל, which means: "Straight (or: upright, honest) with G-d". My understanding is that in his fight with the angel, Jacob totally overcame his *yetzer ha-ra* and achieved such a high level of spirituality, morality and ethical behaviour that his evil inclination left him completely for the rest of his life.

I have written all of this in order to share my passion with you and to provoke you to open yourselves up to the truth about life and explore our great wealth of literature, in order to find your own niche there.

At a time when traditional values are under attack and seriously threatened, people's will and the ability to connect with their true essences for the sake of meaningful existence is more essential then ever.

The goodness in humans is their G-dliness.
The G-dliness of humans lies in their behaviour.
That is up to each and every one of us.
This is the essence of life itself.

5: Water, Life and Numbers

The sun, shimmering on the water. The sweet salt breeze wafting the eucalyptus aroma of the sub-tropical rain forest hanging over the golden shining sands of the Pacific coast beach. Relaxing and inspiring. Walking barefoot on the warm sand where it meets the sea, my feet touching the soothing, salty ripples of the warm and gentle waters, where they meet the sands.

Virtually in my natural state, in bathing suit only – walking – singing to myself – thinking – walking.

The waves forming out of the swell, as they move in from the ocean onto the sandy beach. The sheer power and natural majesty crowned in a frothy foam gently caressing the beach before retreating into the shallows; a soft mixing and mingling with the next racing wave.

The ripples felt underfoot in the sand washed by ripples on the surface of the waters.

Reflections of deep blue from the skies around and of clouds above. Reflections of light, sun and images. Refraction of light, colour and images.

Distortions. Diffraction. Symmetry.

Light separating from darkness and colours separating out of the light.

Walking and talking. Counting and singing. Thinking and dreaming. Exploring, yet aware of the beautiful harmony of nature. Creation – life and living – the connection between the finite and the infinite. My shadow, a colourless silhouette in the water and on the sand, extending from my feet, synchronised in motion with me in real time.

Life was formed within the waters, where it thrived; reproducing, living, ceasing to live. Life and water are closely tied together.

According to the Torah, G-d spoke as He created the universe.

A beautiful Kabbalistic interpretation of creation is that G-d first created the letters of the Hebrew alphabet.[25] With these letters and their corresponding numbers, G-d formed the entire universe. He separated "somethingness" from "nothingness". He formed the fluids and then the solids, as He separated "the waters" and the colours, as He separated the light out of the darkness, as He created nature and life.

My thoughts reflect on the beauty and symmetry of nature all around me. My mind plays games with two Hebrew words: "*mayim*" (water) and "*chaim*" (life). *Mayim* is spelled *Mem, Yod, Mem*; and *Chaim* is spelled *Chet, Yod, Yod, Mem*. Both words sound similar and both have the same spelling in their last two letters. The little letter *Yod* is also one of the letters of G-d's name. The double *Yod* spelling of *chaim* (life) seems to connect life with G-d right from the beginning.

Mayim – water. *Chaim* – life. The *chaim* can be split between the double *Yod* (i.e. G-d's name) into two words meaning *chai* – (being alive, i.e. living) and *yum* – the sea. As the *mayim* can be split just before the *Yod* into *Mem* followed by *yum* ("from the sea").

Water and life are closely related. Nature and G-d are closely intertwined. Nature, with its patterns, colours and symmetry and with all of its life cycles playing out in front of our eyes, is a constant reminder of the power of G-d in our universe.

Our universe has its own purpose. There is symmetry, harmony and balance. Everything is connected with everything else. I'm in tune with the rolling waves and the patterns that they imprint into the sand.

Why is ten such an important number? Notice: it is made up of the two most basic numerals – zero and one. In the binary system, on which all computer systems are based, everything is either "on" or "off", it either exists

---

25   The Hebrew original of the verse "In the beginning G-d created the Heaven and the earth" has, between the words "G-d created" and "the Heaven", the small word *et*, which does not really have a meaning of its own. This little word is made up of two letters: *aleph* and *tav* – the first and last letters of the Hebrew alphabet.

or it doesn't. These are the two fundamental universal symbols. Everything else is made up of them and both of them are contained in everything. Ten, then, is the combination of "nothingness" with "somethingness", where even the "nothingness" contains everything. The Number 1 is "completeness", as G-d is one. The combination of the zero and the one symbolise the unique G-dliness of our universe.

Each of the 92 chemical elements naturally existing in our universe is defined by its atomic number (i.e. the number of protons in its nucleus). Water, H_2O, is made up of two atoms of hydrogen and one atom of oxygen. The atomic number of hydrogen is 1, and of oxygen 8. Thus, the 2H and the O make 10! And the Hebrew word for water, *mayim* (spelled *m-y-m*), reflects the atomic structure of the water.

Humanity is a living combination of the physical or material together with the spiritual; a living partnership between body and soul.

Life is given to us by our parents through a physical union, along with the living results of our choices and actions.

Unfortunately for humanity, the randomness of people's value systems is largely due to the fact that they tend to give priority to their "feel goods" and "instant gratification". These are fuelled by people's senses of "re-creating the wheel" and the inevitable consequences that follow – namely, a generally self-indulgent society with no moral and ethical value system to speak of.

There is no need for us to "re-create the wheel". What we do need is to learn the many uses of the wheel and optimise its numerous benefits, which can certainly improve the quality of our lives. We have inherited a value system which works, which has withstood the erosion of time over the millennia. Our system of laws, ethics and morality has survived history.

As we know, our Torah contains a total of 613 commandments. These three digits themselves, when added to each other (6 + 1 + 3), recombine into the number 10 – the primeval combination of the zero and the one, the convergence of the infinite with the infinitesimal. And this convergence is man, whom G-d created in His image and gave him His holy Torah as the blueprint to life.

Some people are more interested in number plays and numerical connections than others. Some of the great Torah commentators connect wonderful thoughts and ideas with *gematrias*.[26] However, *gematrias* are an acquired personal taste popular only with some people.

My awareness of letters, numbers and gematria became aroused after attending some *shiurim* (Torah classes) which were inspiring.[27] During one of these *shiurim*, about twenty years ago, I became aware of some fascinating advanced statistical research work which was being undertaken in the postgraduate mathematics department of the prestigious Hebrew University in Jerusalem. This scant information drew me like a very strong force field to find out more detail for myself.

For those who are unfamiliar with what a Torah scroll looks like, I mention here that the handwritten parchments contain only Hebrew letters and no punctuation. These letters form words and there are gaps and spaces, both between words and sections, which have all been meticulously copied by the scribe. There are no paragraphs, as we would expect in a book, no page numbers, no division into chapters. The text just flows and learned people

---

[26] *Gematria* is a method of interpretation of words or phrases according to their numerical value. In Hebrew, each letter of the alphabet has a numerical value (e.g.: *aleph* = 1; *bet* = 2; *kaf* = 20; *kof* = 100; etc.). Some Sages attach mystical significance to the numerical value of each word and also claim that there is an inner connection between different words that have the same numerical value. See, for example, *The Spice of Torah* – Gematria, by Gutman G. Locks, New York, Judaica Press 1985.

[27] When I originally wrote this chapter, I genuinely played mind games with Hebrew words and their numerical equivalents. I enjoyed "mental gymnastics" by adding and subtracting and condensing these numbers as well as connecting ideas to them. However, when I sat with Rabbi Steinsaltz in Rome, during our interfaith residential conference next to the Vatican, working through this book, he figuratively "threw this chapter out of the window". Despite my stubbornness and my cheeky sense of humour, I was unable to even "sneak some of it back from out of the window, back inside our room through the little high opening". Thus, for quite a while, this chapter gathered dust, isolated and discarded. The Rabbi was, of course, completely correct in his judgment. I accepted it, but still found it difficult to totally delete all of these beautiful fun numbers; until finally, I did throw all of my number games out of the window once and for all and then rewrote this chapter.

know how to read it. People who read modern Hebrew can also find their way through Torah script.

The Torah has remained unchanged throughout the generations. Our rabbinical scholars and Torah commentators provide us with many levels of interpretation and deeper understanding. Often there are multiple layers of information hidden within Torah text.

No other written work in the history of our world can be compared to the Torah. In fact, it is actually a great pity that there are so many translations of the Torah available, in so many languages, which are totally devoid of the wisdom and meanings conveyed by the commentators. Hebrew is a unique language. The Torah is incomparable.

In our Kabbalistic literature we find some fascinating mathematical connections in the Torah. Some sequences of letters and numerical patterns are known to exist. There was a very learned rabbi from Czechoslovakia called Rabbi Michael Dov Weissmandel, who lived during World War II. He made a most amazing discovery: he became aware of an equidistant letter sequence in the Torah, as follows: in the Five Books of Moses, the word "Torah" is "cached" so that from its first letter, *tav*, the next letter, *vav*, is fifty letters ahead; the third one, *reish*, is again fifty letters ahead, and so is the fourth letter, *hei* (50 is a very significant number: 7 x 7 + 1). But while in the First and Second Books this word is spelled in the usual form, forwards, in the Fourth and Fifth Books it is spelled backwards – yet in the same equidistant letter sequence. In the Third Book, instead of the word Torah we have the Tetragrammaton – G-d's Name that contains the Hebrew letters *yod, hei, vav, hei* – hidden within the text in an equidistant letter sequence of seven spaces.

Together, all of this creates a *menorah* (candelabra)-like form, in this case drawn as a hand, in which the Third Book, i.e. the middle one, forms the branch that figuratively binds these four "Torah" words together. Here, then, is a fascinating illustration of a pattern which appears to connect the five Books of Moses together. *[fig. 1]* (see figures 1–5 between pp. 120-1)

I was excited no end by this sudden discovery. But at the same time I was also thinking to myself: this should have been so obvious to me! Now, in our sophisticated computer age, we have very high-speed ways of searching for all kinds of mathematical patterns and sequences, as well as the ability to analyse such findings.

And indeed, such advanced mathematical analysis does exist and I have been shown some of its results. The "brain children" behind this are Dr Eli Rips (an outstanding Russian-born statistical mathematician) and Doron Witztum (an Israeli-born physicist). Together, they created a computer program that can scan the Torah text for equidistant letter sequences and then correlate these sequences with other sequences and/or statistically analyse each of their findings according to the probability of their random occurrence within the Torah text. They also created a more advanced analytical method to enable comparisons with other texts as well as to locate minimum equidistant letter sequences.

Their findings are truly mind blowing; they have proven that such letters or space sequences occur not randomly, but deterministically.[28] These equidistant letter sequences and their convergences with other critically relevant information within appropriate areas of the Torah text were like codes. Here are a few examples, randomly picked from among the very many examples in their book:

- In the passage in Genesis that describes the arrival of the angels to the home of Lot in Sodom and the behaviour of the Sodomites in that occasion, are hidden the Hebrew words for "HIV", "virus", "destroyed" and "immunity". *[fig. 2]*

- In the passage in Genesis that describes how Joseph accuses his brothers of being spies, are hidden the Hebrew words for "Dreyfus", "prisoner", "calumny", "major" (Dreyfus' military rank), "trial", "culprit", "military", "documents". *[fig. 3]*

- The name of Aaron the High Priest, spelled both backwards and forwards, is hidden numerous times, in various sequences, in the chapters in Leviticus that speak about the sacrifices in the Tabernacle. *[fig.4(a) & (b)]*

---

[28] The likelihood of random occurrence of letter sequences was increased by permitting spacing/sequencing errors of plus and/or minus one, two … five letters etc., only to find out that randomly spaced significant letter sequences failed to occur more often than precisely spaced equidistant letter sequences do.

- The Hebrew names of the seven species of plants that are typical of the Land of Israel (wheat, barley, grape vine, fig, pomegranate, dates and olives) are hidden in the passage in Genesis which describes the Garden of Eden, along with the names of some 25 other trees. *[fig. 5]*

In all these cases, these special words have no other significant hidden appearances in the rest of the Torah text which occur at these minimum equidistant letter sequences, thus giving prominence to their actual location within the text.

We should really not be all that surprised by such things, but rather should expect to find them. The Torah is a Divinely inspired text and contains many levels of understanding. Just like *gematrias* and other numerical associations, such mathematical codes should also contain concealed information.

In fact, the Torah is said to be interpreted on four fundamental levels, known as *Pardes* (literally: "orchard"). This is an acronym for *pshat* (literal rendering), *remez* (allusions), *derash* (homilies) and *sod* (deep secrets). It occurred to me that it is quite possible that with time, the discovery of many such coded messages might in turn reveal another pattern or even patterns of codes which might then unlock information regarding future events.

How exciting!

But ...

Lifestyles in our modern world are so contradictory. Originally, I called this chapter "The Numbers Game" because I was playing mind games with the numerical values of a few Hebrew words while I was walking on the beach. I had fun. It was personal, light-hearted, and quite harmless. This process also stimulated my thoughts about life and living life.

Lifestyles: how many people degrade their lives by falling into the trap of believing that their fate is dictated by "luck"? Who would seriously base their entire future existence on some random betting in a casino or on gambling on a horse, a lotto draw or a poker machine?

Life is not a game of chance. By blaming "bad luck" we are merely trying to absolve ourselves of responsibility for our disappointments and suffering. Life is about taking responsibility, not about the signs of the zodiac! We create our own luck by making choices and exercising our free will. We make mistakes, we hopefully learn from them and we mature in how and why we make choices.

Our choices should be informed choices, not random ones.

G-d is all-knowing and all-powerful. He is the past, the present and the future; from His perspective, there is no random chance!

But we humans are no robots. We do not live our lives by operating blindly and senselessly to the signals of some remote control device. We cannot take the lazy choice of passivity.

How could the statistical-mathematical research of Eli Rips and Doron Witztum produce minimum equidistant letter sequences for so many of the names of our history's most famous rabbis, with their acronyms and dates of birth and death? Was it random chance? Or was it the Torah code of determinism?

Your choice!

Obviously, the whole concept of "good and evil", "sin and atonement", "life and death", "the world we live in and the world to come", are about our free choice and how we exercise our free will. We do have free choice. We are not living as a token in a dice game: we are real, thinking, feeling, living entities.

In typically "Ronny fashion", I decided to find Eli Rips and Doron Witztum myself, in order to see and experience what they were doing. During my next business trip to Israel I made time, while in Jerusalem, to start my search. It was both exciting and challenging.

There were no white-collared technicians or receptionists attending long lines of curious onlookers. Both Eli, a not-so-new immigrant from Russia, and Doron, who grew up in a non-observant family in Tel Aviv, are *baalei teshuvah*.[29] Both have found their lives dramatically impacted by their academic research.

Both men are modest, unassuming, quiet personalities. I spent many hours in deep discussions, mainly with Doron, and encouraged him to publish his work. His book is in my library at home.

So what?

So nothing!

---

[29] Jews from a non-religious background who became religiously observant.

All of this is purely academic, like so much of the information accumulated in our world today. What does matter is how we live our lives and what we can derive out of this to improve our lifestyles.

No man is an island! The majority of people interact with other people. A child learns from its parents and as it grows and matures it emulates the behaviour it experiences.

How many modern parents set the correct examples (namely, free choice) and transmit to their children the message "do as I do", rather than to "do as I say"? How many of them tell their children, with words or without: "You must do this and that; but I don't actually have to do so myself, because I'm the parent"?

In the workforce, an employee expects the manager to act appropriately. But in reality, how many managers truly lead by example, rather than through using their position of power? How many leaders (elected or unelected) truly care for their people and seriously take on the yoke of responsibility for the welfare of their people and of society, without giving much thought to themselves?

Free choice: no random numbers, no casting of the dice, no irresponsible game of living life, but rather personal responsibility, along with its inevitable consequences.

Who makes the rules?

Who knows the rules?

Who cares about the rules?

Who follows the sustainable rules of living life?

All this, and more, came to mind as I was walking along the beach, basking in the sun, feeling the sand with my bare feet. But (rules? choice?) the time came to move off the beach and prepare for Shabbat. There I was, then, going back to the mundane in order to ready myself, ourselves, for the spiritual.

The *Kabbalat Shabbat* service[30] was happy, warm and friendly. Over one hundred men, women and children joined together in the main function room of the Sheraton Hotel in Noosa.[31] A convergence of holiday-makers, a kind

---

[30] Literally: "greeting the Sabbath," a prayer recited around sundown each Friday. (Shabbat is from sundown Friday to Saturday night.)

Fig 1:

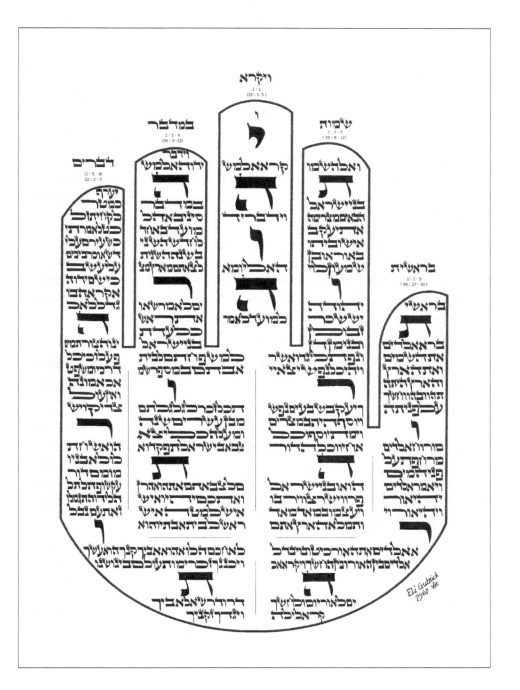

"The Menorah of the Torah" *(in our case, drawn within a hand form)*

The five branches of the Menorah consist of the opening and closing passages of the five books of the Torah. In each of the four branches stemming out from the centre, the word T'O'R'H' (Torah) appears at intervals of 49 letters between each letter. Counting from the first *Tav*, for example, of the word *Bereishit*, after an interval of 49 letters, the 50th letter is the *Vav* of *Tehora* (abyss). Again another 49 letters brings us to the 50th, the *Resh* of *Vayar* (and he saw) and 49 more to the *Hey* of *Elokim* (G-d).

This same design is found at the end of *Bereishit* as well as at the beginning and end of *Shemot*. At the beginning and end of *Bamidbar* and *Devarim*, the last two books of the Torah, the word T'O'R'H' appears backwards as H'R'O'T', on the 49th and 50th letters.

At the top of the central branch, another word appears encoded in the text. At the very beginning of *Vayikra*, the central book of the Torah, the name YKVK (G-d) appears at intervals of seven letters. Also in the seventh *parsha* of the book of *Vayikra*, *Kedoshim* (you shall be holy), the name YKVK appears again at intervals of 49 letters.

The total picture afforded us here is that of the word "Torah" moving from the extremities towards the centre. Perhaps this is the central theme that is expressed by this structure. The authority of the Torah derives from its central, all-inclusive source, the name of YKVK.

Both Torah and YKVK are encoded in the text at intervals of 7 or 49, indicating this profound relationship. In summary it is, needless to say, a great wonder that these and other codes were not made known by the author of the Torah until discovered by Rabbi Michael Dov Weissmandl of Warsaw before WWII. The global character of this particular code, spanning the entire text of the five books and uniting them, bespeaks a single authorship and reminds us of the 8th verse in the 10th Psalm: "The Torah of *Hashem* is whole and perfect, restoring the soul ..."

Fig 2:

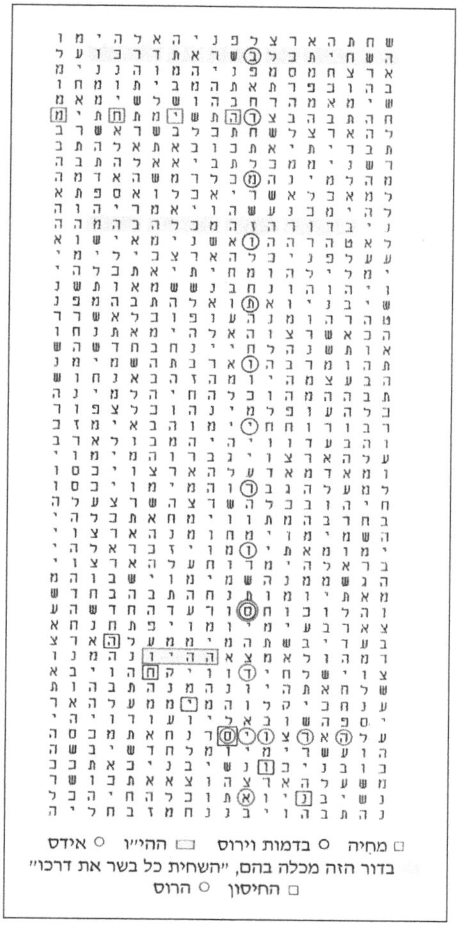

Here we see the following words:

"Bador Hazeh Mechaleh Bahem" – (in this generation it destroys them)
"Bidmut Virus" (in the form of a virus)
"HaHeYV" (the HIV)

We also see the following words (appearing with the least spacing between letters):

"HaChisun" (the immunisation)
"Harus" (ruined)
"Ayds" (AIDS)

The word *"Harus"* (ruined) is marked (vertically) by an equidistant spacing of letters.

Fig 3:

דריפוס ○   אסיר ○   מאסר ○   "באה אלינו הצרה הזאת", "ויתן אתנו כמרגלים את האר[ץ]

We now look at a table of words centred on the appearance of the word "Dreyfus" (vertically appearing with the least spacing between letters).

Here we see a combination of the words "Dreyfus" and "Asir" (prisoner).

The word "Asir" appears here with the least spacing between letters (there are another three occurrences of this word with the same spacing).

This "Asir" (prisoner) is placed in the "Maasar" (prison). The word "Maasar" also appears here with the least spacing between letters.

Just a few sentences after the appearance of the words "Dreyfus", "Asir" and "Maasar" we read (Genesis 42:21) Joseph's brothers pondering why "this trouble has come to us" and further on (42:30) they tell their father Jacob "The master of the land spoke harshly with us and accused us of spying the land."

These same words could have been said by Dreyfus too.

Fig 4a:

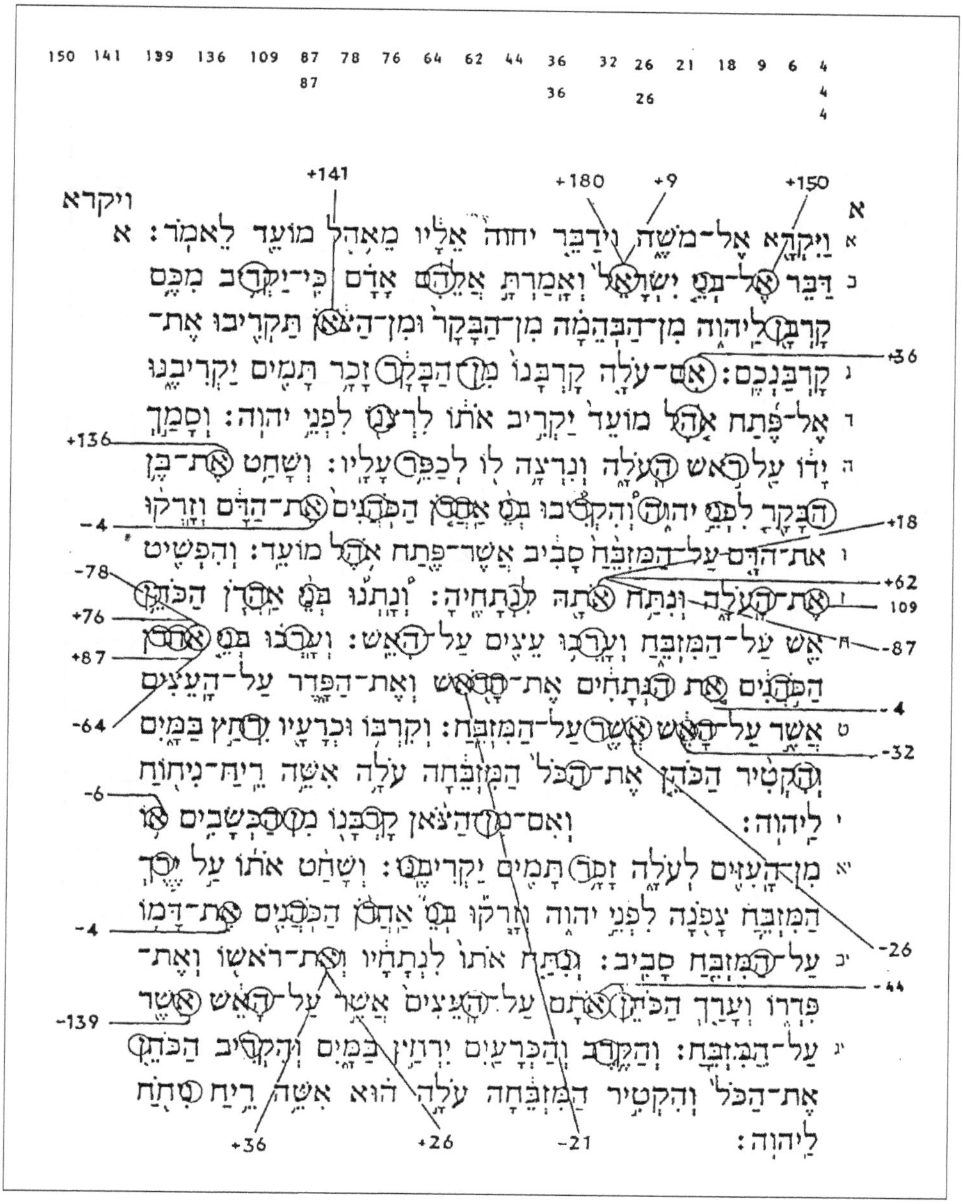

150 141 139 136 109 87 78 76 64 62 44 36 32 26 21 18 9 6 4
87   36   26   4
                                      36   4

+141   +180   +9   +150

ויקרא

א ויקרא אל־משה וידבר יהוה אליו מאהל מועד לאמר: א

ב דבר אל־בני ישראל ואמרת אלהם אדם כי־יקריב מכם
קרבן ליהוה מן־הבהמה מן־הבקר ומן־הצאן תקריבו את־

–36
ג קרבנכם: אם־עלה קרבנו מן־הבקר זכר תמים יקריבנו

+136
ד אל־פתח אהל מועד יקריב אתו לרצנו לפני יהוה: וסמך

ה ידו על ראש העלה ונרצה לו לכפר עליו: ושחט את־בן

–4
+18
הבקר לפני יהוה והקריבו בני אהרן הכהנים את־הדם וזרקו

ו את־הדם על־המזבח סביב אשר־פתח אהל מועד: והפשיט

–78
+62
ז את־העלה ונתח אתה לנתחיה: ונתנו בני אהרן הכהן
109

–87
+76
ח אש על־המזבח וערכו עצים על־האש: וערכו בני
+87
–4
הכהנים את הנתחים את־הראש ואת־הפדר על־העצים

–64
ט אשר על־האש אשר על־המזבח: וקרבו וכרעיו ירחץ במים
–32
והקטיר הכהן את־הכל המזבחה עלה אשה ריח־ניחוח

–6
י ליהוה: ואם־מן־הצאן קרבנו מן־הכשבים או

יא מן־העזים לעלה זכר תמים יקריבנו: ושחט אתו על ירך

–4
המזבח צפנה לפני יהוה וזרקו בני אהרן הכהנים את־דמו

–26
יב על־המזבח סביב: ונתח אתו לנתחיו ואת־ראשו ואת־
–44
פדרו וערך הכהן אתם על־העצים אשר על־האש אשר

–139
יג על־המזבח: והקרב והכרעים ירחץ במים והקריב הכהן

את־הכל והקטיר המזבחה עלה הוא אשה ריח־ניחח

ליהוה:

+36   +26   –21

Fig 4b:

Statistical test: the number of appearances of Aharon at unequal intervals

y x	-5	-4	-3	-2	-1	0	1	2	3	4	5
-5	5	9	10	6	7	11	8	7	5	9	9
-4	9	5	5	8	8	8	9	7	8	2	9
-3	5	10	7	3	4	8	2	5	3	4	10
-2	5	8	5	8	6	10	4	5	6	3	7
-1	8	7	9	4	8	10	7	7	11	8	9
0	9	8	14	6	8	(25)	5	8	4	6	15
1	8	5	10	11	7	6	8	8	5	5	10
2	9	4	10	9	5	8	8	7	5	9	9
3	5	11	8	12	9	5	5	4	12	5	8
4	11	9	6	4	6	9	6	7	8	7	6
5	4	8	11	5	8	9	7	8	6	6	9

Statistical test: other combinations A-H-R-N

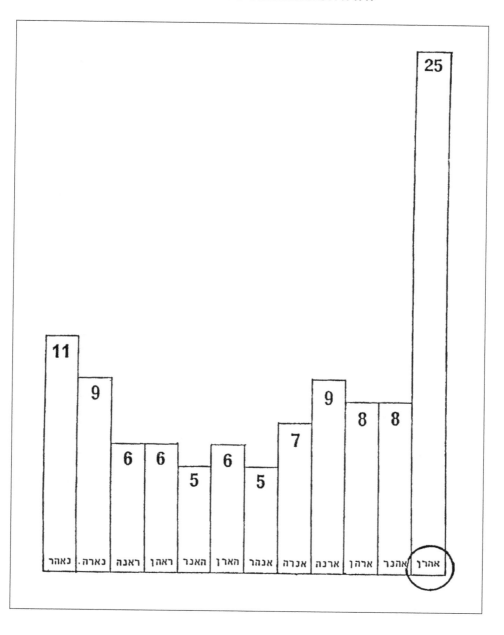

Fig 5:

חיטה	5	
גפן	10-	
ענב	6-	
ערמון	44	
גבח	5	
שטה	3-	
אטד	7	
ארז	5-	
בטן	13	
תאנה	14	
	15-	
רמון	8	
אהלים	6	
אשל	2	
אלון	17	
לבנה	85-	
קרה	7	
שקר	5	
אלה	2-	
סנה	9	
לוז	16-נ	
זית	3	
הדר	נ-	
גמר	8	

1. wheat
2. vine
3. grape
4. chestnut
5. dense forest
6. date
7. acacia
8. brambel
9. cedar
10. peanut
11. fig
12. willow
13. pomegranate
14. aloe
15. tamarisk
16. oak
17. poplar
18. cassia
19. almond
20. mastic
21. thorn bush
22. hazel
23. olive
24. etrog
25. fir

ו אֶת־כָּל־פְּנֵי הָאֲדָמָה: וַיִּיצֶר יְהוָה אֱלֹהִים אֶת־הָאָדָם עָפָר
מִן־הָאֲדָמָה וַיִּפַּח בְּאַפָּיו נִשְׁמַת חַיִּים וַיְהִי הָאָדָם לְנֶפֶשׁ חַיָּה:

ח וַיִּטַּע יְהוָה אֱלֹהִים גַּן־בְּעֵדֶן מִקֶּדֶם וַיָּשֶׂם שָׁם אֶת־הָאָדָם אֲשֶׁר
יָצָר: וַיַּצְמַח יְהוָה אֱלֹהִים מִן־הָאֲדָמָה כָּל־עֵץ נֶחְמָד לְמַרְאֶה

ט וְטוֹב לְמַאֲכָל וְעֵץ הַחַיִּים בְּתוֹךְ הַגָּן וְעֵץ הַדַּעַת טוֹב וָרָע: וְנָהָר
יֹצֵא מֵעֵדֶן לְהַשְׁקוֹת אֶת־הַגָּן וּמִשָּׁם יִפָּרֵד וְהָיָה לְאַרְבָּעָה

יא רָאשִׁים: שֵׁם הָאֶחָד פִּישׁוֹן הוּא הַסֹּבֵב אֵת כָּל־אֶרֶץ הַחֲוִילָה
אֲשֶׁר־שָׁם הַזָּהָב: וּזֲהַב הָאָרֶץ הַהִוא טוֹב שָׁם הַבְּדֹלַח וְאֶבֶן

יג הַשֹּׁהַם: וְשֵׁם־הַנָּהָר הַשֵּׁנִי גִּיחוֹן הוּא הַסּוֹבֵב אֵת כָּל־אֶרֶץ

יד כּוּשׁ: וְשֵׁם הַנָּהָר הַשְּׁלִישִׁי חִדֶּקֶל הוּא הַהֹלֵךְ קִדְמַת אַשּׁוּר

טו וְהַנָּהָר הָרְבִיעִי הוּא פְרָת: וַיִּקַּח יְהוָה אֱלֹהִים אֶת־הָאָדָם
וַיַּנִּחֵהוּ בְגַן־עֵדֶן לְעָבְדָהּ וּלְשָׁמְרָהּ: וַיְצַו יְהוָה אֱלֹהִים עַל־הָאָדָם

יז לֵאמֹר מִכֹּל עֵץ־הַגָּן אָכֹל תֹּאכֵל: וּמֵעֵץ הַדַּעַת טוֹב וָרָע לֹא
תֹאכַל מִמֶּנּוּ כִּי בְּיוֹם אֲכָלְךָ מִמֶּנּוּ מוֹת תָּמוּת: וַיֹּאמֶר יְהוָה

יח אֱלֹהִים לֹא־טוֹב הֱיוֹת הָאָדָם לְבַדּוֹ אֶעֱשֶׂה־לּוֹ עֵזֶר כְּנֶגְדּוֹ: וַיִּצֶר
יְהוָה אֱלֹהִים מִן־הָאֲדָמָה כָּל־חַיַּת הַשָּׂדֶה וְאֵת כָּל־עוֹף הַשָּׁמַיִם
וַיָּבֵא אֶל־הָאָדָם לִרְאוֹת מַה־יִּקְרָא־לוֹ וְכֹל אֲשֶׁר יִקְרָא־

כ לוֹ הָאָדָם נֶפֶשׁ חַיָּה הוּא שְׁמוֹ: וַיִּקְרָא הָאָדָם שֵׁמוֹת לְכָל־
הַבְּהֵמָה וּלְעוֹף הַשָּׁמַיִם וּלְכֹל חַיַּת הַשָּׂדֶה וּלְאָדָם לֹא־מָצָא

כא עֵזֶר כְּנֶגְדּוֹ: וַיַּפֵּל יְהוָה אֱלֹהִים תַּרְדֵּמָה עַל־הָאָדָם וַיִּישָׁן וַיִּקַּח

כב אַחַת מִצַּלְעֹתָיו וַיִּסְגֹּר בָּשָׂר תַּחְתֶּנָּה: וַיִּבֶן יְהוָה אֱלֹהִים
אֶת־הַצֵּלָע אֲשֶׁר־לָקַח מִן־הָאָדָם לְאִשָּׁה וַיְבִאֶהָ אֶל־הָאָדָם:

כג וַיֹּאמֶר הָאָדָם זֹאת הַפַּעַם עֶצֶם מֵעֲצָמַי וּבָשָׂר מִבְּשָׂרִי לְזֹאת

כד יִקָּרֵא אִשָּׁה כִּי מֵאִישׁ לֻקֳחָה־זֹּאת: עַל־כֵּן יַעֲזָב־אִישׁ אֶת־

כה אָבִיו וְאֶת־אִמּוֹ וְדָבַק בְּאִשְׁתּוֹ וְהָיוּ לְבָשָׂר אֶחָד: וַיִּהְיוּ שְׁנֵיהֶם

ג א עֲרוּמִּים הָאָדָם וְאִשְׁתּוֹ וְלֹא יִתְבֹּשָׁשׁוּ: וְהַנָּחָשׁ הָיָה עָרוּם מִכֹּל
חַיַּת הַשָּׂדֶה אֲשֶׁר עָשָׂה יְהוָה אֱלֹהִים וַיֹּאמֶר אֶל־הָאִשָּׁה אַף

ב כִּי־אָמַר אֱלֹהִים לֹא תֹאכְלוּ מִכֹּל עֵץ הַגָּן: וַתֹּאמֶר הָאִשָּׁה

ג אֶל־הַנָּחָשׁ מִפְּרִי עֵץ־הַגָּן נֹאכֵל: וּמִפְּרִי הָעֵץ אֲשֶׁר בְּתוֹךְ־הַגָּן
אָמַר אֱלֹהִים לֹא תֹאכְלוּ מִמֶּנּוּ וְלֹא תִגְּעוּ בּוֹ פֶּן תְּמֻתוּן:

of extended feeling of family, a closeness, a sharing and caring experience of bonding. We all joined in to sing together, clapping, humming, smiling, relaxing – harmonising. A vastly different medley of individuals, otherwise unconnected, melding for a short while into a harmonious group with common ties. A congregation of Jewish people, a nation of families; many similarities out of so many more differences.

These are our roots and this is our heritage. This is the family of Israel – the Divine spark – our spirituality – as it ignites and intertwines; the living waters of our universe – the spiritual and the mundane, the material and the altruistic.

Then, as is the custom, someone – this time, a good friend of mine (Dr Mark Baker, now, Professor "Marky") – stood up and shared some Torah thoughts – a message for us to reflect upon during the Shabbat ... and then on the beach.

> *And G-d spoke to Moses and said to him, I am the Lord and I appeared to Abraham, to Isaac and to Jacob by the name of G-d Almighty, but by My Name, The Lord, I was not known to them. (Exodus 6:2-3)*

Here we have the "*speaking*" and the "*speech*" and the "*revelation*", all from "*The Name*".

During Biblical times, G-d revealed Himself to our forefathers, who were able to communicate with Him. Later on, G-d's messages were transmitted to the people through the prophets. Today we live in a time where G-d seems to be in hiding – so much so that many people reject the whole idea of G-d's existence. As a result, each generation is feeling increasingly isolated, neglected, deserted and very much separated, spiritually – especially from any form of visible Divine intervention. We are experiencing a void of revelation and Divine speech. And yet we exist; we are a part of human continuity and our Jewish survival testifies to the existence of a time-proven "recipe" for spiritual survival.

---

[31] Noosa Heads is about a two-hour drive north of Brisbane, Queensland. This region of Australia is fondly called the Sunshine Coast.

Where does all of this leave us? On the beach, inside the water or up in the air?

There is a spark of G-dliness in each of us. We have the freedom of choice and the power to search for it and nurture it with "soul food", which will grant our lives purpose and spiritual tranquillity. By transcending the mundane, we can connect with our spiritual being. This is real living.

In this kind of a life, our value system becomes more and more positive and others around us also begin to experience things that have the potential to ignite their own spiritual awakening. Let us not risk losing so much living along the way by trying to "reinvent the wheel": it was invented a very long time ago; let us just make better and better use of it.

Our Jewish "wheel", so to speak – or, in other words, the blueprint to life and living – was given to us by G-d. It is in our Torah. It was there when He created the universe. Our history and traditions are oozing with it. There are signs and signals all around us – just like traffic signs, road maps, rules and regulations, criteria for acceptable and unacceptable behaviour, restrictions, limitations, consideration and courtesy. If we accept traffic regulations because we understand their importance, how much more should we wish to seek, find and comprehend the "laws of living"! These laws, like the wheel, need not be reinvented: they already exist. They are there to chart the courses of our relationships, our priorities, our value system – our lives.

At the end of the day, civilisations thrive when they are based on ethics and morality; and they crumble if abused and assaulted by a "free-for-all", self-serving thirst for endless self-gratification.

Community life suffers because its members give priority to individual fulfilment, at the expense of others. Moreover, personal fulfilment is better achieved in a healthy society. Hermits live very isolated and lonely lives; they cannot create thriving communities. Such communities can be created only by committed and well-balanced individuals who contribute to the overall welfare of the group. Within such a framework there is tremendous scope for personal expression and an enormous potential for deriving much happiness and satisfaction in life.

Life is about people, not persons; the interaction and relationship between persons to form a people, the balance between the individual and the group. Life provides a lot of personal space and flexibility to express individuality and enjoy privacy, but it also requires commitment to community.

Where can we find some clues that will give us a head start in our journey through the maze of living? I have found some exceptional "triggers" in some of the daily prayers in our prayer book, the *siddur*.

Is your prayer book gathering dust somewhere? Is it in someone else's library? And even if you do open it every now and then, how often do you actually read the words or try to understand their deeper meanings?

Let me highlight two seemingly trifling, but truly mind-blowing phrases in our prayer book:

In the first blessing before the Shema in the morning, we say, among other things: "... *yotzer ohr u-voré choshech, ose shalom u-voré et ha-kol*" (... Who forms light and creates darkness, Who makes peace and creates all things).

At the conclusion of the Shabbat, once a week, we recite the Havdalah (literally – "separation", or distinction between the Shabbat and the rest of the week, which serves as a model for all other kinds of separations or distinctions between key aspects of our lives). We say: "... *ha-mavdil beyn kodesh le-chol, beyn ohr le-choshech, beyn Yisrael la-amim, beyn yom ha-shevi'i le-sheshet yemei ha-ma'aseh*" (... Who makes distinction between the sacred and the profane [or: the holy and the mundane], between light and darkness, between Israel and the nations, between the seventh day and the six working days.)

These are two very profound statements. When applied to the issues that confront us in our daily lives, they can serve as directions for us in exercising our free will in the many choices we have to make. They help us understand what's what and thus establish the right relationships between things and understand what we are supposed to embrace and what we have to reject, etc. This is what creates the difference.

Shall we grope in the darkness of random living?

Is this what life is really all about?

Or shall we apply our minds to the issues of our lives and exercise our power to choose and control?

Is this not what life has to offer?

Are we "quantity" people, or "quality and consistency" people?

How much value and long-term fulfilment have we derived from our actions?

Do we care about tomorrow, or just go through life living for today?

Do we live like humans – or like sub-human creatures?

Each of us has in-built "good" and "bad" inclinations; but these inclinations are not predetermined for life, nor are they unchangeable: they can be controlled, or nourished, or suppressed. A non-conscious, "drugged" life is a life of ongoing conflicts between these two opposing inclinations in our minds and lives, because we ignore or try to avoid them rather than dealing with them. We're hiding from ourselves; it's nothing but self-deception.

However, when we deal with these conflicts consciously, within a framework of absolute values and out of sincere commitment to lead a moral and ethical existence, we become much better human beings. With time we are also bound to experience much less internal conflict and much greater peace of mind. Searching for true meaning will make us uncover many hidden treasures of immeasurable value; by separating light from darkness, by associating more closely with our people and our tradition, by separating the seventh day from the six working days, we will gain wisdom and good judgment and will be walking the paths of peace.

Investigating and studying our heritage, history, religion and tradition will make us feel a loving closeness with our Judaism and identify with it, rather than take it for granted or shrink away from it because we see it as a burden.

G-dliness is truly alive within us and all around us. We have the ability to uncover its otherwise hidden values and meanings. We can draw life out of the waters.

Shabbat observance is a combination of physical and spiritual actions: the lighting of the candles, the Shabbat meals – each of which consist of the ritual washing of the hands, eating *challah* bread,[32] singing, *Divrei Torah* (Torah-based talks and ideas and blessings) – four prayer services, *Kiddush* and *Havdalah*.[33] A conscious, willing and active participation in the physical as well as the spiritual actions will grant us true enjoyment of the Shabbat.

---

[32]   Challah bread is a special – usually braided – bread for the Shabbat meal. In every one of the Shabbat meals, there are two such breads on the table.

The *Midrash*[34] tells us that G-d created the world for people to live in and to enjoy – and also to keep and guard. Yet we are also commanded "to guard and to keep" the world, just as we are commanded to "guard and keep" the Shabbat. The Shabbat was especially designated for humankind as a separate day, a day of rest, holiness and distinction – a magnificent manifestation of the unity of humans with their Creator. But the enjoyment of the Shabbat is a true personal gift.

Funny, isn't it? However hard people may try to deny G-d's existence, they are unable to escape from Him. G-d is always present and we are inextricably connected with Him, no matter what.

Is G-d hiding from the world – or is He hidden only for those who deny His existence?

G-d is unlimited by definition, while man is finite. Should man risk futility by denying G-d's existence? Or should he make use of the possibilities to improve his own life, by searching for the G-dliness within himself and all around him?

In Kabbalistic sources, the first verse of the Book of Genesis is translated in a way that is quite different from the standard translations. Instead of interpreting the first word, *bereishit*, as "in the beginning", the Kabbalists understand it as "within the beginning". According to that definition *reishit* (beginning) is the primordial matter, the stuff (time/space and energy/matter) out of which G-d created our universe. From this *reishit* G-d made two things: the *shamayim* (heavens – or space/time) and the *aretz* (earth – or energy/matter).

Here, right at the beginning, we start off with the two most basic numbers in existence: the zero, which is the "nothingness" and the one, which is the "somethingness".

If G-d had created the *reishit*, "somethingness", by separating the

---

33   *Kiddush* is the ceremony with which the Shabbat is greeted; it is done twice: on Shabbat eve before the evening meal, and on Shabbat day before the morning meal, usually over a cup of sacramental wine. *Havdalah* is the ceremony with which we bid the Shabbat farewell and usher in the new week.

34   Ancient homiletic commentary on the Torah.

"nothingness" into two "ones" (a positive one and a negative one) and instead of separating His creation, had He added these two "ones" again (by "recombining this separation"), the end result would have been "nothingness" $(0 + 1 - 1 = 0)$.

"Somethingness" from "nothingness" and "nothingness" from "somethingness".

The *reishit* is the two ones: a physical/material "one" and a spiritual/holy "one".

Living life is synthesysing the *reishit* within each of us.

This essay is bracketed between two beautiful beaches. It was begun on an Australian beach in a Southern Hemisphere summer and concluded on a beach in Sardinia, Italy, in a Northern Hemisphere summer of the same year, where I was blessed with a treasured four days together with some of my children and grandchildren.

So there I was, once again walking barefoot on the beach of the Gulf of Marinella near Porto Rotondo, where the sea meets the sand and the sand meets the sea: thinking, singing, counting, dreaming; walking in the warm and gentle Mediterranean waters. The sun shimmering on the sea.

Some of these lines were written quite far away from any beach, such as in an airport lounge, in transit, waiting to board a flight home. I am in one time zone, my family in another – in the morning of a day which for me has not yet begun: an evening and a morning, different times in different places, yet all of them existing at the same instant.

Is your life being tossed around by the waves out at sea? Or are you floating on your life's waters, playing with the waves and steering within the tides?

Is your life being influenced by a random "numbers game"? Or are you making your own free choices and exercising considered control?

Do you live in the past – or in the present or future – or in a combination thereof?

Do you just live for today, or do you actually engage your mind with your tomorrow? Is life deterministic? Do things happen by random chance? Do we have free choice? Or are we living a meaningful life in a sustainable society lifestyle?

Your call!

Roll your dice!

6: Happiness

What is the path to happiness? Does one first have to be free to feel happy, or need one first be happy to be able to become free?

Is there a connection between happiness and freedom? What is the difference between them?

Let me begin with a short story about a young woman and a young man.

It was three days before Passover eve, on an autumn[35] Sunday afternoon. Tammy and Joel were to be married in the garden of Tammy's parents' home. Family and friends were gathering around. The bride and her bridesmaids were already dressed and the photographer was busy taking all kinds of shots. Joel and his groomsmen were on their way to the *chatan's tisch*[36] hosted by the parents of Tammy's brother-in-law, up the street from Tammy's home.

The tradition is that both bride and groom fast on the day of their wedding. The wedding day is a kind of *Yom Kippur* – personal Day of Atonement – since the wedding day is a kind of rebirth in purity. Indeed, on their wedding day, the bride and groom actually recite one of the special *Yom Kippur* prayers.

Tammy was already in a high spiritual frame of mind as she said the special afternoon prayer with *kavanah* (deep intentionality) and *kedushah* (holiness),

---

35   In the southern hemisphere Passover is in the autumn.

36   A *Chassidic*-style gathering of (male) family members and friends before the wedding, together with the groom where songs are sung and blessings and prayers are said. It is now a rather common practice to hold something similar for the bride and her (female) family members and friends.

before going out to sit in the garden on a beautiful white wicker chair placed on a red-carpeted platform; very much like a royal princess, sitting on her throne before being coronated as the queen.

The bridal party was breathtakingly beautiful.

People were wishing them all well.

Joel and the boys arrived at the *tisch*, where a *minyan* (a quorum of at least ten adult men) prayed the afternoon service together. Joel, too, recited his *Yom Kippur* afternoon prayer in a deeply spiritual frame of mind. His *kavanah* and *kedushah* were plainly obvious to all present. He looked serene; almost transcendental.

The men started to sing and clap. The atmosphere was thick with happiness and celebration. The pure joy became infectious. People forgot their own problems momentarily as they were dragged, so to speak, out of their individual selves and sucked into the unison of the group; almost like the coagulation of droplets of a liquid into a cohesive fluid mass.

Meanwhile, Tammy and her bridal party looked resplendent, sitting together out in the magnificent green garden, under the flowering shrubs and trees. The sunlight streamed through the clouds above and illuminated them with warm rays of sunshine filtering through the canopy of leaves and branches.

There was a sea of smiles, a multitude of happy faces, both young and old.

Tammy was waiting for Joel to arrive and cover her face with the wedding veil.

Meanwhile, the *tisch* was "rocking and rolling". The atmosphere was electric. Singing. Clapping. Chanting. One warm camaraderie, observant and non-observant alike. Togetherness.

Then it was time for Joel to be brought to the *chuppah* (wedding canopy). The fathers dressed him in a *kittel* (a white robe which many men wear during the High Holydays, especially on *Yom Kippur*).

As we left the *tisch* and moved out into the street, a few droplets of rain started to fall.

The group danced and sang with gusto as it moved down the street towards

Tammy's house. The rain also gained pace. People opened umbrellas and held them above Joel and his entourage, who were oblivious to the sudden inclemency of the weather.

The rain droplets transformed into rainfall. Tammy and the girls moved from the garden to a bench under the front verandah. More and more people were arriving. The garden had filled with human life standing between the trees. There was a throng of people trying to take cover wherever there seemed to be some shelter.

The dancing and singing men arrived at Tammy's place and squeezed through the gate; people squashing against people. Somehow Joel found himself standing in front of Tammy. They hadn't seen each other for a week. This is our tradition. They smiled. They were so happy. They just smiled.

Joel covered Tammy's face with the veil and both fathers blessed her with the Biblical priestly blessing: *"May G-d bless you and safeguard you. May G-d illuminate His countenance for you and be gracious to you. May G-d turn His countenance to you and establish peace for you."* Then both families prepared to walk to the *chuppah*.

As is customary, Joel's family, together with his groomsmen, went first. The rain had picked up; it was heavy and was becoming even heavier. The *chuppah* had been erected on a platform at the southern end of the tennis court at the back of Tammy's house. It faced northwest, towards Jerusalem, which is also customary. Live music was playing. People were crowding under large white market umbrellas and also under a multitude of colourful ladies' umbrellas. The rain kept on getting heavier and heavier.

Meanwhile, the bride's family and bridesmaids were ready to exit Tammy's house onto a red carpet strip which had been laid on top of the green carpeted surface at the northern end of the tennis court. Tammy's parents held beautiful glass candleholders in their hands. The candles were lit.

Tammy's class of prep students had planned a surprise for their favourite teacher, "Miss G.", on her wedding day. They had planned to form a guard of honour on both sides of the red carpet and had secretly practised singing "Sunrise, Sunset" from *Fiddler on the Roof* for their Tammy.

The bride proceeded out of her home into mother nature's domain. The rain was a flood of warm water. There was no wind.

We waded through a shallow stream of warm water which soaked into our shoes. Our faces were beaming. We were oblivious to our surroundings. We passed through a sea of faces – all smiling – under a mass of colourful umbrellas – there was a hum of noise, a cacophony of sound. Our clothes were soaking. The candles had been washed out by the waters. We were standing together under the *chuppah*.

Tammy's little children were all so sweet. They were huddled together on the raised platform on one side of the *chuppah*. Little faces. Girls and boys dressed in soaking white shirts and soaking blue skirts and pants, little wet faces under dripping hair. They were singing to their Miss G.

The saintly rabbi stood there, under the *chuppah*, next to another rabbi, a Kabbalistic figure, ready to participate in the seven holy blessings of the marriage ceremony as well as the public reading of the *ketubah* (marriage contract). A third rabbi, a *Cohen*,[37] was also standing under the *chuppah*, ready to extend the priestly blessing unto the newly married couple. And there were, of course, the wedding witnesses.

Friends were trying to be helpful by holding umbrellas over the family. Tammy circled Joel the traditional seven times under the *chuppah*.

Then Tammy and Joel were standing side by side. Joel's *tallith* (prayer shawl), which Tammy had bought for him, was covering them both. They looked angelic together.

The rainfall had become a real torrent. The air was filled with water. The ground was a shallow lake. Everyone and everything was soaking wet.

And totally happy.

A bridal couple, standing together under the *chuppah*, two individuals joining together into one life, with all of its dreams and promise for their future; a new partnership, a new family, two individuals concerned for each other and committed to each other.

The parents suddenly experience a high speed snapshot of their own lives –

---

[37] A Jew who is in direct patrilineal descent from the Biblical Aaron, older brother of Moses, with an honoured status of "priesthood" in Judaism.

from their own marriage to their children's birth, development and growth and then, to this separation of sorts from their children. For the bride and groom it was a rebirth, a new start sprouting out of the roots of their lives, nourished by their home environments.

The flood continued according to no rhythm – the waters just descended – warm waters, living waters. The essence and continuity of life, mother nature's domain. Water poured down from the umbrellas like mini waterfalls. One such waterfall was pouring right into the top of the rabbi's black hat, filling the rim, then down the front over his face and nose, then down his saintly white beard as he stood, erect, with the typical trancelike expression in his eyes. These are eyes that do not stare or pierce you through, but rather contain deep wisdom, insight and compassion. Like water.

The rabbi who conducted the marriage ceremony was likewise adorned with a waterfall, which flowed from him to his prayer book.

After we had all kissed each other and wished each other *mazal tov*,[38] we waded back along the red carpet into the house. Tammy and Joel needed to be together, alone, in their *yichud*[39] room (with witnesses guarding the door). Then they had the opportunity to eat and drink something to break their fasts.

The rains had blessed the inside of our home also. Our kitchen, meals area and family room were flooded – towels and mops appeared and all was dried away.

As soon as the bridal couple entered the house, the rains started to ease and quickly abated. The clouds parted and sun's rays smiled down into the garden, illuminating the people and the plants, warming the ground as the waters subsided.

The people outside waved through the glass windows, smiling and blowing kisses, their faces dripping wet and their hearts exuding warmth and happiness. We were all looking forward to the wedding reception.

---

[38] Literally: Good Luck; meaning, "best wishes."

[39] A locked room where the bride and groom spend their first moments alone together after the wedding.

Water and life are closely intertwined. Jewish life is also closely intertwined with cycles of events. We have such a richness of laws, customs, traditions and observances. At the core of Jewish life is our calendar, around which our days, weeks, months, years and personal times are organised. Our daily prayers, too, are set around both times and events. There are three daily prayer services, after our three patriarchs, Abraham, Isaac and Jacob: the morning service, *Shacharit*, after Abraham; the afternoon service, *Minchah*, after Isaac; and the evening service, *Ma'ariv*, after Jacob.

Although every prayer exalts *Ha-Shem* (G-d), every service builds up to the main prayer – the *Amidah*.[40] One very interesting inclusion and variation in this prayer is all about water. In the half year from the end of the festival of *Succoth* – the festival of harvest – to the beginning of the festival of Passover – springtime (in Israel) – we say *"mashiv ha-ruach u-morid ha-geshem"* (He makes the wind blow and the rain descend). In the other half year, from the festival of Pesach to the festival of *Succoth*, we replace this phrase with *"morid ha-tal"* (He who makes the dew descend).

The Jewish calendar is a combination of the lunar cycle and the solar cycle. During leap years we add an entire lunar month (i.e. thirteen months to the leap year instead of the twelve months of a regular year), thus realigning the lunar cycle with the agricultural (solar) cycle.

Similarly, our calendar is based upon two separate, but intrinsically coinciding principles of life: the physical, or agricultural cycle and the metaphysical, or spiritual cycle.

Oddly enough, the Jewish New Year is on *Tishrei*, which is the seventh month of the Jewish year. Why is that so? Because in the physical sense, the first month of the year is *Nisan*, the month of spring; but, in a spiritual sense, the beginning of the year is in *Tishrei*.

Thus, the Jewish year has two starting points, diametrically opposite each

---

40 Literally – "standing up"; the main prayer, made up of nineteen (originally eighteen) blessings, which is recited standing.

other (actually, it has more than two; but we won't get into that here): two separate halves, united into one whole yearly cycle – six months of rain and six months of dew.

Which comes first?

Does it matter?

The Torah names the Passover festival *Zman Cheruteinu* (the season of our freedom) and *Succoth – Zman Simchateinu* (the season of our rejoicing).

Understanding the concept of freedom, at least superficially, is rather easy.

Historically, Passover commemorates the exodus of the Children of Israel from Egypt, about three-and-a-half thousand years ago, after over four hundred years of slavery and oppression. Liberation from such pain and suffering denotes freedom. But this form of freedom is a physical and emotional one in its early stages. Spiritual freedom may or may not be connected.

The Exodus took place in the first month of the Jewish year, *Nisan*. This is the month of our redemption, the season of our freedom. Materially, *Nisan* signifies the beginning of the agricultural cycle. In the northern hemisphere it is spring, a time of planting and growth. Therefore, the second name of the Passover festival is *Chag ha-Aviv* (the Spring Festival).

Passover is also called *Chag ha-Matzot* (the festival of the Unleavened Bread), which is what the Israelites ate when G-d brought them "out of the land of Egypt, [out of] the house of bondage" (Ex. 20:2).

The zodiac sign of *Nisan* is Aries, whose attributes are much more of a physical, material and manly kind; typically, a group of fire – active, strong, fierce-tempered, impatient, bold, courageous, physically skilful, in a hurry.

The overriding sensation is one of material and physical activity.

The seventh month of the Biblical year, *Tishrei*, is also the first month of the chronological year (the Jewish New Year occurs on the new moon of *Tishrei*). The Aramaic word *shera* or *sherei* means "to begin".

Tishrei is a very special month in the Jewish calendar. It is filled with religious events and festivals.

Every new moon is heralded in with a beautiful prayer on the preceding Sabbath, in the course of the morning service, in which we ask for a range of good things, both material and spiritual. *Tishrei* is the only month of the calendar year which is unannounced, because we believe that G-d Himself blesses *Tishrei* on our behalf.

The zodiac sign of *Tishrei* is Libra and its symbol is the scales. Its attributes are much more of a human, esoteric kind; typically, balance and harmony, behavioural characteristics of diplomacy, companionability, friendliness, intelligence, pleasantness and thoughtfulness.

The overriding sensation is one of spirituality.

The whole month of *Elul*, which precedes *Tishrei*, is a period of time to prepare for the New Year, which is also the birthday of Adam – hence, of the human race. On the Jewish New Year, the whole of creation is examined, so to speak, to see whether or not it deserves the gift of yet another year of existence.

The ten days between *Rosh Hashanah* (the beginning of the Jewish New Year) and *Yom Kippur* (the Day of Atonement, ten days after *Rosh Hashanah*) are called the Ten Days of Repentance. This is an awesome time for people to reflect on their lives and to prepare for the Day of Atonement, which falls on the tenth day of *Tishrei*. On these days, people undertake an in-depth "stocktaking" of their spiritual assets and liabilities and voluntarily undergo repentance (*teshuvah*). Even though *teshuvah* is something which each of us is supposed to do, it cannot be forced – it must be conscious and sincere. *Yom Kippur* is a day of cleansing and then, only then, can one really rejoice – during the festival of *Succoth*, the time of our rejoicing.

Our Torah prescribes that G-d has given us Sabbaths for rest, festivals for rejoicing and Feasts and Seasons for gladness.

All of these special events in our cycle of life provide spiritual and non-physical experiences and feelings – although usually, physical effort is also required in preparing for them. These are all "injections" of very positive non-routine variations, each having its own specific meaning.

In addition to being the beginning of the Jewish New Year, *Tishrei* is the start of the Northern Hemisphere autumn. The festival of *Succoth* is therefore also called *Chag ha-Asif* (the Feast of the Harvest) and marks the end of the agricultural cycle. It is the time when crops and fruits have ripened, a time of plenty.

One of the Torah commandments regarding *Succoth* is very difficult to comprehend: the Torah prescribes, "And you shall rejoice in your feast ... and you shall be altogether joyful" (Deut. 16:14-15). How can anyone be commanded to be happy? However, it is obvious that *Succoth* is all about happiness.

Succoth is also an "action festival" – we are commanded to build a flimsy little hut, called a *succah*, which we are to dwell in during this festival. In addition, the Torah commands us to take the "four species" – *Etrog* (citrus fruit, which has both taste and fragrance), *Lulav* (palm branch) which has taste (the dates, that is) but no fragrance; Hadas (myrtle), which has fragrance but no taste; and *Aravah* (willow branch), which has neither taste nor fragrance.

This is a most beautiful connection between nature and spirituality. It contains a message for us to reflect upon life and living and to get back to basics – the simple things which are full of meaning and value. Nature itself is so beautiful, serene and simple on a superficial level, yet so intricate and complex in its very detail. When we take these "four species" in our hands we ask G-d:

> *... that through the fruit of the etrog tree, date-palm branches, twigs of the myrtle tree and brook willows, the letters of Your unified Name may become close to one another, that they may become united in my hand ... that evil forces may be fearful of approaching me ... When I wave them, may an abundant outpouring of blessings flow ...*

Here we are confronted with a mind-blowing spiritual concept. Our *mitzvah*[41] of these four species is equated to having performed the entire 613 commandments in the Torah. It is an act of unification of G-d with humanity on both an individual and a group basis; now and into the future. This very special commandment has many other esoteric aspects.

Wow! What an incredible spiritual experience! Isn't this the essence of freedom and happiness? Isn't this a symbol of the "convergence of the infinite with the infinitesimal"? (The G-dly spark within man.)

---

[41]   A religious act; a good (meritorious) deed

During the *Hallel* prayers in the morning service (in which we recite and sing Psalms 113-18), we each wave our four species in the air, the sound of the palm branch combining with our singing, while we parade as a community around the synagogue.

During *Succoth* we also celebrate *Simchat Beit ha-Sho'eivah*, the water-drawing festivities, commemorating the only time of the year when water, rather than wine, was poured onto the Temple altar by the priests. It is celebrated every night in music, song and dance. In the Temple era, for *Simchat Beit ha-Sho'eivah* they used to light gigantic torches that would illuminate the entire city of Jerusalem.

After the seven days of *Succoth* comes the eighth day, which is a festival in itself called *Shemini Atzeret* and *Simchat Torah* – Assembly of the Eighth Day and Rejoicing in the Torah. On that day, we finish reading Deuteronomy, the Fifth Book of Moses; and right there and then we start reading the first part of Genesis, the First Book of Moses. The entire Torah scroll is then rewound from its end to its beginning. This reading, too, is accompanied with many hours of singing and dancing with the Torah scrolls.

Along comes the last Sabbath of *Tishrei*, which has a special name: *Shabbat Bereishit* – the Sabbath of Genesis, in which we read the story of Creation. On this Sabbath we also announce the arrival of the new month of *Cheshvan*, the second month of the new year.

So much joy and happiness, communal togetherness, a lot of action, so many details – intense spirituality combined with material symbols. The "big picture" – global view – is enlightening and fascinating, but the sheer beauty and happiness is in the detail.

This is a conundrum of sorts. There are people who are very much involved in all of the details – yet they miss the general view and have become starved of the beauty. And there are those who are full of ideas, but know nothing about the details. And there are those who simply don't know.

In this modern world of "information overload" there is really no reason at all for ignorance, except for laziness. Education is open to everybody and there is no substitute for self-education. Ignorance is a very sad condition. Blissful ignorance of an ongoing nature is a very sorry self-delusion.

The harmony and balance lie in the combination of facts together with flavour, materiality and spirituality.

Happiness is a wonderful personal feeling. No one can be forced to be happy. One can be invited to participate, but voluntary participation is different from participation out of duty. If our hearts are not in it, how can we enjoy? When we enjoy, it is much easier for us to feel the enjoyment of others. The "me/myself" turns into "us". The individual becomes part of the group, part of the give and take, of giving and receiving.

There is the "me", the "you" and the "us".

I now wish to share two thoughts; one derived from *Succoth* and the other from Pesach.

Succoth: happiness, materiality and spirituality

In the *Succoth* prayer book there is a strange little section called *Ushpizin* (literally: guests), which is recited before we enter the *succah*. It is an invitation for seven of our ancestors – Abraham, Isaac, Jacob, Moses, Aaron, Joseph and David – to join us in the *succah*. And in the Grace after Meals, we add the phrase, *"Harachaman hoo yakim lanu et sukkat David ha-nofalet"* (The Compassionate One! May He erect for us David's fallen booth).

On the first night of *Succoth*, after reciting the *kiddush* (blessing over the wine), washing our hands and breaking bread in the *sukkah*, I welcome all our family members and guests before seriously "digging into" the gastronomic banquet my dear wife Dina has prepared. We are usually an intimate group of twenty-plus people and the wood fire helps add to the feeling of warmth and togetherness. We sit outside under the full moon.

I connect our happiness with our close feeling of family, which I extend to the wider family of the Jewish people. On a spiritual level all of our souls are connected, as are our past, present and future. This, to me, is the symbolism of our *sukkat David ha-nofalet*, which we say as we sit in our own *sukkah*, together with our spiritual and "flesh-and-blood" guests.

This all-inclusive approach provides us with a feeling of freedom and eternal security which, in turn, creates happiness within us. The potential for this great happiness is derived out of the commandment to rejoice on *Succoth* and is enhanced as one grows out of the "me, myself" into the "we". Thus a limited, negative, restricted and closed way of thinking turns into a positive, open, fresh, sharing and unrestricted experience.

In the *sukkah*, we share this happiness without the trappings of the material luxuries we have generally become accustomed to; rather, we experience it under much more modest conditions and closer to nature. It is an opportunity to get back to basics and to live life in closer connection to our spirituality and to each other.

But the *Ushpizin* – are we consciously and honestly including such auspicious guests together with us at our table? If so, where are they to be seated? My understanding of this is that we open our homes and hearts unconditionally to enable all those present to experience and share the beauty of our collective continuity and thus derive happiness and fulfilment out of the very essence of life itself. Such auspicious and respected guests can only be seated at the head of our table and must be honoured. We, in turn, must feel humbled to be included in such company.

We are a living and feeling part of Jewish continuity.

This is the happiness that the festival brings to us.

Passover: freedom and happiness

In contrast, the month of *Nisan* starts off in a more physical manner.

Our preparations for Passover are laborious: shopping, cleaning and changing over the whole of the house, cooking, setting up the Passover eve *Seder* Table.

The Torah commands us to "teach our children" and for every Jew to re-experience the Exodus of the Children of Israel out of Egypt every year, on the night before the fifteenth of *Nisan* – as though each and every one of us was present there, reliving the Exodus out of the land of bondage into freedom, illuminated by the full moon.

Picture the *Seder* night: People start arriving. There is an air of light and expectation. People feel tired from all of their work and preparations.

Everybody is also a little hungry, having stopped eating all leavened products that morning. The children feel excited about what they have learnt and also about the prospects of the late night ahead. The *Seder* table is beautifully set up, with all those items which have been specifically laid out for the *Seder*.

The festival candles have been lit and are flickering.

Finally, the last guest arrives – usually late. We all sit down at the table in readiness to begin. Usually, the father of the house stands up, lifting the first cup of wine to make *kiddush*. I, actually, very much enjoy singing this most beautiful blessing, which has such a lovely melody.

Then we all sit down again, lean to the left, as a sign of freedom, drink the whole cup of wine and start to discuss the many symbols and customs surrounding this festival. We ask questions and answer them, the hungrier ones trying to hurry things along, while others persist with more stories, comments and explanations.

"Yesterday we were slaves and today we are free people."

The *Matzot* (unleavened bread) are uncovered and, raising the symbolic Pesach plate, we continue:

> *This is the bread of affliction that our fathers ate in the land of Egypt. All who are hungry – let them come and eat; all who are needy – let them come and celebrate the Passover. Now we are here, but next year may we be in the Land of Israel; now we are slaves, but next year may we be free men!*

The youngest child asks the "four questions" (sometimes each child has his or her own turn). Then, everyone sings the traditional response:

"We were Pharaoh's bondsmen in Egypt."

Then we go on to read about and discuss the Exodus and our duty to tell the story of the Exodus to our children. There is a lot of singing. Everyone is in a happy mood.

After some more reading comes the part about the "four sons" – the wise one, the wicked one, the innocent one and the one who does not know how to ask – followed by a fascinating philosophical discussion about the "four sons" and what is the right educational way of approaching each one of them. This is soon to be followed by the both lively and harmonious song of *Ve-Hee She-Amdah*, which says:

> *And this [Divine] promise [of redemption] has stood by our fathers and by us [in every generation]. For not one alone has risen up against us to destroy us, but in every generation there are those who seek to destroy us; but the Holy One, Blessed be He, delivers us from their hands.*

More than forty years have passed since I first conducted my own *Seder* for my immediate family in Lugano, Switzerland, a few weeks after my skiing experience (discussed in the next chapter).

All these years, there were parts of the Passover *Haggadah*[42] which we have always rushed through; for instance, the part before the "four sons", which speaks about five rabbis who were sitting and talking about the Exodus all night. Only this year have I begun reflecting on "these rabbis".

But why?

Is this story really boring? Let's see: Who are these rabbis? When and where did they live? Why is this story included in the *Haggadah* in the first place?

This is how the story goes:

It once happened that Rabbi Eliezer, Rabbi Joshua, Rabbi Elazar ben Azariah, Rabbi Akiba and Rabbi Tarphon gathered together in Bnei Brak and they discussed the Exodus throughout the night until their disciples came and said to them: "Our teachers, it is time to recite the morning prayer of Shema!"

Of all these names, the name "Rabbi Akiva" is the most familiar. According to the Encyclopedia Judaica, he lived in the period when the Second Temple in Jerusalem was destroyed by the Romans. Some of his famous teachings include: "Everything is foreseen and free will is given" (meaning, there is no contradiction between people's free will and G-d's omniscience). His biography is spectacular: until the age of 40, he was an illiterate shepherd; subsequently he became one of the most outstanding scholars in Jewish

---

[42] The book containing the story of the Exodus and the ritual of the *Seder*, read at the Passover *Seder*.

history and had 24,000 disciples; later on he joined the Bar Kokhba revolt against the Romans and died as a martyr.

A famous story (tractate *Makkot* 24b) describes Rabbi Akiva and some of his learned colleagues walking in Jerusalem, where they saw a jackal roaming the ruins of the Holy Temple. Everyone is reduced to tears at the sight, except for Rabbi Akiva, who is happy. When his puzzled colleagues ask him how so, he says that just as the prophecy of the destruction has come true, so will the prophecy of the future reconstruction be fulfilled.

And who were the other rabbis mentioned in the *Haggadah*?

Two of them, Rabbi Eliezer ben Hyrcanus and Rabbi Joshua ben Hananiah, were among Rabbi Akiva's first teachers; Rabbi Tarphon was his teacher later on in life; and Rabbi Eleazar ben Azariah was, despite his young age, one of the most eminent scholars of his day.

What we have here, then, is a Passover *Seder* celebrated by some of the most prestigious rabbis of the period, nearly two thousand years ago. It is taking place in Bnei Brak, near the coastal area, away from Jerusalem. These are times of terrible Roman persecution, fear and insecurity. Religious teachings and traditional practices have been declared illegal under pain of death. The teachers are visiting their prize student rather than the other way around. The *Seder* is conducted in hiding; the students have to come and inform their rabbis – who are engulfed in the story of the Exodus – that it is time for the Morning Prayer!

Were they free men? They were re-experiencing redemption at a time of suppression and persecution. Just as some exceptional Jews did in the Nazi concentration camps during World War II.

And all of us today perpetuate their teachings.

In our *Seder* we also say:

> *Now we are here, but next year may we be in the Land of Israel!*
> *We were slaves and now we are free people.*

What does this mean? If we continue to pass time in robotic fashion and continue to repeat the same formulae year after year, will anything change? How will we be free next year, if we are not free this year? And what does this say about our freedom this year, relative to last year?

In fact, what is freedom?

Let's go back to Egypt for a moment. In Egypt, the Jews were slaves. In addition to the forced physical labor, Pharaoh decreed that every Hebrew baby boy must be thrown into the Nile; before that, Jewish babies were put inside building blocks. The Hebrews suffered so much that they could not even articulate themselves: they just cried wordlessly.

Nowadays, with all the material prosperity and, ostensibly, freedom, many people are in a kind of spiritual imprisonment, mental bondage; they suffer a lot and have very little happiness or enjoyment in their lives.

These two major forces – the material and the spiritual – influence our lives and living.

We need the material and the physical for our immediate survival. With it we feel good; without it, we feel bad (or don't feel at all). We also need the non-material and the non-physical. These are just as real as the "feel-goods" and "feel-bads," our psychological fodder which includes our satisfactions and dissatisfactions, happiness and unhappiness, the balance and harmony (or lack of them) in our daily living experiences.

We have already pointed out that people want to belong and to feel liked and wanted. People do not wish to be disliked nor unwanted. We know that our world comprises both odds and evens as well as real and unreal connections.

Happiness is about creating some kind of equilibrium between the positives and negatives of our life; a harmony of existence. Happiness is a relative state of mind. It actually requires very little, but provides very much.

Obviously, physical and material things, in themselves, cannot provide happiness. Those who focus their minds on obtaining physical or material things only, as soon as they get them will experience the need to obtain something else. This often turns into an uncontrollable, insatiable desire. In contrast, the non-material and non-physical things in life create the best feelings and memories and carry the greatest value that can provide quality living experiences for us.

Most people are not hermits living in total isolation from other people; rather, they mix and interact with other people, forming groups and associations, friendships, families and communities. Consequently, our lives are often affected by external influence or group pressure.

Let us briefly look at Western society in today's "civilised world".

Our world has now moved into a new millennium according to a calendar which represents no more than the ticking clock of time.

Where did we start and where will we end? Or, more importantly, how will we end?

The Western world is pushing ahead at an ever-increasing pace to constantly improve the "standard of living," while the third world continues its daily struggle for mere survival.

What is our quality of life made up of? Even more importantly, how much responsibility do you take in living your life? What choices do you actually make?

The "New Kingdom" of the liberalised democracies of the western world no longer knows right from wrong, it has ceased to distinguish between good and evil. In fact, it hardly ever uses those terms anymore. Its notion of freedom knows no boundaries. One can say that it has entirely divorced itself from the bondage of absolutes, along with unshackling its collective conscience from historical truths.

Furthermore, its modus operandi is purely relativistic. Its primary concern is to recognise multifaceted viewpoints. In fact, "liberalised democracy" is committed to maximising individual freedoms and individual rights. This materialistic kingdom cares much more about all kinds of rights and freedoms than about their consequences. Needless to say, it also places the individual much higher than the group.

What has become of morality and ethics?

What happened to "good" and "evil"?

What is happening to humanity?

What kind of individuals and communities are we producing?

How did "liberalised democracy" gain such power?

Where is it leading us?

I believe that the major driving force has been people's loss of respect, belief and confidence in religions.

Why? I think that the major reason has been the exposure of corruption in leaders of various religious organisations. This has caused many people to feel cheated or misled and to lose their trust in the "establishment". One of the most unfortunate direct consequences has been a rejection of religious faith, which has caused people to abandon religious education, traditional values and, even more importantly, absolute concepts such as "right and wrong" and "good and evil".

Here's one of the puzzles of modern living: when a hungry or thirsty person goes to a shop or a restaurant which serves food or drink not to his or her liking, they will quickly figure out the cause for their distaste and next time around they will try some place else and perhaps even complain and seek recompense.

However, people will generally react in a diametrically opposite manner regarding their thirst or hunger for spirituality. So often, when they have a negative spiritual experience, they respond by totally rejecting the whole thing, rather than criticising the perpetrator. This rejection is usually manifested by a conscious suppression of spirituality.

The truth is that there are many hues and flavours to organised religious expression. In a certain sense, spirituality is as personal as is the taste for physical pleasures. Thus a bad spiritual experience ought not to produce total rejection of spirituality, but rather should motivate a search for appropriate fulfilment "in another shop or restaurant".

The basic forces of our universe are those of attraction and repulsion. This is a foundation stone of physics. Similarly, basic psychology of a human being involves acceptance and rejection.

People generally like to belong and to be liked and accepted. People want others to accept them just as they are. This is the connection between the individual and the group. It is the driving force for modifying one's behaviour; a kind of moulding process to enable the individual to fit into the image of a group, to feel accepted.

We are all driven by our perceptions and misperceptions of things around us. These form our individual concepts of reality. The interplay of these perceptions and misperceptions influences our needs and reactions.

Our reality resides within our conscious as well as our subconscious state of mind. The form of this reality is of a physical nature, while its flavour is of a spiritual nature. Our feelings are very much tied to our concept of reality at any particular point in time. This drives our behaviour.

Thus, a physical person strives to survive and enjoy the material gains, security and pleasures available to him, whereas a spiritual person elevates his life above the physical.

We have the intellectual ability to encourage and to suppress our desires. We also have the capacity to learn from our experiences and to modify our expectations. We can influence our own reality by actively interacting with our perceptions and misperceptions to rationalise our experiences and expectations. `

Our spiritual interaction with others becomes a "religious sort of an experience". Its physical form is more of a ritual based upon participation. Acceptance and rejection both play important parts in the group's behaviour. As much as individuals might try to suppress the non-physical (spiritual) forces within themselves, they do still have an impact.

What about a person as a living member of a group of people? Our Torah gives humanity very important guidance regarding the organisation of a group or a community. In Deuteronomy (14:18-20) we are commanded:

> *Judges and Officers shall you make for yourself (i.e. appoint) in all of your gates ... and they shall judge the people with righteous judgment ... Justice only justice shall you pursue, that you may live ...*

What is the point of this commandment?

Obviously, members of a group who wish to exist together within a framework of equity must have a governing set of rules and regulations:

minimum standards, a code of conduct, morals and ethics and the like. What follows is that in order for these rules and regulations to be effective, whatever is deemed to fall outside these boundaries must be sanctioned; hence the need for "judges" and "law enforcement officers".

Communities should strive to make life as pleasant and favourable as possible for their constituent individuals. At the same time, communities should find it comfortable and safe to interrelate with other communities.

Each individual member should strive towards "a righteous way of living" – according to the group's generally accepted morals and ethics, which our Bible provides within a universal, absolute framework of good and evil – as well as towards recommended values of living and models of behaviour.

Human beings are not required to be "absolutely righteous"; such a degree of perfection is reserved for the angels. We need to feel our frailty and weaknesses – and yet strive for betterment.

What is the prognosis for the future of groups that survive by mainly reacting to their own "feel-goods", rejecting the idea of absolute morals and ethics? The *Mishnah* (end of tractate *Sotah*)[43] says:

> *When R. Meir died the composers of parables were no more. When ben Azzai died there were no more industrious scholars. When ben Zoma died there were no more interpreters. When R. Joshua died goodness ceased to exist in the world. When Rabban Simon ben Gamaliel died the locusts came and troubles multiplied. When R. Elazar ben Azariah died wealth departed from the Sages. When R. Akiba died the glory of the Law came to an end. When R. Chaninah ben Dosa died men of great deeds ceased to exist. When R. Jose Katnutha died the pious*

---

43   This tractate deals with the case of a woman who stands accused by her husband of having been engaged in adultery. She has her rights and her remedies and is innocent until found guilty by a fascinating process, which is not relevant here but worth reading about (See Deuteronomy 5:11-31). The point is that, according to the Torah, immorality starts out from such an individual act of unacceptable conduct. For how does the "evil inclination" operate? It applies temptation of a physical kind onto the spiritual existence. A person's only true defence is the "good inclination", which enables us to deflect, repel or resist the ways and means of one's evil inclination. All of this, as you'll see, is relevant to happiness.

ceased to exist. And why was his name called Katnutha (literally: smallness)? – Because he was the very least of the saintly. When Rabban Yochanan ben Zakkai died the glory of wisdom ceased. When Rabban Gamaliel the Elder died the glory of the Law ceased and purity and restraint died. When R. Ishmael ben Piavi died the splendour of the priesthood ceased. When Rebbi (Rabbi Judah the Prince) died humility and the fear of sin ceased.

R. Pinchas ben Yair says, When the Temple was destroyed the Fellows and freemen were put to shame and went about with lowered head and men of great deeds were enfeebled; but men of violence and men of glibness waxed strong; and there is none that expounds and there is none that seeks and there is none that enquires.

On whom can we rely? – On our Father in heaven.

R. Eliezer the Great says, From the day the Temple was destroyed, the Sages began to be like Scribes and the Scribes became like public officials and the public officials like common people and the common people are themselves deteriorating and there is none that seeks.

On whom can we rely? – On our Father in heaven.

With the advent of the Messiah, presumptuousness shall wax great ... and produce shall soar in costliness; the vine shall yield its fruit but the wine will be costly; and the heathens shall be converted to heresy and there shall be no rebuke. The house of meeting shall become one for adultery. And Galilee shall be devastated and Gablan shall become desolate; and the people of the border shall wander from town to town and none will show them compassion. And the wisdom of the Scribes shall be decadent and those who fear sin shall be loathsome; and truth shall be absent. The young shall put the elders to shame and elders shall rise up before little ones ... the son dishonours the father, the daughter rises up against her mother, the daughter-in-law against her mother-in-law, a man's enemies are the people of his own house. The face of the generation is like the face of a dog and the son will not be shamed before his father.

And on whom can we rely? – On our Father in heaven.

Note the sequence of events as society deteriorates step by step, sinking lower and lower. Once a low point has been reached, some kind of revolution finally takes place where the once silent, suffering majority has had enough and reinvents itself as the vocal majority, which becomes a positive force to contend with. Then, and only then, the downward spiral becomes arrested; it turns around and, bit by bit, slowly but surely, begins the long ascent on a step-by-step basis.

This may very well be the reason why the Talmud chooses to finish this section with the following passage, which is most surprising in this context, because it delineates the path of ascent:

> *R. Pinchas ben Yair says, Zeal leads to cleanliness and cleanliness leads to purity and purity leads to self-restraint and self-restraint leads to sanctity and sanctity leads to humility and humility leads to the fear of sin and the fear of sin leads to piety and piety leads to Divine intuition and Divine intuition leads to the resurrection of the dead and the resurrection of the dead shall come through Elijah of blessed memory. Amen.*

This is how people as well as groups function. History is full of examples of the consequences of people's aspirations and actions. However, most people are too busy "reinventing their own wheel" to have the interest, motivation or presence of mind to study the experiences of others.

In Egypt, too, the Children of Israel had descended to one of their lowest points of spiritual existence prior to their exodus from Egypt. This diametrically opposed process began to reverse and their spirituality grew out of this lowest point to their highest point, when they reached Mount Sinai and received the Torah in the heart of the desert. During the seven weeks between Passover and *Shavuoth* (Pentecost, the festival of the Receiving of the Torah) we relive this process; we ascend one level per day, symbolically, as we associate with this important historical event and identify with our people, as well as humanity at large.

What is the path to happiness? What is the connection between happiness and freedom? What is the difference between freedom and happiness?

There is a basic level of minimum physical needs: drink, food, shelter, personal security etc. Obviously, even these basics vary from person to person. But do they make a person feel happy?

There are no absolutes in happiness. A half-filled glass of water – is it half full or half empty? Is our focus on the positive – on what is and what we have – or on the negative – what isn't and what we don't have?

Our Sages say: *Eizehu ashir? Ha-sameach be-chelko* (Who is rich? He who is happy in his lot).

This is not to advocate complacency or laziness. People thrive on challenges; and even though they very much are "creatures of habit", they also have the ability to adapt well to changes. What we call "happiness" is but a state of mind.

A good analogy would be to compare our self-perception to the accepted way in which our solar system was viewed during the Middle Ages in Europe. The authoritative doctrine of the time was that the earth was flat and that the sun revolved around it. Galileo, while being a believing Christian, proved that the earth is round and that it revolves around the sun in an elliptical orbit. What is the axis around which our lives revolve? Is it homocentric or theocentric? Do we submit to a G-d-centred universe, or are we blinding ourselves to believe in a man-centred existence? Is the dog wagging the tail, or is the tail wagging the dog?[44]

Mere physical gratification is short-term. The ancient Aramaic word for money is *zuzim*[45] which comes from the same root as "to move". Money is "fluid", it moves around. Wealth in itself is nothing; it rolls around from this person to that. And it is only relative. True wealth is what people do and

---

[44]   The *Mishnah in Pirkei Avot* ("Ethics of the Fathers" 1:2, 18; 2:20; 3:1) offers us some exceptional advice. We are taught that: *The world stands on three things: on Torah, on the service [of G-d] and upon acts of loving-kindness.* Also: *The world functions through three principles: justice, truth and peace.* Furthermore: *The day is short, the task [work/challenges] is abundant, the labourers are lazy, the reward is great and the Master of the house is insistent.* And finally: *Consider three things and you will not come into the grip of sin: know from where you came, where you are going and before Whom you will give justification and reckoning.*

[45]   As in *Chad Gadya*, the last song in the Passover *Haggadah: De-zabbin abba bi-trei zoozei* – "[the lamb] which father bought for two *zoozim*."

how they go about doing it, their behaviour and their consideration towards others.

A person cannot be spiritual if he lacks the minimum for physical sustenance. However, sustenance is a long way short of indulgence, overindulgence or sheer gluttony.

True happiness is derived from a harmonious balance in life. It is a non-physical factor, yet it is the essential ingredient in living a life of value and meaning. Meaningful happiness is connected to true fulfilment and it comes mainly from all the "little" things which life has to offer – our relationships with other people and our true inner self-perception.

Inner happiness is contentment. It is goodness. It is a saintly kind of a virtue.

What is Man?

The *Mishnah* in *The Ethics of Our Fathers* (3:1) points out that we all start out from "a putrid drop" and end in "dust, worms and maggots". Not a very heart-warming thought.

But this is the physical part of a person. One's spirituality exists perpetually. I see G-d's creation of physical man as lying within the DNA molecule and *"His breath of living"* (Genesis 2:7) is man's spirituality. This manifests itself in our conscience, which is our spiritual connection and in the ongoing conflict within us between the "good inclination" and the "evil inclination".

Each one of us must strive to connect with the G-dliness within us. Our goodness lies in our G-dliness. We must come to terms with our "evil inclination" rather than try to hide or escape from it. Hard as we may try to suppress our spirituality, we cannot deny its existence. It is our spirituality which connects us and which provides us with our true quality of living. This is our happiness.

> *And light came into existence ... the light was good ... and He separated the light from the darkness.* (Genesis 1:3-4)

Likewise, we must separate the good from the evil within us. This is what life is all about; this is our challenge and our fulfilment. Life consists of our choices: what we do, why we do it and, even more importantly, how we do it.

The prayer for rain or dew – water: the sustenance of life;
The "Time of our Freedom" together with the "Time of our Rejoicing";
Freedom and happiness;
The physical and the spiritual;
The agricultural cycle intertwined with the spiritual cycle, both synchronised in harmony. Nature – G-d's creations.
HAPPINESS IN LIVING LIFE.

7: Science or Religion and Religion or Science

All things have a beginning, but often the beginning is lost, obscured or clouded. So let's try to start at the beginning.

For me, the story starts when I was about thirteen-and-a-half years old. I went to the Beau Soleil boarding school high up in the Swiss Alps, in the French province of Villars-Sur-Ollon for five months. The few non-French (English-speaking) boarders enjoyed morning tuition from an American couple named "the Wolfs" (there was "big bad wolf" and "who's afraid of ..." and others too; but that's another story) and all the resident students skied and ice-skated every afternoon.

While socially and psychologically I was having a hard time, my intellectual world was exploding as I found myself in the boundless, magnetically enticing realms of the sciences, the classics, history, civilisations and new cultures. I read copiously: biology, astronomy, nuclear physics, the Odyssey and the Iliad, Greek and Roman mythology and philosophy, mathematics, chemistry, American history and Norse Legends. My mind was alive with snapshots of the universe, the vastness of space and the microcosm of cells, atoms and molecules. Life was wholly new and challenging. There were no boundaries, only time and time itself had a floating feeling of timelessness.

For me, G–d was always a given: the Creator of the universe – A "father figure" – all-knowing, all-powerful and infinite. I don't know why, but I always had a close relationship with G–d. I often talked to Him, thanked Him for looking after me and for protecting me – but never asked Him for anything at all. Was this a one-way relationship? I don't think so. I felt warm and somehow secure and quite complete; I was contented. My existence was a very positive and meaningful experience.

One sunny afternoon, a group of us ascended the alpine ski slopes by cable car − a sort of half-hour high-wire experience for those foolhardy enough to look down through the narrow windows. Upon disembarking at the top station we divided into smaller groups to ski back down to the village along different slopes in the mountains. My group took two successive T-bar lifts further up the slopes and then started skiing down. It was exhilarating: the freedom of speed and the freezing fresh air stinging my exposed skin where it was not protected by a woollen hat, scarf or goggles. The snow was fresh powder, blindingly white, brilliant in the sunshine.

As a Swiss boarding school student I learned to be a proficient skier; a Swiss bronze medallion was pinned onto my orange skiing parka as a symbol of my status. I was at home in my own environment at the top of the world. Schussing, paralleling, jumping over bumps and rises, stem christie into parallel, straight down like a shooting bullet, spraying out fresh powder snow with each turn and then a fast stop, grinding across the tilted edges of my skis, spraying another burst of snow outwards, ahead of me. A momentary feeling of boundlessness.

There I stood and waited, my heart pounding, my muscles taut in expectation. I looked around and waited. There was no one in sight. I waited some more, all alone.

It was 1963. Black-and-white television had appeared on the market only a few years earlier. There were no videos; even colour postcards were a rarity back then.

Was this my end? I didn't like to think about it. Where was I? Where were the others? Foggy clouds started to quickly roll in, blocking out the sun. Looking up the slope, I saw the sky and the ground joining together into one greyish-whitish mass. It was rolling in, closing in on me. I could feel my heart beating; my whole body was throbbing and thumping, but the rhythm had changed. I looked down the steep slope and saw nothing but white snow all around.

Then something very strange started to happen inside my head. I heard myself talking. A voice in my mind was reassuring me. Instructions flowed – gently, but accurately. A full-colour travel guide flashed through my brain, slowly, edited in detail, always only slightly ahead of me in time, clear, colourful, serene and purposeful.

I gained courage. I set out down the slope, always peering ahead for familiar landmarks and terrain features, constantly making conscious comparisons with the clear pictures in my brain.

"Ski down schuss – as fast as you can go – don't feel frightened – in a few minutes this slope will end and there will be a long flat area to ski across." Down I went – fast, straight, skis parallel, the cold air refreshing. I started skating using my skis, shifting my weight – left, right, left, right – my muscles coordinated, working, pushing.

It was tiring. I was feeling hot. My heart pounded and my muscles throbbed.

"Keep going. Don't stop. Soon you will see a forest up ahead. Approach the forest but stay to the right of it."

I kept on going step by step, skis skating left, swinging right and left, bending right again. There, up ahead, was the forest. I skied to the right.

"Good, very good. Keep moving. In a little while it will become easier and the slope will start to angle downwards again. Keep moving. In a few more minutes you will start to see some rocks to your right. Stay to the left of these rocks and to the right of the trees."

I did. My skis started sliding downhill and my muscles relaxed a little. There! Up ahead, just as I was expecting. I felt so at home.

"Stay to the left of the rock wall. It is for the train. A few more kilometres and you will see a small tunnel through the wall. Turn right and ski down through the tunnel, down into the forest."

I kept moving, feeling more and more reassured. It felt as though I had been here before and yet I knew that this was a definite first experience. I had never been here before, nor had I seen this in any books, posters or movies. This was all very strange, but not at all frightening.

"Watch out! You need to ski through the forest. Watch closely and follow the path. Snow plough! It's quite steep, don't ski too fast, you have to make many turns. Be careful, don't fall. Don't crash into any trees. Slowly!"

I did my best to stay on the path. It was hard work trying to snow plough. The path was narrow, steep and winding. Oops! My right ski jumped, but my left ski dug in and, ouch! I was wrapped around a tree. Stay calm, I told myself. Nothing injured. Take it slowly. So down I skied, along the narrow forest path.

Some time later on I suddenly skied out of the forest into a clearing. It was foggy and it had started to snow. I skied down onto a roadway and saw some buildings up ahead.

At first I did not recognise where I was. As I skied into the village I noticed something familiar up ahead. I thought to myself that I could always knock on a door and ask for help. Then I realised that I had arrived back in Villars, but from the other side, which was out of bounds to us boarding school students. I skied on and found the entrance to Beau Soleil, one of the very rare times I looked forward to re-entering this "happy establishment".

I paused outside to thank G-d for showing me the way home.

My watch told me that I had been en route for more than four hours since leaving the cable car and lost for nearly half that time. I felt comforted rather than frightened and never really tried to understand this experience.

Was it an end or a beginning?

We all have many beginnings throughout our lives. We all search for our roots and try to find our own beginnings. What comes first – goes the famous philosophical question – the chicken or the egg? When does a chicken start its life: in the egg – or when it breaks open its shell and goes out into the world?

I don't think I know of any chickens with the intellectual wherewithal to contemplate this question. We humans, however, are limited only by our own limitations. Throughout history we have endeavoured to rise above the mundane, to extend all boundaries. Our thirst for knowledge and understanding has pushed us to question and to analyse. We are a combination of the spiritual and the physical. One of the main drivers of humanity is the search for harmony, the quest for a natural balance in life.

Such a balance is unnatural, due to the simple fact that this defies equilibrium. Equilibrium is a principle of physics which requires a static central point, a fulcrum to move around and a reference point upon which to relate. It can be defined in absolute terms. We humans, however, require constant changes in our central reference points due to our ever-changing moods and feelings. Thus we find ourselves subjected to relative, temporary equilibrium, which requires frequent adjustments. This makes our ongoing attempts to maintain our equilibrium seem unachievable as a constant.

We search for all kinds of things, but most of all for our roots. This fundamental search to uncover how it all started out is, in fact, the search to reveal our essence. Who are we? What are we here for? We try to locate in order to connect; and we seek to establish equilibrium by harmonising the spiritual with the mundane.

So I commenced my search, my own journey into the depths of the past, which I have been seeking to connect with my present and project into the future, within one continuum of experiential time.

My journey commenced with two unshakeable certainties:
- I firmly believed that the scientific foundations of the universe, as observed and analysed in the realms of the physical sciences and in the history of ancient civilisations, were factually based.
- I firmly believed in the existence of G-d.

Thus, not unlike the ancient explorers, I set out to navigate towards the beginning.

It is interesting to experience different points of view; to delve, to question, to attempt to reconcile, remaining open-minded and analytical without compromising one's own fundamental beliefs.

Very soon I was hitting closed doors and massive walls. Despite my unrelenting efforts to uncover the truth, I found only superficial answers which defied my sense of logic. My sense of harmony was out of balance.

I encountered two divergent schools of thought, each of which claimed to encompass all knowledge:
- The physical world, under the auspices of science, claimed that no G-d existed or was necessary;
- The religious world, claiming Divine authority, insisted that the

Scriptures suffice as the spring of all knowledge and that there is no need for science.

I found both views impossible to accept. Each was illogical and biased. Are these two truths mutually inclusive – or mutually exclusive? I was searching for the convergence of these two truths, but kept finding divergence everywhere I looked. I do not propose to provide cross-references or lists of quotations. This is nothing but my own story. Anyone is invited to read the sources, personally experiencing their profound messages.

The first truth

The Bible is quite clear and specific. It says that G-d dictated the Five Books of Moses directly to Moses, who passed this Divine document verbatim down to Joshua who, in turn, continued to pass it down in its original form through the generations. There is no shortage of source materials, explanations, opinions, commentaries and analyses. Some are fun to read; some are enjoyable and inspirational; others are heavy going at best, boring at worst. Each one of us must invest the time to delve into those sources, which inspire us to uncover the foundations and connect us with the Revelation.

My journey has taken over thirty years – exploring, sampling and piecing together. Some journeys never end, because voyages lead to more voyages. This is what life has to offer.

No one can experience all experiences. We must be selective; often, all we can do is ascertain the beauty, hidden value and meaning of things many years after we have superficially dismissed them. Sometimes, however, in contrast, some subtle little glimmer seems to attract our attention and draw us in, bedazzling us in a unique hypnotic bond which beckons to go deeper and deeper, to connect our subconscious with our conscious. So, too, began one of my first true love affairs, which has only kept growing since. I fell in love with the first chapter of Genesis, the First Book of the Bible. In Hebrew it is called *Bereishit*, which translates as "beginning". And what an awesome beginning this is!

A rather fascinating fact is that so many of the prayers written in Hebrew –

for weekdays, Shabbats, festivals and other events – state: "I am the Lord your G-d who took you out of the land of Egypt, out of the house of bondage". The Exodus is a historical fact, which occurred nearly three-and-a-half thousand years ago. Although there are no known descendants of the ancient Egyptians to interview, there are massive legacies of the ancient kingdom of Egypt to be seen, touched and felt: artefacts, archaeological findings, videos, museum exhibits, books, even computer databases – and, of course, the mighty pyramids, sphinx, rock sculptures and graves in the desert and mountains along the Nile River. All these attest to one of history's most powerful ancient nations.

The ancient Hebrews lived in Egypt. We read how 70 descendants of our three patriarchs, Abraham, Isaac and Jacob, went down to Egypt to escape famine in the land of Canaan. In Egypt these few people, all of one family, were fruitful, multiplied and became abundant, building a high profile, out of proportion to their numbers. The Egyptians, who became jealous and fearful of them, enslaved the Children of Israel and inflicted hard labour on them. They built the cities of Pithom and Ramses.

Scholars of ancient civilisations, including archaeologists, anthropologists and historians, will readily show you hieroglyphics, calligraphy and paintings carved in rocks and pottery and on papyrus depicting these stories in vivid scenes. One day, over two-and-a-half million people, a "mixed multitude", led by Moses, went out of the land of Egypt and walked through the desert for 40 years on their way back to their Land of Israel. These slaves were emancipated. They became free men, women and children and in the desert, en route, they received the Five Books of Moses at Mount Sinai, after experiencing many supernatural events. They became a nation: "the People of the Children of Israel". They returned to the land of their forefathers, Abraham, Isaac and Jacob, their promised land.

Another beginning.

Some beginnings are much more obvious and dramatic than others. Each beginning affecting a single human being is deeply meaningful for that single living entity and can also affect others. A national beginning, collectively experienced by a multitude of people in a most dramatic manner, occurs very much less frequently – in fact, it seems to have occurred only once – but has had a much more lasting impact on all of humanity.

The Bible has been translated into many languages, into some of them more than once. Consequently, there are many English translations, quite different from each other, since every translation is also an interpretation. Tradition has it that along with the written text of the Five Books, Moses also received an oral interpretation thereof. This can be likened to the lecture notes given by a lecturer. Both the notes and the explanations must be digested together in order for the student to gain a true and deep understanding.

The first verse in the Bible contains seven Hebrew words. The entire text does not contain punctuation, which makes it even more prone to multiple interpretations. The most common English translation reads: "In the beginning G-d created the heaven and the earth." (I shall return to this later, in a different context.)

We are then taken through a rapid recounting of the first seven days of G-d's creation, all of which "are good" and all of which contain "and there was evening and there was morning" ... for each new day. The creation of man is at the end of the sixth day, on the eve of the seventh day, the Sabbath, when "G-d rested from all of His work which He had done" (Genesis 2:2).

Everyone who follows the Hebrew calendar knows that we are now in the year 5770 (2009) since Creation. People don't seem too fussed whether this is literally measured from the time of the creation of man, or "a few days before", from the beginning of the creation of the universe. It is relevant to note here that there are no observed or documented scientific or historical contradictions with the Bible post-creation. When we study the scientific theories concerning the creation of the universe we discover an uncanny sequence of events and lack of contradictions with the Biblical story of Creation.

Let's take it one step at a time.

The other first truth

As a young man who was not into black magic, it seemed obvious to me that there were things which had existed on our earth for more than 5,000 years.

There were fossils, which were hundreds of thousands of years old.; dinosaur bones and animal skeletons which vastly predated the Hebrew calendar; rocks which were dated as being millions of years old.

Thus my first problem; and that's how my journey commenced.

My own beliefs were never under attack, nor did they in any way become diluted. However, the more people in the religiously observant world whom I consulted, the more annoyed I became. Generally speaking, there were two kinds of answers. One was dogmatic: the world of science is wrong – how should we believe anything that contradicts the Holy Bible? Obviously the world is only five and three-quarter thousand-odd years old and that was that! The other school of thought allowed things to be "older than the Bible", but obviously G-d had created them that way because He was G-d and was all powerful to do as He chose to do.

How insulting! I thought to myself. I believed firmly in G-d who was infinite – why should He be doing "tricky things" at all?

Then I questioned why G-d should ever rest and what actually is the meaning of this G-dly "rest" upon completing His work of Creation and sanctifying the seventh day, which we call the Sabbath and which we observe according to strict laws and customs.

To me, both the Bible and science are truths. What appeared to be lacking was the harmony. After all, if G-d created the universe, then it clearly followed that He also created science – the laws of physics, the laws of nature, the intricate beauty and the miracle of life itself. Science was not something to be dumped: it was something to be loved and respected.

Maimonides[46] wrote that it is man's duty to study the holy religious scriptures along with pursuing worldly knowledge in a structured and balanced manner. Maimonides guides us to study and to delve into in-depth learning and try to resolve apparent contradictions by finding a set of conditions where

---

[46] Rabbi Moses ben Maimon, b. Spain 1135, d. Egypt 1204, one of the greatest Torah scholars and Jewish leaders of all generations; world-renowned philosopher, scientist and physician. Wrote *The Guide for the Perplexed*, Commentary to the *Mishnah* and *Mishneh Torah* – the most encompassing Code of Jewish Law ever written, as well as many other books and letters.

both worlds can coexist in harmony.

(I strongly recommend to everyone to have a "taste" of Maimonides – if possible, in the original Arabic or Hebrew texts, with translation or together with a scholar. The language is so beautiful and powerful. His unique clarity of mind, the strength of his belief and character and the force of his intellect will surely leave an indelible mark.[47])

There are many books and articles which have been written, some in technical jargon and others in layman's language, seeking to explain the creation of the universe and the beginning of time. Some are more interesting to read than others. This has to do with individual free choice and market forces. It is so easy now for people to browse around and glean snippets of information, as well as new angles on established concepts. The catalyst is only to trigger the interest, to create the opportunity.

During my travels I have read two books which are memorable for the excitement they aroused in me. Gerald Schroeder's *Genesis and the Big Bang* and Stephen Hawking's *A Brief History of Time*. Both books made a profound impact upon me as they exposed me to new ideas and provoked my thoughts. It was almost like being back in boarding school, living inside atoms and discovering how they interacted.

Such experiences are the inspiration and the passion behind great voyages of discovery.

One of the main arguments between theoretical physicists is whether the universe was created once, at the beginning of time – known as "The Big Bang Theory" – or whether creation has occurred more than once in the history of time (i.e. a cycle of creation followed by annihilation and re-creation etc.).

Trying to keep this simple: we can all observe that our universe is expanding. The concept is that the universe will continue to expand; however, the gravitational forces work to slow down the expansion and therefore, at some future time, the universe will stop expanding and will start to contract, as matter tends to "pull itself together". Thus the universe will become smaller and smaller until, ultimately, it will all "implode into itself" – back

---

[47]   See Rabbi Steinsaltz's articles in the second part of this book.

where it all originally started. This is called "The Big Crunch". Then, almost simultaneously, another "Big Bang" would eventuate and off we go again with another cycle of creation and annihilation.

At some point, the atheists appeared to have won the day as, after all, science had all the answers, religion being only for the narrow-minded, the uneducated and the primitive.

But science continues to advance towards newer and greater achievements and so does humankind's ability to observe, measure, deduce, explore, delve, search and predict. Over recent time, physicists have developed the means to measure extremely low levels of radiation in space. The Big Bang theory mathematically predicted that there must be a residue in space of the radiation energy emitted about 15 billion years ago, when the Big Bang took place. If there had been a previous Big Bang, or Big Bangs, so too must there remain evidence of that. The estimated temperature during the earliest instant of time was in excess of 10^{32}°C, i.e. 10 million-billion-billion times hotter than the centre of the sun (14 million °C).

Such evidence has recently been found. We can measure an even flow of 4°K radiation in every direction of the universe. There is no other similar background radiation observable. This means that there was only one Big Bang, which was the one and only beginning.

Now science is faced with three fundamental problems:
- Where did all of this matter/energy originate from?
- How did it all become concentrated into an infinitely dense/hot point in "time/space"?
- As time can only be a real, positive measurement in absolute terms, how/who/what initiated the original compaction/expansion of all of the energy/matter which exists in the universe and how could anything/anyone have existed before time = zero (i.e. the Big Bang)?

This is not a thesis in cosmology: it is an excerpt of my journey which I wish to share. I shall therefore not spend too much time on the details of these exciting, highly stimulating matters. Please browse through the literature and become fascinated and provoked by people who are far more learned and interesting than me. However, I do wish to share some points.

Recently, Stephen Hawking made some calculations regarding the observed average density of the universe, which he then related back to the very beginning. He proved that even the amount of matter existing in the universe is of critical importance. If the original density of matter one second after the Big Bang had been greater by only one part in a thousand billion, the universe would have re-collapsed into itself within only ten years. On the other hand, had its original density one second after the Big Bang been smaller by only one part in a thousand billion, then the universe would have been essentially empty after only ten years.

Another fairly recent estimate is that the universe contains 10^{50} (1 with 50 zeros) tonnes of matter. Furthermore, if the net sum of all of the energy contained in the entire universe is actually zero, it is because the "gravitational energy" is negative and equals all of the positive energy contained in the atoms and photons. Interesting!

Later on I shall propose a "net zero" concept for creation of "somethingness" from "nothingness"; however, an unbelievably exceptional force, to be applied at time = 0, is required in order to "create" this outcome.

Cosmologists have been placing greater and greater emphasis on the absolutely critical nature of the initial conditions of the Big Bang. In fact, some of these theoretical physicists have become more intrigued by their quantification of various initial conditions at the point of creation than with the fact of creation. The major importance of minute variations in these initial conditions and their consequent impact upon later events point to the improbability of randomness in the Big Bang. This is yet another "fingerprint" of Divine intervention.

A future "Big Crunch" – another theory – also seems to be extremely unlikely, as this would appear to defy the second law of thermodynamics ("entropy"), which predicts a tendency towards a state of increasing disorder rather than a natural tendency towards order in any system. Thus the coming together (concentration) of all matter within the universe would be opposed by the continued and further scattering (expansion) of matter.

Science cannot offer all of the answers to all of G-d's wondrous creations on its own and neither can religion; nor should we expect them to do so. G-d has provided us with His living universe to have "dominion over". Dominion contains awesome responsibilities which are in high priority to any consequential rights, rewards or benefits. Great humility is required in order to appreciate this dominion, as a prerequisite to going through the motions of everyday living.

Harmony between ethics, morality, codes of conduct, controlled restraint and awareness of the environment will lead us to possess the consideration and respect, so essential to maintain life in perspective and proportion.

There is no religion without science. There can be no science without religion. Science cannot be an end unto itself; nor can life.

This brings me back to my original dilemma: how to reconcile the scientific dating of fifteen billion years' existence of the universe since the Big Bang with the Bible's recounting of the five thousand seven hundred-odd years since Creation?

In order to understand this apparent contradiction, we must gain some insight into the essence of time itself. Early in the 20th century, Albert Einstein published his now famous Theory of Special Relativity. In it, he provided us with an apparently simple mathematical equation defining time and space not as absolutes, but as relative to the speed of travel.

This is a very difficult concept to visualise. Our experience is based upon our own sense of standing stationary on the surface of our planet Earth and therefore we usually feel comfortable to measure time and distance relative to a stationary reference point.

If we try to visualise a traveller in a spaceship which is moving quite fast relative to the earth, looking at us as he sees the earth spinning around its own axis and revolving in its orbit around the sun, we may be able to "feel" that time and measurement on planet earth and in the spaceship can be two different things.

The Theory of Special Relativity predicts that time slows down and physical dimensions actually shrink as matter travels faster and faster, approaching the speed of light. It also sets the speed of light as the uppermost limit of speed. Maybe this can be a little easier to accept if we take into account that matter and energy are directly interrelated, as can be seen from Einstein's famous equation $E = mc^2$.

Imagine two consecutive pulses of light separated by a finite amount of time (say, one second) on day one of Creation. With the continuing expansion of the universe it may be easier to imagine those two pulses of light becoming more and more separated from each other as time moves on. For example: a one-second interval on day one of creation would be equivalent to more than one hundred thousand seconds of separation when measured some years later on.

Another way to try to imagine the relative dilation of time and distance is to picture a rubber balloon which is slightly blown up, with a small insect walking on its surface. If you were to measure the time it took this insect to walk, say, ten millimetres and you would have marked two dots on the balloon to record this distance, it would be easy to describe your observation and experience to someone else. Now, if the balloon is blown up more, the distance between the two dots will also become expanded and the time required for the same insect, travelling at the same speed, to walk between these two dots would be much longer.

In the Torah (Genesis 2:4) we are told: *These are the generations ... in the day that ...*

Following such relativistic measurements of time, it is possible to conceptualise how one twenty-four hour day during Creation could so easily be equivalent, when experienced at that particular time, to a vastly larger time-scale when viewed retrospectively from today's point of view. Using two identical clocks, one which stayed on earth when it was created and the other which travelled through the universe in our time frame, each would truly record the elapsing of time from that particular event − but differently. From earth's point of view, looking into the future, it would have been created some six thousand years ago, whereas from our point of view, looking back into the past, its creation would have occurred much longer ago. Thus the same event can be measured and described in completely different time frames, depending on the relativistic nature of the observer.

If we view Genesis as G-d's story told to Moses, especially in regard to the first six days before the creation of man, it will be a little easier for us to understand how six days can be six actual days of time in G-d's frame of reference, but billions of years in earth's (or the human) frame of reference.

Looking at time from both biblical and scientific points of view can thus coincide and the apparent conflict can be resolved. Thus what appears to an earthly observer as fifteen billion years can be six days for an observer travelling close to the speed of light and vice versa: six days in the beginning of creation moving forward in time can equal billions of years when looking back into time.

Whenever the Torah repeats a phrase, it is alerting us to take a careful look at something very significant hidden therein. In Genesis (5:1) we are once again told, *These are the generations of the heaven and of the earth which they were created, in the day when the Lord G-d made earth and heaven.* Please note the allusion to the relativity of time: one day for G-d is equated to many generations for man.

It is interesting to note that Psalm 90,[48] written by King David about 3,000 years ago, alludes to this relativity of time. In verse 4 he says: *For a thousand years in Your eyes are as yesterday when it is past and as a part of the night.*[49]

The most beautiful explanation I have ever heard about "G-d resting" is related to this question of the relativity of time.

Jews make a ritual blessing over wine every Friday evening, before the Sabbath meal. (We call this *kiddush*, which means "sanctification" [of the Sabbath]; the word Sabbath – or, in Hebrew, Shabbat, literally means "rest".) The core of this benediction is the recounting of the sixth and final day of Creation, as described in the Book of Genesis. Every Friday night, when I sing this *kiddush*, I feel a very special emotion swelling inside me, as well as an unusual spiritual uplifting. In my mind we are commemorating the unique

---

[48]   This Psalm is read by all Jews as part of the morning prayers of every Sabbath and festival. Strangely enough, is the only psalm which starts as "a prayer to Moses, the man of G-d".

[49]   The standard translation – "a watch in the night" – is misleading. According to Jewish tradition, there are three parts to the night, each of which is called a "watch", and most sleep during that time, and do not feel the passage of time.

universal event when "G-d's universal time frame" coincided with "man's earthly time frame" – or, in other words, these two time frames became at rest, relative to each other – and thereafter, in relativistic terms, the history of the world continued to be measured according to human experiential time on planet earth.

Try as I may, it is impossible for me to even attempt to share my innermost feelings during these very special moments each Friday night, as my essence becomes intertwined with the closeness of the most holy universal awe together with the most intimate and fragile existence of humanity. It is almost as though past, present and future instantaneously intersect – time becomes timeless – life is simultaneously vast and integral with the entire universe and infinitesimally small, almost inconsequential. This is, perhaps, the meeting point between the individual soul as a singular, whole consistency and its being a part of the overall community. In other words, it is living with a feeling of free will, or self-independence, yet being the personification of a collective group – the intersection of the unique singular with the unique plural. We sit, drink the wine and all wish each other a happy and peaceful Sabbath.

For me, this was a particularly exciting discovery in my voyage through life. As already mentioned, for a long period of time, this particular conflict about the measurement of time troubled me more than most other issues. Finding the resolution where "everyone was right and nothing was wrong" restored my sense of equilibrium and harmony.

Many people talk about Darwin and the Theory of Evolution. As with all things, the "warm and fuzzy" generalisations we all enjoy are mostly superficial, especially after one looks for detail. Darwin himself was troubled by this very fact – about which he wrote in his thesis – that the fossil record simply does not support his theory that all living species, in all their diversity, evolved from one common ancestor.

Darwin, in fact, devoted the entire tenth chapter of his book to this problem. "Why then is not every geological formation and every stratum full of such intermediate links?" he asks. These missing links ("transitional forms") concerned Darwin already back in 1859. Now, more than 140 years later and with most of the world well explored with far more advanced technology, it is quite clear that there is just no fossil record to support the proposition that humans systematically evolved from one prehistoric original living cell. Furthermore, *Homo sapiens* have existed without visible change ("evolution") for the past 40,000 years or so.[50]

Another problem is that the palaeontological fossil record clearly shows a sudden proliferation of a vast profusion of animals in the Cambrian period (the earliest part of the Palaeozoic period – about 570 million years ago), quite in contrast to the pre-Cambrian period, where gigantic creatures have been discovered to have lived, rather than the "microscopic ancestry" which logically were to be expected.

To date, biologists have been able to classify about 9,000 species of birds, 4,000 species of mammals, 6,000 species of reptiles and nearly one million different species of insects. Furthermore, insects, too, did not evolve gradually, as Darwin's theory predicts; rather, they appeared in the middle of the Palaeozoic period in a population explosion of historically unmatched proportions. Again, by contrast, the Jurassic era (mid-Mesozoic period – about 150 million years ago), which occurred about 400 million years later, was the age of the massive prehistoric reptiles, which happened so much later than it "should have". On the whole, the sequence of events just isn't what we would expect it to be! Both birds and mammals appeared at about the same time and only after the Palaeozoic Era (from about 225 million years ago).

Thus the fossil record, while it contradicts Darwin's Theory of Evolution, confirms the order of creation of the main life forms as recorded in the Bible!

Further: the "evolutionary history" of modern human beings is one of sudden appearance some 40,000 years ago. The Cambridge Encyclopaedia of Archaeology (1980) concludes: "there is no evidence to indicate the local

---

[50] Nathan Aviezer, in his book *In the Beginning – Biblical Creation and Science*, provides an excellent overview of the biological development of the species.

evolution of Neanderthals into anatomically modern people." Furthermore, Neanderthal man, who appeared only about 100,000 years ago, existed without change for some 60,000 years (The Torah [Genesis 6:1-4] talks about relationships between *Homo sapiens* and other kinds of humanoid creatures).[51]

History has also proven that the most radical changes in the life of humans have all occurred within the past 3,000–4,000 years. The Bronze Age (*Tuval-Cain* in Genesis), the Iron Age, the age of communication and the ages of mechanisation, the industrial revolution and the development of modern technology are all very recent within the time frame of our universe. Civilisation, communities, organisation of groups, royalty, social classes, politics, military campaigns, explorations, colonisation, education, law and order and the information explosion are all recent results of our evolution in the most recent time.

Our planet Earth has experienced many massive climatic changes, which have impacted on life most dramatically each time they occurred. It is well accepted that cellular life can have existed only for a relatively short time period, due to the known conditions on earth throughout history.

The process of mutations, survival of the fittest, adaptation and evolution of life has been closely studied by zoologists, microbiologists, anthropologists, paleontologists and geneticists for some generations of scientific research. The chemistry of the DNA and RNA molecules is also better understood. In fact, cellular microbiologists have completed "mapping" the protein structure of DNA. This important work was performed thanks to the cooperation of a number of teams of medical technologists around the world, utilising the most advanced hi-tech equipment. It is called the "Genome Project".

DNA contains about 3 billion chemical bases. A chemical base is a complex molecule in itself, which we loosely call a protein. Two DNA strands are paired together between the bases according to intricate chemical bonding rules. The four key bases are now well defined: Adenine (A), Thymine (T), Cytosine (C) and Guanine (G).

One of the most fascinating observations is that cells can live only under

---

[51]   ibid., "The Sixth Day (Part I)".

relatively limited environmental conditions and replicate according to programmed sequences of events. The DNA needs the proteins to catalyse the reaction, but the proteins are only produced by the DNA code itself. Here, in nature's microscopic world, only a millionth fraction of a millionth of a millimetre in size, we are once again confronted with another "chicken and egg" paradox. It would seem extremely arrogant of us to be flippant about life and to achieve blind intellectual satisfaction by relegating the creation of life to some random, lucky event, whereby many moons ago a few atoms had a party inside some hot rocks or in a biological minestrone soup, were struck by lightning to become energised and bound together and then started to reproduce – thus having haphazardly become the pioneer molecule of evolution.

Every living cell is comprised of DNA, which consists of about 100,000,000,000 atoms, all joined together according to a specific "blueprint", with each and every atom precisely placed according to a very carefully programmed pattern of sequences. All of the genetic information is fixed within the DNA molecule. A small protein may typically contain 100 amino acids of 20 varieties. There are 10^{130} different possible arrangements of the amino acids in one such molecule. The odds against producing the proteins of a DNA molecule just by chance have been calculated at something like $10^{40,000}$ to one!

One DNA chain, if stretched out, would be nearly two metres long. This is most probably the largest and most complex natural molecule in the universe.

There has been a great deal of research done concerning mutations of cells and their reproduction rates under a variety of conditions. Some years ago I read a report that presented a statistical analysis which calculated the theoretical amount of time required for the basic atoms (carbon, oxygen, nitrogen, hydrogen, phosphorus) to combine together in a "biological soup" in order to form a basic living cell and then mutate, at random, under very favourable conditions, to form a complex protein chain similar to DNA as a basis for a living organism. The result was well over 10^{18} years.

Considering that the scientifically calculated age of the universe is 15×10^9 years and life-supporting conditions have been available for much less than this, there has obviously been a vast shortage of time for life to have evolved at random by itself.

I often wonder at the logic of the illogical.

The fossil record on earth clearly establishes the known ages of various life forms which have existed during the history of our planet. Modern man (*Homo sapiens*) appeared only some 40,000 years ago, in the later Paleolithic period; and agriculture, as well as animal husbandry, are recorded significantly only during the Neolithic period, which commenced in fairly recent times, some 10,000 years ago. Prior to modern man, Neanderthal man is found from about 100,000 years ago. The last of the major ice ages commenced about 18,000 years ago, at the end of the Paleolithic period, and finished only 10,000 years ago, at the beginning of the Neolithic period, when the earth warmed up again. This abrupt transition of modern man includes many unprecedented developments in civilisation. For example: the Bronze Age was only about 4,400 years ago.

Think for a minute about human reproduction: under the most favourable conditions there would not be more than five or six consecutive generations every 100 years. A 10,000 year span would involve a maximum of 600 generations and 100,000 years of continuous reproduction would involve about 6,000 generations.

We are well aware that even the most minor mutations of the DNA molecule produce quite dramatic changes. There is no question that mutations are taking place continuously and that species have an in-built ability to adjust to their environment by genetic adaptation and natural selection – but within strict limits.

However, evolution by mutation does not have to move only in one particular direction: random mutations can, in principle, move not only forward but also in reverse direction or sideways. There is no record of one particular species giving birth to another species, not even as a random event. There is, then, a great deal more to DNA chemistry than the random bonding of protein molecules.

The most fascinating thing about reproduction of higher life forms is the chemical-biological combination of the male and female DNA and RNA. On the surface, the joining together of the male and female of one species is rather simple and often quite brief (different species usually cannot mix); but in that short interval, an extremely complicated and intricate event takes place. In the microscopic world of the DNA, the pre-programmed combination of 30 billion (!) base pairs, whereby each base meets and connects with its appropriate pair. This very specific combination then goes on to replicate itself, forming a unique new living entity.

There is no question that mutations and evolution are ongoing processes and that life adapts, as much as it can, to the environment in which it finds itself. But this modifiability is only one of the factors involved that provide the potential for life to vary and adapt within an otherwise set framework.

The full blueprint of life itself is programmed into the DNA. When male and female meet and combine, all of the genetic information is present. On one hand, individual cells, too, have the natural ability to divide and renew themselves, replacing the old with an identical new one. But every living organism also ages and inevitably comes to its end. This is the majesty of the cycle of life.

At this time of publishing, an explosion of new biological information is being discovered about cells, stem cells and genetics. It seems that living cells contain complex signalling pathways, which enable micro information systems to operate, whereby some cells actually can migrate to specified locations within an organism. Cells can be programmed to replicate, mutate and/or die off. Activity sites can be switched on and switched off. Some chromosomes of viruses and bacteria can actually replicate themselves within 20 minutes and other genetic material requires many hours to replicate. Vast amounts of cell matter can be grown within a relatively short amount of time.

Obviously, human procreation is based upon the actual reproduction of those cells participating in this intricate process of cell division, usually requiring about nine months of time, for the precise sequencing process to become completed .Even though individual cells have the propensity to mutate, the reproduction of one human being is far more complex and involved and, in a strange way, predetermined, within the DNA molecule.

The fossil record also does not provide any evidence of "hybrid" or "transitional" species. What it does prove clearly is the rapid appearance and disappearance of species in the course of the history of life on earth.

An illustration of the sheer magnitude of random events follows in this rather silly scenario. Consider a large room full of monkeys hammering away on typewriters or computer keyboards. Most of what they would "write" would be garbage, but very occasionally, by pure chance, they would type out a word which makes sense, possibly even a sentence.

Stephen Hawking calculated the probability of the following random occurrence: the English alphabet has 26 letters. Therefore, the chance of choosing a word consisting of only three predetermined letters at random is 26 x 26 x 26 (one in twenty-six chances for each letter).

What is the probability of a monkey typing, by lucky chance, one of William Shakespeare's sonnets? Let's choose Sonnet No. 18 which begins, "Shall I compare thee to a summer's day?" – which contains only 488 letters. The chance of randomly typing these 488 letters in the correct sequence – neglecting the spaces between words – is one in 26 multiplied by itself, 488 times, which is one in one followed by 690 zeros!

Compare this trivial little example with the age of the universe – fifteen billion years, which is one followed by "only" nineteen zeros ... seconds of time. Now try to picture a DNA molecule, even under favourable conditions, forming at random within a similar time frame.

I mention the above only to illustrate how a concept can so easily provide us with a "warm and fuzzy feeling of contentment" on a superficial level; but when thought through in greater detail and quantified, can be proven to be a ridiculous concept which defies reality.

I have often heard the argument that proteins have a propensity to join together into more complex chains, according to certain more favourable sequences. Polymerisation reactions under catalytic conditions also tend to produce a range of products; yet these do not occur so much at random in nature, but rather according to patterns. The obvious paradox is as follows:

- All living cells require both proteins and nucleic acids, or else life simply ceases to exist.
- However, proteins are only produced by nucleic acids, and nucleic acids cannot replicate without the presence of proteins.

Here biologists are confronted with their own "chicken and egg" puzzle, which does not support the theory about the spontaneous origin of life.

I do not believe that life (DNA) came into being as a lucky random event. I firmly believe that G-d created DNA as a blueprint for all of life and that it contains the programming of living existence in much the same manner as Nahmanides[52] tells us (in his commentary to Genesis 1:1) that during Creation, G-d made the stuff from which everything is made.

My journey is now more than thirty-five years long. It has been extremely exciting, motivating and satisfying. It has endured many obstacles and progressed in fits and starts, but progress it always has.

No journey is complete until it is ended, which inevitably occurs with the finality of the traveller's existence; although each journey has its own individuality about it, it usually intersects with many other journeys, which inevitably impact upon one another. I feel privileged to have had the opportunity of experiencing my own journey and the ability to share it with so many others. Now we are coming to a new frontier.

Maimonides taught and encouraged people to seek the reconciliation of

---

[52] Great 13th century Spanish-born Jewish Sage. In addition to being a Torah scholar and the author of a most unique Biblical commentary, he was also a doctor and scientist. He is often remembered for his public disputation with Christianity, held in Barcelona in July 1263 against the very powerful apostate Pablo Christiani. This disputation was held in the presence of King James and the leaders of the Dominican and Franciscan Orders. The Bishop of Gerona was so impressed with Nahmanides' presentation that he encouraged him to summarise his views and arguments in a book (known as *Sefer Ha-Vikku'ah* – "The Book of Debate") and the King rewarded him in appreciation. In 1265, however, Pope Clement IV demanded that the King of Aragon punish Nahmanides for writing this book and Nahmanides narrowly escaped from Spain to the Land of Israel, where he continued to work and write until his death in 1270.

apparent contradictions by finding an appropriate set of conditions which may provide both truth and understanding, in harmony.

The following ideas are a consequence of the deepest thoughts which came to me as I was wrestling within my mind during my journey.

G-d, by definition, is infinite and eternal. What commenced in the beginning is still being created today and will continue to be created into the future. What did G-d create in the beginning (*Be-reishit*)? (We are told that G-d is the past, present and future.) Where is G-d? (We are told that G-d is everywhere – all knowing and all powerful and yet no living being can see Him.)

Nahmanides embraces the Kabbalistic view that the *Reishit* is the stuff that everything is made of. The "evening" (*erev*) and "morning" (*bocker*) are chaos/disorder and order.

G-d created ascending degrees of order out of disorder, from one day to the next. This is something that just cannot possibly happen by itself at random; it defies Laws of Thermodynamics.

In trying to open my mind and to unshackle my imagination, I have continued to search for a reality by extrapolating knowledge and reason outside the apparent bounds of reality.

It seems to me that Chapter 2 of Genesis provides some deep clues to the understanding of Chapter 1 (and Chapter 5 adds a great deal to this understanding). The first verse in Chapter 2 tells us that nothing living existed yet, as G-d had not caused it to rain. I therefore see Chapter 1 as telling us that G-d created the master plan, the blueprint of all life. The Bible, however, does not present this as a detailed account, but rather as a philosophical concept.

A close reading of all of the verses referring to human life in both chapters provides very interesting illumination. I prefer to understand "Adam" as "mankind," and hence deduce that G-d is telling us that He initially created the male and female sexes (in plural).

My understanding is that G-d created the DNA molecule (in concept) and then duplicated it, separating the female chromosomes from the male chromosomes. The potential and future of humankind were programmed decisively and intentionally by the Mastermind for posterity. Humanity was brought into existence in kind only later on, after being first created in concept.

A literal translation of selected verses from Genesis follows, to illustrate my concept:

> *Let us make man in our own image after our likeness and let them have dominion over ...*

> *And G-d created man in His own image, in the image of G-d created He him; male and female created He them and G-d blessed them; and G-d said unto them: Be fruitful and multiply and replenish the earth and subdue it; and have dominion over ...*

> *These are the generations of the heaven and of the earth when they were created, in the day that the Lord G-d made earth and heaven. No shrub of the field was yet in the earth and no herb of the field had yet sprung up; for the Lord G-d had not caused it to rain upon the earth and there was not a man to till the ground; but there went up a mist from the earth and watered the whole face of this ground.*

> *Then the Lord G-d formed man of the dust of the ground and breathed into his nostrils the breath of life; and man became a living soul.*

> *And the Lord G-d caused a deep sleep to fall upon the man and he slept; and He took one of his ribs and closed up the place with flesh instead thereof. And the rib, which the Lord had taken from the man, made He a woman and brought her unto the man. And the man said: this is now bone of my bones and flesh of my flesh; she shall be called woman, because she was taken out of man. Therefore shall a man leave his father and his mother and shall cleave unto his wife and they shall be one flesh.*

While writing this story about my journey through life with my thinking inspired by some of Stephen Hawking's most recent publications, I became fascinated with the whole concept and human experience of time.

Before I illustrate what I wish to express, I need to draw a few reference points.

Hawking has uncovered some remarkable facts about our universe in his ground-breaking work on black holes. We can all see a myriad of stars in the night sky illuminating the darkness. In fact, the most recent estimates are that there are at least 10^{19} stars in the observable universe (later on in Genesis, G-d blesses Abraham that his descendants would be like the stars in the sky – although this may allude more to the propensity of illumination through darkness than quantity). Stars are like the sun in our own solar system. The sun is a few thousand degrees centigrade hot, due to nuclear fusion (converting hydrogen into helium – like in a controlled H-bomb), which results in emitting energy out into space. This radiation is the light we see and the warmth we feel. Our sun, then – and in fact all stars – are constantly losing "energy/matter". Therefore, even if stars can exist for millions and billions of years, each star has a limited "life span".

The force of gravity is trying to pull matter together, thus making stars smaller. The heat created through the process of nuclear fusion generates a pressure that enables the sun and other stars to resist the attraction of their own gravity. However, with time, stars have less and less "energy/matter" and their rate of nuclear reaction decreases, as does their rate of emission of "heat/light". As they continue to shrink in size, their own internal forces of gravity dramatically increase, as the density of their residual matter increases. This process can result in a "black hole" in space.

Scientists can measure the effect of gravity on light through the observable bending of light in space, due to the gravitational effects of large masses. As a star comes close to the end of its existence, its gravitational forces "pull back" onto the light energy it is releasing. This "bending back" of its radiation and the density of its residual matter, keep increasing as the star continues to shrink. "Black holes" are very small – only a few kilometres in diameter, and they emit almost no light because most of their light is fully bent in a circle. Their densities would be tens of millions of millions of tons per cubic metre. By comparison, white dwarfs (stars which are nearly burnt out) have diameters of thousands of kilometres with densities of some millions of tons per cubic metre and neutron stars, or pulsars, have diameters of about 30 kilometres with densities of hundreds of thousands of millions of tons per cubic metre.

Our sun has a diameter of 1.4 million kilometres with a mass 330,000 times that of the earth and an average density of 1.41 tons per cubic metre by comparison.

Our earth's diameter is 12,753 kilometres with an average density of 5.5 tons per cubic metre.

To get a notion of the magnitude of the gravitational forces, consider that the density inside a black hole is millions of millions times the density of our earth, whereas its diameter is less than a thousandth of the diameter of our earth!

When a black hole, or any other star, finally ceases to exist, this point in time/space disappears – to reappear at some other point or points in time/space, which may or may not be apparent to observers in our universe, depending upon the circumstances. This instant in time/space is a singularity which is simultaneously infinitely large and infinitesimally small. All mathematics and physics cease to exist at a singularity. Philosophically, a singularity is an unimaginable and unpredictable point.

It seems to me that time is a relative quantity not only in terms of speed of travel within our universe, but also relative to any particular singularity to which it is being referred. For example: we can easily understand the concept of "negative time" to describe an event which occurred in the past, when considered relative to the present. We often hear about something which occurred so and so many years ago – namely, at minus so and so many years before today. We know that our universe was created about fifteen billion years ago. In other words, time on our earth within our universe commenced at minus fifteen billion years from today.

I now find this concept most fascinating when I try to compare singularities.

In my mind, if a black hole "exploded" today and simultaneously one or more new baby universes were created somewhere else in time/space, we must be able to accept the following propositions:

- The "old black hole" ceased to exist at such and such time, as measured by an observer existing in our universe.
- The new baby universe came into existence (i.e. was created) at

time = o, as measured by an observer within the time/space of the new universe.

If the new universe is connected to the existing universe, then these two times will be related in some way; but as the new universe was created at a singularity with the existing universe, it would seem impossible to establish any such relationship from within the new universe.

If the new universe is not connected to the existing universe, then each will remain concealed from the other.

I now return to the questions I posed above.

The creation of our universe (The Big Bang) occurred at a singularity. Obviously, all of the energy/matter must have pre-existed within another realm, which religious people define as G-d's realm and scientists describe as imaginary time/space. Otherwise, G-d separated "nothingness" into what we understand as "creation" at time = o within our universe. Time = o is, by definition, separated from whatever might have been before that. What transpired before time = o will always remain concealed from us.

Indeed, Nahmanides' commentary on Genesis, alluded to before, translates the first three words of the Bible not as "In the beginning G-d created", but rather as "G-d created the beginning". He goes on to explain that the beginning was like a most tenuous kind of matter which had no substance but in which everything else was compacted, and which had the potential to assume form, and therefore was the source of all subsequent forms. He thus taught the modern-day concept of the duality of mass and energy and also the understanding that events prior to Creation are outside the sphere of human investigation.

We have no way of knowing whether the preceding realm has ceased, or still continues to exist. Religious people believe that it continues to exist, much the same as scientists can conceive a black hole within our own universe coming to an end at a singularity and disappearing from our own universe, which continues to exist, while appearing at a different point in time/space, which is concealed from us.

The Bible tells us that humanity has gained the knowledge of "good and evil", but not of "life and death". Humans have been given dominion over all living things, but not over all of the universe and, in particular, not over time/space. In fact, mathematics and physics work well within well-defined limits or boundary conditions, but not in absolute terms. They can be used to interpolate within these limits, but cannot extrapolate into singularities.

Even as Albert Einstein was able to reason that the maximum limit of speed of any particle in the universe is the speed of light, Stephen Hawking recently proved that some photons of energy actually exceed the speed of light for very short periods of time over very short distances even though their average speeds are the speed of light. Only recently, just before publication of this book, I discovered that there is now doubt about this phenomenon. New opinion attributes collisions of high energy atomic particles travelling within black holes with atomic matter situated at the boundary of such black holes, as being the cause of matter/energy observed escaping from black holes.

Theoretical physicists are now exploring all kinds of virtual concepts, such as imaginary time, negative matter (which, when combined with "positive" matter, makes both disappear) and imaginary energies in imaginary universes.

What conclusions will flow from this? What benefits will mankind gain? All this is as yet unknown.

I often smile to myself when I see "religious people" looking up at the sky as they appeal to G-d, or focus their thoughts away from the sky when they think they are hiding things from G-d – like small children who cover their eyes and think that because they cannot see, they are also invisible.

Many years ago I recognised that G-d is both infinitely large as well as infinitesimally small. There is a part of G-d in every living being. He is right inside all of us, a living part of our existence. We can't hide from G-d, nor can we hide from ourselves. Our conscience tells us what is right and what is wrong and we have free choice over our actions and decisions.

Instant gratification often deludes us regarding the consequences of our choices. But what provides us with goalposts for the present is that G-d tells us about our connection with the past and into the future. We must be aware of the awesome responsibilities and inescapable consequences entailed by the "dominion" granted to us.

Physics deals with "action/reaction". Perhaps one day science will connect imaginary time with another place, also called Utopia, The Garden of Eden or "The Heavens".

How can "somethingness" arise from "nothingness"? Here is a creative, crazy explanation:

Waves are a fascinating phenomenon. They have their very own majesty of movement. Picture wave motion in water. Picture a still, limpid pond of water, into which you throw a stone. This will cause a ripple effect – a wave pattern moving outwards in a concentric, symmetrical manner; beautiful perfection of harmonious motion. Now picture a seaside setting: blue skies, bluey-green water and shimmering sands. The waves continuously move through the water towards the beach. Some waves overtake others. Some waves seem to bounce off the shallow waters close to the sand and simply move back into the sea, passing through stronger incoming waves. Occasionally, an incoming wave overtakes another wave: sometimes one wave will pass through the other and sometimes, it will merge with the other and both will continue their motion as one enhanced wave.

It is so easy to take wave motion for granted.

We all see and feel the sunlight warming our bodies – which are light waves. All of us also use radios, microwave ovens, TVs, cellular telephones – all of which base their operation on waves of various kinds. It is not difficult to imagine wave motion through the atmosphere. It is also not too difficult to feel comfortable with the concept of waves moving through a fluid medium, whether liquid or gas. But, how can we truly feel comfortable with the notion of wave motion through a vacuum? Space, by definition, is a vacuum, with some energy and matter dispersed through it; but basically it is "nothingness", a void. So how can we picture radio waves or sun rays moving through vacuum, through space?

It is not difficult to imagine a space ship, a satellite or a ball moving through space, as Newton's laws of motion describe: they move in straight lines. But even if energy is described as little "packets of energy/matter" (usually referred to as "photons"), it is still very difficult to rationalise, conceive and accept experientially, a sinusoidal, wavelike motion, rather than motion in a straight line. Furthermore, when we replace the linear model with the more complex model of a curve-shaped space/time, we expect to observe energy to propagate in a curved trajectory rather than as a wave.

Physicists have developed neat models to describe wave propagation; their algorithms produce simple mathematical equations that accurately predict such wave motion.

If we had videoed our pond scenarios and then viewed our video played backwards, we would experience the circular pattern of waves moving inwards and finally coming to a standstill, as the stone that was thrown into the water comes out of the water.

Let's picture two stones being thrown into our pond simultaneously, at two separate points. We would observe two expanding concentric wave patterns – meeting at certain points. If we focus our attention on those points of intersection, we will see the waves moving through each other, as though unaware of each other. If we relocated our point of observation and move closer to the point of intersection of these two waves, as they move towards each other, we would observe the net changes in the shape of these two waves, as they join together.

If these two waves happened to be of precisely the same shape and one of them would be "upside down" (i.e. inverted, or symmetrically out of phase), then at their points of intersection these two waves would actually cancel each other out and we would observe no disturbance on the surface of the water.

Now imagine that the point where our stone first splashed into the pond is a point of creation. The energy introduced into the pond by the impact of the stone has been converted into wave motion, which can be observed outside the point of impact. If we consider the pond an isolated system, then from the point of reference inside the pond, it can be likened to a singularity. This comparison with the singularity is only for the sake of illustration; but for our purposes, if a finite, however vast, amount of energy was introduced into our own universe (i.e. space/time) in the Big Bang, if we work backwards in time to the singularity of Creation, a comparable model will emerge.

This model helps illustrate three points:

- The measurement of time is absolute when observed from within a system and when measured from that point, can be traced backwards to a fixed "zero" starting point for this system.
- Within the system, the singularity forms its boundary with all outside systems; but from any point of reference outside the system, any such singularity, by virtue of its very occurrence, came into existence due to a disturbance that involved the transfer of energy/matter from that "outside" system.
- The wave model of energy/matter shows us how a wave can be brought into existence "from nothingness" (i.e. in a vacuum) by a force that separates the nothingness, dividing it into two symmetrical waves which move outwards from their point of creation.

Although this is quite abstract and philosophical, it is almost like a "positive and negative" energy having been produced out of nothing, where we experience the effect of the "positive" (i.e. real) energy, but not the "negative" (i.e. unreal) energy within our own framework of existence.

Another way of looking at it is, that if the wave was caused by a disturbance at the point of singularity – which represents our universe's zero point of time at its creation out of nothingness – and continued to move from its singularity within our universe, then there would be an equal – yet opposite – wave "outside of our universe", moving away from the singularity, representing the point in time and space where a "new universe" came into existence (keeping this illustration simple, as waves can be added as well as distorted).

By definition, that "somewhere else" remains hidden from us due to the boundary condition at the singularity. However, if in that "somewhere else" there were an observer who was lucky enough to witness the event, this observer would be able to establish precisely the time in which it occurred. Such an observer should also be able to observe and measure the wave moving out of the singularity, at which point "our universe" came into existence.

Similarly we, within our own universe, should be able to determine the time and location in which a black hole ceases to exist, as well as when a new baby universe comes into existence or has branched off our own universe, or when a new star is formed within our own universe. Obviously the tools

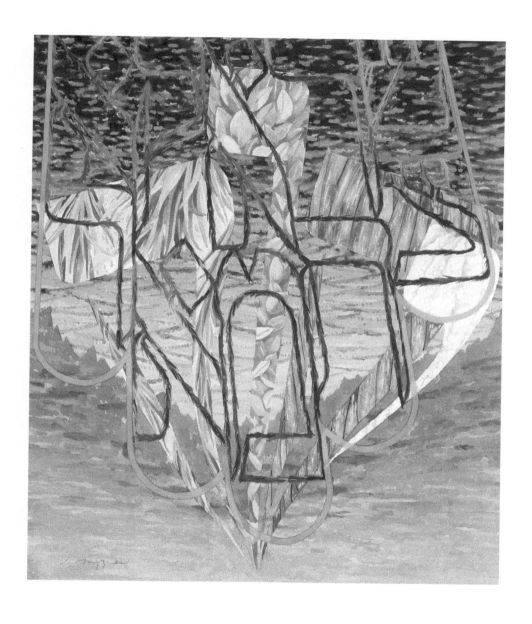

8: Unification of G-d's Name

(watercolour 57 x 51 cm) 2009

You can view/download the paintings in original full colour, free of charge at:

www.mysteryofyou.com

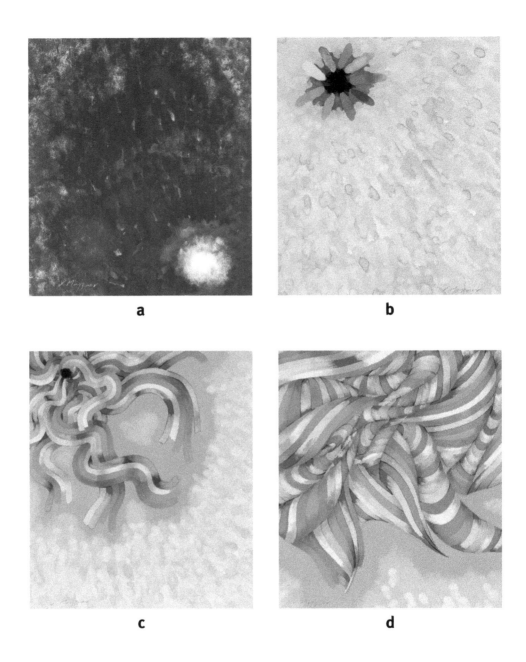

a

b

c

d

9: Yetzer Ha-Tov versus Yetzer Ha-Ra = the constant battle

(watercolour, each frame 29 x 25.5 cm) 2009

You can view/download the paintings in original full colour, free of charge at:

www.mysteryofyou.com

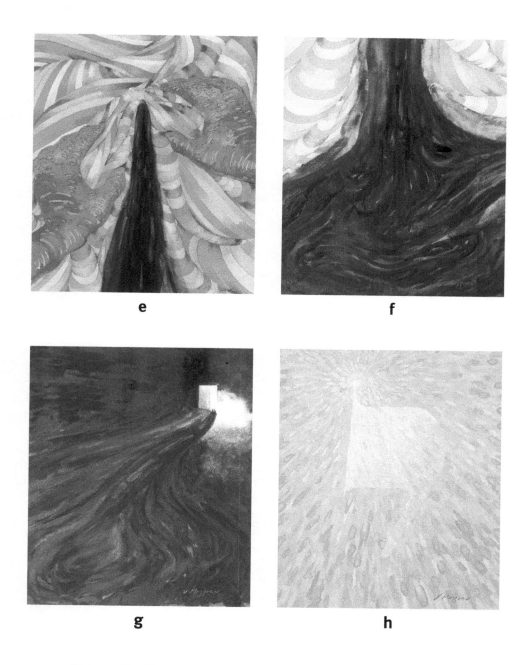

e

f

g

h

9: Yetzer Ha-Tov versus Yetzer Ha-Ra = the constant battle

(watercolour, each frame 29 x 25.5 cm) 2009

You can view/download the paintings in original full colour, free of charge at:

www.mysteryofyou.com

10: Numbers

(acrylic on canvas 76 x 56.5 cm) 2008

You can view/download the paintings in original full colour, free of charge at:

www.mysteryofyou.com

available to us at present, together with the sheer vastness of our universe where we experience the practical limitation of the speed of the light, make any such observation extremely unlikely.

One of the strangest properties of electro-magnetic waves is the shape of the propagation of the wave energy, as it radiates out from its source. A rather stupid, but illustrative, model is a "mass/energy interchange", where the relative mass ("photon" or "particle" of energy) is moving forward in a straight line (= Newtonian motion, in the absence of forces or curvature of time/space), whereas the "non-mass" is acting like a disturbance within the medium, at the point of intersection of the mass with the medium. If you "add and subtract" the mirror images and allow for the motion, you can visualise the shape of a wave propagating as energy.

A new school of thought which is becoming more popular among theoretical physicists, called String Theory, also makes no sense, but seems to work mathematically. It would seem that modelling the universe as a string or strings of "mass/energy" yields some very interesting convergences of mathematical formulae, which appear to consistently predict observed phenomena in time/space. Some say that String Theory will ultimately provide the solution to the Unified Theory of Relativity, which Albert Einstein worked so hard to discover but was never able to derive.

"Action/reaction" is unquestionably a fundamental property within our universe. Spinning and vibrating electrons and other charged particles generate electro-magnetic force fields. The concept of temperature and heat being related to motion, with particles "colliding", is probably easier to comprehend than the concept of gravitational force fields between masses. Conservation of momentum and energy within a system appears to be reasonable, whereas radiation of heat through space (a vacuum) appears to defy logic.

I do not think that a mathematical model of a string, that happens to fit all of the equations that can accurately predict events in the universe, is of much consequence with regard to the Big Bang theory – simply because no strings have been reportedly observed in the universe. Does it follow that there are no strings attached?

My journey is now nearing a crossroad where I shall embark on further exploration of new horizons.

I wish to share the following observations.

Throughout the history of human life on earth, we have searched for answers and have always felt the need to ask many new questions.

Philosophers and scientists have been able to formulate "laws of physics" based upon numerous observations. These laws have been algorithmically expressed and the mathematical equations, in turn, have been used to predict events. Interpolations have generally produced plausible results which could be confirmed and fitted in comfortably with our experiential patterns of observation. Extrapolation, on the other hand, has involved more speculation and risk, despite often being subject to practical observation and requiring confirmation.

Every now and then – though quite rarely, fortunately – there is a divergence between observable fact and theoretical prediction, and reality contradicts prediction. One really good example of this is our very well accepted Newtonian Laws of Motion. These laws assume the existence of absolute measures of time and distance. As we now well know, Einstein's Theory of Special Relativity provides us with new tools to adjust the Newtonian Laws of Motion in situations of high-speed frameworks, as the measurement of both time and dimensions is not absolute at all, but varies, relative to the speed of motion of the framework under consideration. Newton's Laws worked perfectly on earth, which was viewed as being at rest, despite the fact that our planet is both spinning on its own axis and rotating around the sun, as well as moving through space with our entire solar system. But when applied to space travel, radiation of wave energy or sub-atomic particles, Newton's Laws did not work.

Why am I coming back to this now?

It is obvious to me that, in regard to physics, there is no "chicken and egg" paradox at all. To me, it is blatantly obvious that the universe was created first; physics followed some billions of years later, as a result of our thirst for knowledge and creative logic. Physics resulted from our rationalisation of our observations of the universe. Our "laws of physics" are a mathematical description of our observations from planet earth within our universe. When I read a theoretical physicist's statement to the effect that the creation of the universe must comply with the laws of physics, I smile, take a deep breath and contemplate the sheer arrogance of humanity. It seems to me that some of us, despite our education and our intellect, got things a little mixed up. It is quite simply the other way around. Creation was creation. If our laws of physics break down when applied to extrapolated situations and particularly if applied close to singularities, bad luck to our laws of physics.

It is our man-made laws that have to comply with nature and accurately model its behaviour; nature and creation do not have to comply with anything.

Determinism – or random, lucky chance?

This is a very personal question. The answer depends only on whom you ask and in any case will always remain unprovable.

My feelings on this matter are very clear. We were created with an intellect implanted in each individual with our own unique experiential awareness of free choice about nearly everything – except for the certainty of one's own limited existence. I am sure that none of us evolved by some lucky random sequence of events which followed, by itself, from the singularity event of Creation of our universe. The Bible gives us the clue. G-d created our universe with particular attention to every detail. He organised everything in a very precise and deterministic manner. From then on, the entire universe has continued to evolve, with particular attention to our world where humankind abounds.

The Bible then tells us about the "blessings and curses" we can expect to encounter. When we follow the correct path, we "become blessed" and, in the bigger picture, will derive the advantages and benefits of "our blessings". When we make the wrong choices in life, we alone must face the consequences; so long as we continue to avoid the many opportunities we have to make amends, we will "bring curses upon ourselves".

The whole point is that we have the opportunity of exercising our free will; at the same time, though, we must accept responsibility for our actions and face their consequences.

We have free choice. If humans accept the responsibility that comes with their dominion over nature, they must limit their free choice. This freedom of choice is exercised within a framework of absolute laws regarding conduct, ethics, morality and approach to life here on earth. The ultimate significance of these laws is to "choose life over death" (see Deut. 30:15-19). We can fool ourselves by making short-term, convenience-based choices, usually involving instant gratification, while abrogating ourselves from the responsibility we bear for the continuation of existence. The "curses" involved in such choices are nothing but what inevitably follows from such acts; and these acts affect not only the individual who chooses unwisely, but also future generations.

Free choice can also result in compromises. But compromises lead to further compromises, until ultimately compromising the intrinsic quality of life itself. Humanity, both collectively and individually, thus has the opportunity of living with free choice – and also with the consequences of free choice.

G-d, who created the universe, also created humankind. G-d gave us His very special gift, which includes a set of absolute rules and regulations to live by. It is not we who make the rules; however, we can choose to obey the rules for our own long-term benefit. No "G-dless society" has survived in history. The foundation stones of any sustainable laws in any society or civilisation are the moral and ethical principles laid down in the Ten Commandments. No military dictator in some atheistic right-wing country, nor any people's chairman in some left-wing state, can create a lasting set of laws that will ensure the survival of its people. Only G-d-given laws are absolute and timeless.

Most "normal thinking citizens" may very well be offended when they examine the current intellectual thinking and official positions in the area of morals and ethics in any of the major prestigious universities in the USA; there, animal liberation and rights to exist are being defended to the extreme, while humans' rights to live are seriously compromised. Isn't this a bit mixed up?

While the universe was created at the Big Bang singularity of time, as measured within our realm of space/time, the concepts of "good and evil" and "right and wrong" are timeless absolutes. These concepts are not relativistic and cannot be subjected to the ever-changing norms of a self-regulated society. Morals and ethical behaviour cannot be relegated to the "warm and fuzzy feel-goods" of individuals. People come and people go. We all come and then go. Fundamental ethics and morality are absolute properties of human existence, just as birth and death are. "Thou shalt not kill" or "Thou shalt not steal" are equivalent to a human being having one head, two arms and two legs. But while these are absolutes, we have the free choice to accept them for our own wellbeing or to reject them at our own peril.

Did humanity create G-d as a buttress against the unknown and to pacify its fears, insecurities and inadequacies?

I don't think so – not at all! G-d created the universe, placed human existence inside it and gave it great potential.

If "what is" is separated from "what is not" in our universe and becomes further divided down into its most minute, all that we have left is a range of subatomic particles. Some have either a positive or a negative electronic charge and others are neutral. The positive and the negative seem to be able to exist and also to coexist and combine under certain conditions to form an individual particle of neutral electronic charge, which, under other conditions, is also able to split and yield two oppositely charged particles.

Some of these subatomic particles have a small mass, while others are so minute that their masses become almost insignificant. They are so tiny that often their existence is surmised rather than being truly observed. It is mathematically difficult to define/predict the influence of even a few of these particles upon each other, let alone large numbers of them. The Heisenberg Uncertainty Principle (uncertainty due to unpredictable fluctuations), which evolved earlier last century, is now considered one of the foundation stones of modern quantum mechanics. According to this principle, there cannot be accurate measurement of the position and the momentum of any particle at the same time. It also establishes that it is impossible to determine the energy and time of any particle simultaneously.

Do we really feel comfortable with the thermodynamic principle of transferring energy to matter or do we feel "more at home" with the notion that it is the fundamental motion of particles (vibration, rotation, translation) which is what energy is all about?

Let's not get into how electromagnetic radiation travels though a vacuum or where the "gravitational fields" really are which cause matter to be attracted to other matter through "nothingness".

When I discovered myself searching for the truth and the meaning of life, at the beginning of my journey of discovery, the ski slopes in Villars-Sur-Ollon offered their temporary illusion of "weightlessness".

How many degrees of freedom did I truly possess then and how many were my own temporary illusion?

How long can one experience the exhilaration of schussing down a slope of fresh powder snow? What proportion of one's life can be weightless?

What happens when one reaches the bottom of the run?

Where are the goalposts and who are the goalkeepers?

Who really makes the rules?

Who has free choice?

Where does the "real" start and end and what are the boundaries of the "unreal"?

How much comfort do any of us truly derive from what we actually experience and from what we are personally able to comprehend?

Life is full of opportunities, excitement, contentment, happiness, new experiences, challenges, memories, privacy, fulfilment, emptiness, searching, sharing, solitude, pain, suffering and futility; the positive and the negative.

That is all that we have and all that we can expect.

Who has all of the answers?

Science, in isolation, certainly does not. Although science tends to present itself as the monolith of absolute truth, it can only achieve relative truth, based upon human observations of the universe and upon human logic. Science alone is no more than the study of one particular discipline, albeit an exciting, interesting and fascinating one.

Blind faith, too, is shallow. Rather than being a truth unto itself, it is an abrogation of human responsibility from free choice. The Rambam

(Maimonides) put it so very clearly: the challenge of human existence is in finding the harmony of G-d and the universe by studying both the Holy Scriptures and the physical world.

Science and religion constantly defy the relentless human search to delve into their cores in isolation from each other. Yet both science and G-d connect well together if contemplated in harmony. In fact they comfortably belong together, because that is the nature of existence.

Two truths derived from one absolute truth.

Most probably, the only human being in history who "had it all" was King Solomon. He had no boundaries or limits in everything he desired or imagined: wealth, power, wisdom, influence, prophetic inspiration, G-dliness – King Solomon experienced everything life could possibly offer a human being.

And in the very final analysis, what is the advice that this person left us? In the concluding verses of his book Ecclesiastes he says:

> *The end of the matter, all having been heard: fear G-d and keep His commandments; for this is the whole man. For G-d shall bring every work into the judgment concerning every hidden thing, whether it be good or whether it be evil.*

Eastern religions are focused on people's search for equilibrium in existence: balance and harmony between the mundane and the intellectual, the material and the spiritual, the real and the surreal, the natural and the artistic. Such harmony between the physical and the spiritual is best achieved by connecting with the beauty and balance of nature, as well as through art, music, contemplation and control of one's senses.

In reality, what really matters is to be a good member of society; and the definition of "good," despite being of a personal nature, is not relative, but absolute. When G-d created the world and life, He also provided it with His Divine blueprint regarding the acceptable and unacceptable codes of behaviour. These codes of behaviour, or laws of life, are absolute as well as timeless; they apply to all people at all times.

When individual creatures live their short lives to the fullest extent, the many joys that life can offer give them a sense of timelessness within the otherwise limited timeframe of their existence.

This is the continuity of the cycle of life.

Thus the story of "Me", "Myself", "So What?", which is actually about "You", is entitled **"The Mystery of You"**!

Afterword

B*echol Dor Va Dor*
Le Chol Dor Va Dor

In every generation and for every generation.

It is May 2008. Late spring, early summer. Here we are, again, in Jerusalem, in the Old City emerging from a tour of the Western Wall tunnels.

We have walked through the archaeological excavations under the famous Western Wall of the ancient Israelite Temple which King Solomon, the son of King David, originally constructed over 3,000 years ago on the rocks of Mount Moriah, where Abraham, our patriarch, had walked about 4,400 years ago.

These 488 metres of tunnels, rooms and public halls resonate with history: the Levites, Prophets, Maccabeans, Priests, Kings and people, wars, destruction, rebuilding, pain and suffering, hopes and dreams, trials and tribulations.

Life and Death.

The life of the Jewish people. The crossroads of civilisations.

Dina and I emerge into Arab East Jerusalem, a short walking distance from the Damascus (Shechem) gate. We are with our tour guide, Eldad, an Israeli, aged mid-thirties, who specialises in Middle Eastern geography, history and culture. Eldad's parents survived Nazi Europe and restarted their lives in Israel, where he was born, educated and served in the Israeli Army.

We feel secure and happy. The narrow alleyways are abuzz with Arabic people, young and old, men, women and children. Life and trade are brisk on the streets. Open markets. A few beggars. The muezzin's shrill, singing voice resounds through loudspeakers, echoing off the stone walls, calling the people to prayer; the sounds and smells and flashes of colour from clothes hanging on string lines stretched between windows above, dance in the breeze.

There in front of us in the souk are fresh pastries and Middle Eastern delicacies made of semolina, sesame seeds, dates, nuts, honey and sweet syrups. We stop to buy a selection. "*Shukran*" (thank you) we smiled. "*Salam Alaikum*" (peace be upon you, or hello to you) was proffered, to which we responded "*Alaikum Salam*" (to you – peace or thanks, hello to you also).

People – feelings – culture – history and survival. Honour and self-esteem. Respect towards others and respect for one's self. Eldad speaks some Arabic. He is very concerned about the plight of the Arabic populations in general. We have already spent some days together touring Israel with our family. There has been a heated discussion with one of my sons-in-law who objected to Eldad's blaming of Israel for the misfortunes of the Palestinians. Eldad believes that we Jews should have done more and should be doing much more to help them. Eldad feels that Israel is at fault.

As we emerge from the Old City through the Damascus Gate, we stand by the steps waiting for our minibus driver to pick us up. We give most of our pastries to the Arabic children milling around us.

We are waiting in the sun.

I ask Eldad why he blames "us" for "their" problems. We talk. It is a friendly and positive discussion. I point out to Eldad that we Jews seem to expect perfection from ourselves. I say that this is most probably a very good thing. We are human beings. We are not perfect. All human beings make mistakes, but, maybe, it is a good thing for us Jews to aim high, to expect perfection and to punish ourselves (feel bad and seek to improve) when things go wrong.

Eldad approves of my thinking. We had taken him with us when we visited certain charity projects which our family has been actively supporting for many years. Eldad had not previously been exposed to Jewish problems – orphans, battered women and children, soup kitchens for the underprivileged and new immigrant absorption centres.

I remind Eldad that his own parents had suffered from persecution. Persecution for being Jewish, nothing else. They most probably had a lot to hate but had not allowed hatred nor politics to trap them into being lifelong refugees. They had started new lives. They had worked and built and created. They had tried to escape from their own sufferings to provide a better future for their children, for Eldad.

As much as there are many wrongs in the world, we can only try our best within our resources and possibilities to make the world a better place. Modern Israel is only 60 years old. It has absorbed millions of refugees from all over the world in its short, independent, democratic nationhood. It started with rocks, sand, malaria-infested swamps, little water and hostile neighbours. It was forced to fight many battles and wars which were imposed upon little Israel and Israel had to defend itself against the open threat of destruction. Even if there is suspicion of an injured or killed civilian Arab, most Israelis feel saddened by such casualties and often grieve for their surviving families. Unfortunately, the reverse is not the case. Many Palestinians take to the streets, celebrating in public joy and ecstasy when their brother and sister terrorists succeed in maiming or killing innocent Israeli women and children.

I say to Eldad that there is a fundamental difference. Most of us try to move forward with our lives and to build a better future. What do we expect of ourselves? Israel is only about one-third the size of Tasmania – the smallest state in Australia. Israel is about 800 kilometres long (like from Melbourne to Canberra, about two-thirds of the way to Sydney) and 20 to 50 kilometres wide in its most populated area to 100 kilometres wide across the desert. It has only about 6 million in population and no natural resources.

There are over 100 million Arabs with massive oil and gas resources and a vast amount of land that could easily help solve the poverty and social problems of their coreligionists, rather than waste massive amounts of money funding terrorism.

When Israel became independent in 1948 about 400,000 Arabs fled to neighbouring Arab countries, although many stayed and continue to be Israeli citizens. At the time, the Arab League inflated the "official" figures for political manipulation by about 150,000 people according to the United Nations. The estimated total population of Palestine under Ottoman Turkish rule in the mid-nineteenth century was only about 300,000 people. There was general immigration into the region under the British Mandate in the first half of the twentieth century. These 400,000 or so people became refugees in their Arab host countries, which many of them and their descendants continue to be. However, more than 650,000 Jews who had lived in the world's twenty-two Moslem countries (excluding but a few), most for many generations, many families for over a thousand years, as good citizens and neighbours, became refugees and were mainly absorbed into Israel, without compensation for their losses.

I am not saying that there is any moral equivalence. A wrong is not righted by another wrong. I am saying that at least we Jews do try to do the right thing and do try to help others. But! We first need to try to help ourselves as no one else is out there helping us. We are not trying to kill, destroy or colonise/occupy our neighbours. We do try to live peacefully within our neighbourhood and to care for it and our neighbours.

Unfortunately, many of our neighbours hate us and constantly threaten us.

Who is focused upon annihilating whom?

Who is dreaming about peaceful coexistence?

Thus, we must first look after ourselves and use the major part of our limited resources for our own people – for our own survival. We have many problems of our own and many of our own people with serious problems. Our first priority must be to help our own people. Only then can we afford to help others as we do help others all the time.

Just look at the humanitarian aid which Israel sends into Gaza every day and often in the face of rocket attacks, bombs and shooting. The poor people living in Sderot who are under constant rocket attack are the victims, not the aggressors.

Eldad agrees. I ask him what he thinks are the necessary human values in any society to make it sustainable. He thinks for a moment and then says that people have to be good people.

"Yes," I reply, "but what is 'goodness' in people? What is the value system?"

Eldad thinks on this and explains that people need to live by ethics and morality. They need peace. To feel it. To feel peace themselves and be peaceful. To be gracious, kind and compassionate to other people. They need to be fair and to be helpful or charitable to others around them.

"In other words," I ask him, "to treat others as they would like others to treat them?"

"Yes," he responds. "Much like that."

So I say that I fully agree with him. This was what our famous Sage, Rabbi Hillel, had said about 2,000 years ago. Hillel said that this was the basis of living life – it is the basis of Torah. To do unto others as you would have them do unto you and not to do unto others as you would not wish them to do to you.

How can people and society develop these values?

Only by education. It starts in the home by the parents to their children leading by example, investing time and value into showing and teaching children right from wrong.

The first and most important lesson is "no". There are limits and boundaries. There are laws and restrictions. "No" is such an important part of the most basic human behaviour.

The next and equally important lesson is about sharing and consideration of others, such as sitting at the table even though the child is not eating or has finished eating, just because it is nice and proper and the right thing to do out of respect for the others present who are still eating.

This is the opposite of the egocentric modern world.

The "me, myself", the "you" and the "us".

What follows is "the today", "the tomorrow" and "the day after tomorrow," rather than "the here and the now for myself". The importance of the impact of the individual upon society as well as the impact of society upon the individual.

These values differentiate humans from the animal kingdom and make for sustainable lifestyles within sustainable societies.

---

53   A prayer recited on the eve of *Yom Kippur* asking for the annulment of vows to God and forgiveness for transgressions.

Eldad stands and looks at me with a gentle smile on his handsome face. We wait for our minibus to arrive.

"I have enjoyed meeting you and your family," he tells me. "I have never met a family like yours and I have learnt so much during our time together. My family was not religious and we also were not so close," he says. "You are religious and maybe some of you are not so religious, but you are so close and also know so much about Israel and life. Before I met you, I thought I understood a lot and now I have seen so many new things. I want to thank you," he says.

"Thank you, too," I reply. "We have also learnt a lot from you."

Dina is enjoying the discussion as she stands with us in the sun, observing the people all around us. Eldad then turns to her and asks Dina what she thinks is the most important quality of people within a society. How did she, as a mother and grandmother, feel about raising a family in today's world and what was important?

Dina gently responds immediately. "You have to be a *mensch*." I smile to myself. Not bad for my "Sephardi princess", expressing herself with a word in the Yiddish language. "What is a *mensch*?" asks Eldad. Dina replies, "A good person. A decent, honest, moral, considerate and well-behaved person."

Eldad agrees. In fact, he says, that this is what he has said to me just before.

So we all agree. A society is generally civil when its people are good human beings. The person makes for the society as the society influences its people.

I then ask Eldad: "Tell me, you are not a religious person, are you?"

"No," he replies, "you already know that I don't believe in religion. Religion causes too many problems and conflicts in the world!"

"What do you do on *Yom Kippur*?" I ask.

"Of course, I fast," Eldad responds, "and, sometimes I might just visit a synagogue for a short while to catch up with friends."

"Tell me," I continue, "do you know how the Kol Nidrei[53] evening service starts on *Yom Kippur*?"

"What do you mean?" asks Eldad.

"I mean, what is the most important Jewish principle which is emphasised right at the beginning of *Yom Kippur*? The core issue which every Jew must struggle with?"

"Oh, that's easy," responds Eldad. "Everyone knows that *Yom Kippur* is all about begging G-d for forgiveness of sins."

"Is that so," I start to press him. "Do you really believe that *Yom Kippur* is as easy as that?"

"Well, I'm not religious and I don't believe in G-d," Eldad exclaims. "I told you, if there was a G-d, He would run the world differently. People would not have to suffer. There would not be wars, no diseases, no extreme poverty nor injustice!"

"You are 100 per cent correct," I say softly, "but according to you, there is no G-d and the world is a rotten place. Now, tell me please, let's get back to my question about *Yom Kippur*?"

Eldad looks at me, then at Dina and then at me again. "What do you mean?" he asks.

"I'll explain this to you," I offer. "You see, every person who is preparing themselves to enter that truly awesome day of *Yom Kippur*, before they feel their first tears of fear, trepidation and guilt as the Kol Nidrei prayer starts, must first have made peace between themselves and their fellow human being.

"*Beyn Adam Le Chavero* (between people) comes before *Beyn Adam Le Makom* (between a person and G-d). G-d is not interested in us asking Him for forgiveness of anything if we have not first sought the forgiveness of our fellow human beings, whom we have sinned against, Eldad, or 'wronged' if you prefer that word to the connotation of the word 'sin'. So, you see that there is actually no difference between your world and my world. We both live in the same world. It is the people who are causing all of the problems, not G-d and it is the people who can and should solve all of these problems, because these are people problems.

"The only difference between us is that I have a solid reference point. A set of absolute rules and regulations which I believe are G-d-given and inviolate. I don't have inner conflicts about this framework, although I do have conflicts and problems. For me, these are no more than my daily human struggle between my *yetzer ha-ra* and my *yetzer ha-tov*. I am lucky. You are less lucky because your conflicts are not only the same as my conflicts, but you have even greater conflicts to contend with, because you don't start with a fixed framework. You and everyone else like you are searching for and trying to rationalise your own individual frameworks."

We both agree; in fact the vast majority of humanity agrees that people should be "good" and that "ethics and morality" are essential in sustainable societies. The problem is only that every individual in Eldad's kind of society chooses or needs to choose their own definitions, interpretations, rationalisations and rules and regulations. In my kind of society, we only need to try to behave accordingly.

Thus on one hand, there is no real difference between "good" and "bad" in a religiously believing or non-believing person. Both can be either "good" or "bad". On the other hand, there should not be conflicts about what constitutes "good" and "bad" from a G-dly-orientated perspective.

A human's fundamental shortcoming is egocentricity. When we place ourselves at the centre of the universe, there are simply too many centres of too many artificial universes, and society becomes unsustainable.

In a G-d-centred universe, we don't anymore have the "me, myself and now" attitude to life. A very selfish philosophy! Instead, we have a "you, us, tomorrow as well as today and, even more importantly, the day after tomorrow" approach to living life.

"The no and the yes." "The we and the us." Where the "me" is much more part of the "you" than trying to make the "you" part of "me". One world, one universe, but, two diametrically opposing philosophies of life.

We all become silent. We feel a kind of personal serenity – a release and relief. It is peaceful.

Our minibus drives up and we greet our driver as we climb aboard. "You know what," I continue saying to Eldad. "I think that the key words which you would write down to try to define goodness in humanity would be righteousness, justice, kindness (loving-kindness), mercy (compassion) and fidelity (faithfulness)." (*Tzedek, Mishpat, Chesed, Rachamim, Emunah.*)

"Yes", he agrees, "let me think on this some more, please."

"Why not?" I say with a smile, "but do you know where these words were written a very, very long time ago? In the *Tanach* according to the prophet Hosea.[54] Funny coincidence!" I continue. "This is actually read as the *Haphtarah*[55] of the weekly Torah portion of *Parashat Bamidbar*,[56] you know, so there you have it." We all go on living our lives day to day and minute by minute. We all encounter the inner conflicts which life challenges us with. We question. We live. We try to survive. We enjoy the many little joys which life brings. In fact, every morning when we put on our *tephillin*[57] before morning prayers (*Shacharit*) we repeat precisely these five words as we bind our *tephillin* strap three times over the middle finger of our passive hand, both as a renewed covenant with G-d, as well as a reminder to ourselves.

Bechol Dor Va Dor – in every generation people need to experience their own experiences and in so doing, re-experience previous experiences of others. Rather than choosing to try to re-create or reinvent the wheel, it is easier and more beneficial to try to re-experience the revelation which took place at Mt Sinai.

This provides the sustainability – *Bechol Dor Va Dor* for *Le Chol Dor Va Dor*, within each generation as its legacy for each successive generation.

Ageing.

Belief and bureaucracy.

Continuity.

Behaviour.

Water, life and numbers.

Happiness.

Science or religion and religion or science.

---

[54] Hosea Chapter 2, Verses 21 & 22

[55] A section from the Prophets chanted during Sabbath services and festivals.

[56] Bamidbar – this is the first chapter of the Fourth Book of Moses. It mainly deals with the Census of the Children of Israel as Israel becomes a free nation. A Holy Nation – "A light unto the world!"

[57] A set of phylacteries.

I suppose that the fundamental question is "how?"

Life is relevant in each time and in each place. We can only try to imagine our own re-experience of the Exodus from Egypt and the revelation of Torah on Mt Sinai, but, our experience is impacting us in the here and the now, not the past.

This is the "magic" of the relevance of Torah in every generation. Torah is the present which connects us to the past and guarantees the future.

The beauty of the interaction of the Oral Law with the Written Law is that, through *Halachah*, it applies to the todays and continues to be consistent and relevant to the tomorrows.

Judaism, as life, did not get stuck in a particular time in history at a particular geographical location. Yes, we have our traditions and, yes, we love and respect our patriarchs, but, no, we don't live in the past. We live in the present. We survive the "here and the now". Our lives must be relevant to the times and we cannot try to hide from the truth. This ensures our future.

Torah is truth (the *emet*).

I heard a cute story about evolution. In a literal sense, an "evolutionist" should have more respect for his children and grandchildren than for his parents and grandparents. This is because he believes in evolutionary improvement of his species. The link to the past is to some genetically lower species as the genetic path is towards perfection in the future. Conversely, a G-d-believing person views perfection in the past, in G-d's creations and thus time moves us further away from perfection.

Similarly, an egocentric view of life sees "the ultimate person" in themselves in the here and the now.

Interesting! There is much "good" in the past, the present and the future. There is also "bad". The only perfection is in G-d. Humans are imperfect. Humans have the potential to change.

Ancient Egypt philosophised on these issues and attributed good and evil to external, supernatural forces of personality, motivation and dynamics, as did the ancient Greeks later in history (e.g. Eos, Isis, Osiris, Horus, Demeter, Hathor etc.)

This conflict between "good" and "evil", "right" and "wrong" is ageless.

It is the individual conflict of every person as they live their lives in every age, in every time, in every culture and in every generation.

In today's world, at the dawn of the twenty-first century, civilisation is hotly debating the moral and ethical issues relevant to modern medicine. Questions about definitions of life and death. Stem cells, abortions, organ transplants, quality of life, in-vitro fertilisation, pre-implant genetic diagnosis, degenerative diseases – the lists and the issues go on. It is interesting to note the many differences in approaches and attitudes as well as the pressure groups and the dogmas which are being imposed onto the debates. Monotheistic religions tend to cherish life, albeit with conflicting definitions and approaches. Secular ethics tend to value autonomy and individualism as over-riding principles. The outcomes affecting the population vary according to political decisions which impact upon laws and standards. Yet, in the Jewish world, a *Halachic* one based upon many scholarly opinions and disputations, there is an overwhelming consensus in this area. There are two very significant differences in the Jewish approach to dealing with these very sensitive issues. The first is that the definitions of the critical parameters can be *Halachically* derived to be consistent. The second is that the *Halachic* approach is one of looking at each individual situation and then facilitating an appropriate outcome, in contradistinction to all other approaches, which are to apply the rules and regulations to any general case.

For modern civilisation to remain sustainable, its morals and ethics must be consistent and relevant to the times. These principles of life must speak/call to each individual rather than be relegated to personal redefinition. My point is clear. We each have the free choice to do or not to do, to learn, question and try to understand the relevance of morals and ethics to ourselves, our lives and our society at large and then to apply them to the contemporary issues and challenges facing our world. We do not really have the free choice of trying to create our own individual charters of morals and ethics, even though we surely feel that we may possess that flexibility.

Egocentricity! Personal rights!

Deus-centricity (G-d centred). Personal responsibilities.

Rights, responsibilities, obligations and outcomes.

The me, myself, so what?

Humans do not make the rules and regulations of life. The Creator of all life made these rules. We apply or fail to apply the rules for our own benefit, detriment or destruction. We can only try to fool ourselves for so long. The consequences are visible all around us.

We are commanded to "love our G-d". How can anybody love someone whom they have never met and thus do not have a relationship with? Sounds incongruous. Feels sensible.

One practical way is to appreciate the physicality of the world and to respect it. To learn to love the creations which the Creator created. Through this awareness, one can gain greater appreciation and a relationship actually commences. Such a relationship can grow into true love and such love can be experienced as a very wholesome and fulfilling intellectual/spiritual, lasting relationship.

I have often been perplexed by one of our fundamental and most beautiful blessings. It is the *Barchu*. Literally, in Hebrew, it goes like this: *Barchu et Ha-Shem Hamevorach*. Loosely translated: Blessed be the G-d (i.e. the name of G-d) the One who is blessed (i.e. the source of blessings. *Baruch Kevod Ha-Shem, Mimkomo* − Blessed is the Glory of *Ha-Shem* from His place).

My problem is more a grammatical one, with the word "*et*", which seems to me to be superfluous in the literal context. A simple reading would have been *Barchu Ha-Shem Hamevorach* (Let us bless G-d, the Blessed One).

Only recently did I start to feel the importance of the inclusion of the "*et*" within the context of blessing the creations which G-d created and He blesses. You may recall my mention of the Kabbalistic allusion to the "*et*" in the first seven words of Genesis in the Science and Religion chapter of this book. The Kabbalists interpret the "*et*" there as the *Aleph to Tuph*, i.e. first letter of the Hebrew alphabet through to its last letter. (The basic building blocks of creation.)

Isn't this beautiful here too?

"Blessed be the *Aleph Tuph* (i.e. physical creations) which G-d the One who is the source of blessings, created."

Me, myself, so what?

Who am I? Where did I come from?
What kind of a life am I living?
Where am I going?
What impact am I making on others around me and on the world?

Bechol Dor Va Dor	In every generation
Beyn Adam Le Chavero	Between humans
Beyn Adam Le Makom	Between a human being and G-d
Le Chol Dor Va Dor.	For every generation.

Righteousness, justice, kindness, mercy and fidelity.
Who makes the rules?
Who defines the definitions?
The evil inclination and the good inclination.
The G-dly spark in the soul of every living person.
Searching ... Connecting ... Living.
The journey through life rather than the destination.

The Confrontation of the
Yetzer Ha-ra

Before one can confront one's *yetzer ha-ra*, one needs to be able to recognise it.

Before being able to recognise one's *yetzer ha-ra*, one must have first become aware of its existence and have experienced it at work to understand its influence and power.

The Talmud tells a fascinating story about the *yetzer ha-ra* and *Succoth* provides a unique opportunity through its protective power to raise one's spiritual awareness – *but* – more on these later.

I told this story to Victor Majzner. The story is full of drama and imagination. Victor could see the process. He was able to live the experience and his artistic talents became inspired. The result is included in this book, painted like a strip/narrative in eight frames. This is the story.

Let the confrontation begin!

You are well armed and prepared. This is going to be one of your most difficult and challenging battles of your life and yet it will also be an easy one because you have chosen to win it.

You are spiritually strong, feel well nourished and you fully understand the nature of your free choice and your ability to harness its true power. You are totally committed to your *yetzer ha-tov* as the real illumination of your life and, equally, you recognise your *yetzer ha-ra* as the evil illusion which it thrives within. You have prepared your fences and gates and you are well armed to commence as well as to complete this Don Quixotian mission.

"A little bit of light takes away a lot of darkness" (as my four-year-old grandson, Giladi, says of his fears, before falling into peaceful sleep in his room at night).

You look inside yourself. It is quiet. Empty. It is dark, but the darkness contains its own kind of serenity. You look. You wait. You look.

You sense something else present. You allow your consciousness to become aware of it. You feel some kind of feeling of familiarity. It grows. It starts to warm. It starts to reveal itself. Images appear. There is movement. Your senses open to become stimulated by the attractions and illusions which progressively appear to be more real and alive.

You encourage your *yetzer ha-ra* to come closer to you. To move and to allure. To beguile and to deceive. You hide your own innermost power, your choice to deceive the *yetzer ha-ra* by exposing it.

The encounter increases in its intensity. Two opposing forces engaged in a battle of superiority. The stronger and most committed will overpower the other. The stakes are high. The *yetzer ha-ra* is supremely experienced and adept in the arts of deception and seduction as in self-preservation. Your *yetzer ha-tov* is simply, purely, "goodness", but so far inexperienced in these manoeuvres and untested for domination.

The *yetzer ha-ra* can come and go. It can grow and diminish. It can conceal itself. The *yetzer ha-tov* illuminates.

Your choices control. You allow your *yetzer ha-ra* to perform its tricks. You pretend to succumb to its illusions. You encourage it. You nurture its attractive powers to grow, to intensify. You open yourself to its vivid theatrics and you draw it closer.

Your *yetzer ha-ra* feeds on its success. It fills with colour and movement. It projects live images so real and enticing. It rages its consuming fires in anticipation of success. It flaunts itself, hypnotised by its own exposed vulnerability. It prepares to climax its evil intentions.

You unexpectedly reach out. You engage your *yetzer ha-ra*. It is bewildered. You are well prepared and determined in your outcome. You grab hold of its cloak of deception and seize it most strongly with both hands. You tear it open.

Your free choice remains determined and uncompromising. You gain brute strength. The *yetzer ha-ra* tries to free itself. Its bright and dynamic illusions start to fade, despite its innate ability to twist and contort – to transform and transpose.

You tear its cloak open. It shrieks! You tear and expose!

Its ugliness pours out. You rip apart its garb, which becomes ever weakened as the dark putrescence outflows. Foul, black, oozing fluids fill the void. The *yetzer ha-ra* becomes limp and seeks to retreat.

You feel revolted by the sight and repelled by the smell. The stench is repugnant. Its ugliness sickens you. This is almost unbearable, but you persevere.

You draw strength and respite from your *yetzer ha-tov*. It is shining light. Its radiance illuminates as the *yetzer ha-ra* dissipates.

You become aware of a little opening in the far corner of your mind, where the *yetzer ha-ra* is seeking escape and the light filling the darkness is taking shape. Renewed strength. Victory is near. This mission is dear. Your confrontation is clear and almost complete.

As the *yetzer ha-ra* moves towards the light in the corner and your *yetzer ha-tov* fills all of your darkness with warmth, you expel the *yetzer ha-ra* out through the little opening in the corner to the outside and immediately shut the gate to banish it from within your fence.

You feel weightless. Your energy is sapped. You feel totally exhausted but elated. Safe. Serene. Strong and clean. You lie back and drift, eyes closed. Enormously relieved. You ponder. You dream.

You have emerged victorious in your battle against your *yetzer ha-ra*. You have overpowered its negative influence over you. You have ejected it and now have gained the power of your *yetzer ha-tov* to resist the bad influence of the *yetzer ha-ra* in the future.

The experience is yours. You have the insight to recognise the *yetzer ha-ra* and to expose it. To literally undress its cloak of disguise and deception by revealing its true ugliness which lies within it.

Your memory of this milestone event in your life is your experience as well as your unique insight. You possess the power of free choice in your understanding of the true nature of the negative illusion of the *yetzer ha-ra* and the positive influence of your *yetzer ha-tov*.

Living life with free choice.

The Talmud relays a fascinating story about the *yetzer ha-ra* (Sanhedrin tractate 64a and Yoma 69b). It is most interesting to note that the tractate Sanhedrin deals with issues pertaining to the highest court of law and Yoma deals with the Holy Temple service on *Yom Kippur* (the Day of Atonement) conducted by the High Priest in the Holy of Holies. Both versions of the story cover the same event but, in Yoma, we are told some additional details.

The story reveals that the *yetzer ha-ra* has its purpose in our world and without the *yetzer ha-ra*, life does not function. Thus the *yetzer ha-ra*, as a force or an entity, cannot be destroyed or annihilated from existence but people need to be able to deal with its potent, negative/destructive influence/power.

Thus my story. Meeting the *yetzer ha-ra* by discovering its ways and being able to recognise it. Choosing to confront it by revealing/exposing its true ugliness and thus becoming empowered to negate its beguiling influence by illuminating its darkness and expelling it outside of your mind.

Succoth provides a very special spirituality as a unique window in our annual cycle of time. Commencing four days after *Yom Kippur*, at the full moon (middle of the month) of Tishrei, we experience the unique *mitzvah* of the four species. We are told that our performance of this *mitzvah* is the "unification of the four letters of G-d's name", due to us having spiritually performed the entire 613 commandments within our Torah. This is the ultimate pinnacle of existence which any human being can achieve.

Then, on the last day, so to speak, of *Succoth*, which is elevated by the special name of *Hoshana Rabbah*, another unique *mitzvah* is performed. It is the beating of the five willow branches, which is also compared to separating these four letters of G-d's Holy name again (back to how they usually appear throughout the year).

Succoth closes with the festivals of *Shemini Atzeret* (the closing/departure of/on the seventh [day]) and *Simchat Torah*, when we read both the last chapter (part) of the Torah (*Ve Zoth Ha Berachah* in Deuteronomy) and the first chapter (part) of the Torah (*Bereishit* in Genesis).

Thus we have moved up in spirituality as we approach the month of Tishrei and are being returned (moved back down, so to speak) as Tishrei concludes and we move again into the next month. These few days of *Succoth* provide an opportunity to reach the pinnacle of spiritual intensity. This unique period of time in the year assists us to deal with the *yetzer ha-ra*, whose influence becomes much diminished and also to connect very powerfully with our *yetzer ha-tov*.

Living life to the fullest.

Exercising free choice.

Choosing the paths illuminated by the positive light of your *yetzer ha-tov*.

Excluding the negative illusions of instant gratification by the deception and temptation of the *yetzer ha-ra*.

> *... and [Eve] perceived that the tree was good for eating and that it was a delight to the eyes.* (Genesis 2:6)

Perceptions, or rather, misperceptions are the ways of the *yetzer ha-ra*.

It fuels our imaginations and activates our senses. It feeds our desires and unfulfilled expectations with fantasies as it works to encourage our actions/reactions. These perceptions/misperceptions mould our behaviour and cloud our judgment. It is our free choice which controls us and provides us with the real consequences of the outcomes of our actions.

Our *yetzer ha-tov* illuminates our path but we have the innate ability to dim its light and to repress its influence.

Our *yetzer ha-tov* will stand up to public scrutiny and is real for the day after tomorrow as it resists the forces of the *yetzer ha-ra* which is only concerned about the here and the now.

The yetzer ha-ra
Knows you from afar
It plays with your senses
It doesn't like fences
It's earthy, material, imagination enhancing
It teases and tempts, emotions are dancing
Provoking fulfilment with short-term illusions
Promising pleasant, indulging conclusions
Working to stimulate body and mind
With all sorts of images of its own kind.

The yetzer ha-ra
Is a creature of night
It thrives in darkness
Avoiding the light
In the deepest recesses
Of your living soul
It plays out its mischief
For grief is its goal.

An explosion of colour
A sight to delight
Sounds most symphonic
Such sweet perfumed fragrance

Enhances the sight
With touch, erotic, sublime yet so slight.

The subtle scent permeates
The touch which electrifies
The mellow, soothing sound
The taste more delectable
The sight to ignite
The thoughts which stir and arouse
The passions of the soul
In the beating of the heart
No finish – just start!

Lurking in the dark recesses of the mind
Never out in front but always from behind
Stalking vulnerability, feasting on deceit
The yetzer ha-ra is plotting your defeat.

Always there to help you,
Especially when you're down
Cloaked in darkness through and true
Disguised as friend, adorned with crown.

I'm with you but you're not there
I'm next to you, you're unaware
I move closer but you don't see
Your world does not include me
The void of despair
The emptiness, depressingly bare.

No affection, no feeling, no one to share
Living in darkness, an absence of light
The blindness of sight in the darkness of night
Emotionless sadness everywhere
And your yetzer ha-ra is lurking there.

Outpouring of heart
Parched, sad soul
The darkness is filled
By illusion, whole
Seduced by deception
The unfulfilled dream
Sucks dry the emptiness
Appealingly seen.

The yetzer ha-ra will make you feel good
With new beginnings, follow, you should
No thoughts of endings
Nor journey, nor face
Just race to the now, at your quickest pace
Your yetzer ha-ra
Draws near from afar
But the door is ajar
With the light of the night.

This is your moment
Your time to prevail
Gather your strength
And you shall not fail.

Let the light in
And open that door
You want to win
As the law gives you more for sure!

Your yetzer ha-tov will illuminate
All that you love and all that you hate
Bring in the light
With all of your might
You'll hear the roar

As your yetzer ha-ra
Is expelled out of the door
Your yetzer ha-ra can deceive you no more.

Its cloak of illusion
You ripped apart
Exposed of delusion
Before it could start
Its routine of deception
Its negative ways
You revealed your selection
The luminous rays.

Your yetzer ha-tov
Leads you forward, ahead
Nurtured through strength of
All being said
And considered and chosen
And not being led.

Your yetzer ha-tov rules and prevails.
Your yetzer ha-ra is exposed and it fails.

Ron Goldschlager
13 February 2009

Rabbi Adin Steinsaltz

"Jewish lore is filled with tales of formidable rabbis. Probably none living today can compare in genius and influence to Adin Steinsaltz, whose extraordinary gifts as scholar, teacher, scientist, writer, mystic and social critic have attracted disciples from all factions of Israeli society."   TIME, 1980

Rabbi Adin Steinsaltz is internationally regarded as one of the leading scholars and rabbis of this century. He was born in Israel in 1937 to a secular family. At age 23, he became Israel's youngest high school principal.

Best known for his commentaries and translations of the Babylonian Talmud, Rabbi Steinsaltz works with teams of scholars and editors in producing the 41 Hebrew, 21 English, 21 French and five Russian volumes which have been completed over the past thirty years. The Rabbi expects to conclude the Hebrew Talmud project with a total of 44 volumes during the next decade.

Since 1988, Rabbi Steinsaltz has founded the Jewish Universities of Moscow and St. Petersburg, a publishing house in Moscow, and *Lamed*, the national Jewish teachers organisation. He travels to Russia and the Republics frequently for lectures and meetings with students, teachers, politicians, journalists and key decision-makers, serving as *Duchovny Ravin*, a historic title bestowed upon him in 1995, indicating his role as spiritual mentor of Russian Jewry.

Founder of the Israel Institute for Talmudic Publications, Rabbi Steinsaltz has published over 60 books on the Talmud, Jewish mysticism, religious thought, sociology, historical biography and philosophy. These books have been translated into Russian, English, French, Portuguese, Swedish, Italian, Japanese and Dutch. Rabbi Steinsaltz has also translated *Pirkei Avot*, the Ethics of the Fathers, into Chinese with an introduction and commentary.

In Israel, Rabbi Steinsaltz is Dean of the *Mekor Chaim* network of schools in Jerusalem, encompassing kindergarten through high school, as well as *Yeshiva Gevoha*. In 1988, Rabbi Steinsaltz received the Israel Prize, the country's highest honour.

Rabbi Steinsaltz has been a visiting lecturer and resident scholar at leading academic institutions in Europe, China and the United States, including Oxford University, the Sorbonne, The Academies of Social Sciences in Beijing and Shanghai, Yale University, University of Cape Town, The Institute for Advanced Studies and the Woodrow Wilson Center.

Rabbi Steinsaltz lives in Jerusalem with his wife, and has three children and thirteen grandchildren.

The following articles are arranged to follow the same themes and order as the chapters in the first half of this book.

Preface

Ron Goldschlager is neither a writer nor a philosopher. His everyday occupations do not define or characterise him; what does define him is that he is a good man, whose head is full of thoughts.

These thoughts are, in his own personal way, thoughts about the universe and about all those things that are "under the sun" (Ecclesiastes 1:9), as well as what is "above the sun": the Almighty, His relationship with the universe, and sometimes also His relationship with Ron Goldschlager.

Ron has shared with me the various stages of the creation of this book when it was developing from within the recesses of his heart. I would listen, comment, sometimes add or delete. Needless to say that Ron is always pleasant company, be it when he tries to help me find a new constellation in the sky or to fathom the secrets of creation.

Philosophy books, good or bad, are attempts to construct systematic thinking, either on a specific topic or about the world as a whole. This book does not even attempt to construct such a complex structure. However, it contains interesting and even important ideas, as well as some worthwhile statements, which call upon the reader to continue thinking about them, either along the same lines or in an opposite direction.

Every book is a certain reflection of its author, his musings and his dreams. This book, too, is a window to the personality of its author. A peek through this window provides not only the trivial aspect of superficial acquaintanceship, but also a much deeper knowledge of his person than even his relatives and friends may have. Some of the ideas in this book are well known while others are surprising, yet all of them are adorned with the unique contribution of the author's personality. And although it is impossible to weave from them an entire tapestry, the reader constantly comes against precious threads of thought that should be dealt with further.

My articles, which Ron graciously added to this book, are his choice, and I hope that the reader will find some interest in them as well.

Adin Even Israel Steinsaltz
Jerusalem, Israel 2010

Starting in the Middle

It is a Jewish tradition to start everything from the middle. No Jewish book except Maimonides, perhaps, who was a very organised person – so organised, in fact, that sometimes it is difficult to figure out his orderliness – ever starts from the beginning. They all begin somewhere in the middle; the beginning is then found somewhere within the book, and the end is usually not at the end. This is so because the world we live in is not orderly and organised – not in terms of how reality is, but in how we humans experience it.

We always experience the world from the middle; a baby is born into an existing world, trying its best to understand it – always starting from somewhere in the middle. Thus, for instance, a child learns to say "mummy" and "daddy" long before it gradually figures out what that really means. This is the reason why, even though Jews have always been learning, there are no traditional Jewish schoolbooks. All the great Jewish books are "adult" books, which children have been studying throughout the ages. Can we really make an introduction for children to the grammar of the language they speak? Or can we prepare them for the structure of the world they live in? Not really; we begin to live and learn; and as we progress we keep revealing things, and somewhere along the way we also get to the beginnings. The organised, well-structured approach is artificial. It may have justification for the sake of organising subject matter, but it has no existential basis in human experience. The natural way is to starting from somewhere in the middle.

The One and the Many

Generally speaking, the Jewish way is not only for outstanding individuals but for the nation as a whole. Each and every one of the Torah commandments pertains to the entire Jewish people; there is no commandment or teaching that involves only a select, special section of the people. Moreover, one of the aspirations and ideals of Judaism is the *tikkun*, betterment, of the whole world.

The inherent value of the many is expressed also in the fact that rulings are made according to majority opinion. "To decline after the many to wrest [judgment]" (Exodus 23:3) is a principle of Jewish law that applies even when an individual's opinion seems to be the correct one – as was the case with Rabbi Meir, whose companions could not fathom his thinking and ruled against his opinion, or the more dramatic case of Rabbi Eliezer ben Hyrcanus, where the *Halachah* was decided against his opinion, despite the many proofs that he was right – because his was a minority opinion.

This is also why Jewish customs often serve as the basis for *Halachic* rulings and quite often also "a custom abolishes a ruling". Wherever the *Halachah* is uncertain, we are called upon to see how the people conduct themselves. An extreme expression of such a case is found in the *Midrash* (*Tanhuma, vaEthanan* 6), where Moses says: "Let Moses and a thousand like him perish, and not one single Jew". This is the epitome of the submission of the greatest personality to the majority.

On the other hand, however, there is a diametrically opposed approach, whereby the many are nullified vis-à-vis the individual. The basic parameter here is truth. Whatever the claim of the many may be, it becomes immaterial when faced with truth. In fact, the place of the Jewish people among the nations is a salient example of this principle: the Jews are a very small minority; but since the minority is the one that chooses the truth, all the others do not matter at all. The Jewish nation has chosen the path of truth, and therefore it stands alone in front of the multitude of false prophets and does not take them into any consideration. It is the same in Jewish law as well: an erroneous custom, even if it is followed by many, cannot continue, and it is annulled by the choice few.

The *Midrash* (*Tanhuma, vaYeshev* 1) explains this idea with a parable: there was once a king who lost a diamond in the waste piles, and he fumbled in those piles – until he found the diamond; then he discarded the piles altogether. So too the Almighty sustained all the generations from Adam to Noah, until Noah arrived, and all the generations from Noah to Abraham, until Abraham arrived; then He set aside all the rest. This *Midrash* expresses the relationship between the one and the many as follows: the many are secondary to the individual; they do not count at all: it's the individual that matters.

In truth, there is no contradiction between the two approaches. But what is it that distinguishes the "right" kind of a multitude, which is therefore viewed positively, from the "wrong" kind multitude that is viewed negatively? It is not a question of justice or injustice: in fact, even when the People of Israel sins, Moses still considers it more important than himself, the loftiest individual. Where, then, does this difference lie?

There are two aspects to any multitude: that of "people" and that of "mob". Both a people and a mob are not just a large number of individuals, but an entire organism made up of many individuals, the sum total of which is more than the sum of its parts. But whereas a people is a multitude that is unified in a way that allows, at least potentially, the higher powers of the soul to rule, a mob is a group of individuals that activates the base and lowly aspects of the human soul. According to this definition, a people is preferable even to the best of individuals, because the group powers are of a more sublime nature. This is the reason why, whenever there is a *Halachic* dispute, the ruling is decided according to the majority opinion (*Berachot* 37a): "Where an individual joins issue with the majority, the *Halachah* is determined by the majority." But when the multitude is a mob, its numbers are insignificant; on the contrary: the higher the number, the greater the disadvantage. Such a multitude, vis-à-vis the individual, is like the waste as against the diamond. The Talmud (*Sanhedrin* 26a) puts it as follows: "[King] Hezekiah was afraid, and said: 'Perhaps, Heaven forfend, the mind of the Holy One, blessed be He, is with the majority ...' Thereupon the Prophet came and reassured him (Isaiah 8:12): 'Say ye not a confederacy [= conspiracy], concerning all of whom this people do say, a confederacy'; it is a confederacy of the wicked, and as such cannot be counted [for the purpose of a decision]." In other words: the mob, even if it is the majority, does not count at all.

The difference between mob and people is not in who its members are, but rather in the way in which they are united. The same group of individuals can be either a multitude or a mob, depending on its state at any given time. It follows, then, that everything that the many do or say must be checked, in order to see whether it is "the majority of the people" or a "conspiracy of the wicked".

There are two ways of influencing the multitude: by turning to the "people" aspects of that multitude, or by appealing to the "mob" aspects. Appealing to the "mob" is by lowering oneself to mob values, seeking their acceptance by stooping to the lowest common denominator. An example of this is the religious reform. On the face of it, it looks like the Reform movement is so very considerate of the needs of the multitude; but in truth, it is an appeal to the mob, because it belittles Judaism. The traditional Jewish way, on the other hand, is the appeal to the "people" aspect, because its intention is to raise it to an ever higher level.

But how does one do that? How can a multitude, which is like amorphous matter, be turned into a people, which is a form that makes for further progress and ascent? Appealing to the mob is easy, because the lowly sentiments that are the cohesive element of the mob can be easily aroused. But a people cannot be created in this way. The creation of a people is a personal process that involves an extended, ongoing process of education, that lasts until this goal is attained. This is where the outstanding individuals come in. Such individuals serve as the educators of the public; they lead it towards becoming a people, and continue to guide it even after it has turned into a people.

This explains the two-faceted attitude towards the individual: certain individuals may be worth as much as a multitude, or even more: "Moses our Teacher is equal to 600,000 Israelites" – (Deuteronomy *Rabbah* 11:10), but they also have certain roles vis-à-vis the multitude. On the one hand, the role of the individual as the guide and mentor of the public makes him highly important, much beyond his value as an individual. However, this importance is related to the mission that he has to fulfil for the sake of the multitude, as it says about Moses: "The Holy One, blessed be He, said to Moses: 'Moses, descend from thy greatness. Have I at all given to you greatness, except for the sake of Israel? And now Israel have sinned; then why do I want you?'" (*Berachot* 32a).

The entire Jewish nation vis-à-vis the rest of the world is like the individual leader who leads the multitude. Israel is the guide to all humanity on its way to fulfilling G-d's will. All of Jewish history is marked by those superb personalities who are at the forefront of the Jewish people and educate the Jews in the way of the Torah. This educational process is slow and may last for generations, or even more; but the final goal is in the hands of the true educators of the people, who aspire to raise the nation to their level, rather than lower themselves to the level of the multitude. The prophets of Israel were also the educators of the people. It took many years until their messages were absorbed, but eventually, they succeeded in overcoming all the false prophets and eradicating idol worship.

The Sages of Israel, the Pharisees and the *Chaverim*[1], too, eventually succeeded in leaving their imprint on the life of the nation, and in educating even the simplest folk – *amei ha-aretz*[2] – a social group that in the course of the Talmudic and Geonite periods disappeared completely. In fact, there are many Jewish customs that originate not only in the desire to perform the commandment in the best way possible (*hiddur mitzvah*): great individuals have, through their educational influence, succeeded in instilling their ideas and practices in the entire nation. Some examples are the lighting of the Hanukkah candles, which nowadays is done according to the strictest opinion; another example is the custom of wearing a hat, etc.

To conclude: even though the way of Judaism is a path for the many, the role of educating and influencing the people is in the hands of a small number of choice individuals. The individual, in and of himself, is of great worth, but his value increases when he acts as leader of the multitude. The leader's actions and endeavours to elevate himself must always be vis-à-vis the multitude. Finally, we must keep in mind that the most desirable way for the nation as a whole is the way of the leading, pioneering individuals.

---

[1] The Torah Scholars who are very strict in every aspect of Jewish observance (including the laws of purity, which were very difficult to observe).

[2] The simple folk, who could not always be counted on to properly observe the laws of tithes and purity.

From Childhood to Old Age

The Inner Aspect of Education

Every educational method, anywhere the world and at all times, is based upon
certain ideas, ideals and worldviews. However, quite often – possibly, almost
always – educators (or whoever else is in charge of education) are only partially
aware of the fundamental ideas, goals and aspirations that are at the basis of
the education they impart; and among non-professional educators, the degree
of awareness is even lower. But in the final analysis, what determines education
is the ideas, and not the degree of awareness of their existence in the minds
of the educators. Thus in every society, even the most primitive, education
is influenced by the educator's desire to mould the students' personalities in
ways that suit his own private views, or those of his society.

There is a great variety of educational approaches that change with time,
place, social status etc., and so many good intentions on the part of educators
who wish to impart certain worldviews and ways of life. Generally speaking,
however, all existing educational forms can be divided into two major groups.

The first approach is based on the desire to prepare the child for life.
Children are taught whatever they need to know in order to live on. Only little,
if any, attention is paid to children's needs and desires, and if so, it is done
in the negative way – namely, by trying to prevent the child from engaging in
childish things and turning his attention towards what he is to do as an adult
and making him want whatever adults want. The main aim of this kind of
education is to erase, as much as possible, the child-like aspects of the child
and turn him into a little adult as fast as possible.

The second educational approach works in the opposite way. The child is
taken care of and given maximal freedom, while his desires are fulfilled to

the maximum degree. The adults want the child to be a child, and not bother with the tough ways of life; they want, for as long as possible, to leave him in some kind of paradise in which he will grow and develop according to his inner inclinations. The child leads a life with many rights and very few duties.

These two basic approaches to children – children as apprentice-adults or as social protégés – can be found in practically almost all the societies of this world, either in their extreme forms or in various intermediate forms, in which the child's position is shifted this way or that, in a kind of compromise between these two opposing trends. Modern Western education basically aspires to give the child as happy and pleasant a life as possible; still, it must take into account the facts and possibilities of life, and therefore it also prepares the child, to some extent, for the future. Similarly, educational systems whose aim is to turn the child into an adult, nevertheless place the children in some kind of paradise in which they do not have any real duties – except for one: "To study well and to behave properly". In short, if we analyse all the "intermediary" educational forms, we shall discover in every one of them elements of these two major educational approaches which have existed throughout the ages.

Even though the difference between these two forms of education seems huge, they do share one similarity. In fact, these two approaches can be seen as two different conclusions drawn from one common concept: that adult life is the life. The child's life is not real life, but a preface to "life", which is adult life.

The influence of this concept can be easily discerned in the first educational approach, the approach that sees education as preparing the child for "life". But the second approach is also based on this very same idea: the child is given whatever his heart desires, is surrounded with comforts and unrealistic conditions, almost no demands are made on him and he is completely exempt from responsibility. Yet all this is not because childhood is seen as the ultimate ideal; on the contrary: it is because the adults want to give the child some respite before starting "life itself". Once life itself begins, his situation will change completely.

Both educational forms, then, are based on one and the same idea, the only difference between them being their attitude towards the child in this "introductory" period of life: should children be trained and prepared ahead of time – or should they be allowed to enjoy themselves until "life" actually begins?

The Ideal of Adulthood

The idea that "life" is adult life has a tremendous, all-encompassing influence, not only in the limited sphere of child education, but also in all spheres and stages of the life of every individual.

Education that is based on the assumption that "real life" is somewhere in the future, that it is yet to come, also contains some implicit assumptions about the nature of this "real life". To be sure, every society has a different concept of what "life" is; but "life itself" is always seen as that period in which one is physically mature – namely, those years of one's life in which one is at the peak of one's physical development. In other words, "life" is the life of the young adult, in full possession of all his bodily powers, whose eyes can see and whose heart can covet whatever the world has to offer. Education, then, unconsciously postpones all the wishes, aspirations and ideas about this desired happiness to the period of adulthood. Moreover, the ideal is not only adulthood, but also all the cravings and passions of that age. There are many other ways of enjoyment, but if adulthood is presented as the ideal, then if one cannot, for whatever reason, fulfil all the wishes and fancies that are related to adulthood, one feels miserable.

This ideal of adulthood, which turns the child's life into a "preface", has a deep influence on the old person's life as well. Just as the child is educated to see childhood as a mere preface to life, so the old man, influenced by the same concept, sees his life as an epilogue. An elderly person no longer has the same physical powers and abilities as the young adult, and consequently feels as if he has lost life entirely; from middle age on, he no longer feels that he is living, but only expects death. Indeed, the spiritual pain and general unpleasantness of old age is, to a large extent, the result of the fact that the old person feels that life has passed; "life" was when he was a young adult, and now he cannot live in the present. This also accounts for the tendency of old people to live in their memories.

Looking into the Ideal of Adulthood

The ideal of adulthood has tremendous influence on the life of every human being – from the very beginning, when the child either is forcefully dragged into the adult world or kept completely apart from it, until old age, when people feel that they are degenerating, going from a state of near-perfection towards death. If childhood is the introduction to life, and old age its final scene, then "life itself" is that time span in between them.

But even a superficial look will reveal that there is something strange here: according to this view, most of our life is lived in preparation for a rather limited period of time which is "life", whereas all the rest of the time is not "life" but only "appendages" to it. Moreover, this view of "life" does not include every possible form of life, but rather only specific forms and conditions thereof. The ideal of adulthood is closely related to physical health and the ability to enjoy the possibilities that the healthy body offers. Consequently, the adult person can enjoy the possibilities and pleasures that pertain to "life" in only a very small portion of life, since a major portion of adult life is spent preparing towards the "real thing", either by studying or by working.

This ideal, then, makes people devote most of their lives to preparing for what is actually a very small chunk of the whole of life. The child looks forward to "when I grow up"; the old man ruminates about "when I was young"; and the young adult thinks about and plans for "when I have some leisure, when I save some money, when I get married", etc. Thus, instead of actually living, people only *want* to live. This ideal, then, if closely examined, makes no sense. How much life is wasted because of this kind of education!

A deeper look into the contents of this ideal makes it look even worse; for what, according to this ideal, is the *inner content* of a life? Does this kind of life bring happiness? If so, then adulthood should be considered as neither better nor worse than any other period of life, and the forms of happiness of adulthood should be seen as neither superior nor inferior to the forms of happiness that are adequate for other periods of life. True, adulthood has its own distinct forms of pleasure and happiness; but the child and the elderly person, too, have their own sources of happiness. If adulthood-related happiness is not life's one and only goal, why should the child be made to look to the "future"? And why should the old person be made to long for the bygone past?

A sort of life that is constantly looking forward to "something" grand, which is supposed to happen in the close or distant future, is a strange life indeed. The child who is told to look to the time when he grows up misses out on so many childhood experiences, either of his own will or because of his training. But when the child grows up, he finds in adulthood no significant happiness, nor any overall improvement that would justify his being robbed of his childhood. He finds out that he has merely substituted one form of life for another. Similarly, the old person keeps longing for the days when he was "young" and daydreams about a past which, in fact, was not better than his present – instead of making the most of the present.

The Ideal of Life

This ideal of adulthood, which focuses all of life on one meaningless point, can be juxtaposed with the Jewish-human ideal of life: the ideal of living life in its entirety, living life as it is at any given time. It means not dreaming about some remote happiness, in either the past or the future, but rather living the happiness that real, actual life can offer. In other words, to live life in the present, to accept the entire course of life as it is, and to live accordingly.

This ideal says that to the extent that there is perfection in life, it can be found at any point in life; and that life can be improved in its entirety. The ideal of life, then, is to find good and pleasure in every day and every circumstance, without making any comparisons with other periods of one's own life or with other human beings. Living means appraising and understanding life on its own terms, and enjoying all the possibilities that life offers in each and every stage of life.

The human aspect of this ideal can teach us to live life in a complete, total way. But beyond that, there is a higher, more fundamental aspect: the religious sphere, from which comes the inner significance.

From the human point of view life is life, and its main goal is life itself. Religious Jewish life, however, is not "just" life: it contains certain goals and missions. According to this view, proper living means fulfilling the purpose and mission of life. This mission contains many parts and details, but its focal point, its main idea, is to perfect the body, the soul and the world, in the framework of an ever-evolving relationship with G-d. This mission is not restricted to a certain age or period of life: on the contrary, it can and should be fulfilled in each and every part and circumstance of life.

Indeed, all of the Torah commandments show us that there is nothing – no time or place – that does not somehow pertain to G-d's worship and to the desire to perfect the soul and elevate the world. Every single aspect and detail of the life of the Jew is surrounded with commandments, and the Jew is obligated to fulfil the commandments at each and every moment of life. So long as he does, he attains the goal of life. While everything has its proper time and age, there is no time or age when one is exempt from worshipping G-d. In every age one has different roles, according to one's abilities at every time and circumstance; so just as the young adult has his own roles and obligations, so there are other roles that one is supposed to fulfil as one progresses along the course of life.

Judaism, then, does not perceive the course of real life as an ascent towards adulthood and then descent towards death, but rather sees it as an uninterrupted journey "from strength to strength" (Psalms 84:8). Man starts life as an amorphous, inchoate mass, a vessel that has not yet taken shape; he then become more and more formed, and continues to become better and better defined through study and good deeds as well as the perfection of body and soul, when directed towards the real goal of life. Seeing life as a totality, all of whose parts are equally important, leads to a very different evaluation of life. Once man develops the ability to live in the present moment, to live life as it is without any imaginary ideals, he can be as happy in old age as the young adult in the peak of his vigour. The physical changes of old age, albeit inevitable, are usually accompanied with spiritual changes that lift all the emotional burden from them. Thus, putting aside all the imaginary, unfulfillable aspirations enables us to make the most of every point along the path of life – to live life itself.

Education for Life

Accepting the ideal of "life" calls, of course, for a fundamental educational change. In other words: once life is not seen as focused around a specific period, the two major forms of education described above become invalid. The ideal of life says that there is no reason to put the child apart from "life". Life spans from the moment of birth to the moment of death. While one goes through the path of life, one's task is to do so in the best way possible, given all the gifts and abilities that one is endowed with.

According to this view, the sole aim of education is to help the student – in this case, the child – to live life properly. A child should be taught to live as a child and to draw happiness and pleasure from this, as well as from any other situation in which he will find himself. To be sure, the child must be prepared for the adulthood that lies ahead; however, just as the child should be prepared for adulthood, so should he also be prepared for all other periods of life; he should, therefore, be taught at the right time not only what he should know at the age of twenty or thirty, but what he should know at the ages of ten and seventy.

Generally speaking, then, studying means preparation for every period of life and for every situation that may arise. Today people think that one finishes studying when one reaches "life", because then there is no longer a need to know anything new. This, however, is not so: studying and education must continue throughout life. At no time does one finish to study and begin "life". Education to live, and life itself, are eternally intertwined; the more one learns and lives, the more does one know *how* to live – provided, of course, that one wants to live, and does not content oneself with dreaming about life.

Thus, just as there are no boundaries between the child and "life", as far as studying is concerned, so too the obligation to keep doing, to continue perfecting ourselves through our bond with the Almighty, has no limits. Moreover, just as the adult has duties, so does the child – not in the same spheres of life, of course, but in terms of the relationship between doer and deed. In other words: just as the adult has duties, mainly to do good, so too the child must perfect himself and his world. Naturally, the child's duties are fewer, and his understanding of what he is doing, too, is more partial; but even this does not constitute a fundamental difference between one age group and another. Whoever progresses through life eventually realises that his previous understanding or actions – in whatever sphere of life – were far from perfect. On the other hand, whoever feels certain that he already knows everything is bound to soon find out that his childish understanding was superior to his present one.

To sum up, then: it is not through imaginary ideals, but by walking in the real path of life itself and putting all of the Divine vitality granted to us by G-d throughout life to the best use that we can, that we live all the years, days and moments of life in a real, palpable way.

When ...

In *Pirkei Avot* (2:4), Hillel the Elder says: "Do not say: 'When I have leisure I shall study'; perhaps you will not have leisure." The scope and significance of this saying can be applied to many more areas of life. "When I have leisure I shall study" is, in fact, just one example of a much wider principle. Although this saying is surely valid for its own sake, many more things follow a similar pattern.

There are so many instances in which one says to oneself: "When such and such a thing happens, when a certain event takes place, when the suitable time arrives – then I shall do a certain thing." All those things which get postponed to an "auspicious time" or to "the right moment" are things that one truly wants to do. Moreover, paradoxically, the more something is deemed important, the more one wants it, then the greater the desire to put it off to another time, to do it under different, better conditions.

Whoever says, "When I shall have leisure, I shall study," does not say it in response to other people's prodding him to study; one who really does not wish to study can always find a myriad of excuses. Such a person will not say, "When I have leisure I shall study," because he does not intend to study even when he does have leisure. Rather, such a statement is made by one who does want to study; but it is because he wants to do it perfectly, in the best way possible, that he finds it so difficult. Such a person thinks: "What is the value and benefit of studying hurriedly and under pressure? Surely, such learning will not go well; not only will I not get any pleasure from it, but I will also not be able to do it well. It is therefore better to push it off it to the proper time, to an hour of leisure, when the spirit is free of worries and stress and there are no external disturbances. In such a time of leisure my studying will surely go better and will be more fruitful."

The same applies to a long list of good things that people want to do. The present seems to be an unsuitable time, for a variety of reasons – which may all be true and even objective. And there always seems to be "another time" in which all the obstacles will be removed and then ... then one will be able to and will do all those wonderful things that his heart desires.

The things that create this "when ..." are as numerous and varied as human beings and the things that they would like to do. Some wait for "when I grow up" or "when I am older". Others wait for propitious external circumstances: "when I get married"; "when I have children"; "when the children grow up"; or for an improvement in their economic situation: "when I have more money"; "when I build my house".

About all this, Hillel expressed the fear that "perhaps you will not have leisure". This also applies to all the other things that depend on the realisation of desires and plans. So many of these hoped-for or longed-for circumstances or events may never arrive – not only unrealistic dreams and wishes, but also things that people assume will happen naturally.

But in fact, there is another, more serious concern. Often, a person reaches the long-awaited moment or circumstance, only to discover that he no longer wants to, or can do, whatever he had wanted to do. One who waited for the time when he will be free of business or worries finds out that he is no longer able to study in the free time that he now has, be it because his physical or mental powers are no longer what they used to be, or because the desire to learn, which was sincere at the time, is no longer there.

Moreover, a new situation in life does not change only one aspect of life, while all the other variables remain the same; any change in a person's life – in time, place or lifestyle – brings along changes in the totality of that person's life. The boy who turns into an adult, gets married, builds a house etc., is no longer the same person he was, but rather a new personality. And in that new state of being, or rather, in that new personality, he may find out that the dreams that he entertained in a different time and stage in life are no longer meaningful to him now.

Finally, even a person who still holds on to the very same heart's desires may find out that the new situation that he looked forward to not only does not provide a solution to the problem, but is also the source of new problems. Just as there is the trial of poverty, so there is also the trial of wealth; once the problems of loneliness are solved, there arise the problems of living within society; and the problems of youth may indeed evaporate along with youth – but they are sure to be replaced by new problems.

Are You Satisfied With Where You Are Now in Your Life?

Basically, I'm not satisfied. A part of it is a personal trait of not being satisfied with any kind of achievement, any situation. Whatever the achievements in the past were, there are always new horizons. To put it metaphorically, when you climb a mountain, the higher up you are the wider and more distant the horizons become. So whatever I've been doing just means that now the horizons are opening up, and the distance to get to what I can now see becomes ever bigger. This is on the personal level.

In a more general way, the whole notion of being satisfied is basically a non-religious, perhaps even anti-religious attitude. Our main target is not to achieve a certain position or situation; the main goal is always infinity. Therefore, the more you know about infinity, the more you realise that you are always in the distance; and since the distance always remains infinite, you can never be satisfied. The strife never diminishes. If it does – if one feels that one has achieved something worthwhile, something one can remain with – it is an indication of some kind of weakness of character or of a failure, because there is always the drive to get farther and higher.

In a yet broader sense, life is an unceasing attempt to reach more, to achieve more, to get more. We stop struggling when we die; but so long as we're alive, we cannot be satisfied to remain in the same station. Sometimes one becomes too weak or frail to do very much about it; but the fact that one cannot do things does not mean that one should be satisfied. Rather, it is an unpleasant situation that is thrust upon one; it is not a matter of one's own choice. There is a Jewish aphorism that says: "One who has 100 wants 200, one who has 200 wants 400" (*Midrash Kohellet* [Ecclesiastes] *Rabbah* 1). The more you have, the more your dreams and ideas grow. With time and with anything, whatever we do, the gap just keeps growing.

The Fear of Loneliness

Night. Out of the darkness the cry of a little child is heard: "Mummy, come here, I'm scared of being alone, come to me." This is not the cry of a spoiled brat who wants attention; it is a cry that echoes a deep fear that shakes the child's soul – the fear of loneliness.

At first this may seem like a childhood ailment only. Like the teeth that grow and fall out, or like the dreams, fantasies and tears that come as the child develops, the childish fear of loneliness is bound to disappear; an adult person no longer fears loneliness. Indeed, so it seems from the outside.

But is that really so? Or is something still hiding behind the seeming calm of the lone adult? A grown-up person does not usually disclose a fear of being alone – not necessarily because he does not have that fear, but due to sheer shame. The adult is ashamed to express this fear publicly, and therefore must restrain himself and hide his real feelings, from himself as well as from others. Thus, the fact that adults do not cry is no proof that they have indeed liberated themselves from the childish fear: it may still be crouching deep within them.

This may, at first, seem strange: why should brave and resolute people who do not fear true dangers, fear loneliness? How could we even think that strong, intelligent people, braggart youths or fickle girls, still retain even a measure of this childish fear of loneliness?

But let us go out to the streets of big cities at times when people are at leisure and observe what is going on: the streets are flooded; people are walking to and fro, chattering in merry groups or rushing to the movie theatres – always in groups, never alone. They flock into the movie halls and are herded out of them. They go to cafés, fill club halls, attend youth movements, roam about – always in company, either in groups or pairs; never alone. In their hours of leisure, they leave their homes and go downtown, to the tumult of the multitudes. Because they cannot bear the loneliness of their rooms and apartments, they flee from their loneliness into the crowd, the herd. Look at a lonely person walking in a deserted street; such people always move quickly, awkwardly, as if fleeing their loneliness, making their way back to the haven of society.

This shows that even grown-ups have not yet grown up: they are still afraid of being alone. Even when there is no overt reason for fear, most people, when alone, feel profound unpleasantness and dissatisfaction, confusion and vague apprehension.

The fear of loneliness, then, does not belong only to children; it may stay with a person throughout life, as a shadow in the background of the soul. Whatever changes may occur in this feeling are only external – from the overt fear of early childhood to the hidden panic and distress of the adult years. The same thing that causes the child to cry in bed is what drives the adult out onto the streets; and just as the child is eventually soothed in its mother's lap, so too the adult is soothed in the lap of society, once again feeling calm, happy and reassured.

But why do children cry? Why is the baby afraid of loneliness? A young child who was feeling happy at a certain place will often start feeling distressed when left there alone, and this feeling grows and grows until it becomes a profound fear that erupts in tears. People say that children fantasise about all sorts of scary beings. Perhaps; but why does this happen only when they are alone? Clearly, it is not something about the place they are at, or any objective change that occurs there. The fear of loneliness exists in the light as much as in the dark, in a familiar room full of toys as in an unknown place. This fear, then, is an internal fear. It is not caused by anything in the outside, but the self. In fact, the cause for this is not even a change that occurs within the self, but rather the uncovering and removing of a veil from existence.

A child cries and asks for help and reassurance because it feels insecure, weak and insignificant. So long as the child is surrounded by adults, it feels it has someone to lean on, and can thus forget its weakness and inability to do things or to defend itself against danger. This feeling of weakness is the core of the fear of loneliness; this is what makes it so terrible for the child, but it is not what creates the fear. The child, whose heart and mind are filled with scary images and realises that it cannot defend itself against them, becomes frightened. But what is it that actually evokes these frightening images in the child? What creates in the child such a desire and need for defence?

Let us look at a little child that has been left alone somewhere; let us assume that it was given enough toys to keep busy for a while. So long as the child is taken with its games, it pays no heed to its loneliness. The same applies to the child who wakes up at night: at first, it will spend some time in thought, and only then will it begin to feel the fear of loneliness. And then, instead of being bored – as would have been the case were the child in the company of other people – the child feels emptiness. For when a person – child or adult – is alone, he feels things more deeply. When in society, lack of occupation or interest brings about a feeling of boredom, which is the external expression of emptiness. Boredom is the result of lack of content, and therefore a person who has inner content is never bored. In company, people always find someone or something to blame for the boredom. But when a person is alone, he can blame nobody; only his own emptiness. Obviously, little children cannot define or understand what emptiness is; but they certainly can feel it right away.

The distress that the child experiences when alone and with nothing to do is the feeling of emptiness. This feeling is far deeper than merely having nothing to do. Unlike pain or pleasure, emptiness is relative. An adult who is occupied with things that concern a five-year-old is undoubtedly a very empty person, whereas for a five-year-old it would have been perfectly all right. Emptiness, then, as in the physical world, is the gap between vessel and content. A person whose vessel – namely, spiritual powers and capacity of understanding – is relatively large, whereas its contents are poor, is an empty person. Emptiness is a fact; but the *feeling* of emptiness is created when the great desires and ambitions of the soul are confronted with a meagre, petty psychological reality. The child who feels emptiness when alone is, in fact, victim of the gap between its relatively great desires and its limited capacity to fulfil them; for children usually do not yet have enough in them to nourish their own souls.

So long as the child is among people, adults or peers, this has no practical importance, since he *does* feel the reality. Social life being a relative network in which one always compares oneself with others, can make one evade self-criticism. But when one is alone one is assaulted with this feeling of emptiness, which is created by the unquenched thirsts of the "I". This emptiness, the vacuum within the self, is what awakens the fears that torment the lonely child. The subject matter of these fears is the inner emptiness; the actual form they may take varies according to the education and the environment, and can assume the shape of devils and witches, thieves and robbers, or nightmares.

So little children are afraid of being alone; why should adults not feel the same? The inner emptiness of the adult person can take different shapes, not necessarily the form of a devil; but so long as it exists, it is accompanied with the feeling of loneliness. So long as there still is this enormous gap between vessels of the soul – which have the potential of containing the whole universe – and their actual content, which may be almost negligible, there is room for the fear of loneliness. It is with good reason, then, that people flee from their empty, frightening homes into the safe streets.

The most common expression of this emptiness in adults is the nullifying of all values. All those things that are so thoroughly enjoyable in company seems so utterly pointless, insipid and insubstantial in solitude. For instance: people who read jokes when they are alone hardly ever laugh. It is as if there is no place for laughter and merriment in the gloomy hours of loneliness.

The reason for this is that the lonely hours are a time which stimulates people to look into themselves. Since no one else is around, one just has to confront oneself. All good manners and external achievements melt and vanish outside of the society that endows them with meaning. When one is alone, one is forced to wonder: "Who am I? What am I?" Indeed, in society one can always compare oneself with others: "I'm wiser that this one, greater than that one"; but when alone, all these relative measurements become meaningless. Then one asks: "When I am by myself, what am I?" This is, indeed, the big question. When one is alone and feels one's own emptiness, then one becomes aware of the fundamental gap between what one could and should have been and what one actually is. Then, all kinds of strange questions begin to surface: Is this the true purpose? Is this the right way to live? What is my life, except for standing in the void and feeding on nothingness? Who am I? … Nothing.

These are the kinds of thoughts that people have when alone. They feel that they cannot stand their own selves. They feel that the loneliness, and the thoughts about and feelings of emptiness, destroy all of their well-established notions and the false persona which they had built for themselves. They then remain naked within the nothingness of emptiness.

This is why people leave their rooms – so as not to remain alone. They flock together, they stick to each other, lean on each other, in an attempt to sustain their faltering entities.

Death Shall Be Defeated

It is one of the many paradoxes of Jewish history that whereas the Jewish people has known premature and unnatural death as a constant companion, probably more than any other nation, culturally and spiritually the Jews are remarkably not preoccupied by death and the hereafter.

In the Exodus from Egypt, the Jews left a vast civilisation that was obsessed with death and devoted much spiritual energy and material resources to preparations for the hereafter. This cult of death was one of the evils from which Moses led the Children of Israel, guiding them towards a more wholesome outlook that put the stress on life.

The Jews never equated death with holiness. Cadavers, far from being treated as objects of sanctity and adoration, are regarded as impurities from which one must keep a distance. Of all the many forms of ritual defilement listed in Jewish law, the gravest is that caused by a corpse. And when a Jew, like a Cohen in the synagogue or a priest in the Temple, is called upon to serve in holy function, he has to take special precautions to avoid contact with death in any and every form. The same is true of the *nazir* (a man dedicated to G-d), who voluntarily undertakes to follow an especially holy way of life.

In Judaism, holiness is first and foremost the sanctity of life. Where life abounds, holiness is at hand. "Life" is a synonym for all that is most exalted in Creation. One of the names of G-d is "the G-d of life". The Torah is described as "the Torah of life". The Torah itself speaks of "life and goodness" as of one and the same thing (Deuteronomy 30:15). "Living waters" are seen as a source of purity. It is thus not surprising that the Jews rejected all forms of the myth of the Dead G-d. Death is the negation of the Divine reality in all its manifestations.

The Jewish belief that "this world is the antechamber to the next" may well have inspired massive Gentile speculation on heaven and hell and purgatory but, by contrast, Jewish literature and tradition engage in scant exploration of paradise. Judaism makes no attempt either to forget death or to smother it in false jubilation. "The dead praise not the Lord, nor do they who go down into the silence of the grave. But we will bless the Lord from this time forth and fore ever more, Hallelujah!" proclaims the Psalmist (115:17-18); characteristically, he disdains death, but he does not, he cannot, ignore it.

The natural reluctance to accept death is expressed in the conviction that the truly righteous do not actually die but rather "depart" or "ascend" to a different realm. Thus Maimonides writes of Moses (*The Guide for the Perplexed*, part 3, ch. 51) that there occurred in him what in other people is called death. It is said that "the righteous live on even in death, while the wicked are already dead when alive" (Jerusalem Talmud 15b). Here again we have the parallelism – goodness is life and life is goodness, whereas evil is death and death is evil.

The Jewish approach to death is that it is a problem to be solved by and for the living. Death, preparation for death and mourning are all worked into the fabric of day-to-day life. The essence of mourning is not sorrow for the deceased, but rather compassion for the surviving relatives in their loneliness. "Weep not for the dead man who has found rest," said an ancient eulogist, 'but weep for us who have found tears" (tractate *Mo'ed Katan* 25b). Jewish law prescribes that all eulogies made at funerals are to life and to the surviving members of the family. Grief is defined within, as it were, concentric ripples of diminishing intensity. The ripple on the first day of death is the strongest and most critical. Also powerful, but somewhat less so, is the first week of mourning. The succeeding periods, the first thirty days and the first twelve months, are getting less and less grievous. At all times, precautions are taken against unseemly outbursts of violent keening. There is an express injunction against self-mutilation as a token of sympathy for the dead, let alone suicide in order to accompany the dead (see Deuteronomy 14:1 and Ibn Ezra there).

The personal confrontation with death, perhaps the harshest test of a personality and of a culture, is of course frequently encountered in Jewish lore. But all the many variations of this theme have one feature in common – the encounter with death is looked upon as a major moment of life, which must be met worthily. Unlike many other cultures, Judaism does not accept that any particular kind of death is glorious per se – with one exception, to which we shall return.

Even in Biblical times, a hero's death was not regarded as a glorious achievement; the ideal was for a man to "sleep with his fathers" and to pass on the wealth of his life and strength to those who come after him. A special tome called "The Book of Departure", which describes the deaths of the fathers of the nation, harps constantly on the need to maintain a calm, confident stance in the face of the archenemy death, to stand up to the Angel of Death and to be prepared in all tranquillity to return "the bond of life to the Lord your G-d" (I Samuel 25:29).

Nevertheless, there is one exceptional kind of death which the Jews do consider glorious, and which we term "sanctification of G-d's Name" (*Kiddush HaShem*) – martyrdom endured for the sake of sanctifying G-d's Name. It is a public act performed in the midst of the holy community, whereby the sacrifice imparts an added sense of sanctity to the living. Yet even when martyred in this way, the Jew embraces death for the sake of the survivors, so that their dedication to the Jewish way of life may be strengthened.

In this context, we can understand the extraordinary character of the *Kaddish*. Initially this ancient prayer had no connection with death or the dead, and was an ordinary part of the liturgy. Only at a relatively late period – in the early Middle Ages, when mounting persecution brought frequent martyrdom – did the *Kaddish* become a death-related prayer. However, there is no mention of death in it, and it is also devoid of even the slightest insinuation of reproach to G-d, who is throughout praised, glorified and sanctified.

The basic attitude of Judaism to death – which, it is said, was ushered in with Adam's expulsion from the Garden of Eden – is that it is not a natural, inevitable phenomenon. Death is life diseased, distorted, perverted and diverted from the flow of holiness, which is identified with life. So side by side with a stoic submission to death, there is a stubborn battle against it on the physical and cosmic level. The world's worst defect is seen to be death, whose representative is Satan. The remedy is faith in the resurrection. Ultimately, "death and evil" – the one being tantamount to the other – are dismissed as ephemeral. They are not part of the true essence of the world. And as the late

Rabbi Kook emphasised in his writings, man should not accept the premise that death will always emerge the victor.

In the combat of life against death, of being against non-being, Judaism manifests disbelief in the persistence of death, maintaining that it is a temporary obstacle which can, and will, be overcome. Our Sages, prophesying a world in which there will be no more death, maintain that we are getting closer and closer to a world in which we shall be able to vanquish death, in which we shall be above and beyond death.

The Significance of the Giving of the Torah

The giving of the Torah came after the great miracles of the Exodus, the splitting of the Red Sea and all the major events that the Jewish people underwent before arriving at Mount Sinai. What was the purpose of all the preparations, as well as of this sublime revelation itself? The actual contents of the Ten Commandments – faith in G-d, honouring one's parents, not killing, etc. – is the cornerstone of human morality, and can also be reached logically. Moreover, it says about our father Abraham that he fulfilled all of the commandments even before the giving of the Torah. What, then, has the giving of the Torah actually added to the world?

Every Jew has a "Divine spark" that is the innermost core of his spiritual life. This spark is always there, even when we cannot see beyond all the concealments. This spark is the "holy of holies" of the soul, and is the reason why we always aspire to G-d, whether we are aware of it or not. Some people seek philosophical closeness with G-d; others may be led to seek His closeness by the events of their lives, by delving into the mysteries of nature, or by examining Jewish history.

Another way of answering the desire for closeness with G-d is by looking into oneself: "From my flesh shall I see G-d" (Job 19:26); it is the understanding that G-d is the source and essence not only of the entire universe, but also of my own individual soul.

However, even when the desire for closeness with G-d turns into a conscious drive, even when it pushes us to seek G-d, we're in the dark: "Where is the place of His glory?"

The first thing that the G-d-seeker usually wants to do is to transcend the limitations of matter and soar to the abstract and the spiritual. Our material body, and the physical world around us, seem to be the greatest obstacles on this path. Sometimes, one can reach peaks of love for the Divine and leave this world. But is this really the right way?

Furthermore, if we think more deeply we will realise that whatever we do, we will never be able to comprehend G-d. Whatever we may feel of G-d's life-giving light is but a minute, dimmed spark, whereas the Almighty Himself is far beyond anything that even the most sublime human mind can apprehend. To Him, not only physical matter but even the highest degree of spirituality is nothing.

It follows, then, that all human efforts to get closer to G-d are bound to failure. However high one may ascend, there will always remain an infinite, unbridgeable gap between him and G-d. We may feel the desire to come closer to G-d, but we have no means for fulfilling it.

This is the point of the giving of the Torah. We humans are incapable of reaching G-d; but G-d, in His infinite loving-kindness and goodness, and also in order to fulfil the aim of Creation, lowers Himself, so to speak, to us. The Revelation on Mount Sinai is much more than just a series of commandments that instruct us on what to do and how to behave: it is an expression of G-d's will through the Torah and commandments. It reveals to us the way to actually unite with G-d – namely, by fulfilling His commandments. Indeed, the Hebrew word for "commandment" – *mitzvah* – comes from the word *tzavta*, togetherness – being united with G-d.

By "descending", so to speak, on Mount Sinai, G-d "brought down" His unlimited, undefinable essence into the definitions and limitations, fences and constraints of the Torah and the commandments that He has given to us. The Torah, then, is the expression of the Divine, it is G-d's wisdom and will, and therefore it is much more than "A Torah from Heaven": it is Heaven itself.

Thus there is a fundamental difference between the external manifestations of the commandments, as we understand them, and their essence; they are all ways of connecting with G-d. "Thou shalt not kill" as a human law, arrived at through human reason, may be a great achievement of human ethics and morality; but it does not transcend the human realm. But the "Thou shalt not kill" that was revealed on Mount Sinai is a Divine commandment, part of the bond that the transcendent G-d is making with us.

The commandments, then, are finite tools meant to help us reach the Infinite. In the pre-Revelation world man strove to reach G-d, but despite all of his efforts he remained distant. The giving of the Torah has opened for us the path – the Torah path – to reach G-d. The Almighty Himself descended and revealed Himself through the Torah, thus giving us the way, the possibility, to overcome the obstacles of our human nature and come close, and adhere, to G-d.

The Religious Question

The most important of all human questions has been, and will always be, the religious question. But is it really the time now for this abstract metaphysical question? Are not issues of war and peace, blood and fire and existence, much more burning, actual and important? When our very existence is in jeopardy, when we are asking ourselves how to live all together, is there room for any other questions? But the opposite is true: this question is not abstract at all; it is a vital, fundamental question that is far ahead of any other question. Compared to it, all the urgent questions seem very distant, mere immaterial shadows. The question of preserving life is preceded by the question about the essence of life – or, in other words, the religious question.

What values do concepts such as state, homeland, family or life have, when they are preceded by the question about life itself, the innermost point of existence, the very existence – G-d?

Just as in any scientific or philosophical system there is a fundamental question that cannot be evaded, a question that recurs in every nook and cranny, so too this question is the most general question that pertains to all spheres of life and that cannot be escaped. There is not one single phenomenon or event, either in nature or in man's soul, that is outside this question, and it is impossible not to deal with it or leave it unresolved. Every thing, every act or deed, is a reply to this question, and every possible position is a position in regard to this question; there is always a "for" or an "against", and there is no way out. This question must be raised before everything else, and it must also be replied before everything else. And between the "yes" and the "no" lies infinity.

Let us present this question in its simplest and clearest form: is there or is there not a G-d? Is the Torah binding or not?

Strangely, but in fact not strangely at all, no one is asking or answering this question – and yet people live their lives as usual, running around and seeking and finding everything – except for the great question. But how do people really live without an answer to this question of all questions? Now here is the great wonder: everyone has an answer. The question is not asked, the solution is not sought, because it's there already; everyone has it and everyone knows it – although there are still differences of opinion as to what it is. Some say yes, others say no, but that's not important: the question should not be asked any more, because the solution is already there. Only little children and fools keep asking this question, and they don't know that it's a shame to ask, because the answer is already known. Nevertheless, we shall raise this question again, overtly, simply and clearly: is there or is there not a G-d? Is the Torah binding or not?

The main reason for evading this question is its fundamental importance. No one really cares whether, or how, the Theory of Relativity will be researched. Whether it is true or erroneous, one's life will continue to flow as usual, and breakfast will be consumed on time. Not so with religion: the answer to this question will uproot and change everything, from the minutest everyday matters to the very foundations of life. Thus, when it occurs to a person to investigate this issue, a problem comes up: "What if it turns out that I was wrong? What if I find out that all my life, from beginning to end, was one big mistake? All will have been lost; what shall remain for me?" Such an investigation, then, is far too dangerous; questions such as, "What was in the beginning? What will be in the end?" are frightening and shocking. It is better, then, to read the evening newspaper; such reading will not shake the foundations of life.

However, not every person can push this question off just like that. People are somewhat ashamed of themselves, and ... of faith, and so they dwell in religiosity just as they would dwell in all the other pleasant nonsense, or, if they are born without it, they turn to the other option: thought. The headline is:

"Believing in G-d's existence is faith;

Believing that G-d does not exist – that's thinking."

Thus, the question sometimes arises (among those who, for some obscure reason, still debate this): "You say that there is a G-d? Prove it!"

If no proof is found, or if someone brings a proof that is rejected, it follows that the mind obliges us not to believe. This conclusion is based on two logical mistakes. The first one has to do with general logic: the replacement of negation with juxtaposition; the other is ignoring the nature of the problem – namely, that it is a dispute not about a theory but about a reality. When we explain a phenomenon with a certain theory, the theory does not have an independent existence; when the justification for this theory disappears, the theory also vanishes. This is not the case when the issue is related to the objective existence of something: here there is no point in bringing proof. The existence of a green grasshopper or a white elephant will not be affected by the fact that there is or isn't proof for their existence.

So too in regard to this issue: let us assume that there really is no decisive proof for the existence of the Creator (even if, philosophically speaking, there were such proof). In any case, there surely is no proof for His non-existence. The situation, then, is that a person can believe, for whatever reason, in G-d's existence, or believe in His non-existence, for whatever other reason. Both this belief and lack of belief are beliefs; although they go in opposite directions, they both belong to the same sphere of pure emotion.

This is equally true in regard to the Torah. People say: "Bible Criticism proves …" – but Bible Criticism, again, is based on beliefs. The premise that the Bible can be treated like any other book is an assumption that can be believed or not believed in, and this is true even without making any investigations about the reliability of Bible Criticism in general, or its various pre-assumptions such as the negation of the possibility of miracles, the impossibility of prophecy, etc. In addition, this whole system of investigation, which usually involves an assumption, a question, a rewriting of the text and an additional assumption based on this rewriting, out of which springs a further question etc., is a good method; its only disadvantage is that it can be applied to everything. Would it not have been great if this method could be used also in the natural sciences? By the way, if both opinions are based solely upon faith, then the share of the positive believer is better, logically speaking; for a person who believes in G-d at least has some sort of intellectual reasoning, however feeble, with which to bolster his faith, whereas the poor believing heretic has no logical explanation for his faith.

There are some careful people who seem to have found a sharp-witted way out of this maze. Their reply to the question of G-d's existence is, for instance, "I don't know", or the more philosophical version: "There is no way of knowing". Seemingly, they accommodate everybody, because if it ever turns out that there is a Leader to this world, then they did not negate that possibility; and if not, they never really said there was. However, this solution is good for only one side of the issue, and the less important one, too – namely, the intellectual aspect. But what about the emotional aspect? Does or does not such a careful person believe in G-d? When it comes to emotions, one can either believe or not believe (namely, have a negative faith); there is no in-between option and even those who extricate themselves from the emotional tangle, by no means rid themselves of the profound question that touches the innermost depth: what should one believe in?

Freeing oneself from the prejudice that the clash between religiosity and irreligiosity is the clash between faith and the intellect, and understanding that it is, in fact, a matter of two different kinds of faith, creates a completely different picture. When it is the intellect that is juxtaposed to faith, the choice is not between the object of intellectual recognition and the object of faith, but rather between the way in which we know things intellectually and the way we know things through faith. However, when the tools of knowing are equal, then one must investigate the reason for faith.

One possible criterion that should be used whenever (as in our case) the intellect cannot give a decisive opinion is the point of *benefit* (in the purer sense). And indeed, when one looks into the issue of benefit of both these faiths, an argument that is often raised (by religious and irreligious people alike) is as follows: life, in and of itself, is good; however, it is somewhat bland, and that is why we add religiosity to life. In other words: religiosity in life is like salt in the soup or a patch on a pair of trousers: one can manage without it, but it is more pleasant with it. This view is the source of the mistake of those who choose negative faith because they think that it is possible to manage without the religious spice. Because in fact, the state of things is entirely different. Religion is not an addition to any sort of main thing; it is, itself, the main thing, it is the centre and essence of life, and parting from it is tantamount to parting with life. Every kind of reality exists only against the background of religion; Judaism is the main thing, whereas all of "life" is but its ornaments. It is impossible to bring direct proof for this, because it is impossible to exit the region of religious influence and see what is left of the world when there is no religion. The most secular human being contains such great amounts of religiosity that he himself can serve as a religious sample. It is, however, possible to prove in regard to certain elements that religion is the root of their very existence. To show that existence itself means religion is impossible, because a world without religion is inconceivable; the only thing that can be done is to create the full picture from the various details.

Let us take morality as a first example: what is ethics in and of itself? What is the factor that draws man – who, everyone agrees, is not a moral creature from birth – towards morality?

There are two aspects here: the first aspect is morality from the utilitarian aspect. While the moral imperative deprives us of pleasures that harm others, it also protects us from other people's pleasures that might harm us. The second aspect is morality as a fundamental law that grows out of religion. The innovative aspect of the Ten Commandments was not in the theological part, but rather in the moral part. Honouring one's parents, or not killing, not committing adultery or not stealing surely were ancient and well-known moral principles in every human society even then, but there is a tremendous difference: here, the moral imperative is not utilitarian; unlike in the past, "thou shalt not kill" does not mean "don't kill because it's not worth it"; from now on it means "do not kill because it is *forbidden* to kill." Everything shifts from the sphere of relativity and calculations to the sphere of absoluteness: "Thou shalt not kill!"

This difference is not merely theoretical: it is the fundamental difference between real morality, which began with the Torah of Moses, and all the "moralities" that either preceded or followed it. The secular, utilitarian morality can be analysed, discussed, calculated and weighed whether or not it is worthwhile. Thus, when there are no special considerations, all is well and good; but when the practical calculations that call for moral behaviour are undermined, then there is no longer a need for "bourgeois morality" or for "Jewish slave morality". But morality that is religion-based is absolute and leaves no room for calculations. It is an unshakeable Divine commandment. It is indeed typical that the two anti-religious societies that got to rule the world – Bolshevism and Nazism – are characterised by the undermining of morality that followed the downfall of religion.

Let us now take another example – science. Science, too, is built on the foundations of religion – not in the sense that this or that formula is taken from the prayer book, but in the sense that the inner content of science is religion. If there is one principle that is shared by all sciences at all times, it is the principle of the unity of phenomena, or the possibility of attaining scientific precision. Even pure materialism (which, by the way does not exist today, nor has it ever existed), and even idolatry, do not provide any basis for this. Phenomena remain detached from one another because after all, nothing is ever exactly like other things, and things remain different. The idolatrous personifications of the powers of nature, too, cannot serve as a basis for science; the idols can clash with each other at will, and therefore no generalised law or nature can grow out of them. Science can exist only after man feels, out of his own religiosity, the unity of the universe, the existence of the One Cause for everything; only then can there be a possible basis for the creation of science, for making use of the formula that expresses the unity of all phenomena. What happens when this religious basis is gone? The known facts are not forgotten, but they become disconnected. Science becomes a craft, and phenomena break down again into single units; experience teaches us how to make use of them, but the intellect does not find any way of unifying them.

Culture, in general, is also one of those things whose "soul" is religion. If we take anthropocentricity and the idea of progress out of the foundations of Western culture, what will remain of it? The two Jewish ideas – (a) the centrality of man (in the moral and spiritual sense) as the final purpose of Creation and his creation "in G-d's image", on the one hand, and (b) the idea that the world can, and should, be brought forward towards the better and the best – these are, in fact, the basic ideas of final redemption, the redemption that is in the hands of man. The collapse of these two foundations means the collapse of the entire culture.

Consider Liberalism, Socialism, Communism: these methods, in both their idealistic and materialistic versions, are based on the fundamental idea that all men are entitled to equal opportunities (legally, socially and economically). This idea is in complete contradiction to all the worldviews which claim that human beings are not equal. In whichever way we may want to examine and according to whichever criteria we may use on things, we shall see differences in level between people. What, then, is the origin of this idea? This idea comes from a Jewish Biblical source: all the souls are equal, because all human beings are the descendants of Adam. These ideas have spread not only because of the emotional factor, but also because of the hidden spiritual principle. Because even behind the militant materialism of Marx lies the idea that all human beings are equal because they have souls. Once we pull the religious foundations from underneath the constructions of humanity, there will remain only rubble, destruction and waste; man will turn into a beast.

All this is even more conspicuous in regard to the specifically Jewish issues. It is totally impossible to speak about Jewish or Israeli nationality without the Torah. Jewish religion and nationality are inseparable – firstly, because the existence of the Jewish nation is tied to the Jewish religion from the very beginning. The Jewish people never existed without the Jewish religion, so that they cannot conceivably exist without it. The separation of Jewish nationality from the Jewish religion results in ridicule. It is no wonder that every young child who is not totally stupid will find the study of "nationalistic" Jewish history boring: exile, anti-Jewish decrees, persecution, death for the sanctification of G-d's Name (what on earth is this? And what is it good for?), more exile, more decrees, etc., etc. The fact that in the time periods between one exile and another, or even during the exiles, there was religious cultural life and some great personalities lived and operated, makes no difference whatsoever. What is the importance of the Talmud, with its 3,000 pages, or of its commentators who added many more thousands of pages to Talmudic literature? To a person for whom Jewish culture is no more than archaeology, what value is there to all the Jewish literature that is related to the Talmud or to the Kabbalah, the *Midrash*, or to liturgical poetry?

The same will happen even when we go back to the Bible; the Bible is a difficult book to read, and not a very interesting one. One can either relate to the Torah as Torah, or not relate to it at all. The commonly accepted way – "the horse path" – is nonsensical in every possible way. How sadly ridiculous are the struggles of a nationalistic historian who is debating with himself what to decide about the Hellenised Jews: on the one hand they considered themselves men of the world, scientists, cultured people, and therefore quite close to the views of our historian; on the other hand, though, they were an anti-nationalistic element that the Jewish people ejected with disgust and treated as a horrid symbol. So our historian does not know whether to give them a positive or negative mark. The teacher who tells with great enthusiasm how old Mattathias stabbed to death the Hellenised Jew who sacrificed a pig does not usually think that he himself is very much like that Hellenised Jew, and that, had he fallen into the hands of Mattathias, he would have not fared differently. All of the major Jewish figures, from the dawn of its history, are a blatant contrast to that band of "nationalists" who keep trying, despite everything, to find one or two persons whose company they can keep. Subconsciously, they try to reconstruct the figures of all those who tore themselves from the main body of the Jewish nation, to praise them and find all sorts of virtues that they had or did not have. But this never works. When the nationalists take a great Jewish personality and imagine that he is similar and close to them, it is usually a disappointing mistake. When, for instance, they take Maimonides, admire him, burn incense (so to speak) in his honour, celebrate his birthday and voice their favourite opinions about him to each other, do they really know what he would have thought of them? If they really want to know, let them kindly read the part of his *Halachic* book *Mishneh Torah* that deals with apostates, and they'll surely find out.

We speak about the Land of Israel, about the historic connection between the Land and the Jewish people. These are all jolly things that are good for internal consumption. If our people has a historic right to the Land of Israel because it dwelled there for a while, then it also has a historic right to Iraq, Egypt, Persia, France, Germany and Italy. Basing our right to the Land on the fact that it was once conquered by our forefathers is based on a void. One conquest annuls a previous conquest, and our right as conquerors will be just as valid if we decide to conquer Antarctica. The same applies to our "right" to build the Land of Israel and make its deserts flourish – which so many people still take as a serious argument.

We do have a right to the Land of Israel, but it has nothing to do with all the babbling about history: our right to the Land comes from G-d's promise to Abraham and his descendants. That is our sole right to the Land and our connection with it.

The only ones who have really taken the Jewish nationalistic ideas at face value are the "Canaanites", and they are also a living proof of how "pure" nationalism destroys itself. "Canaanism" is a natural, graded, and most of all, logical continuation of secular Jewish nationalism. The comedy of Jewish "nationalism" would have turned into a tragedy, had the "Canaanites" not been such a wretched lot. Out of their great zeal, they have completely severed the roots of their spiritual existence, and soon they found out that they are in a void. The logical thing to do in the death throes of the Canaanite spirit was to leave the Jewish religion and revert to the resuscitation of an ancient foreign myth. Their anti-religiosity brought the Canaanites to a "religiosity" of groundless intellectuals which is insane and full of complexes. This is the natural end of a Jewish nationalism without religion. All the other Jewish nationalists avoid this sort of an end only because they allow themselves a life of stupidity and thoughtlessness.

It seems, however, that one could still say that although in the past, many things used to be based on religion, there have always, and everywhere, been non- and anti-religious people, and the world continues to exist as always: morality is morality, science is science, culture exists and Socialism spreads, and just as the world existed with religion, now it continues to exist without it. Zionism, too, has established a state which was not made up of religious people. However, all this is only apparently so. If we look more deeply into things we shall see that religiosity still is the cornerstone of the world. A person who mocks religion may be a very moral person, but this morality is nothing but the continuation of the religious morality to which the non-religious person continues to adhere – be it out of habit of mind, because of stupidity, or as a result of the fact that this morality has taken such root in his heart that he takes it as a vital component of his life. The scientist who seeks to solve the mysteries of the universe, to unify the theory of the magnetic fields with gravitation may not be a religious person, but within him there is at least one residue of the religious spirit that still works: the search for unity within multiplicity. The non-religious Communist holds on to his views not for theoretical reasons, but out of the religious sentiments aroused in him by religious Communism. The Israeli nationalist can be as much of a transgressor as he may be, but he imbibes his devotion from the ancient religious Judaism; willy-nilly, he is a link – albeit a somewhat rusty one – in the chain of Jewish generations. Everywhere there still exists the relationship of "They left Me, but kept My Torah" (Jerusalem Talmud, *Hagigah* 6b); people may leave religious Judaism as much as they wish, but even within the most secular of secular people, all the sublime elements are a religious inheritance from their forefathers. Rabbi Israel of Rhyzhin once said: "Had the evildoers known how much pleasure they give to the Creator, they would have burst with anger!"

One could claim that even if the foundations of human existence stem from religiosity, and religion has fulfilled an important role in shaping them, it does not follow that we must have any sort of relationship with religiosity. We must honour religion for the role it fulfilled, but this has nothing to do with the present. We can dump the inner religious content and keep only its fruits: morality, research, culture and progress, as well as our national existence. But this, too, is impossible. All these things are like limbs that were severed from the body. Nothing can continue to exist unless it is linked and attached to religion. Surely, things that were created with great effort and investment in the course of many generations cannot be completely destroyed in one or two generations, and therefore, after this cutting off everything seems to look the same, just as it did before. But the gradual weakening is inevitable, and will necessarily be followed by destruction.

Theoretically, it is simply understandable: all the foundations of our existence as human beings and as Jews are by no means rational; they are inexplicable and cannot be proved beneficial. Once the reason for them is gone, they themselves remain like an ancient inheritance of our forefathers. In the first and second generations, things still remain quite the same, out of habit; but eventually people change, and one day they will look at those ancient relics and condemn them to perdition. Destroying them will surely lead to their own destruction as well, but when the results of their actions are apparent, they will no longer be able to understand them.

Let us consider some practical examples: Marxist Communism is gradually losing touch with the inner-religious sources of its spirit, which are its true foundations (namely, the equality of the soul). It is no wonder, then, that the country that professes this principle is the place of greatest inequality in the whole world. The same applies to the Nazis, when they consider the foundations of morality: how ridiculous this wretched relic of religious tradition seems to them! But this is not surprising, because when the religious basis is missing, these feelings also vanish, and the practical results are well known to all. Jewish nationality – or, in its true name, Judaism, or Jewishness – is expressed by the Canaanites, who see their strange spiritual forebears who are not religious, but nevertheless maintain their meagre, baseless nationalism.

More and more people sober up daily and understand that if there is no religion, then also everything that is related to it loses its value, and hence – "every man does that which is right in his own eyes" (Judges 21:25), people seek their own private interests, or idleness, or the fulfilment of their own desires. The end result of all this is, of course, destruction. But meanwhile, everyone realises that there is no need to stay bound to one place. The fetters have not been cut loose; rather, they are no longer tied to anything, one can run free with the fetters. Indeed, full freedom has been attained – the freedom to progress towards nothingness.

This is not to say that the importance of religion is in its being a indispensable basis for the existence of morality, science and nationality. Although this is surely true, we must gain a deeper and more comprehensive understanding.

Putting together the various details of human existence should lead us to a general conclusion about religion as the basis for human existence in general. *Being equals being religious.*

Between the Robot and the Chimpanzee

Not only an examination of the roots of things pushes man towards his true foundation; in our day and age, science and technology do so too. The new physics totally undermines scientific self-confidence. Certainty and stability vanish: no size is a constant size, no map is permanent, the tangible and solid are no longer such, matter and energy are interchangeable and so, on the one hand, we have a multiplicity of forms, endless transformations; and on the other, we vaguely sense the underlying unity. The atom and hydrogen bombs also sometimes make us think: our bonds have become far too loose, destruction is behind the door. But more than all these, there is another thought-provoking invention, even though it is not so very revolutionary: the robot.

The electronic mind robs man of the attribute that till now was his alone: the mind. Robots do many things that are beyond the ability of the human brain; they operates with precision, with nearly zero mistakes, and they also keep becoming more and more elaborate. We hear now about robots that have a memory, and other robots that have perception. Vain attempts are made to distinguish and separate between the essence of the human mind and the robotic "mind". The difference between these two – which is quantitative rather than qualitative, keeps shrinking constantly, and they are becoming more and more similar, to the point of complete identity. Man is being deprived of the unique crown of the human creature; man is on the point of becoming bereft of identity. He is about to lose his uniqueness, for now the world of the mind is not solely his. Thus, man remains standing between the chimpanzee and the robot; he no longer considers himself a lofty creature, and the comparison with the machines is not always to his benefit. Consequently, man feels as if he were standing in the void and nothingness.

Man wants to find the secret of his power, the mystery of his separate existence. However, the philosophical garb that man puts on the deepest secrets of his thoughts is not always adequate; sometimes the ideological husk hides the inner content. We must therefore understand the real meaning and significance of religiosity and religious thinking.

The answer must be given with a clear head and full heart. But when the answer is even somewhat imperfect, the result is that instead of Judaism we get wild growths of Reform. The most common motivation for reform is comfort, both in the spiritual and in the physical level. Many people think that the rigorousness and strictness of Judaism are seen as a burden by large segments of the Jewish people who would, perhaps, have come back to a Reform kind of Judaism (moderate or extreme), but will never return to Orthodox Judaism. In fact, the very essence of Reform Judaism is self-contradictory: does the Reform Jew believe that the Torah is binding – or not? If he believes it is, then there is no basis for reform; one cannot "reform" a Torah that was given from Heaven. The Torah is what it is, regardless of whether or not it is nice and convenient or not.[3] If, however, he does not believe in a Torah from Heaven (namely, if he believes in lack of belief), then he has no link to the Torah and the commandments. Even if the commandments are cut down to the barest minimum, it will remain ridiculous so long as some Jewish nucleus remains. But Reform Judaism is ludicrous not only in terms of its basis, but also in terms of its hope that a cropped-up Judaism will be more attractive and viable than the full-fledged Judaism. In whatever way Judaism may be cut down from whichever direction, there remain two options: to create a Judaism that will not be a burden at all for its followers, or to construct a Judaism that will be a bit of a burden. A "Judaism Lite" that is no burden at all (if such an option can be meaningful at all) does not have to be created: it already exists, and even has the upper hand, in the State of Israel. Every non-observant Jew in the State of Israel fulfils a part of the Commandments – that part which he does not consider a burden. But if that "cut-up" Judaism will contain some burdensome parts, the problem will remain, and people will once again say: there are some superfluous parts here that are not to the taste, and against the worldview, of the younger generation, and must therefore be uprooted. A Jew who did not live his life as a full Jew but rather became a Reform Jew in order to get rid of the difficult aspects of Judaism will rid himself of the difficulties of Reform Judaism in the very same way. The result will be a Reform Jew who will eat three meals on the Sabbath, but will not refrain from working on that day, will hold a Passover *Seder with Chametz* – and in short, will be totally devoted to Judaism, so long as it is not in his way.

---

[3] Making changes for practical reasons, e.g.: to help the newcomer to Judaism, is a different matter.

The inner relationship of the believer to a faith that is sewn or undone according to the latest fashion must be a rather weird one. This kind of lifestyle was already described by the Prophet Isaiah: "He burns the half thereof [= of the log of wood] in the fire; with the half thereof he eats meat; he roasts roast, and is satisfied; yea, he warms himself, and says: 'Aha, I am warm, I have seen the fire'" (Isaiah 44:16-17). Similarly, first the Reform delete from their prayer books Zion, the Temple, Redemption; and in another generation, as per the newest fashion – the holy Fathers, the heroism and the holiness, and whatever does not speak of Zion. Later on, as they continue to develop, perhaps they will also delete the Almighty from the prayer book (which is not all that inconceivable, given that a Bible without mention of G-d has already been published). And after cutting off all the disruptions, and appeasing all those that should be appeased, then – "The residue thereof [= of the same log] he makes a G-d, even his graven image; he falls down unto it and worships, and prays unto it, and says: 'Deliver me, for thou art my G-d'" (ibid., v. 17). A religiosity such as this has only one explanation, which is also written in that same chapter: "For their eyes are bedaubed, that they cannot see, and their hearts cannot understand" (ibid., v. 18). Eventually no one should be too surprised if one day everyone will understand that a religiosity that constrains the Almighty to jump according to everybody's whims is nothing but a log.

Despite the inherent stupidity of Reform Judaism, those who follow it are usually not stupid: they are mistaken, and their mistake stems from a lack of understanding of the way of *teshuvah*. The followers of Reform are those who are interested in Judaism for some utilitarian reasons (and not necessarily crass utilitarianism), and they all think along one path: either because they are worried about morality, fear for the Jewish nation, or even more deeply, feel the existence of a painful void in the heart and mind; still, they are all united by one thing: for them, Judaism is a good means to attain morality, a useful adhesive for Jewish nationality, or straw with which to fill a soul that feels its own emptiness. And because, for them, Judaism is but a means, they want to compromise with it, and this compromise begets all sorts of ideas whose skin, so to speak, cannot contain their flesh, stillborn ideas.

Alongside this sublime utilitarianism there is another factor: sentimentality, nostalgia, childhood memories. The heart fills with yearnings and a good will to return to the old nest, the old melodies, even the food from olden days. The *shtetl*, the Jewish family, the page of Talmud that has not been studied since one fled from home – all these things are so very enticing. The heart thirsts for a simple recitation of a chapter of psalms, and the lips sometimes whisper (not always knowingly) various excerpts. And those people, who are so full of longing, want to return to Judaism; but they do not have enough energy for a full-fledged return, so they, too, seek compromise.

Would it not be nice if one could wrap Judaism up in a small package (tied with a pink ribbon) and present it to the nostalgic Jew? But no; it's impossible. The G-d of Israel has remained just as mighty and great as ever; He cannot be folded. It's impossible to return to Him partially, or in bits and pieces. He is a Jealous G-d, without partners and without compromise. One can only be entirely with Him, or entirely without Him. Even when the soul yearns for a life of Jewishness, even when it is truly thirsty for that, when it really longs to be filled with a new light from a distant time and place – how close is the voice that says: "I am the Lord your G-d", I am Who I am, the one and only.

Even in a full-fledged *teshuvah*, return to G-d, there are different aspects and levels. *Teshuvah* must not be the return or surrender of one who lost one's way and is now returning to his original place exhausted, broken and beaten up; it must be a return of victory, of progress. The wanderer finds not a place of rest but a new path. It is not a return of descent, of locking oneself up inside religiosity, of finding solace and calm in holy stupor. *Teshuvah* is not a return to the past, but finding a future; it is a return of knowledge and mind, of a full and wholesome heart. It is not rest, but unceasing work; not of fatigue but of eternal enthusiasm. One reaches the path to G-d not in order to stay put there, but in order to walk (see Zachariah 3:7); what yesterday was the sky above our heads should be the ground underneath our feet today.

When one knows why to return and how to return, he must also know where and to what to return. When one wants to make a true return to Judaism, he is faced with the question – is there where to return? And is it possible to return without having to reduce and seclude oneself? Will this return not be suicidal? Will bringing the soul into an ancient world, which is so very distant from the present reality, not be a sort of hazy world of hallucinations in the nowhere? This problem is not only the problem of the returnees to Judaism; it is just as much the problem of all religious Jews. It is difficult to hold on to a fossilised Judaism that belongs to a different world. The religious Jew stretches his life over the gap between the world of Judaism and the world in which he lives. And this split between the worlds results in a sort of schizophrenia and collapse.

In every generation and in every change that occurs in this world, a new parallel aspect is discovered within Judaism. Degeneration and crisis happen when it is not found, whenever the connection between Judaism on the one hand and man and reality on the other is disconnected. A connection between Judaism and the world does not mean an *identity* between them. The attitude of Judaism to the world does not have to be positive; on the contrary, quite often it can and should be negative and contrary; but what should always remain is the very relationship and connection. The main problem of religious Judaism today is this lack of connection and the resulting duality and inner split.

The path and ideas that we propose as a solution for this problem is currently acceptable to a small group of people only. We do not know whether it will spread, but at any rate, it is the path towards a true Torah, not a dead and frozen Torah but a Torah of life for the entire nation. This path can be called "renewed *Chassidism*". In essence, it is a new wave of the *Chassidism* of the Baal Shem Tov, the *Chassidism* of our generation.

Different Types of Human Knowledge

The Limits of Human Consciousness

Human consciousness strives to perceive and to know all and to understand everything that exists in the world, possibly also things that do not exist. However, man has realised that even though the desire to know is boundless, the human ability to know is limited.

Some of the limits of human consciousness can be overcome through various technical means: by improving technical thinking, or upgrading the instruments we use to explore reality. But alongside things that are or were inaccessible to us for purely technical reasons, there are also things that are inaccessible in essence. Many great philosophers have attested that our thinking will improve when we get to know in which areas our thoughts can operate and in which areas they cannot. Such knowledge will help us organise our thinking, while preventing us from wasting mental energies.

Unanswerable Questions

One of the pivotal teachings of Rabbi Nachman of Breslav deals with the various questions that may arise in one's mind. According to him there are two types of questions: (a) questions that are aroused by the reality of this world – such questions are answerable, and therefore it makes sense to ask them; (b) unanswerable questions which it makes no sense to ask; it may even be forbidden to do so, because dealing with them creates problems that cannot be solved in any way. Rabbi Nachman calls questions of the latter kind "questions that come from empty space" – in other words, questions that stem from the inherent otherness of Divine hiddenness, which is the source of the universe.[4] Since these questions arise because we are such limited and defined creatures, any attempt to delve into them is doomed to fail, and they will only lead us into the depths of scepticism.

But even Rabbi Nachman himself does not give a complete definition of these questions, and leaves it to the reader. Therefore, one could say that according to Rabbi Nachman, "questions that come from empty space" are those inherently unanswerable questions that try to negate faith, or to prove that it is an illusory figment of human imagination.

Knowing Reality and Knowing the Essence

The highly structured Chabad literature provides many definitions of the permitted and the forbidden, as well as of the ways for investigating them. By defining which areas of Divine knowledge should be delved into and which ones not, the Chabad movement has created a system of concepts and ideas which is also applicable to human consciousness in general. Understanding these ideas about the objects of human consciousness will also help us gain a deeper understanding of superhuman consciousness.

Consciousness – which in the Chabad literature is called "knowledge" – is divided into two separate spheres: knowledge of reality and knowledge of essence. Generally speaking, "knowledge of reality" is the acknowledgment of the *very existence* of an object (physical or spiritual), while "knowledge of essence" is knowing the *nature* of the object whose existence has already been acknowledged.

This idea is further developed and subdivided as follows: there is the knowledge of the reality of reality, knowledge of the essence of reality, knowledge of the reality of the essence and knowledge of the essence of the essence.

- *The knowledge of the reality of reality* is the most basic kind of knowledge, and usually it is on the material level. It is the empirical knowledge

---

4   According to *Chassidism*, which is based on Lurianic Kabbalah, the Creation of the world was made possible because G-d reduced, so to speak, His infinite light and left an empty space in which the world was created.

that something exists, but without knowing anything about its nature or purpose.

- *The knowledge of the essence of reality* involves a certain definition of the nature of the object, for instance: knowing whether a certain thing is large or small, strong or weak, etc. All these definitions relate not to the thing itself, but only to the ways in which it is perceived by us and how it relates to things we already know.

- *The knowledge of the reality of the essence* is the awareness that there is a certain, undefined essence which is as yet unknown to us; it is the recognition that a certain object has an essence of its own, and the recognition that to know that essence means going beyond an external familiarity with it. However, this knowledge does not yet truly connect us with the object of our awareness.

- Such an inner connection is called *the knowledge of the essence of the essence*; it involves knowing the very essence of objects and a fully aware connection with it.

To understand this, let us take the following example: a person is in a completely dark room, and has no idea what is in that room. He starts walking around and bumps into something. Now he knows that there is something in that room. This is the knowledge of the existence of existence – namely, the knowledge that something is there.

Then he begins to feel his way around; he locates the object that he bumped into and figures out its size and what it is made of. Let us say that he finds out that it is of a certain size, that it is made mostly of metal and that it has some screws, springs, levers and buttons. Thus he gains certain knowledge of the essence of the existence of that object; he can now say that it is a machine of sorts. This is already a definition, which is much deeper awareness, far beyond the experiential awareness of the existence of that object.

If the person is familiar with this kind of an object, or if someone switches on the light in that room, he will be able to say: "This is a typewriter, and its uses are such and such." This understanding of the machine and all the aspects of its existence stems from our inner knowledge. It is the knowledge of the essence of essence.

11: Kedoshim

(Watercolour on paper 71.5x56 cm)

You can view/download the paintings in original full colour, free of charge at:

www.mysteryofyou.com

12: Hula Valley from Ramot Naftali

(Acrylic on canvas 137x152 cm) 2007

You can view/download the paintings in original full colour, free of charge at:

www.mysteryofyou.com

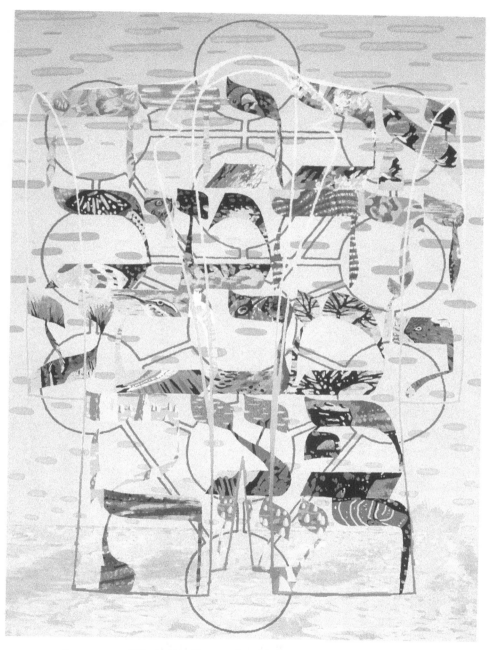

13: Images of Tanya, Gate of Unity and Belief, Chapter 12

(Silk screen print on paper 67x47 cm) 2001

You can view/download the paintings in original full colour, free of charge at:

www.mysteryofyou.com

14: Painting Me Painting

(Acrylic on canvas 91.5x76 cm) 2007

You can view/download the paintings in original full colour, free of charge at:

www.mysteryofyou.com

Knowledge of G-d

These four levels of knowledge – which pertain to all existing objects, both material and non-material – are of special importance in regard to the knowledge of G-d.

In regard to G-d, the first type of knowledge, knowledge of the reality of reality, is the awareness that there exists an entity that we can neither define nor understand, a supernal entity far above and beyond us. This is the awareness of, or experiential contact with, the existence of the Absolute.

In *Chassidic* thought, this kind of awareness is presented as an explanation of the verse, "from my flesh shall I see G-d" (Job 19:26): a sort of fundamental experience, an almost physical sensation of the existence of the Divine. This awareness exists in every human being, from the most primitive tribes to the most highly sophisticated culture: each and every human being has an awareness of something that is beyond us; some call it nature or fate, others call it G-d, but the experience is one and the same – an awareness that there is something there, about which we know nothing.

Then come attempts to find out about the essence of the existence of the Supreme Being. This is the task of the philosopher, who interprets and defines possible ways of making contact with that transcendental Being. In this level of knowledge we define the infinity, greatness, eternity, omnipotence and all the other attributes of Divinity, calling G-d the Supreme Being, the Creator of the world, the King of the universe, etc.

However, we must keep in mind that what the philosophers do is no more than defining a reality that we grasp. Philosophers can define G-d only to the extent that their prior experience can grasp it; our worldly experience, our moral awareness and our feelings of awe in the face of Infinity – they define these feelings and chart their boundaries and limits. However, they have no knowledge or awareness of G-d Himself. The knowledge of His essence is way beyond the reach of experiential knowledge.

The next level is the knowledge of the existence of the essence of G-d. This level is higher than philosophical thinking; it is the level discovered by the prophets and sensed by believers. It is the awareness of what we can understand about a Divine essence that transcends all the attributes that our thinking and knowledge can grasp. The awareness of the prophet, and the prophecy that he experiences, are what enables him to understand that there is something beyond ordinary logic.

In *Chassidic* thought this is defined as the difference between G-d as "He who fills all the worlds" – namely, the philosophical notion of G-d as the soul of the universe, which has an experiential basis – and the supernal, totally abstract essence of G-d that is not connected with the universe at all, and which is called in *Chassidic* philosophy "He who encompasses all the worlds". The prophet experiences the awareness and knowledge that there exists a Divine essence which is above and beyond the reach of our understanding, and which is not related in any way to our ordinary human experience. In this level of knowledge there are different levels; the greater the prophet, the greater also his knowledge of the existence of that essence.

However, knowledge of the essence of the essence of the Divine is altogether beyond human reach; only G-d Himself knows the essence of His essence. "If I knew G-d," said one Sage, "I would be G-d". If we could have attained the knowledge of the essence of essence and come in contact with it, we would have become totally identified with it.

This level of knowledge – knowledge of the essence of essence – is the only level of knowledge that is completely beyond human reach. To know the essence of the essence of the Divine is to know G-d from within; it is an awareness that interprets and explains everything, that gives everything meaning and significance. In Chabad literature this is called "the fiftieth gate of understanding", and it is a level that no human being can attain.

On the Impracticability of Returning

Although the concept of retrogression is quite unpopular in the age of progress, there are always many people who look back to the "good old days" with a measure of nostalgia, if not a strong desire to actually revert to what they see as a better state of things. Amongst modern Jews, the most popular period seems to be about 2009 years ago – a time when, it is conceded, Jewish life had authentic style and vitality and was much richer in content.

But is it really possible to go back to *any* period in the past? Is not the very idea of return self-destructive?

This kind of an endeavour is indeed destructive. Even when confined merely to sentiment, it is a wish to get rid of whatever already exists – and which probably came into existence as a result of this much-admired past. Of course, no one ever openly voices the desire to eliminate whatever is new; it is only implied. Even the most conservative and reactionary do not wish to uproot everything. The desired change is generally confined to making life conform to a certain ideal pattern or idea. And here is the root of the error: the desire to change only one or two aspects of our world is naïve and unrealistic. All the components of any given historic reality are so intertwined and closely bound together, that it is almost impossible to tamper with any of them without seriously upsetting the whole.

Those who feel a strong drive to revert to an old order of things usually are not willing to get into a hopeless conflict with the whole world. They only want to be left alone, to create a kind of a social island or ghetto where life can presumably overlook undesirable innovations of the present. Such attempts, no matter how courageously undertaken, will not withstand for long the pressures of historic reality.

Such a return is not only unfeasible from a practical point of view: it is also very questionable theoretically. Every genuine social, educational or cultural expression must have a definite starting point in a historical setting, out of which it grows, and the same applies to such yearnings for the past. Such yearnings – whether as a mere longing or as actual plans of action – must be grounded in the present, in some part of contemporary reality. Otherwise, it will be an unsolvable inner contradiction.

The answer, then, is not in any form of negating of the past. Human societies seem to flourish in the best way possible when they are well rooted in some sort of tradition and history. Jewish tradition not only allows us to look up to new heights, to strive to supersede the past; it obligates us to do so, as attested by the verse (Deuteronomy 30:5): "And He will make you better and more than your fathers."

Homecoming

Most of the Jewish people are so very scattered and removed from each other that they hardly ever find a common language, or even any language that makes sense to them as Jews. This is what is called assimilation, which is basically the loss of the common heritage. We therefore have to try to reach some deeper levels of the soul, many of them bordering on the unconscious, to help us get back to talking together, to having some kind of a common language.

Jews can hardly be categorised as a nation (even though there is now an emerging Israeli nation); we cannot even be considered a religion in the ordinary sense of a religion with a message which we think should become general, which we want to "sell" to others. Altogether, we are a very different sort of entity.

To clarify what we are, we may start by saying that we are a family, just a family – a large, not entirely biological one, but basically a family. Family ties, sociologically speaking, are far more basic than either that of a nation or a religion. To be sure, the family tie is a very primitive way of binding people, but it is probably the most stable one, as well as the most resistant to outside change and influence.

The concept of the Jews as a family defines us not only sociologically, but also, in a manner of speaking, theologically. In fact, we do not only behave like a family – feeling like a family, and occasionally fighting and hating each other, sometimes at great length – it is also dangerous for a stranger to intervene, because any outside pressure only reinforces the unity and the feeling of the family. We can easily be separated and estranged from each other, but at a certain level we come together again as a family – that is, we feel the unity in the way we conduct ourselves, in the way that we continue to behave in a certain manner, even when we do deceive ourselves about the meaning of it.

Even though at times we may think that we have nothing in common, as happens in every normal family, we still have all kinds of ties and links that are enormously hard for us to explain. What is more, we somehow find ourselves at ease with each other, sometimes fighting, but nevertheless comfortable as within our own family. Understandably, too, we feel a certain amount of safety in being together, and we find it easier to make connections within the family. But of course, brothers and sisters tend to get estranged. They move to different countries, adopt different accents, ways of life, ways of behaviour. Nevertheless, there is this uniting element, very primitive, very hard to define, but undeniably very much in existence.

One can go so far as to say that Judaism, as a religion, is in many ways simply the ways of our particular family. It is the way we do certain things. We walk and talk with G-d and man like everyone else, but we have our own way of doing it. And, as in any other family, we try sometimes, when we are young, to run away, to fight our parents, yet later on we find ourselves resembling them more and more. This particular way, which is called Judaism, is in many respects the way that we, as a family, move together, pray, dress, eat, do a variety of things. We have our own approach to all sorts of matters. For example, in our family we do not eat certain things. This does not mean that we have a special claim of any kind to being "the best family there is"; but as in any group of people, we may have this feeling, and nobody can blame us. Telling myself that "my father is different, my brother is different", is still a very human preference.

At a deeper level, the notion that our people are really our family – brothers, sisters, connected by kin as well as life style – is called in the Bible the "House of Jacob", or "The House of Israel". It has the flavour of a family or tribe – very extended, but nevertheless a tribe, with common goals, and united somehow, even if the unity is obscured by a great variety of individual expression. The connections are so very deep that we usually are not consciously aware of them; but they awaken, and sometimes it is as though we feel that the clan is calling. And then, much to our own surprise, we join in.

This family feeling is possibly one of the main reasons why Judaism as a religion was never very active in proselytising – just as a family would never go out into the streets to grab people in order to have them join the family. It does not mean that Jews feel either superior or inferior; it is only that from the very beginning, it has its own pattern and way of living. Even when members of such a family are out of the family house, even when they wander far away, they still follow the same lifestyle – theologically, sociologically, behaviourally. Of course, members of the family can be severely chastised, and rifts can occur between individuals and groups; but there is really no way of leaving the family. You can hate it, but you cannot be separated from it. After some time people, younger or older, come to the conclusion that they cannot really get away from it, and it would therefore be far better for them to try to find the ways in which they are connected. This connection is beyond choice; it is something we are born with. And since you are stuck with it, it is far better to get to know where you came from and who you are.

For some of our people it is almost like the story about the duckling that was hatched by a hen. Often enough, our ducklings grow up in a different atmosphere; they are taught to think and act in ways which are entirely alien to their nature. In the course of history, Jews have adopted a lot of other cultures, national identities and sometimes even religions. In some cases, there is a very wonderful recognition and return. Frequently, however, it comes as a very unpleasant discovery: I am different, my medium is a different medium. But when I do indeed find water, I will swim in it, even though those who raised and taught me don't. Altogether, finding – in whatever way – to which family one belongs is a familiar theme in literature and life. Knowingly or unknowingly, each person begins at some point to discover it. If the discovery comes sooner rather than later, then it enables one not only to acknowledge the fact that he belongs somewhere (at least so as to be buried in the right graveyard), but also to make his life, in a way, more logical. Paradoxically, freedom comes with the acceptance of a definite framework from which one cannot move away.

To be sure, a family is usually a biological unit; the Jewish family, however, is and is not a biological unit. We speak about ourselves as being the "children of Abraham", or the "children of Jacob". Surely, many of us are, biologically speaking, the children of another patrimony. But in fact, our real legacy isn't a biological one at all. Our tribe is a very different sort of tribe. To quote an old source, when we speak about the father and mother of our family, we say that the father of our family is G-d, that the mother of our family is that which is called the communal spirit of Israel (*Shekhinah*). This is not just a mystical-theological statement: it is the way our family is constructed, and it is what determines how the family behaves and feels.

When we speak about G-d our father, it is not just an image: it is a feeling of integral belonging to the source of the family. This makes for a stronger family, of course; nevertheless, we continue to behave just like an ordinary family. Like all children, we pass through periods of admiring father and periods of fighting with father, even hating father. But we can never come to the point of denying the existence of a father, our father. Of course, some children may express this denial as a mark of revolt, and various members of the family may react in different ways. Sometimes members of the family become very angry at such blasphemy. Sometimes they just wait for the young blood to simmer down a little bit. But always – be it when one hates or loves, or whether one is an ardent believer or a convinced heretic – one remains his father's child.

This basic connection is what is called the Jewish religion: being a member of that family. We have our own history, but that is not the most important part of it. Most central is our relationship to the father and mother of the tribal entity to which all of us belong in one way or another. This is what makes sense to those who have remained.

There are widely dissimilar parts, a great variety of members in our rather large, distressed and sometimes not so glorious family. How much are we aware of these connections? How much are we aware of each other's existence? We often try, and some of us keep trying very hard, to ignore, to deny, and even to remove from ourselves any feeling of pertaining to this family. On the other hand, there are many members of our people who consciously choose to re-enter the family fold. It is not necessarily seeking for "G-d"; often it comes as a result of extended wanderings and far-reaching explorations – and of the feeling that we cannot always describe: the feeling of coming home.

One can point to more beautiful mansions and more exciting sights, but they cannot very much duplicate the home. The roaming and wandering of individuals separated from their family, the desperate attempts to be independent, only lead to a discovery that one must try to come back and find the truth of being home.

The real point of a Jewish person, then, is this recognition: "I do belong" –whether I want to or not. It is the deepest and most important part of my being, one that I cannot cover over with opinions about language, culture, nation or religion. Ultimately, I do belong to the family. The deeper I go into myself, the more important the past becomes. I can reject this past and even cut it off from myself entirely, by playing roles and trying to imitate others, but that does not change what I am. And if I ever want to find out more about it, I follow the long route home. It is not an easy way, but it has its compensations and its own truth.

When animals brought up in a zoo are released, they sometimes do not even know whether they are wolves or deer. They have to find out who they are, what they are. It is a great discovery to discover: "I am this or that", and to explore the right way of being what I am. Such is the destiny of a Jewish person who has been estranged. He may or may not find helpers. He may almost instinctively move into his natural habitat, or have all kinds of strange objections that will forever interfere with his normal behaviour, so that it can possibly be corrected only in a later generation. But whatever happens, he is at least coming to grips with the problem.

Very frequently, the process is accompanied by tragic mishaps – finding, losing, finding again. But basically it is the situation of the person who wakes up and finds out that even though he grew up somewhere in, say, Midwest America, he really belongs to this very old family, with those strange parents, those sometimes lovely, sometimes ugly brothers and sisters. He has to get accustomed to this idea, and then find out what to do about it.

"The World Should Endure Because of the Children; They Deserve It"

(Interview by a young schoolgirl)

Do not think that it is so easy to show up and interview somebody! This time, I was particularly full of apprehension, my heart was pounding. Who am I that I should go and interview the great and famous Rabbi Adin Steinsaltz? They say that he is a genius and a *tzaddik* (righteous person); thousands of Jews throughout the world learn Talmud from the Steinsaltz Talmud volumes which he authored. There are even editions of this Talmud in English, Russian and French, for Jews who do not understand Hebrew. Important people from all over the world come to him for advice, even non-Jewish prime ministers! And now I am going to interview him?! I regretted the whole idea more than once.

Luckily two of my elder brothers, who study at the *Mekor Chaim* Institutions under his direction, went to visit him when he was not well, and they accompanied me. The most difficult moments were when we were waiting for the Rabbi in the simple living room of his home. I was very nervous. Sometimes, grown-ups do not take me seriously, and I feared that the Rabbi would consider the whole thing a joke – he has so often refused to be interviewed for really famous newspapers! But the moment he walked in, I felt relieved. He was very nice to me, and spoke with me as if there were nothing else on his agenda. The topic we discussed was "children". He sat, listened to me and spoke with me calmly, and even when other people, important people, came into his home, he signalled to them that he was busy.

After I left, all sorts of questions that I should have asked came to my mind, and perhaps I missed the opportunity. At any rate, here is the interview.

Q: *Most readers of this interview published in Otiyot [a children's magazine] are below bar/bat mitzvah age. As such, we are obligated to fulfil the mitzvot only as part of the process of our education; we are merely preparing ourselves. On the other hand, we have learned that "the world endures only for the sake of the breath of school children". Even though our elder brothers disagree, we, the younger children, think we are important. What is the real influence of the actions of young children?*

Rabbi Steinsaltz: Young children indeed do not fulfil the mitzvot as commandments; when a young child learns Torah or performs a mitzvah, he does that like a volunteer, and this is a great and important thing. He does all these things even though he is not obligated. Therefore, children deserve that the world endure because of them. When your father performs a *mitzvah*, it is because he is commanded to do so; but when *you* do that, your action is totally holy, it's a 100 per cent volunteering. You are giving the Almighty a gift, and He is happy.

I can no longer give Him such gifts: I *have* to study, I *have* to pray, just like your elder brothers. They, too, are included in the same contract. Do you understand?

Our Patriarch Abraham performed the *mitzvot* not as commandments, because he did not receive the commandments. Nevertheless it says that Abraham fulfilled all of the Torah. That was the uniquely high level of Abraham.

Q: *Many of the readers of Otiyot live in Judea and Samaria. Do you have any advice for these children how to stop the situation [from deteriorating], so that they will have only good experiences?*

Rabbi Steinsaltz: I do not exactly know what a "good situation" is; but whatever anybody does, it should be done with utmost seriousness – each in his own way, each in his own place. Whatever a person does, he should draw strength from it and do it in earnest, that's the main thing.

Q: Including building houses?

Rabbi Steinsaltz: Yes, of course! It does not really matter what will happen afterwards: it is important to build, because this is the Land of Israel. Even though other people dwell here too, it is the Land of Israel. So now I am building a home, or am doing something else in the Land of Israel. Everyone should make something come true in the Land of Israel. This is true not only for the residents of Judea and Samaria. If everybody, wherever they may be, would do their small share in earnest – even if it is only to plant a tree or say a prayer – the situation would be quite different.

Q: Let us go onto lighter matters. I heard that you did not really like going to school when you were young. Do you have a suggestion for students about how to survive school?

Rabbi Steinsaltz: I liked to study – I loved to learn and read; it's the school that I liked a lot less. How to survive school? Some children go to school and really like it there; they have no problem. For children who are not really crazy about school, my advice is that they remain neutral – namely, try to fulfil their duties and obligations to the school, try not to disturb – and also not to be over-involved. Disrupting the class or making a point of not doing one's homework will not really help anyone go through school smoothly, nor will it add to anyone's pleasure. A child who dislikes the school should not think about it all the time; it would be best if he would simply fulfil his duties and find more interesting things to do after school hours.

Q: We Jews attach great importance to garments. Do you think that having a school uniform is a positive thing?

Rabbi Steinsaltz: On the whole I think it is. For most children, it saves a lot of headache, especially for girls. As you know, on the 15th of the month of Av, all the Jewish girls would go out wearing white …

Q: And what about boys?

Rabbi Steinsaltz: They too have this problem. In certain places, boys behave just like girls, so at least during school hours, this problem can be solved.

Q: *What made you establish the* Mekor *Chaim School? And why did you not establish a girls' school as well?**

Rabbi Steinsaltz: I wanted to set up a place that children will love more than they like an ordinary school. Does it work? (The Rabbi looks at my two elder brothers, who are students in that school). That's important. I think that almost all the students there actually like the place, even the younger ones. Other things will come with time.

Q: *But why not a girls' school?*

Rabbi Steinsaltz: Had I had the money, the energy and the people, I would have started a similar school for girls as well. Meanwhile I am doing what I can, and a bit more than that. (Ponders a bit) How old are you? Ten? Perhaps when you are fourteen, you will be able to study at my school, perhaps by then there will be a girls' school. Who knows?

(The Rabbi once interpreted the strange expression *be-khol me'odekha* – usually translated as "with all your might" – in the portion of *Shema* as meaning that a person must do whatever he can to make himself love G-d with all his might, but that one's own might is not enough! *Be-khol me'odekha* means that one must give everything – and then a bit more. We kids, when we play ball we sometimes feel that we have no more energy left; but we know that we can always find a little bit more energy within us.)

Q: *A boy called Elkana Shor from Kfar Chassidim once wrote a story in* Otiyot
about redheads. When you, Rabbi, were young, you were also a redhead. Did it bother you?

Rabbi Steinsaltz: When I was very young, yes. Not all the time, but until I was about five, I used to say that I am not a redhead, but that my colour is golden. Even when I was only two years old (I began talking when I was very young) I used to say that I am golden. But it bothered me a great deal. Once, when I was young, I made a list of all the great Jews that were redheads. It was a very impressive list, even though King David and Esau probably were not part of it. But in later generations, it is an established fact that the Baal Shem Tov, the founder of the *Chassidic* movement, was a redhead, and some say that the holy ARI (who created Lurianic Kabbalah) was a redhead, and Rabbi Nachman of Braslav and most of the Rebbes of Chabad were redheads. But all in all, even though at the beginning it used to bother me that I am a redhead, after a while I got used to that.

Q: Why do you think that King David and Esau were not redheads?

Rabbi Steinsaltz: Because in both cases the word "red" means "red skin". About Esau it says explicitly that his face was red, and I think that what it says about King David also means that he had red cheeks. Once, only very few Jews were not dark-haired; and it is known that Rachel was dark and Leah blonde, and perhaps that is why there are people of all colours among the Jews. It seems that Leah had blue eyes; it says about her that her eyes were "tender", and it is known that people with blue eyes are more sensitive to sunlight.

Q: To what colour would you like to change your hair, if you could?

Rabbi Steinsaltz (smiling): I have already changed my colour (meaning, from red to white) … but I think I would have chosen black.

Educating Desire

I had a friend. He was older than me, but for a time I became his teacher. He was on a long path to religion and it was for him a way of suffering. At one point, I told him about procession caterpillars. They go in a line, one after the other. You see a whole line of caterpillars, each touching the other, and they are going in a procession. They are perhaps searching for food, or whatever. Biologists experimented with them and one experiment had almost political implications. One caterpillar leads. The others follow. Why is the leader a leader? What made him into a leader? And they found out that the leader is a leader because each has the instinctive feeling to follow the tail of another caterpillar. Now, there was one caterpillar who didn't find a tail, so he became the leader. By default. So that's the leader! The one that didn't find a tail.

In order to prove it, they did something which is in a way unkind. They arranged them to form a circle, the first caterpillar touching the last. They work by instinct, and so they walk in a circle. And they go like this until they die. Always in the same circle. I said to my friend that sometimes people go in this kind of circle in their spiritual life and the only way to solve it is to cut it. You have to cut the caterpillar-like circle by will and then you may go in any direction.

The circle means death – moving but staying in the same place. There are people who lead that sort of life for years, and I'm not speaking about material ways of life, but spiritual as well. A person has all kinds of driving impulses, but no solution. You come to the same questions, the same answers, and so you move in a circle. You don't move anywhere.

Things like worry or depression are almost the same. You go into a circle and you can't cut it. Because a worry doesn't have any answer. It can only be cut, not answered. You can go on worrying forever.

I asked my friend what was the moving power in his search. He said it was a verse in the book of Job when Job speaks to G-d and says, "You are yearning for Your handiwork."

And my friend said, "If G-d is yearning for me, how can I say no?" So, there is a yearning. And sometimes I come, and sometimes I don't come. I may have my longing, the Almighty may have His. And we may meet, or we won't ever meet.

Sometimes you make a choice. There are certain things that you just don't want to care about. People make such decisions all the time. Look, some people have an obsession with an absence. An absence of money. And they are obsessed with it all their life. Including people who become very, very rich. But they can't get rid of the yearning, and all the time have same kind of unresolved desire. Other people may have a great yearning for beauty. Some people don't have it at all. So for them, there's no absence, and for them there's no yearning. It just doesn't exist. At a certain point we make decisions not only about what we are going to do but about what we are going to desire.

Some people want power, and others may decide that they are not only not going down this path, they are deciding not to dream these dreams of power and influence. It's not only because it interferes with other things. I just don't want to. Sometimes a decision comes because I am convinced that I am not searching for the right thing. At other times I may think that it's a bad, or a mean thing. Or useless. Or I say it is not important enough for me to go on dreaming about it. In a certain way, it is a matter of educating one's desires.

And we do have this education, all the time, and not always in a completely positive way. There is a certain age at which children will collect things: marbles, or stones, or baseball cards. It takes all of our time and then, somehow, it stops. Sometimes it changes into other things. Those that collected, say, the baseball cards, may come to collect other pieces of paper, green pieces of paper – some people are great collectors. At any rate, I may have still at home a collection of those cards. They no longer mean anything to me. This means that I was, in a way, educated. I don't know if it's a great advance or not a great advance. But I got educated.

Now, in a certain way, part of our problem is that we are yearning for something which is "good". But we have to define what is "good". If we get educated, the notion of "good" changes. I remember when it was so very important for my little daughter to be good at playing marbles and now she no longer cares whether she was good at marbles or not. Supposedly all of us do not care now about it. But for a time, it was an important part of my life, a part of my yearning, a part sometimes of my dreams. If I would pray, sometimes I would pray to be very good at that. I'm just saying that growing up is in many ways the knowledge of how many things I dreamt about that I no longer dream about. I'm no longer yearning though the yearning at that time was a very real one. Everybody is different … sometimes it's a nice pretty dress. You may have it or not have it, but it no longer counts. There is a time when you cry because you don't have something, or are very happy because you got it. You grow up, and it's not important anymore. A problem can arise if when we grow up we stick to the same kind of yearning – some of them we got at the age of eighteen, some of them we got slightly earlier or later. And we stick to them.

We can be educated in making different choices. I can decide that habit, so and so, these things, other things – other, what you call, "points of desire" — I don't want them anymore. I decide I am not going after that anymore. I am changing to something else. And, if I am successful, I'm not bothered by them anymore. I want something else. So I discard the old things. And they don't matter to me anymore. This bus goes in another direction. I'm not riding it. I took another one.

See, for some people the decision for them to go into a religious life, contemplative life, it is a matter of a choice. You can will to be close to G-d. You can have a will like this. What happens if you find that someone is in love with you? You just find out. What is your reaction? For most people it's very hard to ignore it completely. There is some kind of a resonance. In the book of Ecclesiastes, it says, "like a face to the water" (now we would say like a face in the mirror), as one face to the other face in the water, so is one heart to the other heart. The idea is that, if I love somebody they cannot be completely indifferent. When G-d says, "I yearn for you" I may think, "leave me alone. Mind your own business." Some people will answer like this. And for others it's a very compelling power, the power that comes when you know that somebody is yearning for you.

But many responses are possible, and sometimes it is as though somebody changed my mind. Like the points of the compass, I now am pointing in another direction. Just yesterday, I couldn't care less and now it is the only thing that matters. It happens. It happens sometimes when people fall in love. I saw a face, I saw a person, and for some time it was of no consequence, of no importance.

Now there's a click, and it becomes more and more and more important. For some people, it's not a matter of a click. It's a matter of a really slow move. And in some cases, a voluntary move. I want to go in a certain direction. I want to go there. I am in a way channelling my ability, my power, my inner sense of yearning in a different direction. And in some way I think that everybody can and does do it.

Now I am saying that the same ability is there also to shut off, to close all sorts of things. There is a *Chassidic* story about somebody who sent one of his disciples to the home of another one. So, he came to the home, it was night-time. He knocks on the door. No answer. He knocks, and knocks, and knocks again, and again … well, he was commanded to meet the fellow. So he's still there, knocking on the door, and nothing. And then, after some time, the host opens the door and says, "You know what I wanted to teach you? That man has the ability to allow whomever he wants to enter." There are lots of knocks on my door. And I can decide: I don't want to allow it to enter. It's as simple as that. Let them knock or ring.

So I think that this kind of ringing is not only about ringing. Look, I may say there is a whole world ringing. They want from me this thing and the other thing, and people want from me lots of things. Family. Acquaintances. And I may just say I don't want it, I want other things. Just as simple as that. They called you, and you are not going. You are not available. I may say, "I don't care for you." It's a freedom. Sometimes it's, "I don't care for you" full stop. Or, "I don't care for you" not to put a full stop, but "I care for something else." I used to play the piano. I am not going to play the piano. I'm going to play football. And I think it's important, because a change in the desires means eventually also a change of life. When I don't want certain things, they no longer count, and they are no longer a part of my life. They disappear.

Deed and Intention

The performance of the commandments (*mitzvot*) has traditionally been conceived as a dual imperative: the contemplation of the content and inner meaning of the *mitzvah*, and its physical expression. Jewish writings have dealt extensively with the questions arising from this duality, weighing the value of deed against that of intention and seeking the relationship between the two.

Devout men throughout the ages have generally stressed the intention over the deed. Nevertheless, they also felt that while a deed without intention is like a body without a spirit, intention without deed is similarly imperfect, like an elusive apparition, having existence but no substance. Thus for these men, in the realm of *mitzvot*, there was no deed without intention, and no intention without deed.

The questions that prompted the continual discussion of this issue are still with us today. However, what was for our forefathers a complex problem of vital importance has become for us just another question for which a pat, uncritical answer will suffice. The modern Jew tends to avoid confronting this problem by stressing intention to the detriment of deed, resulting in a disintegration of the totality of the *mitzvah*.

For some people, the *mitzvah*-act (deed) becomes a mere expression of good intentions, while for others it is even an obstacle to attaining the true sense of love, awe or communion with the Divine; thus the physical expression or deed itself is nothing more than a symbol, an empty gesture devoid of essential religious content.

This grasp of religion so prevalent in our time has been seen to differ radically from that of previous generations. To fathom such differences in religious outlook, an understanding of three integral elements is necessary:

an understanding of the nature of man, an awareness of the relation between G-d and man, and an apprehension of the essence of Divinity. In Judaism, as in other religions, the changes of attitudes and thought that have taken place with the passage of time have affected each of these elements and thus religious outlook as a whole. Furthermore, the interrelationships between the factors themselves have often accelerated such changes. For example, any development in the understanding of the nature of man alters the substance of man's relation with G-d: as the self-esteem of man increases, acknowledgment of his dependence on G-d decreases. The greater man grows in his own eyes, the more G-d seems to diminish.

Just as increased emphasis on the value of man influences the quality and force of religion, so do today's humanistic aspirations have their effect on the perception of Divinity. If religion requires fulfilling the will of G-d, then whatever one understands of Divine will influence the essentials of religion, such as the nature of Divine service and the tension between intention and deed.

Although a detailed philosophical discussion of theology cannot be presented here, it will, nevertheless, prove useful to inquire into the essence of Divinity as understood by religious people. Consider the following list: table, stone, bird; idea, ideal, dream; G-d. In which category should G-d be placed: in the category of concrete objects or in that of the abstract concepts, idea, ideal and dream?

Most people, religious and non-religious, would quite likely place G-d in the category of spiritual or abstract concepts, rather than with the concrete and substantial. Such a classification has far-reaching significance. It is an evaluation denying G-d many of the attributes of physical reality and concrete existence. If the Divinity is an abstraction, an idea without substance, one may question the degree of reality of G-d and be led to doubt His very existence.

The G-d of such a believer is a shadow – a shadow resting on the soul – about whose reality there is often grave doubt. It is an intellectually experienced Divinity. Once G-d is apprehended in this fashion, certain consequences are unavoidable. If G-d is a spiritual concept, He should be served with ideas, silent prayer or meditation. Is it not a contradiction to serve an abstract spiritual Divinity by concrete physical actions?

However, all Jewish thinkers and philosophers have rejected the view that G-d is a spiritual concept. They stress that just as G-d is infinitely above and removed from the familiar, physical universe, so He is removed from man's conception of spirituality – even in its highest form. It is, therefore, as sacrilegious to attribute spiritual qualities to G-d as it is to attribute physical ones to Him.

The question that then arises is: If G-d is neither substance nor spirit, what is He? The answer often given is that man cannot even begin to know the essence of G-d. One can only hope to experience the actuality of His being. Such an experience of Divinity cannot proceed by a logical or inferential analysis of various aspects of His existence; it is based on the actual experience of His presence. G-d, then, is a reality. He is the real substantiality and there is no "reality" outside of His being.

This brings us back to the problem of the preference of intention over deed. When G-d is recognised as infinite, there is no significance to the distinction between His substantiality or spirituality. Therefore, the spiritual intentions of man, no matter how pure or noble, are not necessarily closer to the Divine will than the most concrete, physical actions – in the eyes of G-d they are equal. G-d is as close to, or removed from, the corporeal as he is to the spiritual, and the simple, physical aspects of the *mitzvot* have as great a religious relevance to the doer as do the spiritual ones.

The essence of this conception is a physical, as well as spiritual, perception of the actuality of G-d at each and every moment, the feeling that "He fills His world and activates all His worlds". For He is able to manifest Himself in every physical sensation just as in the most sublime, spiritual awareness. In performing the *mitzvah* of winding the phylacteries, for example, one is as conscious of performing the Divine will in winding the straps as one is in making the spiritual effort to realise "And thou shalt love the Lord thy G-d". Such a Jew is in true harmony with the Divine will.

Yearly Stocktaking

The last days of the year that lead us to Rosh Hashanah, the Day of Judgment, are days of stocktaking which every individual should do for himself. If the most central component – namely, heartfelt repentance – is there, then one's heart cries out and the stocktaking is done almost by itself. But when this central part is missing, people tend to cover up its absence with excessive detail; it is like the story about the absent-minded fellow who, before going to sleep, wrote down where he put each of his belongings, so that he would be able to find them in the morning; the only thing that he forgot to put in the note was ... himself.

What is the nature of this yearly stocktaking? Surprisingly, the *Rosh Hashanah* prayers do not contain any reference to sin; in certain prayer versions, even the transgressions mentioned in the *Avinu Malkeinu* prayer are omitted, because *Rosh Hashanah* is a festival, and on a festival one does not confess one's sins. Furthermore, although *Rosh Hashanah* is also the Day of Judgment, there is hardly any mention of judgment in the *Rosh Hashanah* prayers – except for the *U-Netanneh Tokef* prayer, which describes the Divine judgment. The reason is that the judgment – which is the outcome of the overall balance of good and evil, credit and debit – has already been made (although not finally sealed).

The theme that is repeated over and over again in the *Rosh Hashanah* (and *Yom Kippur*) prayers is the prayer for the revelation of G-d's glory in the world. Our lives are filled with various kinds of questions, small ones and big ones. The main question that everyone ought to ask on *Rosh Hashanah* is – what have *I* done to help reveal G-d's glory in the world? If we ask it we may find out that in fact, we have not done a single thing to prove that we indeed "bend our knees, bow, and acknowledge our thanks before the King Who reigns over kings, the Holy One, Blessed is He".[5]

In the course of the year we spoil and soil many things. The main point is not to find out why we created damage, or to what extent we have been sullied, but rather to figure out the overall balance of our deeds and of the world as a whole. Throughout the year, "the Holy One, blessed be He, sustains [all creatures], from the horns of wild oxen to the eggs of lice"[6]; on the Day of Judgment He asks: has all of this been worthwhile? Should the world really be kept going for yet another year? The Day-of-Judgment-question, then, does not deal with minor issues and sub-paragraphs; these are dealt with by the "Forgive us, our Father" prayer etc.[7] that we recite three times daily. The *Rosh Hashanah* question embraces the entire world, and it is therefore directed not only to the pious and the righteous, but to each and every individual, as it says: "And every creature that breathes will say: the Lord, G-d of Israel, is King ..." etc.[8] Every living, breathing creature, then, should be wholly devoted to this goal. This is why there is no mention of guilt in the *Rosh Hashanah* prayers; for these prayers describe the world not as it is, but as it should be. Our task is to contemplate this description and compare it with our reality; this comparison will clarify matters to such an extent that there will be no further need for details.

Take a soldier who is preparing for a parade: his buttons are shining, his hat is properly placed on his head and there is not a single speck of dust in his gun. That he has no bullets in his magazine is immaterial, because he does not intend to go to war anyway. Something similar can happen to us on *Rosh Hashanah* as well: we focus on the small details, but behind them there is absolutely nothing. We stand up and cry out on Rosh Hashanah, and sing, and plead – but for what?

The only thing we can say is, "See how wretched and miserable we are; we are so ashamed! Please give us one more chance!" Yet all year long we have

---

[5]   From the *Aleinu* prayer.

[6]   Tractate *Shabbat* 197b.

[7]   From the *Shemoneh Esreh* prayer.

[8]   From the *Rosh HaShanah* prayer.

been catnapping, if not actually sleeping. How much can one possibly improve in one single day? One can, perhaps, make no more than a small, tiny motion; but if this tiny motion means that we are beginning to wake up and live, then we will really begin to do something.

In the very last *Minchah* prayer before *Rosh Hashanah*, we say – as we do on every other day of the year – "bless … this year and all its kinds of crops for the best".[9] At that time, what remains of the year is a mere half-hour or so – and yet we are asking for a blessing for the whole year! The point is that even in that half-hour we can change the meaning of the entire year. In some languages, the only difference between a declarative sentence and a question is the punctuation mark at the end of the sentence. Similarly, even if we cannot change *what* we have done in the course of the year; we can decide to replace a full stop with a question mark, or vice versa. I may have said or done certain things, and now I decide to doubt them; I may have given open cheques for all sorts of things, and now I decide to withdraw them; I may have been carried away, but now, at the very last minute, I can still say that I no longer agree to that. Indeed, on *Rosh Hashanah* eve we do *hattarat nedarim* – annulment of vows – thereby releasing ourselves from whatever we have bound ourselves to in the course of the entire year. This enables us to set ourselves free, to turn our backs on whatever we want to, and to start walking an entirely new path.

---

9   From the *Shemoneh Esreh* prayer.

Strengths in the Soul

The ten *Sefirot* exist in the human soul just as they do in the higher world; the whole gamut of human thoughts, feelings and experiences grows out of the interrelations between them.

The first three *Sefirot* have to do with pure consciousness: *Hokhmah* expresses the power of original light; it distinguishes and creates and serves as the basis for intuitive grasp; *Binah* expresses the analytical and synthetic powers of the mind; it creates and comprehends forms and it looks into the meaning of what comes from the *Sefirah* of *Hokhmah*; and *Daat* expresses the crystallisation of human awareness into conclusions and abstract proofs of facts; it is that which enables our consciousness to move from one form of existence to another, thereby ascertaining its continuity.

The following three *Sefirot* are the *Sefirot* of the higher emotions: *Hesed*, *Gevurah* and *Tiferet*. Hesed, grace and love, is the inclination towards, the desire for, or attraction to, things and beings; the outgoing flow and opening up to the world; that which gives of itself in terms of will or affection or relation. In giving, it opens up to the *Sefirah* of *Gevurah* or strength. *Gevurah* is an inward withdrawal of forces, a concentration of power which provides an energy source for hate, fear and terror as well as for justice, restraint and control. *Tiferet* is harmony and compassion as well as beauty, a synthesis or a balancing of the higher powers of attraction and repulsion; it leads to moral as well as to aesthetic acceptance of the world.

From these we proceed to the three *Sefirot* that are directly related to the actual world of experience: *Netzah*, *Hod* and *Yesod*. *Netzah* is the will to overcome, the profound urge to get things done. *Hod* is striving to achieve and attain that which is desired, as well as the power to overcome the obstacles posed by reality and persevere. Yesod is the power of connection, the capacity and the will to build bridges, make contracts and relate to others, especially as it is in relationships with teachers, parents and meaningful and authoritative figures.

Finally, the *Sefirah* of *Malkhut* is the realisation of this potential; it is the transition from the soul to the external existence, thought and deed. It also affects the transmutation of consciousness back to *Keter*, Crown, which is the first and highest of the *Sefirot* as well as the central point of will which contains within itself all the higher powers that activate the soul from above.

A Torah of Life

In terms of its place in the Jewish calendar, the Festival of *Shavuot* complements the Passover Festival. The relationship between these two festivals is that the epitome and completion of the Festival of Freedom is in the giving of the Torah; the giving of the Torah is the fulfilment of the hopes and wishes aroused in the Festival of Freedom.

The unique significance of the Torah is often blurred by incorrect analogies. Seeing the Torah as a legal book of a certain religious system is a distortion of the Jewish worldview; it is a misunderstanding of the essence of Torah. Calling the Torah "Law" puts it in the same category as "the Law of Gravity" and the like, thus uprooting a most fundamental point: the Torah is unique, and the term "Torah" may therefore be used for one thing only: the Torah.

"Religion" is an ideological and practical system designed to regulate a certain part of life – that which pertains to G-d's worship. But Judaism, as it is expressed in the Torah, cannot and must not be thus stipulated. In essence, the whole of life is seen as a unified system that encompasses every aspect of the life of the Jewish people, down to the smallest details. The Torah contains not only laws that govern religious ritual (*Bein Adam LaMakom* – Commandments between Man and G-d) and social life (*Bein Adam LaChavero* – Commandments between Man and Man), but also history and poetry, moral guidance and prophecies, solid facts and mysteries.

Moreover, all these components are not separate elements that are somehow joined together, but one indivisible totality. One does not have to scan the entire Torah in order to prove this point: even a small "sample", such as the Ten Commandments, reflects this. The Torah, like life itself, like human beings, is not compartmentalised: it is a mixture of everything, of the entire world and all that is in it. Man does, of course, classify things and draws limits and borders; but these are always technical and artificial; for in truth, everything human is nourished, to a greater or lesser degree, by all the other parts of the whole human being.

The Torah, is therefore indivisible. The portion of *Kedoshim* (Leviticus chapters 19-20, which, according to many commentators, is a "mirror image" of the Ten Commandments) flows smoothly from the commandment to respect one's parents to some laws of sacrifices; from the commandment to give gifts to the poor to "love your neighbour as yourself"; from the prohibition to take revenge and bear grudges to the prohibition to wear clothes made from a mixture of wool and flax. And this is precisely why the Torah is what it is,[10] since it both indicates and paves a way of life for an entire nation. Judaism is the sum total of the combination of the Jewish people and the Torah.

Placing the Torah within the limited framework of "religion" – whether it is done by those who believe in the Torah or by those who deny its validity – is to destroy it; it transforms it from "Torah" into something entirely different; it makes it similar to all the other world religions or belief systems. Defining the Torah as "religion" is like imprisoning it within a restricted area; furthermore, it means severing it from the totality of life. A Jew who defines himself as "religious" actually denies the Torah, because the Torah calls upon the Jew to construct his whole life in such a way that everything will be Torah.

The Torah was given to the Jewish people after the Exodus from Egypt in order to complement the Exodus and to forge its character and all the parts of its being. Indeed, the Rebbe of Kotzk said that although the Festival of *Shavuot* is the festival of the giving of the Torah, there is another part to it which is no less important: it is the personal or national event, that has no fixed time or place, of the *receiving* of the Torah. Only then does the Torah truly become a Torah of Life.

---

[10]   The Hebrew word Torah comes from a root that means "to teach", "to point to" and "to show the way".

The Inner Meaning of the Giving of the Torah

The giving of the Torah took place once, some 3,300 years ago. The receiving of the Torah is individual: some of us receive the Torah at a very young age; some may receive the Torah today; others may receive it at some point in the future. Receiving the Torah means absorbing it, becoming identified with it, taking it as a personal message. Receiving the Torah, then, is a highly personal matter, an event that changes one's personality entirely, and it can happen at any moment. But we have to be prepared for it.

I wish to approach this topic through the ideas of the *Alter Rebbe*.[11]

In the giving of the Torah there is a strange verse: *"vekhol ha'am ro'im et ha-kolot ve-et ha-lapidim ve-et kol ha-shofar"* (And all the people perceived the thunderings and the lightnings and the voice of the horn [*shofar*] – Exodus 20:14): how can one see voices?[12] The *Alter Rebbe* asks a further question: why was the main voice that was heard during the giving of the Torah the voice of the *shofar*? If G-d was going to speak, why was there a need for any other voice altogether? And if there was a need for another voice, why not choose something more musical than a *shofar*? Almost any other instrument would be better!

In order to answer these questions we must gain a better understanding of what actually happened, and why. There are also other levels of asking the

---

[11] Rabbi Schneur Zalman of Lyady, 1745-1812, founder of Chabad. The passage is taken from *Torah Ohr*, p. 73c-d.

[12] The questions we ask are an expression of interest and connectedness; we do not ask questions about things that are meaningless to us – we ask because we want to know.

question. In a certain way, most of the Ten Commandments are slightly, or more than slightly, disappointing, because the fact is that most of the ideas they contain are not so brand-new; the notion that stealing, or killing human beings, are negative human behaviours existed in the world long before the Torah. Even the notion of the existence of the Creator was not something novel.[13] So what is so startling about the Ten Commandments? The giving of the Torah was a unique, once-in-human-history event – so why choose such non-startling contents to be given on that occasion? Or, to put the question even more generally: what is there in the Torah that is so special?

The *Alter Rebbe* continues, and asks: "The voice of the *shofar* is a simple, unmodulated sound; it is also a frightening sound which is not pleasant to hear." In historical times, the *shofar* was used not only on *Rosh Hashanah*, the New Year, but also, or even mostly, as an alarm – when war, or some other calamity, was about. "It is a voice that makes people frightened, as the verse says (Amos 3:6): 'Shall the *shofar* be blown in a city, and the people not tremble?'" Why is the giving of the Torah, which is supposed to be a positive experience, accompanied by this frightening voice that is heard all over the world?

The Hebrew word *shofar* comes from a root that means to improve, to make things better and nicer – or, in other words, closer to G-d. And since G-d is the source of pleasure, it follows that the *shofar* has another aspect to it: that of pleasure, of being connected to the source of all pleasures, as the verse says: (Psalms 36:6): "For with You is the fountain of life; in Your light do we see light".[14]

There are different levels in the soul: there is the level of emotions, which all of us are familiar with; above it is the level of the intellect; beyond it is the will. Often, our understanding very much depends on our wills and desires; I want something, and my mind creates the required rationalisations, because the mind gets its order from a more potent source: the will. And the source of

---

13   Indeed, people tend to think that the Ten Commandments are universal, or at least universally acceptable. I once had a conversation with a young Jewish millionaire, who claimed that he cannot observe all the commandments because there are too many of them; however, he said that he observed the Ten Commandments. I checked with him one commandment after the other, and it turned out that he indeed kept the Ten Commandments – so long as they did not interfere with his whims or desires. So every Commandment is just a statement that can be implemented or ignored at will.

14   See also the first *maamar* in *Likkutei Torah* by the *Alter Rebbe*.

the will, says the *Alter Rebbe*, as well as the ultimate source of everything that happens in the mind, is pleasure. The will is about how to get pleasure and how to avoid displeasure. Pleasure is not only very powerful; it also requires no explanation: it is its own reason. Interestingly, the Hebrew word *ta'am* means both "taste" and "reason".

In other words, the reason for things is their taste – just as the reason for eating chocolate is its taste. Pleasure, then, is what creates our will; only then follow all the intellectual and emotional structures that we create around it. According to the *Alter Rebbe*, the notion of life is identical with the notion of pleasure. Furthermore, the notion of pleasure is so powerful because pleasure can be connected with almost anything: taste, smells, beauty, intellectual achievements, etc. and the highest, most powerful source of pleasure is life itself.

The reason why we do not feel that extreme pleasure is that so long as we are alive – even before birth – life is always with us. We get to feel this ultimate pleasure only when we are about to lose it: a person who was saved from grave danger feels an enormous surge of pleasure, which is equalled by nothing else. Life and pleasure, then, are inseparably interconnected; and thus G-d, being the source of life, is also the source of pleasure.

According to the *Alter Rebbe*, then, the *shofar* is two-faceted: it is connected with our deepest fears, but also with our purest and highest pleasures. And precisely because the *shofar* is such a primitive instrument, because there is nothing external about it, it goes right into the very core of things. The voice of the *shofar* touches what is beyond our conscious mind, and thus awakens our real connection with G-d. The voices of the *shofar* in the giving of the Torah made the People of Israel listen to G-d, not in the same way that one would listen to a good lecture, but rather from a very different place, beyond feeling and understanding. In order to listen in such a manner, one must connect with those powers within ourselves that are beyond measure, that cannot be classified or compartmentalised. The blowing of the *shofar* awakens the soul itself to the point of the source of life, the notion of life itself. Hence both the fear and the pleasure: I feel as if my life is moving, trembling, with the voice of the *shofar*.

Let us now go back to the other question that was raised before: why was the giving of the Ten Commandments such a big event? The world did not begin with the giving of the Torah, and even before this great event there were great as well as saintly people and prophets; similarly, both before and after the giving of the Torah, there were evil and vicious people. However, we say that world history can be divided into two periods: before and after the giving of the Torah. What is it about the giving of the Torah that changed the universe?

The Torah is the real law of the world, of existence, and if we do not observe it, it is only because we are imperfect; if we were perfect, we would have kept the Torah naturally, as it says about the Patriarchs – just as we do not have to be commanded to eat or sleep. But we are imperfect, convoluted beings and we act in twisted ways; just as sick people who lose their sense of taste eat things that are harmful to them, so too we do things we should not be doing. This is also why we have to be taught so many things. Similarly, people who have an inborn musical talent simply know how to play musical instruments, while others who are not musically inclined have to be taught. This is also true for every other area of human knowledge and talent. Similarly, a person who is properly built observes the commandments not because he is told, but because that is the natural thing; he knows that he cannot do certain things – not because he has been told that they are forbidden; rather, he knows this in the same way that I know I must not put my hand into the fire, because it will be painful. Similarly, our Patriarch Abraham observed the Commandments not because he was commanded, but because he had an inner understanding of what the Torah is.

If so, what difference does the giving of the Torah make if, in principle, people in a state of perfection can observe it naturally? We can, of course, claim that this holds true only for a very small number of human beings and that for the rest of humanity, the giving of the Torah makes life simpler, by explicitly telling them what is right and what is wrong. But does the giving of a manual justify such a great and unique event as the giving of the Torah, which according to Rabbi Yehudah HaLevi is the most important event in human history, and the basis of the Jewish faith?

So now the *Alter Rebbe* turns to Abraham and asks: what is it that makes Abraham essentially different from us?[15] We can gain some understanding of this through the notion of "genius" – a genius is someone who is born different; it is not a matter of choice or decision. But a person who is born a genius will not necessarily always materialise his special talents: this already is a matter of

---

[15]   See the notion of *tzaddik* in the *Tanya*. A *tzaddik* is is a person who has a special inborn talent for feeling holiness; it has nothing at all to do with one's intellectual level.

choice and hard work. A *tzaddik*, a righteous person, is likewise a person who was born with an ability to feel, and to cleave to, holiness. However, just like the musician, the *tzaddik* too must work very hard in order to make his special talent real and concrete.

Our Patriarch Abraham, then, was not just a person who was born differently; he was also a person who made a lifelong effort to materialise his abilities – as the verse says (Genesis 12:9): "And Abram journeyed, going on still towards the South" – which, on the spiritual level, means: he kept going and going towards the point of being connected with the quality of love, which is connected with the right hand and the South.[16] So Abraham kept going farther and farther in order to be as close as he could to the point of love, until he became a chariot for the quality of love.

Being a chariot is a symbolic expression which means: being a vessel for the Divine, and not an entity with a will of its own. A person who reaches such a level no longer has a self; the only thing that motivates him is not in himself but the Divine; he is no longer an ordinary human being: he is an instrument of the Divine, without will or desires of his own. All of us may sometimes be pushed and pulled and kicked into doing what G-d wants us to do; we do it despite our will, or, sometimes, because we are convinced about it. Being a chariot means that there is no longer a self or a will, there is no longer an "I".

A verse (Kings II, 3:15) says: "And it came to pass, when the minstrel played, that the hand of the Lord came upon him." The Hebrew for "the minstrel played" is *ke-naggen ha-menaggen*, and the *Maggid* of Mezeritch says about this – in a sort of play on words – that when the musician becomes like the instrument, this is prophecy. It means becoming completely selfless, without any wishes, totally submerged in a will beyond one's own. Prophecy, then, means being – even for a very short while – a mouthpiece, an instrument. Indeed, the more humble a person is, the greater a prophet he can be. A person who reaches such a level does only what G-d wants him to do; in other words, he fulfils all the commandments even without knowing that this is what he is doing. But no human being can be born like this: such quality, such a level of existence, is acquired only through very hard work, and even then, the results are not guaranteed.

---

[16]   When you face east, the south is to your right. Indeed, the Biblical word for "south" is *teyman* which is derived from the word *yamin*, the right hand side.

The *Maggid* says this not as a mere story, but as practical instruction; because the point of *Chassidism* is to study not in order to gain knowledge, but in order to identify with what I study and to apply it in my life. If I do not do so, it is a waste of time.

The *Midrashic* book *Tanna de-vei Eliyahu* (chapter 25) says: "Every person should always say: when will my deeds reach those of my Patriarchs Abraham, Isaac and Jacob?" At first glance, this seems very presumptuous: who am I to compare myself with the Patriarchs? But the real meaning is this: the Torah stories are not fairy tales; they are meant to create role models that will direct my life. I have to strive to be like Abraham. I may not be able to achieve his level, because I lack the qualities for that, but this is not an excuse for not trying.

Becoming a chariot, says the *Alter Rebbe*, is the highest of levels. It is achieved only by very few. I may not be able to reach it, but I want to dream about it, I want it to be my fantasy, rather than fantasising about becoming rich or powerful or wise. Why G-d gives one person a great soul, and a very small one to another – that is a question that cannot be answered in this world. But as a Jew, I am born with a superior soul and with an inborn sense of holiness. I can choose to develop and nourish it or to suppress, besmirch or misuse it. The basic idea is, however, not only to be unselfish, not to do things not because I am compelled to do them, but because I identify with them. On a less perfect level, one can now and then have a moment of prayer, of feeling really connected with the Divine; or may fulfil a commandment out of total consent and complete identification, feeling as if G-d's hand were working through him.

This is attainable. Does it happen every day? Possibly not; it may happen, in the fullest sense, once in a lifetime, that we know what it means to be connected. And it requires work. Indeed, the life of our Patriarch Abraham was a lifetime of unceasing movement towards this aim, until at a certain point he really became a chariot for the Divine, he became himself the quality of Divine Love (*Chesed*). Each and every one of us can get this up to a certain level.

This is the meaning of the voice of the *shofar*: hearing the sound of the *shofar* is not just an understanding, but a preparation for the right kind of feeling. Learning *Chassidic* thought is, at best, is like learning to appreciate music or art. I cannot create ears for anyone, but I can say: if you learn about it, when you listen you will get a better understanding and perhaps also a deeper emotion. So just as people can develop a taste for good wine, they can also acquire a taste for a good commandment.

Our Patriarch Abraham was always travelling, just like the beasts in the Divine Chariot are constantly going back and forth (Ezekiel 1:14), oscillating, *ratzo va-shov*. What is the idea of *ratzo va-shov*, this notion of running back and forth? Says the *Alter Rebbe*, there are two basic feelings towards the Divine (or, for that matter, about anything), two main forces: the drive to go towards things, and the drive to flee. That is the basic motion of life – in fact, it is the definition of life. Everything that is alive is oscillating in this back-and-forth movement: the heartbeats, the breathing – when it stops, it means death. The same forces operate also in physics – the basic electromagnetic forces; these are also the basic forces in human relationship and in the relationship between the human and the Divine. All of them are made up of two basic forces: one is the flaming desire, the feeling of a burning need, which is much more than a mere wish; the other is the drive to recoil, to go back.

People's wishes are often weak, but there are also deep human wishes, and one of them is the desire to be close to G-d. It comes from the feeling that nothing else really matters. It is like a fire that burns within, and if one does not stop at the right time, one may be consumed by it. This, by the way, is one way of explaining the sin of the sons of Aaron (Leviticus 10:1-2), which is perhaps the noblest, loftiest, most beautiful of all sins: they were burned in their love of G-d.

As for the other part of this oscillation: there is a commandment to return. In a most ancient Kabbalistic book called *Sefer Yetzirah* it says: *Im ratz libbkha – shuv*, "if your heart is running – go back". There are two versions here; the most common one is *shuv le-akhor*: "go back"; in *Chassidic* books, however, it says *shuv le-ehad*, "go back to the One". This much more powerful version means that the desire to be with G-d is a noble desire which everyone should have, and those who do not have it, instead of crying about not having a source of income or a spouse, should cry about not feeling this desire.

However, since we fulfil our duty as human beings in this world by doing work in this world, we constantly oscillate between our desire to unite with G-d, while destroying all the bridges that bind us to this world, and the commandment that calls upon us to stop and reconnect with the world. But since being completely within this world is also not good, we are bound to constantly oscillate between these two poles of inner drive and obedience, love – *ahavah*, and awe – *yir'ah*. So we come back to this world and do whatever we do in it; but while and by doing it, we have a reawakening of the primal desire to be one with G-d. We Jews have a spark of this desire in our genes. If we do not develop it, we are like retarded people who do nothing with their inborn talents.[17] Whoever does not feel this desire should know that there is something very wrong with him, much more than losing the feeling of a finger or a limb. It is an illness that must be cured.

Being alive, then, means being in this back-and-forth course: on the one hand – wanting to leave this world, which is not such a good place to be in, and on the other – remembering that we have a duty, that we have work to do in this world and we are commanded to return. Some people go through this daily; others, periodically; and some people have to be awakened to this. Some people become aware of this in their early childhood or as young adults, while others discover this only as old people; but whoever is not a part of it is actually dead.

By living this back-and-forth movement we emulate our Patriarchs. We may not be exact replicas of Abraham, Isaac and Jacob, but we may get to the point of being decent copies. Just as there is only one original "Mona Lisa" at the Louvre, but there are also numerous copies of it throughout the world, and some of them are almost as nice to look at as the original. Similarly, there was one Abraham, and there are copies of him: thousands or millions of them, and they are generally inferior to him, but they can still be good enough to look at.

Can we achieve this? Let me finish with two stories, both of them true. A famous Rebbe was once given something to eat, and after he looked at the food he put it aside. A few minutes later someone ran in, agitated, and cried: Do not eat this! It's *treif* (not kosher)! So people asked the Rebbe: "Surely, you must have *ruah ha-kodesh*, the Holy Spirit, for how else could you know?"

And he replied: "It is not *ruah ha-kodesh*; it is something much simpler that anyone can achieve. If you truly promise yourself that when something that you are about to eat is not kosher, it will get stuck in your throat, even to death, then you will get to feel whenever anything is not kosher. In other words, it is possible to cultivate a sense of right and wrong; some people will find it

---

17   People who convert to Judaism are also souls that are the children of Abraham, and are therefore literally called "son/daughter of Abraham and Sara".

easy, for some it will be much more difficult, but it can be done."

The other story is about a small, forsaken Jewish community in India. This community was so cut off from the rest of the Jewish people that they lost all of their books, even the Bible. Around the 16th–17th century, the missionaries arrived in that region and began, among other things, to distribute bibles. They did it gradually, so at first they gave this community the Five Books of Moses, which they took and were very happy about; then they gave them the Prophets, and they were happy about that. Then they were given the Scriptures, and they were happy about that too. Finally, the missionaries gave them the New Testament – but they rejected it; they said: it's not the right thing! – and they remained Jewish. They were very simple people, as ignorant as can possibly be; but because they were Jews and wanted to remain Jews, they had this sense for holiness, and so they stopped at the right point.

To conclude, let me restate what was said at the very beginning: the point of learning is not knowledge – it is internalisation. We have to prepare ourselves to receive the Torah in the right way. This is much more difficult than washing one's face or brushing one's teeth, because it often demands that real changes be made. No real change can take place by just listening to a lecture. Sometimes a person on the bus may say something that you have to hear, and if you are in the right mindset, then you can hear it and absorb the message. Sometimes it happens immediately; sometimes it may take years for one to internalise these things. But in any case, the point of studying is to become one with what we learn. It may be very hard work, but it can be done.

Freedom Without Content
Is Another Kind of Slavery

Shavuot is in many ways the completion of the *Pesach* festival. Its very name, *Shavuot*, or "Weeks", attests to the connection between the two festivals, insofar as *Shavuot* is not connected to a specific day of the month. It relates, in fact, to the counting of 49 days after *Pesach*. And only when this period of seven weeks of the counting of the Omer is completed, is Shavuot celebrated, on the 50th day.

The other name of the festival – *Atzeret* – is also indicative of this special connection. It means "a final festive day". And just as the festival of *Succoth* has its own *Atzeret* on the eighth day (*Shemini Atzeret*), so does *Pesach* have its own. However, this *Atzeret* of *Pesach* does not fall immediately after the festival, as with *Succoth*, but rather 50 days later, on the festival of *Shavuot*.

This link between the festivals of *Pesach* and *Shavuot* is not just formal and external: it is an expression of the intrinsic connection between them. In other words, *Pesach*, the festival of redemption and freedom, is completed only on *Shavuot*, which is the festival of the giving of the Torah. Thus, *Pesach* without *Shavuot* is incomplete and lacking. And in the same way, *Shavuot* needs *Pesach* in order to have a foundation in real life. The two festivals are interconnected. Whoever severs them apart remains with a partial entity, with only one aspect of things.

The *Pesach* festival symbolises the period when our forefathers left Egypt and cast off the yoke of external bondage associated with being slaves in a foreign country. But only after the giving of the Torah did they truly become one unit – a significant entity with its own inner content, with a meaning to its being and a goal for its continued existence.

The Exodus was the casting off of the yoke of slavery, but in and of itself the Exodus did not grant freedom. Freedom is more than the mere casting off of bondage; freedom also has a positive meaning. Slavery and bondage are states in which both an individual and a nation are not free to do what their hearts desire, but are constrained to do what others tell them to do. Thus a state of freedom exists only when a person can do what he wants, and can live his own life.

This, of course, cannot be achieved unless he has a will of his own and an intrinsic direction to his life. This point applies not only to human beings or to specific interpretations of the concept of freedom. It is, in fact, the elementary meaning of freedom. Freedom without an independent will has no essence, and therefore makes no sense.

This notion applies not only to the complex structures of spiritual life, but to every living thing. For instance, it is a well-known phenomenon that animals born and raised in captivity which escape from their cages often do not know how to live in freedom. They are not capable of taking care of themselves, nor do they have the motivation to do so. When in their cages, acting out of a vague instinct, they look as if they are constantly striving to set themselves free. When they do attain freedom, however, it usually takes them no more than a few days to return to the comfort of their pen with its well-known routine and attendant, even if that attendant makes them work.

And if this is true for animals, it is much truer for human beings. For to be free means to have a personality of one's own, to have a life goal of one's own, a goal which is worth striving for despite all difficulties.

Our Sages express this idea succinctly in a famous saying. About the expression in the Torah *harut al ha-luhot* (Exodus 32:16), which means "engraved (*harut*) on the Tablets (of the Law)", the rabbis say: "Do not read the word as *harut*, but as *herut* (meaning 'freedom'), for the only person who is truly free is he who occupies himself with Torah" (tractate *Eruvin* 54a).

This is the paradox of freedom itself. For he who does not occupy himself with Torah – indeed, he who does not *have* Torah – does not have a life of his own. It makes no difference whether the yoke of foreign enslavement is evident or not. For what will he do with his freedom when there is nothing he really wants for himself? He will naturally enslave himself once more to whoever will be willing to be his master and tell him what to do and how to act.

The giving of the Torah is therefore the conclusion of the process of casting off the yoke of enslavement. In *Pesach* we have freedom only in the negative sense. In order to acquire true freedom, we need the festival of *Shavuot*, the festival of the giving of the Torah, which imparts to the Jewish people a positive content.

Attaining freedom by "accepting the yoke of the Kingdom of Heaven" is not a simple or self-evident thing. A penetrating question arises, one which was probably asked by those who came out of Egypt and continues to be asked even today: why can other people, large and small, live their lives without Torah? And why must the people of Israel, of all nations, be exceptional in order to exist?

The answer is connected with the anomaly of the Jewish people, an anomaly which has existed since its inception as a people. It is best expressed in the words of the prophet: "Who has heard such a thing? Who has seen such things? Shall the earth be made to bring forth in one day? Or shall a nation be born in one moment?" (Isaiah 66:8).

Ordinarily, the creation of a people takes many centuries, during which a joint existence slowly binds the individuals into a larger unit, which then assumes its own identity. This was not so with the Jewish people: the people of Israel was "brought forth in one day", in a one-time process.

Since the very beginning of its existence, the unity and unique national character of our nation have not simply stemmed from the fact that "we are here". The development of the People of Israel is not "natural". Consequently, our people cannot satisfy itself with mere existence.

The people of Israel grew as a nation on the basis of a unifying idea, and the nation's continued existence is connected with that idea. Rav Sa'adia Ga'on said: "Our nation is a nation only in its Torah" (*Emmunot ve-De'ot*, 3) and this saying has retained its significance even in generations when most of the Jewish people did not live by the Torah.

The Torah has nevertheless remained the foundation of the life of our people, because ties of identity always draw upon a common past, and this common past is imprinted with the unifying seal of the one Torah.

This uniqueness has not decreased, but has rather increased, with the establishment of the State of Israel. The State, like the Jewish people itself, was born not as the outcome of a situation which lasted for many generations before finding its expression, but as the sudden fulfilment of a wish, the realisation of an idea. This unique characteristic of the State is underscored by two factors. The first is that its neighbour states have largely failed to come to terms with its very existence, and the second is the fact that the State constantly attempts to (and also must) attract new immigrants.

The existential pressures on the State, which affect all those who live here (as well as those who plan to come here), make its existence look very different from that of all other nations. The People of Israel needs a qualitatively different and deeper kind of freedom than that which is required for others.

Messianic times are defined in *Halachah* as being based on the abolition of the yoke of other nations. This can only be relevant against the background of a previous meaningful Torah existence – one that could not reach full expression under foreign rule. Without Torah, the removal of slavery does not lead to true independence; it is only the preliminary step. The festival of Redemption is the beginning; Redemption awaits completion by the giving of the Torah.

Shavuot is called "The time of the giving of our Torah". Of this, Rabbi Menachem Mendel of Kotzk said that the Torah was indeed given in one day. But, he added, the active receiving of Torah happens for every individual separately, when that individual decides for himself to "receive" the Torah. In this sense, *Shavuot*, the giving of the Torah, represents a possibility and a challenge to which the People of Israel in its entirety – and every individual therein – is called upon to respond.

The giving of the Torah is not a final point; quite the contrary. It is, for the People of Israel, a point of departure towards a long and complex path that incorporates both the receiving and the fulfilling of the given Torah.

Diaspora as a Dream

Living in exile is an experience all too familiar to Jews, and not only to Jews. The quality of life in a homeland is very different from that of life in exile. In many ways, life in exile is unnatural, cumbersome and full of suffering; yet it also contains an unexpected sort of freedom.

Peoples living in their homelands behave in a normal way in whatever they do; their thinking, their political activities, their daily conduct are all governed by some kind of rational set of laws which is taken for granted and never questioned. Thus, free peoples living in their native lands are, in a sense, doubly limited: they are limited by the physical boundaries of their native countries as well as by the patterns set by the normal flow of their everyday life.

In exile, on the other hand, people live an abnormal life which in a way is like a dream. What is a dream? Dreams are made up of real elements; one cannot dream about things that are not part of reality. However, these things are put together in ways that do not exist in reality. Indeed, in a dream one can do things that would otherwise be impossible.

In exile, although one certainly cannot do the undoable, one can still create combinations that do not exist in the "real" world.[18] One person living outside his homeland, even if he feels that he belongs to another place is, in fact, deep within this combination of fantasy and objective reality; or, in other words, he creates a dream. Therefore exile may sometimes produce individuals who are very creative in ways they could never have been in their homelands,

---

[18] Psychologists explain why people often dream either of flying or of falling. They say that when we are on our feet, we feel that we have something solid underneath us. When we lie down, however, our feet do not touch anything and the brain gets a confusing message, which it interprets as either going up or falling down. This, then, is an objective situation that creates a specific dream.

because they are not bound by the laws and limitations of the country in which they live.

One such example is Napoleon: had he remained in Corsica all his life, he would never have attained the throne of France. Or Pushkin's grandfather: what could he have possibly become in his historic homeland? Only in distant Russia did he become a general in Peter's army and the grandfather of a famous poet.

However, such "dream people" can use their power either positively or negatively. Individuals in exile might become a part of the underworld; perfectly decent women turn into prostitutes, while honest men join the Mafia. Often, such people do not understand what happened to them; it is as if some kind of a dream has pushed them outside of the boundaries of society.

Not only individuals but even entire nations living in exile may also achieve things that they would not have been able to achieve in their homeland. Nations living in their natural homelands have their philosophers, scientists, workers, farmers, robbers and policemen. In a normal country, the intelligence level of some ten per cent of the population is above average, and they are the ones who are cultivated, while the rest are average or below average, and tend to stay within the circles into which they were born. In exile, however, people are forced to act in ways which would not be natural for them in their homeland.

I call Diaspora a "dream" because it comprises many irrational factors. People in exile may change their very character and achieve things they could not have possibly achieved in their own country. And when such is the state of not an individual but of an entire nation – as was the case with the Jewish people – then paradoxically, it becomes the norm.[19] Thus, the very unnatural existence

---

[19]   I have a family story which seems to contradict my statements, but in truth it does not: During World War I, my family spent some time in Tambov, which is "real" Russia (unlike Moscow, which is more cosmopolitan). In the midst of the tribulations of war, hunger and danger, Tambov passed a number of times back and forth between the hands of the Reds and those of the Whites. Nevertheless, my family's basic notion was that the Russians are good people, not at all anti-Semitic, and that they possess a deep yearning for things spiritual. Indeed, I have read a lot of Russian literature of all kinds from that period, from Dostoevsky to Gorky, and have found there a real feel for the spiritual. Today, I am told, Russians are more interested in money than even the Americans. This, then, may have been the exception which proves the rule; namely, that at that point of great historical changes in Russia, life had a Diaspora-like character: not in the horizontal sense of space, but in the vertical sense of time. It was clearly a "dream" existence.

which Jews led in the Diaspora turned them into a far more spiritual people than peoples living in their own lands. This was one part of the dream existence.

During a normal sleep period people usually dream six or seven different dreams. An entire nation, then, cannot possibly entertain one single dream for two thousand years; surely not when they are dispersed between completely different countries such as Babylon or Egypt, Medieval Spain or capitalistic Germany, conservative Russia or the young United States. But in all those places, at every moment, a dream-existence continued.

The Jewish dream-existence has contributed a great deal to the world. Our nation has produced many talented people, but our main contribution was not Nobel Prize winners, or even the Bible, but rather ideas, in the religious, civil, cultural and scientific spheres.[20]

Not all peoples have such dreams when in exile. There can be different dreams too. The Gypsies, for instance, have been a wandering people for the past fifteen centuries. They made it a point not to belong to any country, not to be bound by any boundaries, and in this they have succeeded. But only very few of them became great writers or scientists. They did not become a chosen people because they did not want to. A law in physics and economics says that it is impossible to get something out of nothing. This holds true for human life as well. Being a chosen people involves paying a price, and the Gypsies did not want to pay it.

In certain places, the Jewish dream was to become unified with the people among whom they lived, to share the same culture, the same philosophy. For instance, the Jewish dream in 18th- and 19th-century Germany was to become good Germans, even better and more patriotic than the native Germans themselves. Indeed, for a certain period the Jews were the most important and creative element in German cultural life. Then Hitler came and woke them up. It was a dream, because the Jews wanted to be identical and different at the same time. It is exactly like dreaming about becoming an animal: one cannot become an animal and still remain a human being.

---

[20]   A humorous article was once printed in the papers, titled "The Influence of Moses on Mao-Tze-Dun". This article explained, in political language, that the basic idea of every revolutionary movement is something which the Jews created, and has since taken different forms, both religious and secular. This idea is not a "natural" one, but rather something which we Jews gave to the world as a gift, and which now exists and continues to influence, whether the world likes it or not.

Today we are facing a different yet similar dilemma: what happens when a person or a nation returns from exile? When a person or a people returns from exile, things go back to normal; but at the same time, some of the wonderful things which they saw in their dreams are no longer possible.

Of course, it is possible to create a dream-existence even in one's native land, and the kibbutzim are an example. The kibbutz was based both on the ideas of Gandhi and Tolstoy about the importance of physical labour and its supremacy over intellectual achievement, and on the Marxist utopia of "everyone working according to their abilities and receiving according to their needs". There was a time when it was as difficult to become a kibbutz member as being admitted to the world's most exclusive clubs. In kibbutzim one would find shoemakers with PhDs in Philosophy, and the best of intelligentsia in fields or cowsheds.

This, again, is not a normal existence. However, contemporary Israeli society, which is made up of the children and grandchildren of these very people, is quite different. We lived in a dream-existence for some 2,000 years of exile, and the first decades of the rebuilding of Israel were also like a dream. But now that we have begun to wake up, we are clearly becoming a normal people. And what is the result?

Diaspora Jews are among the most prominent intellectuals in almost every field, far beyond their proportion in the general population. For instance, in the past 50 years the 15 million Diaspora Jews produced some 85 Nobel Prize winners – an average of more than one per year. How many countries with a population of five million have produced anything outstanding at all? Clearly, abnormal achievements are the result of an abnormal system. And in fact, the State of Israel has produced only half a Nobel Prize in Literature, and none at all in any of the sciences;[21] for here we have not only our own intellectuals but also our farmers, taxi drivers, shopkeepers, etc., so the percentage of outstanding people is going back to normal.

In one of his short stories, Thomas Mann depicts a young writer writing about his life. On the one hand, he is proud of being different; on the other, he always dreams of becoming like everyone else around him.

Zionism has had this ambivalence from its very inception: on the one had, it aimed to turn the Jews into a normal people; on the other, it had this dream of being a "light unto the nations", a different, higher people.

---

[21]   This has changed since the article was written, but still not very significantly.

So what can we Jews be? What do we want to be? This is an issue about which we, as individuals and as a nation, are now called upon to make up our minds.

Divine Providence
and Faith

The path of spiritual life does not run smoothly. Every human being, even the greatest of the great, has ups and downs, periods of elation and depression. This spiritual imbalance is an inherent trait of creation, and not necessarily related to one's own failings.

At a certain stage of his development, man tends to identify himself with his spiritual achievements, experiencing each and every element in the manner appropriate to his nature, so that his spiritual powers find expression in thought, word and deed. However, one should not remain for ever at a given stage of spiritual development but rather keep progressing to ever higher levels.

However, in this process of growth – both when it is purely intellectual or also emotional – there is a certain decline, even "collapse", between one stage and the next. This is inevitable because, in order to acquire new concepts and insights, one must abandon one's previous notions and ideas; if one doesn't do so, one cannot truly reach a new, higher stage of perception and understanding. Furthermore, new concepts can be acquired only in a kind of vacuum, in which most of the notions we already know seem to be forgotten, and one goes back to the simplest bases.

Alternatively, one may attain certain spiritual insights intellectually, which will not generate any emotions such as enthusiasm and excitement. In such a case, it will be impossible to hold onto one's former notions, because the new insights make them irrelevant. However, it will also not be possible, yet, for one to fully comprehend the full significance of the new concepts one has acquired. This, then, is an intermediate stage between a lower and a higher level, which from a spiritual point of view is a "decline".

The advice which *Chassidism* offers in such cases is to study the basic principles of faith. This kind of study may not yield as much exaltation of devotion and enthusiasm as a new insight, but it can provide a safe and solid base to which one can always return in time of need. One who has studied in depth the principles of faith and examined the relationship between man and his Creator may still encounter many pitfalls along his way; but he will not stray from his achievement to such an extent that he will no longer be able to rise back. A person who has a firm grasp of the fundamentals of faith has something to hold onto with full confidence, even when he fails to feel love and devotion, which is what links knowledge and emotion.

Different concepts of Divine Providence grow out of different attitudes to G-d. Thus, Divine Providence can be seen as either general or particular; as relating to all of creation, to the human race, or only to the Jewish people (while the rest of creation is conceived as being under some general kind of Providence).

At first glance, it seems that the more subtle and exalted the concept of the Divine, the more general should the concept of Divine Providence be. The nature of the Divine is beyond anything that can be imagined or grasped by man; the gap between human perception and the Divine Mind is infinite. Therefore, if we perceive the Divine only in negative terms, if we are only aware of the impossibility of describing the Divine with positive attributes, how can we claim that the Almighty, who is so supremely exalted, will "lower" Himself to look after the minute details of the lives of His creatures, even if they are the most perfect and worthiest of men? Those devoted to G-d may deserve His providence, while all other creatures are merely taken care of in a general sort of way by a Divine Will which can bear their existence, but is not concerned with details.

Such a notion, although originating from a deep feeling for, and recognition of, the greatness of the Divine, is not the *Chassidic* way. *Chassidism* offers a different sort of perception of the connection between the Divine and the world, not because *Chassidism* lacks a higher understanding of the infinite distance between the Divine and mankind: on the contrary, precisely because it has studied this issue in much greater depth than others.

Philosophy basically defines the Divine as the "Supreme Intellect", the

Divine Mind which, as Maimonides says over and over again, is in no way comparable to the finite, limited human mind. Nevertheless, even this concept is somewhat limited; indeed, the Maharal, Rabbi Loewe of Prague, insists that the Divine cannot be defined or confined in any way.

Our Sages refer to the Almighty as "The Holy One, Blessed Be He". This appellation says, in fact, that the Divine is in the realm of holiness, namely, beyond any definition or limitations; whereas the notion of Divine Providence as Divine Mind is limited and finite, and therefore contrary to the truth. Such notion of the Divine is somewhat anthropomorphistic, just as seeing G-d as being in some way corporeal.

In relation to the Divine, the loftiest spirituality is in no way superior to the physical or material. In comparison to the Divine Light, even those things that to us seem pure and lofty are finite and small. This understanding of the otherness of the Divine does not negate the existence of Divine Providence on the individual level; on the contrary: it leads to an increased awareness of how personal this Providence is.

However, when we understand that the greatness of G-d goes beyond the limits of both the spiritual and the physical, and that these concepts are meaningless in relation to Him, then we cannot claim that Divine Providence is confined only to the great and exalted; because after all, what is exalted or great when compared to G-d? What difference is there between the greatest man and the smallest insect? In relation to the supernal light, everything is equally insignificant. Divine Presence extends as much towards the greatest saints who devote every moment of their lives to G-d as to the lowliest organisms that merely subsist.

Understanding that G-d is not bound by time or space will lead us to the conclusion that His Providence is all-embracing, since from G-d's viewpoint, the great and the small, the most sweeping generalisation and the minutest detail, are all equal in their infinite distance and total insignificance as against G-d's greatness, and also equally close to Him as recipients of the all-embracing Divine Love.

Such a profound understanding will now give us a proper understanding of the verse from the *Hallel* (Psalms 113:4-6): "Great above all nations is G-d and His glory is above the heavens. Who is like the Lord our G-d, exalted on high, looking down to see the heavens and the earth." This verse describes how Divine Providence works. The gentiles say: "G-d is above all the nations";

Divine supremacy is beyond all the worlds, beyond human understanding, and therefore also "His glory is above the Heavens", and only there does G-d reveal Himself in the fullness of His splendour, in broad, world-embracing spiritual problems; they say that G-d is not to be found in the lowly world of matter, and mostly not in the petty affairs of individual human being and creatures.

The original Jewish concept expressed in the verse "Who is like unto thee, O Lord" (Exodus 15:11) is based on the idea that G-d's Divine Revelation to the Prophets and to those who received the Torah is infinitely greater than what is knowable to those who perceive G-d's greatness through the human mind. The Lord our G-d is infinitely greater and more exalted that even the concept of "His glory is above the heavens" (Psalms 113:4); G-d's greatness is not only above the physical world, but also far above all the spiritual worlds, and even the most sublime intellectual probing: "He looks down to see the heavens and the earth" (ibid., v. 6). However, because G-d created the world, He cares for it and sustains it both in heaven and on earth.

This, then, is the basis for the *Chassidic* claim that Divine Providence applies to everyone and everything. G-d not only "guides the steps of man" (see Psalms 37:23) but also provides for each and every creature in this world, and directs it towards the goal set for it.

The Baal Shem Tov illustrates this idea with a famous image. He says: "If a man stoops to lift a handful of sand and then throws that sand into a pit, he must know that each and every grain will fall exactly into the place assigned to it during the six days of Creation by the Will of the Creator. Whoever does not accept this is a heretic and a non-believer."

The Baal Shem Tov, then, claims that each and every object in this world, even a grain of sand, is under the wings of Divine Providence; it is bound by G-d's will that determines its place and the role it is to play in the world. Denying Divine Providence regarding the minutest details of life is equal to denying the idea of Divine Providence altogether. Acknowledging Divine Providence over individuals and small details attests to the greatness of G-d and to the depth and force of man's belief in Him. Here, too, the Baal Shem Tov illustrates this point with an image: a great storm breaks in a forest, breaking branches and uprooting saplings. Why? Possibly, in order to bring one leaf nearer to the mouth of a worm somewhere in that wood. Divine Providence cares for all the needs of each and every creature, even for those of primitive creatures such as worms who, in the perfect plan of Creation, have their place and a role to fulfil.

Succoth

O f the three pilgrimage festivals that commemorate the Exodus from Egypt, *Succoth* is, in a sense, an exception.

Pesach is the celebration of the Exodus itself, the exodus from slavery to freedom; *Shavuot* recalls the giving of the Torah; *Succoth*, on the other hand, seems to have a far less specific connection with the nation's history, because it relates in general to the forty years of wanderings in the wilderness, a period that, by and large, was not marked by any outstanding miracles or events.

The commandment about the festival of *Succoth* is to be found in the Torah (Leviticus 23:42): "You shall dwell in booths seven days, all that are Israelite born shall dwell in booths." This clear commandment is followed up immediately with the words, "... that your generations may know that I made the Children of Israel to dwell in booths when I brought them out of the Land of Egypt" (ibid., v. 43).

The lack of specificity has always seemed rather strange; according to tradition, *Succoth* commemorates the miracles of the clouds of glory that enveloped the Israelites throughout their long march through the desert, thereby explaining the inner meaning of the festival in a way that can certainly make sense. The clouds of glory were a miracle of a very special kind, and the booths themselves serve as a reminder for this. This explanation, however, is not quite sufficient, and even raises some questions: this truly remarkable miracle does not play any central role in the history of the nation, in the same way that the Exodus does; what, then, is the point of linking the festival with it? And, if the clouds of glory are commemorated, why not commemorate also the miracles of the manna and the pillar of fire? Moreover, the Torah itself does not contain any overt indication of the connection between the festival of *Succoth* and the clouds of glory; it only says, "I made the Children of Israel to dwell in booths".

In order to answer these questions we must first of all go back to the passage in Leviticus: "You shall dwell in booths seven days, all that are Israelites born shall dwell in booths, that your generations may know ..."

The most obvious way of reading this passage is to understand the words "Ye shall dwell in booths" as a Divine commandment telling us that in every one of the festivals we are to return to the booths in which our forefathers dwelt when they left Egypt. *Succoth*, just like *Pesach* and *Shavuot*, is a kind of re-enactment of a historical event, and as such it is a re-living of the forty years of wanderings in the wilderness. However, the connection with these wanderings goes much deeper, for this is not a mere anniversary, commemorating an event: it is a spiritual condition, a symbolic act of return to a state of wilderness, in a way that has a profound impact on our lives.

In one way, the period of wandering in the desert was, for the Children of Israel, an interlude, a preparation for the final goal: conquering the Land of Israel and settling there. At the same time, however, it was also a period in which the Children of Israel were in a state of grace, superior to any that followed thereafter. At that time, the Jewish nation was in ongoing contact with the Almighty; life centred first on the process of building the Tabernacle, and later on – on G-d's worship in His sanctuary. The Israelites were under the leadership of G-d's greatest prophet, Moses, who was in direct communion with Him, and their livelihood came directly from Heaven (the manna) or from whatever they miraculously found in their surroundings. They lived in a very real way in G-d's constant presence, as reflected in the verse (Deuteronomy 8:2-3), "Man does not live by bread alone but by the word of G-d." The Children of Israel could survive under the most unlikely conditions, so long as their mind and purpose were directed only towards G-d and to fulfilling His will. This is why the forty years of wandering in the wilderness have been regarded as a "golden" utopian era to which we should resort as a source of spiritual nourishment, if not an ideal we should aspire to recapture.

Thus, *Succoth* may be defined as a national break from the routine round of seasons and the stability of the settled life, in order to return to a quasi-nomadic state, to the absolute freedom of the hosts of the Lord. It expresses a longing for a return to the primal days of Israel's wanderings.

In the prophets, too, we find repeated reference to the ideal state of the nation in the period of the wilderness. When reproving Israel for vain sacrifices, the prophet asks whether during the wandering in the wilderness they were rebuked for sacrifices and offerings. The wilderness is remembered not only with nostalgia, but with an active longing for a return to such a state of purity. The wilderness is not merely an ideal period of national history: it represents redemption, both the first redemption of the giving of the Torah and the building of the sanctuary, and the ultimate redemption which is still to come.

Ezekiel (20:35) says: "And I will bring you into the wilderness of the people and there I will plead with you face to face" – which seems to indicate that the prophet anticipates that the second, fuller redemption, like the first, will begin with an exodus from a wilderness. Hosea (2:13-14), too, hints to a return to a more perfect state: "Therefore behold I will allure her and bring her back into the wilderness and speak comfortably unto her ... and I will give her vineyards from thence and the Valley of Achor for a door of hope ... and she shall sing there as in the day when she came up out of the land of Egypt." Here again we see a similar idea: the wilderness as the place of Israel's "youthful love" and innocence, which also contains the hope for the final redemption.

In Hosea (12:9) we also find the passage which outstandingly sums up the duality of this symbolism, as it is expressed in the festival of *Succoth*, the ideal state of passionate involvement with G-d at the time of the Exodus and the adamant promise of eventual redemption: "And I that am the Lord thy G-d from the land of Egypt will yet make thee to dwell in tabernacles, as in the days of the solemn feast." G-d, the one G-d of Israel since the days of the Exodus, will again deliver the nation and bring it back to its former state, renewing its days as of old.

Behind the literal meaning of this verse one can discover a second, deeper meaning: G-d will make us to dwell in booths "as in those days" – as a reminder of the wandering in the wilderness and as a promise of the *Succoth* that is yet to come, in which G-d will enable us to dwell permanently in booths, to live in pure and close ongoing contact with Him.

But even after clarifying some of the inner meaning of *Succoth*, we are still faced with the question of timing: the festival of *Succoth* is also the festival of harvest. What is the connection between the booths and the harvest season? This question itself gives us the clue to the answer: the connection is paradoxical. *Succoth* includes two elements which at first glance are mutually exclusive, but which in truth are complementary. The harvest season is that time of year when the farmer can rest from his toil and enjoy the fruits of his fields. Winter is putting a halt on the agricultural work, and the produce is stored to protect it from the coming cold. Often, this is a time of plenty, of rejoicing and thanksgiving. The farmer is grateful for what he has, and the land is grateful to the Jews who settle and till it.

This feeling of wellbeing, of having roots and being connected with the soil, is now being contrasted with the call of nomadic life, of the desert, of the need to be not connected to soil, even when it is tilled as part of a higher goal. In Israel, *Succoth* comes after the harvest time; but instead of sitting back and enjoying the full barns and the tranquillity of a settled-down existence one hears the call to get out of one's home, to search for an earlier, freer way of life, to pursue a higher reality.

And since *Succoth* invokes the memory of the period of wandering in the wilderness and brings us back to an earlier mode of nationhood, it is particularly appropriate that *Simchat Torah* is the Day of Solemn Assembly of *Succoth*, just as the Torah was given on the Assembly of Passover, after a period of wandering the wilderness.

This clarifies another inscrutable feature in the verse in Leviticus (23:42): "Every Israelite born shall dwell in booths." Israelites, in this case, refers to the people who had settled down, found a place for themselves and connected with the soil.[22] Herein lies the most essential meaning of *Succoth*: we are commanded to dwell in booths so that the Israelite will be temporarily uprooted from his settled existence and will once again seek out that early state of the nation, "the kindness of its youth". *Succoth* is therefore the festival which expresses both our joy over our material achievements, and our ability to renounce them and to return to our total devotion to G-d.

---

22   Elsewhere, the term is taken specifically to mean one born a Jew, as opposed to one who converts to Judaism, or lives among Jews.

Preparing for the
New Year[23]

The beginning and end of each year are times that stimulate every human being into thinking. Even people who are not accustomed to make a daily stocktaking (*heshbono shel olam* – "account of this world", in the words of the Talmud, tractate *Bava Batra* 78b) tend to do so at times when people are prone to sum up, examine, plan and think.

Beloved are the People of Israel, who were given by the Almighty times and festivals at the beginning and end of each year that provide opportunities not only for thought, but also for answers to our questions, and offer us challenges for the hopefully better days that are about to come.

We are called upon to think, repent and make good decisions every year, and so much more so in days within the year that do not allow the routine of daily life to block out our deepest thoughts: What is life all about? What do we live for? Where are we heading?

However, our capacity to contain good is also limited. The days of the month of *Elul*, and the following month, *Tishrei*, abound with so many festivals, special days, commandments and prayer. All this bounty might make it difficult for us take in all in; it is liable to make the details look blurry and our hearts insensitive to their messages. Furthermore, the month of *Elul* and the festivals of *Tishrei* demand that we relate to each one of them in a different way. The

---

23   This article is the translation of the introduction to the booklet *Ohr Pnei Melekh* ("The Light of the Countenance of the King"), an anthology of essays about the month of Elul and the festivals of *Tishrei*, the Teko'a Yeshiva, 5762 (2002).

month of *Elul*, which does not have one specific focus, is very different from *Yom Kippur*, which is a single day of total concentration. Similarly, the stern Days of Awe are not at all like the days of *Succoth* and *Simchat Torah*, which are days of relaxation and joy.

Above all, in each case, we are unable to understand or fathom the significance of answers, unless we first pose appropriate questions. A wise person's question, they say, is half the answer; and on a deeper level, a wise person's question contains the seeds of the reply. Therefore, the appropriate way of preparing for the end of the year and the beginning of the next is to contemplate the questions that ought to be asked. By making our questions sharper and more pointed, we create the infrastructure that will enable the answers to be truly effective.

This kind of preparation for the festivals is an ancient custom; our Sages said that an upcoming festival should be studied in public quite a long time before its arrival (*Pesachim* 6a). Beyond the need to learn and remind ourselves of the laws pertaining to the festival, there is also a psychological purpose to such study: to prepare ourselves not only for what we should do, but also for how we are to greet this festival. This is akin to the work of ploughing, which prepares the soil to take in the gifts of Divine bounty and make them grow.

All aspects of spiritual life obviously have a large measure of privacy and individuality, as King Solomon, the wisest of men, says (Proverbs 14:10): "The heart knows its own bitterness, and no stranger intermeddles with its joys." Private, inner experiences cannot be fully shared with others; perhaps only the ministering angels can "accept from each other."[24] Still, G-d "fashions their [= our] heart alike" (Psalms 33:15),[25] and so, despite all the differences and partitions separating one soul from another, all Jewish souls have some binding factor, which enables us to be givers and receivers of even the most profound secrets in the innermost recesses of our hearts. We must therefore try to receive from each other virtues and the points of sensitivity and feeling, so that we will be able, every one of us, to find his own path to the Almighty Creator.

---

24   See *Targum Yonathan* to Isaiah 6:3.

25   Which could also be translated as "He creates their hearts together."

On Science and Religion – Some General Thoughts

The problem of the relationship between religion and science – or, to be more precise, religion and human knowledge – is a long-standing Jewish issue. For over 2,000 years, it has been surfacing in various ways, but the crux of it has always remained one and the same. It is difficult to find a complete solution for it, because its details are so numerous and belong to so many spheres of life, that the mere presentation of the question – even before seeking a solution – is a major feat. However, it seems that as a starting point, we should not look into specific questions; there is no need for that. So many of them have changed; questions have become answers, and vice versa. If we devote our energies to details, we may soon find out that neither the questions nor the answers have any relevance. We must therefore first turn to the general problem and, only then, to secondary issues, as circumstances may require.

Take, for example, the monumental work of Maimonides, who dealt extensively with issues of religion and science, resolved numerous contradictions and answered many questions: with all due admiration of his greatness, our generation cannot solve religion-science problems on the basis of his writings. Maimonides did indeed succeed in reconciling the Torah with Aristotelian philosophy and medieval science, but his philosophical explanations, and even more so his scientific knowledge, are of little or no use for our generation. He devoted so much effort to specific issues, which have proven to be quite worthless. It would have been so much better had Maimonides outlined a general way for dealing with religion and science issues, rather than focusing on the specific scientific knowledge of a specific era. Of course, at his time no one could have imagined that science would change and that so much of the old knowledge would be proven invalid; but whatever the case may be, it is obvious that there is not much point in working out the minute details of specific problems: what is called for is a general approach.

Religion and science are two separate, distinct areas of knowledge. Religion originates from superhuman sources, whereas the source of human knowledge is human. These two types of knowledge often go in different directions which do not intersect. But even in ancient times there were some areas of overlap in both religious and scientific concepts. Religious knowledge and human knowledge do not *have* to reach different conclusions, but it is quite probable that they will. And indeed, there have always been differences, sometimes subtle and sometimes major, between religion and science. The existence of such differences has always been perceived by religious people as a serious problem, and consequently they tried to minimise them as much as possible. All such have one thing in common: they are contrived and artificial, and they are awkward both from the religious and the scientific points of view.

This twofold awkwardness of the attempts to reconcile religion with science has driven many of those who are troubled by these issues to join the ranks of the naïve, who have neither questions nor doubts. In the modern era there are many ostensibly logical reasons to support such a position. Why should science and religion clash in the first place? It is true that at the moment, they reach different conclusions; but experience has shown that scientific knowledge is rapidly changing, whereas religion is stable, and there is no point in comparing a body of knowledge that is in a state of constant mutation with a body of knowledge that is stable and unchanging. What is the point of casting doubts on something in the Torah because of a scientific fact, which will soon probably be proven worthless? They say: when science reaches perfection, when it will be able to solve these problems – if, they always add, such problems will then still exist – feeling quite certain that they will not – then we will be able to look into the science-Torah relationship.

This, of course, is ducking the issue, and does not solve anything. Theoretically one may, of course, claim that it is impossible to rely on the ever-changing science; and it does not solve the problem of what to do if, eventually, the conclusions of the "perfect science" will differ from what the Torah says.

At any rate, this theoretical issue does not touch upon the true root of the confusion; it is like a straw for a drowning person. The root of the matter is not the fact that there are two different opinions on one issue, and that *accidentally* one of them originates from a religious source, while the other comes from a human source. No believer, or whoever has a certain opinion, will doubt that some people do not entertain the same beliefs as he. No Jew thinks that the fact that the ancient Greeks believed the world was created not by G-d but by a group of gods, poses any threat whatsoever to Jewish faith; the Jew relates to such a view with equanimity. The science-religion debate, however, is an entirely different matter. If these two areas of knowledge were of equal value, one could have asked the naïve question: why does science cast doubts on religion? It could just as well have been the other way around! But this is not so: people who are not religious do not usually think that religion contradicts science, whereas for the complete believer, the relationship between science and religion poses a serious problem. Why is that so?

Science seems to us to be based on a very firm basis of verifiable facts, seemingly sound extrapolations and well-established theories. The scientific structure seems unshakable; in fact, it looks as if it cannot be contradicted. Of course, things that seem unshakable may, with time, turn out to be far from certain; but at the time, science seemed eternally stable and positively true. Thus, even the most ardent believer will see the science-religion issue as a problem that must be solved. Even when certain about the truthfulness of the superhuman knowledge, one will still have to ask: what is wrong with religion? And if one does not figure this out, one is left not with a question about religion, but with a question mark. On the other hand, even if a person makes a faulty scientific consideration due to an error in scientific logic, one is still certain that science is firm and unshakable. A person who has not had a spiritual experience, or whose faith is riddled with doubt, has difficulties adhering to his faith, whereas the scientific path seems safe and open to everyone who wishes to take it.

Clearly, as long as science has not reached a point of total certainty (will it ever?), it will be impossible for it to put religion in complete doubt. But for the ordinary person, science = certainty, with plenty of proof, whereas in religion there is always room for doubts and questions. Therefore, even though the theoretical issue can somehow be evaded, the psychological aspect remains – namely, the fact that the Torah says one thing and science another, and that scientific *certainty* seems to contradict religious *faith*.

There are three levels to this clash between science and religion: philosophic, in the natural sciences, and in Bible Criticism. In the philosophical sphere, there are some hypotheses or theses that stand in contradiction to the basic tenets of faith, e.g. the assumption that the universe has always existed, scientific determinism, doubts and questions about G-d's existence, etc. In the natural sciences, the problem area is the clash between the findings of the natural sciences and the Torah. The Bible states certain facts which geology, archaeology, history, physics, chemistry etc. seem to contradict. The third problematic area is Bible Criticism, which dissects the biblical text, plays around with it and amends it, and thus demolishes its reliability in our eyes.

In the Middle Ages, the main area of debate in the science-religion issue was philosophy. Nowadays, however, it is quite irrelevant. One can cast doubts on science on a philosophical basis only when there is one philosophy; today, however, after generations of philosophers have disproved every possible philosophical principle and axiom and when even logic itself is questioned, there is no real room for any philosophical question. Bible Criticism, too, has no real weight in the science-religion issue. Although Bible Criticism does raise some worthwhile questions, the proofs it brings are not decisive, because they are based on certain pseudo-philosophical or scientific hypotheses, which are as good as many others. After all, a critical approach that analyses a prophet's words on the basis of the assumption that a prophet cannot possibly foretell the future, is inherently faulty. Or an analysis which dates the Torah a few centuries later than what the Torah itself says, is based on the assumption that the Torah is false. If it turns out that the parting of the Reed Sea [often mistranslated as Red Sea] and the Revelation on Mt Sinai did indeed happen – which for "philosophic" or other reasons Bible critics find unacceptable – then the entire Bible Criticism will fall apart. In a Divinely-given Torah, there is no place for the kinds of answers that Bible critics provide. In fact, most of the difficulties and questions that Bible critics point to were already noticed by our Sages; but their faith in the Torah led them to different conclusions (= the *Halachic Midrash*), which are just as good as those of Bible Criticism. Of course, a person can always reject the premise that the Torah is Divine, and reach his own conclusions; but the theory that the Torah was written by a number of priests is by no means more valid than the premise that the Torah is Divine.

The main problems in the science-Torah issue arise when we shift from the humanities to the natural sciences. In the humanities, both the philosophical and the literary hypotheses are based on basic assumptions which one can either take or leave, and therefore any structure based on them can be refuted. This is not, however, the case with the natural sciences, which are based on experiments and seem to be certain and objective. Natural sciences intertwine with religion in two main areas: in the logic upon which *Halachic* decisions are based, and in the Holy Scriptures. In many cases, the reasons that *Halachic* deciders bring forth certain *Halachic* decisions are scientifically wrong; in such a case, the question arises: how, then, are we to behave? Should we act according to the *Halachic* logic, which has been proven wrong – or according to the *Halachah* itself, revoking the faulty reasoning? This question is not directly related to the science-religion debate, because it a practical rather then a philosophical question, and in practice we must keep in mind that the reason cited in the books is not necessarily the most fundamental or true reason, nor is it what motivated the *Halachic* decider; rather, it is an attempt to find a reason for an existing *Halachah*.

The greatest difficulties are in the whole area of contradictions between science (that is, natural sciences) and religion. The contradictions between science and post-Torah religious texts are not a religious problem, because there is no reason to assume that even a great person can know everything, yet this does not diminish his spiritual greatness or personal sanctity. Therefore the contradictions between science and the Talmud, for instance, are not problematic in the least. This is not the case, however, with the Torah: whatever is Divine must also be true – or else it is not Divine.

We are all aware of the contradictions between science and Torah in a number of areas, especially geology, archaeology and ancient history. The contradictions are numerous and fundamental, and most religious people provide only feeble answers, which are cowardly evasions of the issue. On the one hand, the basis for these answers is casting doubts on science (i.e. pointing to contradictions that prove nothing, or describing the tortuous path of science, while ignoring the overall scientific progress). In addition, they often resort to the totally unfounded assumption that in previous generations things were different. These two kinds of answers actually evade the issue, because instead of addressing them, they only wait for the "perfect science" – and who knows what its conclusions would be. In addition, there are quite a number of questions that these answers are not valid for. For example: the fact that the Euphrates and Tigris rivers have no common source, and that the river of Pishon (even if it is not the Nile) which flows all around Cush (even if it is near India) is not even near that area, and that there is also no Eden that we know of around those places, cannot be brushed away by stating that "science does not know everything". In other words: seeking refuge in ignorance does not work, especially since, often, such refuge turns out to be quite unsafe and rather vulnerable. After all, the main issue is psychological; a yeshiva student can easily be convinced of the flimsiness of geology – but a student of geology will not be so easily convinced of that.

On the other hand, the science-religion issue cannot be resolved by labelling the story of creation "a mere legend". It is impossible to take the Torah as only 50 per cent holy: either it is Divine, and if so then it is completely true, or it is man-made, and if so, it can be wrong in both Divine and natural matters.

The science-religion debate, then, is a religious problem, and must therefore be resolved like every other issue – namely, on the basis of religion itself; any other kind of solution is fraudulent and baseless. The answer must come from a thorough and honest examination of religious understanding. The Divine origin of the Torah is a basic tenet of Judaism; but despite that, only a few people really look into its inner contents and implications. Saying that the entire Torah is Divine means that not only the ideas expressed in it, but also each and every verse and every single letter: "the entire Torah", says Nachmanides in the introduction to his commentary to the Torah, "is the names of the Holy One, Blessed be He". In this sense, the verse "Hear, O Israel" is not more important than the verse "And Timna was the concubine", nor is the verse "I am the Lord your G-d" more important than "and the sons of Ham are Cush and Mitzrayim". Of course, one must not compare the *idea* expressed in the verse "Hear O Israel" with that expressed in the verse "and the sons of Ham" etc.; but in terms of their Divine value, they are equal, because each and every letter in the Torah is a Divine revelation, and every vowel and sign is a great Divine illumination. The letters of the Torah are the basis and foundation of the Torah. They come in various orders that hint at different things: they are organised in verses, and the verses in paragraphs etc., thus revealing some of their inner content. The main part of the Torah, then, is its hidden content, which is what explains the significance of every word and letter; they are all names of the Almighty.

In addition to the inner content there is also the external content of the Torah – the *Pshat*, or literal level, which should also be understood, although it is only secondary to the inner content of the Torah. It is a random creation in the sense that it may happen that the letters making up a certain mathematical formula will also form a word – which has, of course, nothing to do with the formula. But the Torah is not a random creation, and even though the literal level of the Torah does not encompass the whole of its significance, it is certainly a part of it. Nothing about the Divine Torah is random; therefore, even its secondary aspects are premeditated.

The literal level is not intended to reveal truths: its purpose is to be a simple, external expression of the spirit of the Torah, as well as to teach and educate. The most obvious educational tool of the Torah is the commandments: the Torah points out the good deeds, tells us what can and should be done and what must not be done, directs us to the practical ways of reaching human perfection and to what might lead us away from it. But along with the straightforward teachings of the Torah – through the positive and negative commandments – there are also teachings that come through stories. The Torah stories must be taken not only literally; we are called upon to try and understand their inner meaning as well, since they allude to loftier things.

At this point one may ask: why, then, should we seek an allegorical interpretation only for the stories, and not also for the commandments? This question was already raised by our Sages, who answered it as follows: the aim of the Torah is to teach us and give us directions through Torah learning. Therefore, whatever we can understand as a commandment or directive, must be taken literally. For instance: the verse "and they shall be for frontlets between your eyes" (Deuteronomy 6:8) can be interpreted also as a metaphor; but since it can also be implemented, we must do what it says. This is not the case, however, with the verse "circumcise the foreskin of your hearts" (Deuteronomy 10:16), which cannot be implemented literally and must therefore be interpreted metaphorically. Similarly, about the verse "cities that are great and fortified in heaven" (Deuteronomy 1:28), our Sages say: "The Torah says absurd things" (*divrei havai*). The question whether the Torah stories are true also in the literal sense has no religious significance. The facts that are recounted in the Torah have nothing to do with any external reality, and their historic truthfulness is religiously irrelevant. From a religious point of view, it does not matter if the world has been existing for some 6,000 years or much longer. The Torah stories have a meaning, whether overt or covert; people's life-spans also indicate something and have some sort of inner logic.

There is an inner significance to the fact that the name of the person who discovered metal fusion was Tuval Cain, and that he was a descendant of Cain. However, in terms of the inner meaning, it does not really matter whether such a person actually existed. The Torah stories contain hints about many of the commandments that can be learned from (for instance, we learn that in the phylacteries there should be a four-headed letter ש from the side remark "he should write her a bill of divorcement" [Deuteronomy 24:1]; the commandment to "multiply and be fruitful" [Genesis 1:28] is given as a blessing and not as a commandment; and there are many more examples).

Generally speaking, the Torah stories serve only as sources from which we are supposed to draw understandings; for example, the fathers of the nation are role models for both positive and negative things, and the fact that we are not to understand the stories about them literally does not prove that they are not true, just as it does not prove the opposite. Religiously speaking, this issue is irrelevant, just as it is irrelevant whether there really was a case of a poor man and his lamb, as in the prophet Nathan's allegory (see II Samuel, chapter 12). The Torah is not a historic document, just as it is not the documentation of the story of Creation. Its purpose is to teach and educate us, and it should therefore be seen not as a history textbook, but rather as a historic tale that has a certain purpose and aim. The flow of events described there is not necessarily how things actually happened, but how they should have been. (It surely would have solved many problems had Scripture said: "any similarity to real people and actual events is entirely coincidental ...")

Let us bring one simple example that will prove that there really is no other way of understanding the Torah stories. Take, for example, the list of the Kings of Edom in the Book of Genesis (36:31 ff). The believer cannot simply accept the idea that the author, because of some strange eagerness for historic facts, inserted into his book every list he could put his hands on, and is compelled to seek the significance of these verses. For the religious person, the fact that such kings reigned is not sufficient reason for including them in the Torah; he must assume that there is an additional meaning – which is that they allude to the "breaking of the vessels" in the world of *tohu*, and the like; the believer must also assume that this information is fundamental, and that without it, the book would be lacking. Therefore the names of those people are an integral part of the Torah, regardless of whether such people actually existed or not; the question of their actual existence is something for archaeologists to deal with.

In this way, the science-religion debate is resolved: there is no connection between human science and the Torah stories. The Torah stories may be completely true or only allegorically true, but either way they would only have a random connection with reality. The Torah stories are not legends: they are allegories, allusions and indications, some overt and some covert, and their aim is to instruct man. The literal understanding of the Torah is not the understanding of the literal facts, but rather the inner significance of the stories. Indeed, all the great Jewish Sages have always warned against studying the Torah as a history book, and stressed the need to seek its inner meaning. This is the origin of all the ahistorical interpretations of the Torah: the commentators were not interested in relating what happened, but rather what we are supposed to learn from what happened.

On the literal level, then, there is absolutely no connection between science and religion. Thus, having resolved the seemingly weighty contradiction between science and religion, it will be possible to create a new, deeper and more profound connection which is based on a different understanding of science, and which will bring about the complete unification of science and religion.

Innocence and Modern Man

The Innocence Crisis

The Hebrew word for innocence – *temimut* – comes from a root that also means wholeness, perfection. Although this word is not used in the exact same meaning as "perfection", it is universally accepted that "innocence" entails a state of primordial perfection.

How does innocence find expression? How do we define it? Usually we see innocence as a straightforward approach which is not convoluted, intricate or complicated; rather, the innocent person does not even think that anything can be complicated. It's a simple, direct approach based on trust and without apprehension.

Surely, the innocent approach may not always suffice for finding a solution or unravelling intricacies, be they natural or man-made ones. Innocence can sometimes fall short because it can be deceived and tricked, and consequently it often seems to us somewhat ridiculous and silly.

But however we may relate to it, we must realise that innocence, or rather the innocent attitude towards things, is the most primary, pristine attitude. It is pristine in two ways: firstly, time-wise. During childhood, the first stage of human life, the human being is very innocent. Who can be more innocent than a baby? Innocence is the baby's point of departure – it is his ability and desire to hear, to learn and to believe everything he is told; and it is this attitude that eventually leads him to whatever else he studies. Psychologically, too, innocence is the most basic attitude; it precedes all the other human attitudes throughout a person's life, as well as in the world in general.

Innocence – which is, as we said, the most pristine way of conceiving things, without complications and without problems, but simply the way they are – characterises not only childhood, but also spirituality. Spirituality, as a primary means of conceiving and understanding, must take things in as they are – namely, innocently. When encountering things for the first time one cannot quibble with the facts or analyse them: one must first grasp their very existence. Only then can one begin to investigate, analyse and compare. But at the basis for all that is the simple, innocent understanding of reality.

However, if man is born innocent, and this is how he grasps the world, why does he not remain so? The fundamental cause for this crisis of innocence – as the personal crisis of the adolescent or the more general crisis of sophisticated generations – is embedded in innocence itself.

Innocence, being holistic, cannot possibly make distinctions. Innocence can only be one, and can always be focused on one single object (or a group of similar objects). But at a certain point in human development, man begins to learn about the existence of different objects; at first he learns about them innocently, but later on he finds out that they are different and even contradictory, and can no longer contain this contradiction. Thus, innocence becomes self-destructive. It is then followed by periods of life, as well as by generations, that are convoluted and intricate – but also accompanied by an ever-growing longing for this lost primordial innocence and for the times when everything was so whole and perfect.

Three Types of Error

Among modern men there are different, even contradictory attitudes towards innocence, yet they are all based on one basic premise: that innocence is a lie, whereas complexity and complication are the truth.

In certain people, this will create an attitude of contempt towards innocence along with admiration for all forms of complexity. This contempt for innocence, however, is accompanied with anger and envy. The man in the street, while mocking all forms of innocence and deriding simple-minded attachment to ideals, envies the innocent in his heart of hearts.

A more sophisticated approach is aware of the advantages and value of innocence, as well as of the negative aspects of the loss of innocence. Still, such people, in their striving for truth, are shackled to complexity, saying: How happy are the foolish innocents! Too bad I cannot deceive myself like them.

A third attitude, which differs from the first two, also accepts the premise that complexity is the truth; it consciously opts for innocence, saying: It is better to delve into pleasant experiences that make one happy than to get involved in the difficulties of real life.

This last approach, although it seems to be a form of innocence, is, in fact, nothing but synthetic, sham innocence. A person who embraces such an approach does not become innocent, even if he adopts this view in earnest, because he still believes that his innocence is either nonsense or a lie. In addition, such "innocence" cannot exist for too long, because it goes against the natural flow of life. Life evolves from the simple to the more complex; this is the way of the world. Therefore, any attempt to return to innocence is doomed to fail. In fact, it seems that nothing can stop the further development of ever-growing complexity.

More Problems on the Way to Innocence

Once we realise that whatever path modern man may choose will only take him further and further away from innocence, we must ask ourselves: is the return to innocence possible at all?

One thing is certain: the existing pre-assumptions make it impossible for us to return to innocence; only after we reject it will we be able to see if there is indeed a way back to innocence.

Obviously, the assumption that complexity is the truth and that innocence is a lie is a subjective, psychological feeling that has no intellectual basis. Man's strong fascination with complexity is because complexity is man-made. Man acts without questioning why, and is so immersed in creativity that he has no time to ask himself what is the point of it all. He likes what he does, and feels no need to find reasons for it. At moments of leisure man may perhaps entertain some thoughts about how complicated the world has become, and that it can get much more complicated – to the point of self-destruction; but soon enough he will once again become immersed in his work and continue to do all sorts of things that are sure to bring about his annihilation.

All of this is augmented by the fact that man feels independent, free and mature whenever he is busy with his own work. Only when this freedom and independence – and the responsibility that comes with it – get to be too heavy, does man begin to look back to innocence. Because innocence is weakness, it is the direct result of the child's vulnerability and total dependency; but innocence makes sense only when one has complete confidence in being assisted.

The transition from innocent dependence to mature independence occurs both in the life of the individual and in the history of the human race. In ancient times, man felt his dependency on so many natural and social factors, and at the same time he was also much simpler, psychologically speaking. Modern man, on the other hand, has control over so many natural forces, and the greater his control, the greater his inner complexity; he must, he just has to be, sophisticated and wily in order to get around all the complexities of the world. It is therefore extremely difficult for modern man to admit to his weakness and his dependency on powers greater than himself. Admitting his dependency means giving up on his independence and maturity, and even more so – putting aside his wisdom, that wisdom which has enabled him to overcome the forces of nature and improve the quality of his life, and which heretofore has seemed to him the highest, most supreme kind of wisdom that can leave no problem unsolved.

This wisdom-complex haunts man wherever he goes; being (or at least seeming to be) wise is considered a supreme value, whereas any deviation from wisdom seems humiliating. In this context, a return to innocence seems like a nightmare, and is tantamount to the loss of one's spiritual existence.

The way to innocence, then, is fraught with many obstacles that originate in the psyche and which, although they have no logical basis, are profoundly influential. These obstacles must be examined closely and eradicated through education.

But in fact, underneath all these problems there hide other, more fundamental issues that have to do with the relationship between innocence and today's complex world. The most fundamental issue is the essential disparity between innocence and intricacy. Innocence is a simplicity and oneness that can neither be divided nor multiplied. How can all the myriad of objects and concepts of this world be included within this unity? The other problem is psychological: is life really leading to development and expansion, despite the difficulties? And if so, is it possible to move life in a different direction – or, in other words, is there still a way to regain innocence?

About the Way Out

Being innocent and cunning simultaneously seems impossible. The concessions involved in the return to innocence seem to require a tremendous effort, even when the pain created by complexity is great. It is always impossible to solve one's own life problems when innocence is only a wished-for value within a whole set of values.

In order to reacquire innocence we must turn to a Supreme cause that is above and beyond human values. Only such an Archimedean point of leverage will make it possible to disentangle this mess. A prisoner cannot free himself from his prison. Man can emerge from the labyrinth of his existence only when he feels the presence of a Supreme Entity, for the sake of which he would be willing to give everything.

But there is another, deeper point: is not a simplistic, innocent approach to complex issues a self-contradiction? Can we achieve innocence only by demolishing, or ignoring, complexity?

In order to answer this question we must first make a clear distinction between human deeds and the emotions they arouse. The progress and development created by man are positive, even necessary, and we must not turn our backs on them; at the same time, though, we must not allow them to create within us a feeling of self-admiration. Such a feeling is a kind of idol worship and emotions of this sort create complexity and intricacy and threaten the integrity of the human psyche.

The remedy lies in the awareness that, despite human progress, independence and maturity, man still has to rely on his vulnerability and innocence. He still is as unable as he ever was to nourish his own soul and direct the path of his life from within, and will always need Divine assistance in order to live a good, true and full life. He desperately needs innocence and passivity, in order to be able to come close to the absolute, superhuman truth.

But changing the way we feel is not enough; our emotions must be given an objective, intellectual basis. How can man remain innocent while retaining his own understanding of the complex world around him? In the final analysis, the relationship between innocence and complexity, unity and multiplicity, is the relationship of faith in the One G-d versus the multiplicity of phenomena and myriad of beings of this world. How can man adhere to G-d's simple unity without being swept away by the phenomena of this world?

The resolution lies in the *Chassidic* worldview that says that "G-d's glory fills the entire world" – that the Divine unity is to be found in every single part of our complex universe. Every place, every situation, every psychological and philosophical tangle can lead us to the Creator – because He is within it, because He is revealed within the multiplicity of hues and seeming contradictions. All this multiplicity is but different aspects of one and the same thing, and every phenomenon is a revelation thereof.

This is also the solution to the problem of life versus innocence: everything, all the seemingly contradictory manifestations of life, are reflections of the unity behind the multiplicity, that unity which encompasses all of life and is reflected in each and every one of its aspects. The entire flow of human life, with all its beauty, is the revelation of the unity within the multiplicity.

The solution to the problem of innocence, then, is not to ignore multiplicity but rather to find the unity within the multiplicity. Innocence is not gained by brushing wisdom aside; true innocence can be found within disunion. Man's task is to find the unifying principle of all of reality. Then everyone will see multiplicity as aspects of unity. The very understanding that one cannot escape the One, He Who is found in everything, is itself the key to wholeness and perfection.

Technology Does Not
Change Man's Problems

We asked Rabbi Adin Steinsaltz: What is the spiritual-Jewish significance of the Apollo 8 flight to the moon? In his reply, the rabbi points to a few sides of this issue.

From a Jewish point of view, he says, we should feel proud that man can make such achievements. The queasiness that many religious people feel about scientific achievements is unjustified. Human ability to overcome natural problems does not stand in contradiction to the power of the Almighty; on the contrary: it is a way of making good use of the power to govern this world, a power that was given to us by G-d (see Genesis 2:3). G-d gave us the ability to do things, and we only elaborate it. This idea is stated both in the Talmud and in the *Midrash*: man's actions are the completion of the act of Creation. Every new human achievement is a praise to the G-d who endowed us with our creative powers – "You have made him [= man] a little lower than the angels" (Psalms 8:6). Human beings, unlike animals, are not limited in any area. Thus, rather than weakening our faith in G-d, our achievements strengthen it. Man was created in G-d's image, and his great achievements are praises to G-d.

The second aspect of this issue is the potential benefits of the space project; as G-d said about the generation right after the Flood: human beings are able to achieve whatever they set their minds on (see Genesis 11:6); the only problem is that the benefits of their actions are dubious. Humans tend to invest their abilities in the wrong places. The space project could have been a lot more beneficial, had even a small percentage of the resources been devoted to finding solutions to problems such as the desalinisation of ocean water, food production or global warming; this project would have then yielded positive results that billions of people could have benefited from. Furthermore, the most basic motivation behind the space race is negative – and this is why it is turning into a frightening power struggle.

The third aspect is that technological achievements change life. Technological development has had revolutionary effects on life, but one thing it cannot change is man's fundamental problems. Thus, there is an ever-growing gap between technological achievements and the betterment of human nature. And even though everything is, in principle, doable, the remedy for the human spirit has yet to be found.

The Question of Purpose

Our basic concerns revolve around three fundamental questions: Why, How, and What for; or, in other words, the problem of the reason for things, the inquiry into the essence and manner of existence, and the search for the purpose of it all. Man has been asking these fundamental questions throughout history, and each one of them has yielded a vast amount of knowledge.

In comparatively recent times, however, the third question, the question of the ultimate purpose, has been deemed superfluous; it is considered as having no place in modern scientific investigation or progress. The basic reasoning is that, since human reasoning cannot possibly find an answer to this question, there is no point in asking the question. The only thing we can do, so people think, is to endeavour to find the causes and conditions for the existence of things – or, in other words, revealing whatever reality is prior to anything ultimate.

Furthermore, the more we know the reasons for natural events, and find out that they are based on the laws of nature, which seem not to have any direction or aim, the more certain we are that everything is the result of the past, and that beyond that, nothing can be known. Thus, at least, says modern science.

Is this reason enough to dismiss the "what for" question entirely? There are many other questions which, like the question of ultimate purpose, have no meaning in the realm of scientific thinking. Questions of everyday life, such as: is this beautiful? Or: is it good? Or issues of taste and preference, success and failure, and the like. It does not occur to anyone to "delete" such questions from our conscious lives, just because they do not go with scientific reasoning. So, too, the question of the ultimate purpose remains one of the most constant and significant of human problems.

Mathematics answers the question "How", and does so through formulas and equations which are not time-dependent; the answers to it are always true, and always in the present tense. All other sciences relate to the question "Why", and provide the causes and the history of things and events; they deal with the past.

But what about the future? We have no knowledge of it from within ourselves, as we only have memory of the past; and the various faculties of the mind – which were developed by mathematics and the sciences – are quite at a loss beyond the various theories based on their analysis of the past and the present. The future is a total mystery, to which we cannot relate – except through faith.

By "faith" we do not necessarily mean religious faith; rather, it is the general acceptance of the understanding that many things, which we cannot experience directly, do exist, in some way or other. It is also the belief that whatever existed in the past will continue to conform to the laws of nature, and that what we know about it will be valid in the future as well. Therefore, faith in the future seems to be a part of the human condition. However, the field of knowledge that deals with faith and with the future cannot be the same as those spheres of knowledge that relate to the past (through reliance on memory), or to the present (through the reliance on abstract thinking). Still, it must be well-grounded; even if it differs from science, it should be scientifically reliable.

This calls for a different set of assumptions. Faith, in the widest sense of the term, has to presuppose the existence of some absolutes which are imperceptible and axiomatic; these are the basis for the existence of all transient and random factors, and they are what make it possible to follow things through, from the past to the present and the future. Without such a belief, all our reliance on nature and on any sort of order and regularity would be untenable. It is a faith in that which is beyond nature, in its absolute and unchanging nature and its consistency, irrespective of time and any other factor; in other words, a relationship of sorts to the Divine.

If there is absolute guidance of some sort from the past to the future, there is also a direction and a purpose. And this is the source for the answer to the question of the meaning of the "science of the future", which we call faith. This science views things from every aspect; for known events are only part of an infinite chain of events, and only through such knowledge that is based on the absolute can there be a unified grasp of reality – which will provide answers to all the questions: "How", "Why" and "What for".

To be sure, there can be no proof for the findings of this science, just as there is no proof that anything existing in the present will exist in the future: we accept them by faith. Similarly, one cannot use this "science of faith" to check future events as they turn into the present, because faith, by definition, relates only to the otherwise impenetrable mystery of what will be. Faith does not predict what will be: it only enables us to claim that the future will have certain consistency and relationship with what preceded it.

In other words, the knowledge that deals with the future is religion. It cannot be called upon to prove its pre-assumptions, because they are based on faith. However, it is the sole basis for an all-embracing, general knowledge that will include not only the remembered past and the experienced present, but also the hidden future. Every religion, then, is concerned with the question of ultimate purpose and, in the answers to it, it finds its justification, value and meaning.

Half-Wisdom

There were days, not very far back, when everyone knew that the place of the mind is in the brain and the place of the emotions is in the heart. Our Sages say that the source of all sin is the blurring of the boundaries between the two. In fact, this is precisely how the very first sin, the sin of the Tree of Knowledge of Good and Evil, is described in many Jewish sources: as the blurring of the distinctions between bad and good. The great sinners are not those who want to do evil. No evil, black as it may be, is as dangerous as the greenest blend of good and evil. "Pure" evildoers will never be as harmful as those who have ceased to distinguish between good and bad.

This enormous group of half-way people includes the most distinguished sub-group of the half-wise. What is the definition of "half-wisdom"? Basically, it is partial knowledge that creates an external impression of understanding, but is neither deep nor strong enough to create real understanding. It is sufficient to impress others, but not enough to generate any kind of deeper, independent thinking. Being half-wise is not a pose: the half-wise do not cheat anybody knowingly. It is themselves that they cheat, because they really believe that their wisdom and understanding are not only all that they need, but also all that there is to know.

We live in an age which is, in many ways, the age of the half-wise. For one thing, the well-wishing layman can no longer have a full understanding of anything; he can, at best, be a dilettante. Anyone who wishes to acquire significant knowledge in any field must become an expert in that area. Common sense, which used to be the faithful guide of the simple person, has become a useless tool in a world full of complicated problems. At the same time, though, democracy – which can be defined as the rule of the layman and of common sense – fosters the idea that everyone can and should have a say about everything.

Half-wisdom is not only tolerated: rather, people seem to think that there isn't, and there cannot be, anything else. Today's layman enjoys the greatest amount of freedom to express opinions and make decisions – about issues that are far beyond the grasp of his education and knowledge. Consequently, no one seems to think it strange or improper that high school students have a say in matters of philosophy, that women's organisations are allowed to decide in religious issues, or that illiterate peasants can tip the political scales.

The main feature of half-wisdom is its lack of completeness. It is a kind of understanding that starts out of something positive and clear, but fizzles out without any sense of aim or direction; people may ask questions, but they cannot get to a state of finding real answers; all they get for answers are counterfeit half-wisdoms.

On a certain level, half-wisdom is a necessary stage of human development. We all grow up with a set of basic ideas which we accept without questioning. This is the world of childhood innocence, a perfect world in which there is an answer for every question. Later on in life, mostly during adolescence, there comes the unavoidable clash between these primitive, childish notions and more highly developed notions that are acquired along the way. Our basic notions, which were created in a state of spiritual wholeness where there was no room for questioning, cannot withstand any kind of criticism, and they crumble before the attack of the more intellectualised, sophisticated ideas. So these half-wisdoms are very often victorious.

But when it comes to building a new set of positive notions, the half-wisdom is insufficient, because it does not contain enough knowledge, subject matter or tools required to create spiritual rules, such as the ability to absorb information, to distinguish between good and evil, the important and the trivial, and to formulate ideas that will be able to resist criticism and contradictions.

One very prevailing example of the destructiveness of half-wisdom is the religious crisis that so many people go through. During childhood, so many of us develop a set of religious notions. These notions are all destroyed when they encounter the more complex and highly developed cultural notions, because they seem simplistic, ridiculous, anthropomorphist. But while the old ideas are destroyed, the half-wisdom lacks the ability to rebuild religion in a higher, more mature way. The old notions were destroyed because they were too primitive and too frail; but no new notions were created, because they were too high and too complex.

A similar process happens also in many other spheres of life, resulting in a state of emptiness, which finds expression in pseudo-cynicism. It is pseudo-cynicism because it does not stem from any kind of assurance that there really is nothing worthwhile in this life, that our entire value system is truly faulty and empty; it is there only because people lack the spiritual and emotional tools to create a new, higher set of positive notions.

Half-wisdom is not a psychological trait: it is the fruit of the intellectual ailment of our age. The worst part of it is not the incompleteness, because perfection is universally unachievable. The worst aspect of half-wisdom is its inability to understand its own flaws. The notions created by half-wisdom are so very dangerous because they create an illusion of certitude and profundity, and thus make it virtually impossible to reach any sort of truth.

The Reparation of the Intelligentsia

One of the distinctive features of the modern era is the central role played by the intelligentsia in almost every nation. This social group, which in most cases is a minority (sometimes a very small one), is the de facto leadership of today. Indeed, very often we see in almost every issue, the viewpoint of the intelligentsia almost instantly adopted by the entire nation, and even when differences of opinion arise, the scales are tipped towards the notions held by the intelligentsia. The power that this social group enjoys seems to be growing in proportion to the world's general progress. One of the results of technological development is that so many aspects of our daily life require knowledge above and beyond what the education of the average person provides. In almost every factory, operations that used to be carried out by simple folk are nowadays performed by intellectual experts – in addition, of course, to all those areas that are totally dependent on advanced scientific knowledge. And beyond technology, the overall progress in everyday life has complicated all the fundamental issues of our daily life, assigning an ever-growing importance to intellectual abilities in the army, the government and all other aspects of life.

It is the importance of the role played by the intelligentsia, then, that lends such weight to its ideology.

Beyond the intellectual aspects, the intelligentsia is characterised also by a specific sort of spirituality – the spirituality of the intellect. It is not the IQ but this special nature that moulds the typical member of the intelligentsia. Obviously, the intelligentsia is made up not only of pure intellectuals, but also

15: Ki Teitzei

(Watercolour on paper 71.5x56 cm) 2008

You can view/download the paintings in original full colour, free of charge at:

www.mysteryofyou.com

16: A Planted Garden

(Acrylic on canvas 183x168 cm) 2007

You can view/download the paintings in original full colour, free of charge at:

www.mysteryofyou.com

17: Lights

(Acrylic on canvas 196x166 cm) 1994

You can view/download the paintings in original full colour, free of charge at:

www.mysteryofyou.com

18: The Book is Everywhere

(Acrylic on canvas 152 x 137 cm) 2000

You can view/download the paintings in original full colour, free of charge at:

www.mysteryofyou.com

of professional intellectuals – namely, people who are part of the intelligentsia because of their profession, whereas in every other way they are part of the multitude. Nevertheless, being part of the intelligentsia professionally does bring about a certain measure of spiritual and intellectual refinement in them.

The typical member of the intelligentsia may best be defined as the person who sees the shades of grey. For the average simple person, regardless of his level of morality or of IQ, the world is basically black or white; things are either completely good or completely bad, honest or fraudulent, just or unjust, truth or lie. The member of the intelligentsia, on the other hand, is keenly aware of the endless possibilities and combinations that exist between these polarities, the infinite number of the shades of gray. This is what characterises the member of the intelligentsia in all the spheres of life: practical and theoretical, scientific and moral alike.

For the member of the intelligentsia, this ability is highly advantageous, because this way of seeing the world is not only more beautiful, but also closer to the truth. Life is not a black-or-white matter; on the contrary, every event and occurrence in our lives is somewhere on the gray scale.

In the scientific realm, too, there is great advantage in discerning the shades. In fact, a major difference between the scientist and the layman is in their ability to see minute differences between objects. Understanding small differences and how they are created is the most basic tool for developing in-depth knowledge – be it in science, philosophy or any other sphere of life. This ability grants the member of the intelligentsia control over anything with which he deals; in fact, it is this that has granted the intelligentsia its high status throughout the world.

As an individual, this type of intellectual is a positive, healthy human being: spiritually alert, he is a social and mental catalyst that leads society towards progress. The problem is, however, that this type of intellectual is gradually ceding his place to a different type of person: the "rotten intellectual".

The rotten intellectual is best defined as one who sees *only* shades of gray. This type of person may be far more intelligent than the "healthy" intellectual – but is rotten as a human being. While the healthy intellectual sees the shades of gray as interim stages between the black and the white, the rotten intellectual sees neither the black nor the white: he sees only the shades of gray. For him, there is no good or evil, but only a large variety of phenomena and things that are neither good nor bad. He claims that there is neither truth nor lies, but only relative differences between things that differ from one another, not in essence, but only in quantity or level.

Scientifically speaking, there is nothing wrong with such a view; but spiritually, it is quite destructive. A person who sees contradictions only as differences in level has lost his spiritual focus and is wandering in an aimless universe. If the difference between truth and lies is a matter of quantity only, and not of essence, then the truth is no better than a lie. How odd, yet how very typical, it is that a certain group of people who are capable of discerning minute differences between objects, see no difference between darkness and light! The spiritual significance of such a stance is total chaos and aimless wandering in a meaningless existence. Psychologically speaking, then, the rotten intellectual is miserable, because he lives in an aimless, pointless universe, without reasons or meaning.

Rotten intellectualism is a danger to society and to the nation because it is entirely passive, and therefore likely to succumb to any power. German Nazism is a perfect instance of the growing power of the multitude vis-à-vis a totally helpless intelligentsia. The German intelligentsia did not identify with Nazism, but, typically of a rotten intelligentsia, it was passive and apathetic. The rotten intelligentsia ceases to distinguish between good and bad, and it therefore no longer cares who the ruler is; it does whatever the ruler wants it to do with the same kind of equanimity, regardless of whether this ruler is the finest human being or an insane murderer.

Another reason why the rotten intellectual is dangerous is that he is an inevitable outgrowth of the healthy intellectual, because he reaches conclusions that the healthy individual does not dare to voice. When the healthy intellectual goes down the intellectual path, he will almost certainly become rotten. And once he loses the grip on his soul he is sure to become prey to his lusts and succumb to every crude, coarse force. The spiritual downfall of the choicest segment of society is therefore bound to snowball and sweep the entire world to perdition.

Since the danger of the rotten intellectual is so great, the importance of the remedy to his condition is just as great. Restoring the spiritual health and life of the rotten intellectuals will benefit not only this small group of individuals, but will bring about a major transformation in human society and the recovery of the positive forces behind progress.

The root of the malady of the rotten intellectual is the complete absence of absolute values. This is what makes it impossible for him to decide what course to take, and this is why he ends up wasting his spiritual powers on barren analyses of psychological or intellectual issues. The sole remedy, then, would be to decide on a goal that will guide his mental faculties and grant meaning to everything.

However, intellectual goals and values cannot possibly fill the vacuum in the intellectual's mind and soul, because incessant intellectual probing tends to demolish whatever intellectual structure has been set up. There is a need for values whose origin is above and beyond the intellect – values that the mind can neither touch nor demolish. In other words: the only remedy for the rotten intellectual is religion.

The major problem is that the intellectual believes – and justly so – that the new set of values will penetrate his soul only if he puts aside some of his intellectual hypotheses; but for him, to put his intellect aside, even partially, is tantamount to ceding intellectuality altogether. In other words: the intellectual will attain inner peace only if he completely loses his identity. This is equal to suicide.

The rotten intellectual can be healed only if he weaves into his purely intellectual structure some fundamental values whose origin is in a source that transcends the mind. Even the most rotten of intellectuals still has enough mental power to embrace the fundamental values of religion because, unlike the multitude, the rotten intellectual does not despise the basic tenets of faith; rather, his position is, "I wish I could believe". This is why, if only he would want, the intellectual is more capable than anyone else to embrace these tenets of faith. For such a highly sensitive person it can be really easy to shift from total indifference to sweeping enthusiasm (which the intellectual often experiences as an abyss). While for the man in the street the religious ideas may seem strange and far-fetched, the intellectual may find out that they are very close to his mind.

All that the rotten intellectual needs, then, is the courage to take one audacious step: from "I wish I could believe" to "I believe". Rather than self-deception, this is the revelation of the hidden truths of the soul. A person who says "I wish I could believe" is, in fact, a believer; he has already overcome all the obstacles on his path towards faith. The remaining obstacles are just those old, seemingly immutable customs of religious people.

Once the intellectual has accepted this main principle, he should harness all of his mental powers in order to build a perfect intellectual structure for his religiosity. His ability to discern minute differences will make it possible for him to reach very high levels of religiosity and will open for him vistas that no one else can access. The healed rotten intellectual will become a very positive role model: once the source of all the evil within him is uprooted, all his negative traits disappear. The healing of the individual intellectual and the entire intelligentsia opens new gates not only for them, but also for the society they live in, for their people and for the entire world.

Heroism

I would like to start with what I started out last year: with the feeling that here in Israel, at this time and in this place, we are on a sort of island, isolated from the rest of the world. All around us the world is storming, boiling, full of trouble, while here we are in a kind of a bubble. On the one hand, it is quite pleasant to be in such a bubble; but on the other hand it is not only impossible, but also forbidden for people – and especially for us, as Jews – to reside, even temporarily, in such a world of calm and quiet. Even when one is in high and lofty worlds, one must remember that although the great ladder reaches the heaven, it is firmly grounded in the earth. And the earth is not always a comfortable place; for throughout the world the earth is now shaking, quivering and wet with blood.

This is why I chose to speak, this time, about a less abstract topic: heroism – to try and understand what heroism is.

The simple definition of heroism is the one we can find, for instance, in the story of Samson: heroism is to take apart the gates of the city of Gaza and carry them away; it is to grab a lion and tear it in two; to make a building topple and thus kill three thousand people at once.

But there is also a different definition of heroism. In *Pirkei Avot* ("Ethics of Our Fathers", Chapter 4 *Mishnah* 1) it states: "Ben Zoma says ... who is a hero? He who controls his desire (subdues his evil nature), as it is written (Proverbs 16:32): 'He who rules his spirit is greater than he who conquers a city.'"

Ben Zoma was considered the greatest expounder of homilies, so much so that the *Mishnah* (*Berachot* Chapter 9 *Mishnah* 5) attests that, "When Ben Zoma died, there were no more expounders." The question is, what is the novelty in Ben Zoma's words? It seems that what he is saying is stated explicitly in a Scriptural verse! Is there need for the greatest of expounders just to rephrase a Biblical verse?

But what at first glance seems self-evident is, in fact, not that simple at all. For the verse is actually not telling us anything about the essence of the hero. It also does not say that he who is slow to anger, or he who rules his spirit, is a hero; it only says that one who is slow to anger and rules his spirit is a better person, in moral and human terms, than one who can "rend a lion as one would rend a kid" (Judges 14:6).

Ben Zoma's homily is based, then, on a more inner, fundamental understanding. In presenting the person who is slow to anger and the hero, the one who rules his spirit and the conqueror of cities, as analogous to each other, the verse is actually saying that they belong in the same category. For it is impossible to compare two things that have nothing in common; it is impossible to say, for instance, that an elephant is bigger, or smaller, than a mathematical equation, because they are not things of the same kind. Every comparison is based on the assumption that the things compared belong to the same set, that they are on one and the same scale, and that therefore they can be juxtaposed with each other, and one can try to determine what is greater than what.

Ben Zoma's innovation, then, is that he reads the verse and draws a conclusion from it. He sees the verse as telling us that there are different kinds of heroism: there is the heroism of him who rules his spirit and subdues his evil nature (controls his desires), and the heroism of the hero who can "devour the arm and the crown of the head" (Deuteronomy 32:20). And from the comparison of the two it emerges that one is preferable to the other.

Here, in Israel, we have become acquainted mainly with heroism of the first kind; we have here many lists of warriors who endangered their lives and displayed heroism, bravery and resourcefulness in actual wars. But it is the second kind of heroism that I would like to speak about: a more private and personal heroism – the heroism of the victories within one's own soul. It is a different kind of heroism, not only because it is mostly spiritual, but also because it reveals a different aspect of what it means to be a hero.

We can learn something about this kind of heroism from the second verse of the *Shema* which is, perhaps, the second most significant verse in the entire Torah. This verse (Deuteronomy 6:5) says: "And you shall love the Lord your G-d with all your heart, and with all your soul, and with all your might." The classic commentary of our Sages to this verse is found in the *Mishnah* (*Berachot*

Chapter 9, *Mishnah* 5): "With all your heart – with both your impulses (= the good inclination and the evil inclination); with all your soul – even if He takes away your soul; and with all your might – with all your wealth." According to this interpretation, what seems at first glance to be an ascending order is not an ascending order at all: heart, soul, and … money! Although our Sages state elsewhere (tractate *Hullin* 91a) that, "the righteous ones are fond of their wealth more than of their own bodies", in most cases, when people are faced with the choice of "your life or your money", they (even the most righteous among them) tend to give their money.

And even if we interpret "with all your might" differently, as meaning "more and more and more", giving beyond measure, the question still remains: in what way does "with all your might" create an ascending order within that verse?

I am struggling with this question, not as a commentator, but as one who recites the Shema; and here is the solution I have found: "with all your might" does not mean that a person is commanded, "give your money now!" To negate wealth not as a one-time act, but as an ongoing, constant way of being, means that a person is sentenced – be it by himself or by others – to a life of hardships. In this sense, "with all your might" is not to take a person's life, but to take a person's soul out, so to speak – little by little, day by day, year by year, through poverty, affliction and suffering.

The heroism that expresses itself in outbursts of occasional heroic deeds, such as that of the person who jumps into the fire, is momentary, while the heroism of "with all your might" is a kind of heroism that continues day after day, year after year, in distress, poverty and need, in a state of hopelessness. Incidentally, throughout Jewish history, this heroism of "with all your might" played a much more significant role than that of dying for the sanctification of G-d's Name, of giving one's soul in the literal, immediate sense. Whoever defined himself as a Jew, only seldom had to pay for it with his life. However, the practical significance of defining oneself as a Jew was that a person sentenced himself to live on the fringes of society, to a life in which he must be at least twice as good as the other guy so as to have a slight chance to reach a similar status; a life in which one had to work so much harder and receive so much less; and, in general, a life of poverty and need.

The devotion and self-sacrifice of "with all your might", then, is a continuous kind of devotion, day by day, year by year, without seeing an end to it and without expecting a better and brighter tomorrow.

This worldview involves a heavy price, not only economically but also in terms of how one conceives of life and experiences it. My wife once said to me that in any part where there are Israelis and others, she can immediately tell who the Americans and Europeans are: they laugh. Indeed, in a party in which Israelis participate, it is very rare to find people just standing around and laughing together. It is not because people here are always sad, but because life here is always enveloped in a feeling of dread, pressure, fear and heaviness. Within all this one can, and must, live, and there may even be moments of merriment; but the overall picture is one of "bearing the yoke and keeping silent" (see Lamentations 3:27-28).

It seems, however, that this is going to change; for not only in Israel, but also throughout the world, people are now learning about the need for this other kind of heroism. The world that has seen, and sometimes even admired, the heroism of violence, must now learn the kind of heroism that has nothing to do with swords, cannons and bombs. It is the heroism of the person who lives in an extended state of terror, knowing that wherever he goes it may be his last journey, and that danger lurks everywhere – and still does not break down, and rules his spirit, and does not get easily upset, and keeps going. This heroism is the ability to be in a state of distress and under pressure, yet still live and build, and continue fighting this war in which there are no immediate prospects of victory, and live a life of quiet heroism, of ongoing self-sacrifice. This kind of heroism lacks the grandeur that is the share of the conqueror of cities; for conquerors of cities are honoured with triumphal processions; but nobody makes such celebrations in honour of a person who rules his spirit, especially since tomorrow, and the day after, he will have to do this again and again.

The contemporary hero, then, is not the one described in *Pirkei Avot* (5:20) as "heroic as a lion". In fact, the lion is a very lazy animal that does absolutely nothing most of the time, but it has the ability to reach a very high speed within less then a second, and harness all of its tremendous force in order to do something spectacular. The "heroic as a lion" kind of hero has great powers that are neither constant nor stable, but that are revealed all at once, in one extreme outburst. But it is the contemporary hero, the one whose heroism is not discernible, who is the greater hero. It may be the man who wakes up in the morning and opens his grocery store, even though there was a terrorist attack there the day before; it is the person who does not flee into the realm of oblivion, or to a different place, but rather continues doing all the things that must be done. It is that person who walks with his backpack on his shoulder, and continues walking even when he gets hit; the person whose buildings are destroyed, yet he rebuilds them; whose plants are uprooted, yet he re-plants them; whose descendants are killed, yet he gives birth to new ones.

Thus, we have the level of loving G-d "with all your heart"; beyond that, we have "with all your soul", which is the one-time sacrifice; and above and beyond that is "with all your might", which is the determination to continue indefinitely, although the future is unclear and there is no promise as to when all of this is going to end. This heroism is not fit for movies or theatre shows, but it is a kind of heroism that is suitable not only for great, prominent people, but also for the simple and the small. It is the heroism of "when I fall, I shall arise" (Micah 7:8), of "a just man falls seven times, and rises up again" (Proverbs 24:16).

The just man falls seven times because he is no angel: he is merely a just man. Angels fall only once, if ever; a just man falls and falls and falls again, and there is no guarantee that after the seventh fall there will come an end to the trials and the tribulations and the obstacles. He may even fall seventy-seven times, but always "rises up again". And this is precisely the kind of heroism we need now: the heroism to continue in a situation where no promises are made, in which I know nothing about what is going to happen. It is the heroism of falling and rising up again, and again, and again; the heroism of "in quietness and in confidence shall be your strength" (Isaiah 30:15). I hope that we shall have the strength for this kind of heroism as well, so that we can be "as the sun when he goes forth it its might" (Judges 5:31) – able to keep waking with unceasing perseverance, while constantly emitting light and warmth.

Appendix 1

Publications of Rabbi Adin Even Israel Steinsaltz

In addition to the books listed below, Rabbi Steinsaltz has published over 600 articles, between the years 1956 and the present, on a great variety of topics, including: Bible and Talmud studies, Jewish mysticism, science, Torah and science, art literature, zoology, sociology, education, psychology, politics, philosophy, social behaviours, science fiction and many others. Many of his books and articles have been translated into other languages, including: English, Russian, French, Spanish, German, Portuguese, Dutch, Swedish, Italian, Georgian, Chinese and Japanese.

Books for the General Public

The Babylonian Talmud, vocalised, punctuated, translated and with commentary
> Hebrew (Milta Books, Jerusalem)
> 43 volumes to date, 45 volumes (the entire Talmud) projected
> Small format edition: 27 volumes to date

The Vilna-Steinsaltz Edition of the Talmud: The traditional Vilna Talmud pages on one side of the page, and on the other, all the special features of the Steinsaltz Talmud
> 35 volumes to date

The Talmud – The Steinsaltz Edition
> English (Random House, NY, 1989–2000); 21 volumes
> Bava Metz'ia Vol. I-VI
> Ketubot Vol. I-VI
> Ta'anit Vol. I-II
> Sanhedrin Vol. I-VII

The Talmud – the Steinsaltz Edition
French (Israel Institute for Talmudic Publications and Biblieurope, Paris, 2009)
21 volumes to date
Brachot Vol. I-IV
Bava Metzi'a Vol. I-V
Ketubot Vol. I-II (half the tractate)
Ta'anit
Sanhedrin Vol. I-II (half the tractate)
Sukkah I-II
Sota I-II
Gittin
Pesachim

The Talmud – the Steinsaltz Edition
Russian (Russian Academy of Sciences, Moscow)
Bava Metzi'a Vol. I
Ta'anit

The Talmud – the Steinsaltz Edition
Spanish
Brachot I, II (not published yet)

The Jerusalem Talmud, vocalised, punctuated, translated and with commentary
Hebrew (Milta Books, Jerusalem)
One volume to date: Tractate Pe'ah (available also in small format)

The Talmud – The Steinsaltz Edition – A Reference Guide
English (Random House, NY) (hard-and soft-cover editions) 1989
French (Ramsay, Paris) 1994
Hebrew (Keter Publications, Jerusalem) 1984
Russian (Russian Academy of Sciences, Moscow) 1993
Spanish (in preparation)

The Essential Talmud
English (Basic Books, NY, 1976, reprinted by Jason Aronson, NJ) 1992
French (Albin Michel, Paris) 1987
German (Morascha, Switzerland) 1995
Hebrew (Domino Books, Jerusalem) 1977
Italian (La Giuntina, Florence, in preparation)

Portuguese (A. Koogan, Rio de Janeiro) 1989
Russian (Institute for Jewish Studies in the CIS) 1993
Spanish (Ediciones Aurora, Buenos Aires, Argentina) 1995
Swedish (Bokfrlaget Nya Doxa, Stockholm) 1996
Italian (La Giuntina, Florence) 2000

Teshuva: Practical Advice for the Newly Observant
English (Macmillan – The Free Press) 1987
French (Albin Michel, Paris)
Hebrew (Domino Press, Jerusalem) 1982, new edition (Israel Institute for Talmudic Publications) 2005
Portuguese (Ma'ayanot, Rio de Janeiro) 1994

Tales of Rabbi Nachman of Bratslav (formerly **Beggars and Prayers**)
Hebrew (Dvir, Tel Aviv) 1981
English (Basic Books, 1979, Jason Aronson, NJ) 1993
French ("Le Mantre du Prire", Albin Michel, Paris)
Russian (Institute for Jewish Studies in the CIS) 1998

The Thirteen Petalled Rose: A Discourse in the Essence of Jewish Existence and Belief
English (Basic Books, 1980, Jason Aronson, NY) 1992
French (Albin Michel, Paris) 1989
Hebrew (Milta Books, Jerusalem) 1998
Portuguese (Ma'ayanot, Rio de Janeiro) 1992
Russian (Institute for Jewish Studies in the CIS) 1985, 1989, 1990, 1993
Dutch (Uitgevrej Karnak, Amsterdam) 1983
German (in preparation)
Italian (La Giuntina, Florence) 2001

Biblical Images
Hebrew (Misrad Habitachon) – in two booklets. Men of the Bible and Women of the Bible, 1984
English (Basic Books), Expanded new version (Jason Aronson, NJ) 1994
German (Morascha, Switzerland) 1996
Japanese (Tuttle Mori) 1984
French (Menorah, Paris) 1990
Russian (Institute for Jewish Studies in the CSI) 1995

Talmudic Images
Hebrew (Misrad Habitachon, Tel Aviv) 1987
German (Morascha, Switzerland) 1996
Russian (Institute for Jewish Studies in the CSI) 1996
English (Jason Aronson, NJ) 1998

The Sociology of Ignorance; co-author: Amos Funkenstein
Hebrew (Misrad Habitachon, Tel Aviv) 1988
Russian (Institute for Jewish Studies in the CSI) 1997

The Passover Haggadah
Hebrew (Carta, Jerusalem) 1979, New, improved edition: 1998
English (Carta, Jerusalem) 1983, new edition – 2002
French (Bibliophane, Paris) 2003

Commentary on the Tanya
Hebrew (Milta Books, Jerusalem) 1991 – Present
Vol. I – Chapters 1-12
Vol. II – Chapters 13-26
Vol. III – Chapters 17-37
Vol. IV – Chapters 38-44
Vol. V – Chapters 45-53
Vol. VI – Iggeret Hateshuvah
Vol. VII – Shaar Hayechut V'Haemunah
Vols. VIII-X – Iggeret Hakodesh (in preparation)
French (in preparation)

Opening the Tanya – Discovering the Moral and Mystical Teachings of a Classic Work of Kabbalah
Hebrew text edited by Meir Hanegbi and translated by Yaakov Tauber
English (Jossey-Bass, CA) 2003

Learning from the Tanya – Volume Two in the Definitive Commentary on the Morl and Mystical Teachings of a Classic Work of Kabbalah
Hebrew text edited by Meir Hanegbi, English text edited by Edward Levine, and translated by Edward Levine (Glossary), Tuvia Natkin and Yaakov David Shulman
English (Jossey-Bass, CA) 2005

Understanding the Tanya – Volume Three in the Definitive Commentary on the Moral and Mystical Teachings of a Classic Work of Kabbalah by the World's Foremost Authority
> Hebrew text edited by Meir Hanegbi and translated by Yaakov David Shulman
> English (Jossey-Bass, CA) 2007

The Long Shorter Way: Discourses on Chasidic Thought (on the Tanya)
> Edited and translated by Yehuda Hanegbi
> English (Jason Aronson, NJ) 1988

The Sustaining Utterance – Discourses on Chasidic Thought (on the second part of the Tanya)
> Edited and translated by Yehuda Hanegbi
> English (Jason Aronson, NJ) 1989
> Russian (Institute for Jewish Studies in the CSI) 1996

The Strife of the Spirit: A Collection of Essays
> English (Jason Aronson, NJ) 1988
> Portuguese (in preparation)

In the Beginning – Discourses on Chasidic Thought
> Edited and translated by Yehuda Hanegbi
> English (Jason Aronson, NJ) 1992

Le Chandelier d'Or
> Edited and translated by Rabbi Josy Eisenberg
> French (Martte, Paris) 1993
> English (**The Lamp of God**, Jason Aronson, NJ) 2000
> Hebrew (in preparation)

La Femme Vaillante (The Woman of Valor)
On Proverbs Chapter 31, with drawings by Yitzhak Tordjman
> French (Martte, Paris) 1993
> English (Martte, Paris) 1994
> Hebrew (Milta-Zofia) 2003

The Prayer and The Book (2 volumes)
> Hebrew (Miskal Books, Tel Aviv) 1994
> English (**Guide to Jewish Prayer**, 1 volume, Schocken Books, 2000)

Biblical Commentary in Medieval Responsae
   Hebrew (Keter Publications, Jerusalem) 1978

On Being Free (Collection of Essays)
   English (Jason Aronson, NJ) 1995

Judaism (*Yahadut*)
   Hebrew (The Israel Government School of Tourism) 1966/1982

Initials and Abbreviations in Chasidic and Kabalistic Literature
   Hebrew (Sifriyati, Tel Aviv) 1968 (out of print)

Midrash Haggadol on Leviticus By Rabbi David bar Amram Ha'Adani
   (From manuscripts, with introduction, textual variants and comments)
   Hebrew (Mossad HaRav Kook, Jerusalem) 1976

The Rebbe, 30 Years of Presidency; Co-Editor with Rabbi Hanoch
Glitzenstein
   Hebrew (Kfar Habad) 1980

Pete HaDorot (About the Lubavitcher Rebbe; Co-Editor)
   Hebrew (Kfar Habad) 1983

Les 5 Megillot, with illustrations by Yitzhak Tordjman
   French and English (ERF, Paris) 1990)

Pirkei Avot, Ethics of the Fathers.
   With commentary, Chinese translation
   Chinese (The Chinese Academy of Social Sciences, Beijing) 1996

Sefer HaKen (Editor), Articles about Rabbi Scheur Zalman of Lyadi, to
   mark 150 years since his demise.
   Hebrew (Kiryat Sefer Publications, Israel) 1969 (out of print)

Simple Words
   English (Simon & Schuster) 1999
   French (Bibliophane, Daniel Radford) 2004
   Italian (UTET Libreria) 2007

Reshafim Periodical
Hebrew, 1956-1963 (out of print)

The Candle of God, edited and translated by Yehuda Hanegbi
English (Jason Aaronson, N.J.) 1999

Anthology of Aggada
Russian (Institute for Jewish Studies in the CIS) 2001
Russian (Institute for Jewish Studies in the CIS) 2004

Laisse mon Peuple savoir, anthology of articles and speeches, translated into
French.
French (Bibliophane, Daniel Radford) 2002

A Dear Son to Me (collection of speeches and articles)
Hebrew and English editions (Israel Institute for Talmudic Publications)
2002

The Miracle of the Seventh Day
English (Jossey-Bass) 2003

We Jews: Who Are We and What Should We do
English (Jossey-Bass) 2005

Tehillim
Hebrew (Institute for Talmudic Publications)2005

Appendix 2

Notes on Paintings by Victor Majzner

1: Me

(acrylic on canvas 76 x 56 cm) 2008. [front cover, Ageing]

On an all-consuming/surrounding sea, the monolithic word "ME" is contained within a coat-like outline of a garment. The garment acts as a cage, a container for the ME. Where the garment is fragile, a reference to one's soul, the monolithic ME seems strong and impregnable, perhaps like our ego? Yet on further observation, the ME is made up of the same material as the sea – water and its apparent strength is just that, an appearance, an illusion. In fact the ME, just like the garment, is vulnerable to its "source". A human life, although very precious and important to each of us, like the ME of the painting, is in fact simply a transient and temporary illusion. To stress the vulnerability of a human being, an image of Ron floating in an endless sea is at the same time part of the word ME and partly disguised by the coat.

2: (G-d's) Open hand

(watercolour 57 x 51 cm) 2008. [Belief and Bureaucracy]

Over a condensed landscape of Israel, from the Negev (bottom of picture) to the Galil (top of picture), is painted an outline of an open hand, symbolising G-d's gift of the world to us (with an open hand He gifted). "You open your hand and satisfy the desire of every living thing." Psalms 145:16. The (life) lines within the hand are the G-dly emanations, the ten *Sephirot* with which He creates. "It is a tree of life for those who grasp it and its supporters are praiseworthy ... its ways are ways of pleasantness and its paths are peace." Proverbs 3:17, 18. Each *Sephira* is painted according to the colour code of its function as explained by Isaac Luria (Arizal), the 16th century (1534–72) mystic and Kabbalist from Sefad.

3: Bereishit – In The Beginning

(watercolour 57 x 51 cm) 2008. [Continuity]

Over a field of cosmic chaos, Creation is taking place. Light is being separated from darkness, land formations, plants, animals and birds are coming into being. As G-d created the world through speech, through utterances in Hebrew, each letter of the Hebrew alphabet wants to be the first letter to begin Creation. As these letters juggle for prime position, G-d chooses the letter *Beit* (as this letter was the only one not wanting a prime position) to be the first letter of Creation and of the Torah. *Beit*, being the second letter of the Hebrew alphabet, implies a duality, a separation. Each letter of the word *Bereishit* (in the beginning) is falling into place to form the word, however the letter *Beit* (being first) is given prominence – just like in the Torah. Each letter contains different aspects of Creation (the world) as it tumbles into place (order out of chaos).

4: Fences

(acrylic on canvas 56 x 81.5 cm) 2008. [Behaviour]

Psalms: 111:10: "The beginning of wisdom is the fear of G-d ..." This quote in Hebrew is painted as a hedge/fence within a Pilbara (northwest Australia) landscape. Ron's image is surrounded by this hedge/fence. We all build different fences around ourselves, but this fence is different. The idea is that wherever one finds oneself (in the world) it is good to remember this particular fence as it is the Jewish way towards fulfilment. The first letter of each word of this hedge/fence is slightly lighter than the others, highlighting the fact that the Gematria of these letters is 228 = the same number as *Etz Chaim* – Tree of Life. Such numerical correlations are very important. In this case, the mystical significance of this fence in revealed.

5: The hidden Aleph = letter A of Hebrew alphabet

(watercolour 57 x 51 cm) 2008. [Water, Life and Numbers]

Over Ron's front-yard water garden of fish is painted the diagram of the ten *Sephirot* as a system of refracting light (the emotions) according to Rabbi Ginsberg. Each *Sephira* is painted according to the colour scheme of its function. This diagram is painted as if one is looking through it to Creation. Framing the complete painting is an outline of the Hebrew letter *aleph* (A, first letter of the Hebrew alphabet). At the Creation of the world, the *aleph* was hidden. Yet its potency is such that it permeates everything. The pond, water and fish are symbols of abundant creation.

The letter *aleph* starts out black (symbolising *yetzer ha-ra*), gradually turning white (*yetzer ha-tov*) then gold (G-dly – beyond good or evil) and eventually blue, symbolising tranquillity, the sky, peace = the complete symbolic (colour) process, signifying the meaning of life.

6: The (hidden) Menorah of the Torah (Torah code)
(watercolour 57 x 51 cm) 2009. [Water, Life and Numbers]

The Torah is often referred to symbolically as a garden (of delight, of knowledge, of law, of life, etc.). But mostly it is referred to as the *orchard – PARDES* – the acronym for *Pshat, Remez, Drash* and *Sod*, the four levels of Torah interpretation. Apart from the various levels of interpretation and the 70 "faces" that it carries within itself, there are other codes that are gradually being revealed. One of these is the symmetry of the letters that spell out T'O'R'H (Torah) in Hebrew. In four of the books of the Torah, counting from the first *Tav*, in *Bereishit* and *Shemot* the letters of the word T'O'R'H appear every 50 (49 spaces = 7 x 7 plus the 1 makes 50) letters, and in *Bamidbar* and *Devarim* they appear backwards: H'R'O'T. In *Vayikra* (the third, or middle book) the letters of Y'K'V'K (G-d's Holy name) appear at intervals of 7 (every 8th letter i.e. 7 spaces plus the 1) letters. These "secret" hidden codes point to the Gematria (mystical numerology within the Hebrew alphabet) and contain a deep level of knowledge and inspiration within the Torah. The symmetry of the letters in the words T'O'R'H and Y'K'V'K' within the five books make up a kind of mystical (light) menorah.

7: Tishrei – Nisan – the idea of the two first months
(watercolour, each 57 x 51 cm) 2009. [Happiness]

Nisan is commanded in the Torah to be the first month for the Jewish people. It is the first month of freedom (from Egypt). It has a spiritual significance as G-d delivered us into freedom. It is also associated with spring as the word Nisan in Hebrew means bud. Therefore *Nisan* is also the spring (awakening) of the Jewish nation. The painting is constructed through numerous symbols; the background is of flowers = spring (new buds), the menorah from which emanates light in the painting as well as having its seven lights lit is the symbol of Judaism. The light of the painting comes from the bottom part of the menorah. The original menorah was carved out of one piece of gold by Betzalel on Moses' instructions as directed by G-d. The central column (stem – from the bottom up) = one; it represents G-d's oneness (singularity and infiniteness of G-d). The cups (branches – from the top down) =

seven, representing G-d's "physicality" in Creation. As the chains of slavery and oppression break, the light of freedom, both physical and spiritual (from Egypt = *Mitzraim* = restricted place) illuminates our future. The flames from the menorah shine over a matza (unleavened bread = symbol of Passover). All of these point to the spiritual significance of *Nisan*.

Tishrei: although it is the first month of the Jewish year, it is referred to in the Torah as the seventh month. It is the first month because it is associated with the Creation of Man. Adam was created in *Tishrei.* It therefore has a physical association = from dust/earth (resulting in clay when mixed with water – both suggested in the painting) G-d created Man. In a desert-like landscape, although vegetation has already been created (right of painting), Adam is being created. The bottom part of his figure is like the land (mud), brown and heavy. As the "breath" of G-d is being "blown" into Adam's nostrils (Adam's living soul), he begins to take on an alive (pink) colour and demeanour. Genesis 1:27: "So G-d created Man in His image, in the image of G-d He created him; male and female He created them". The reference to the creation of both genders is suggested in the painting by the template of the female back to back with the figure of Adam, as a *Midrash* suggests. The image of G-d is represented by the range of hands (sky-like images) in the process of Creation (pointing), out of which droplets of water (symbols of fertility) are coming down to earth. This painting is about the physical being created by the metaphysical = the significance of *Tishrei.*

8: Unification of G-d's Name

(watercolour 57 x 51 cm) 2009. [The Confrontation of the Yetzer Ha-ra]

By performing the *mitzvah* of the *lulav* (the four species during *Succoth*) one is unifying G-d's Holy Name as each species carries a symbolic connection to the Tetragrammaton: (Citrus) *Etrog* = *Yud*; (Date Palm) *Lulav* = *Hey*; (Mytrle) *Haddasim* = *Vav*; (Willow) *Aravot* = *Hey*. In the days of the Temple, huge willow branches were brought and leaned against the altar during *Succoth*. The *shofar* was blown and the *kohanim* (priests) would walk around the altar and recite the prayer *hosha na* – "Please bring salvation". Then the people would come in and wave the *aravot* (willows). On *Hoshanah Rabbah* we perform the ritual of encircling the *Bima* with the four species seven times and waving the willows as we do the four species (in commemoration of the Temple service) followed by the thrashing of willow branches five times on the floor or against a chair, to dislodge some of the leaves. As the *Machzor* explains: "The five-time beating of the *aravah* (willow) branches symbolises the breaking of the five vessels which restrain the full force of holiness. The beating of the branches thus causes a 'sweetening' of the strict powers." To paraphrase this: by beating the five willows the intention is to "sweeten" G-d's judgments that are made on *Rosh Hashanah – Yom Kippur* period that "come down" to the "here and now" physical dimension through the day of *Hoshanah Rabbah*.

Over a background of water (symbolic reference to the depth of Torah) the letters of the Tetragrammaton are painted in the art form of the species in their corresponding orders. They are unified towards the central point just as on *Succoth* we hold the four species together. The "thrashing" of the five branches of the willow are symbolised by the Hebrew letters within the image of the hand overlapping the Tetragrammaton. Just as *Succoth* is the festival in *Tishrei* which immediately follows the spiritual heights of *Yom Kippur* (ascended during the previous month of Elul to *Rosh Hashanah* and the Ten Days of Repentance), *Succoth* bridges this spiritual high point as it brings us towards the new month of *Cheshvan* in the cycle of the year.

These letters are a symbolic reference to the five *Megillot* (five scrolls) of the *Tanach*: Each of these is symbolically referred to as:

Shir Hashirim (Song of Songs) – *Tzedek* = Righteousness,
Ruth – *Chesed* = Kindness,
Eichah (Lamentations) – *Mishpat* = Judgement,
Kohelet (Ecclesiastes) – *Emunah* = Belief,
Esther – *Rachamim* = Mercy.

The first Hebrew letter of the *Megillah* (scroll) and the first letter of its symbolic connotation are combined within the image of each "finger" of G-d's hand: *shin/tzaddek, reish/chet, aleph/mem, koof/aleph, aleph/reish*. This combination of the ten letters are a pointer to the ten other utterances of G-d = Creation and the Ten Commandments. In a visually symbolic manner this painting represents the totality of the Torah.

9: Yetzer Ha-Tov versus Yetzer Ha-Ra = the constant battle

(watercolour, each frame 29 x 25.5 cm) 2009. [The Confrontation of the Yetzer Ha-ra]

Yetzer ha-ra = external, evil force; *yetzer ha-tov* = G-dliness in each of us. Imagine that these two opposing forces play within the "consciousness" of the individual. Maybe it is the soul of the person influencing their conscience and their free choices?

Painted like a strip/narrative in eight frames:

Frame 1: Within a person, the place of **yetzer ha-ra** is dark, like a dark and frightening tunnel or a pit: emptiness, nothingness and a sense of foreboding. However, as the world was created by **Elokim** through judgment/righteousness, so even within the darkest and most empty habitat of **yetzer ha-ra** there remains a tiny dot of light, of hope, of redemption – of **yetzer ha-tov**.

Frame 2: As soon as the light (goodness) of **yetzer ha-tov** confronts **yetzer ha-ra**, the latter appears to begin to withdraw and the light of **yetzer ha-tov** illuminates the darkness. It corners and surrounds **yetzer ha-ra**, at which point yetzer ha-ra appears to sprout colours, to disguise itself.

Frame 3: Although **yetzer ha-ra** is innately black (dark/evil) and preys upon one's vulnerability, it disguises itself as being beautiful, sensual, attractive and desirous. It beguiles with a mirage of colours as it attempts to allure and mislead.

Frame 4: **Yetzer ha-ra**, disguised in a veil of beauty and colour, goes through a seductive "dance-like" series of movements or self-preservation manoeuvres in order to distract and hypnotise **yetzer ha-tov** into a false sense of security, as its goal is to dominate by whatever means is available. Genesis 2:6: "And the woman (Eve) perceived that the tree was good for eating and that it was a delight to the eyes ..." However, this colourful charade proves to be only a thin veneer of a disguise, as it has been identified and recognised for what it truly is.

Frame 5: As soon as this disguise is torn open/exposed, out pours the reality of ugliness and repugnance of **yetzer ha-ra**. Its destructive work is exposed. The forces of **yetzer ha-tov** need to have been able to overcome the forces of **yetzer ha-ra** to have approached it so closely and taken hold of it to tear off its disguise.

Frame 6: Its true nature exposed, the forces of **yetzer ha-ra** are gathering and multiplying in strength. A serpent-like (dark/repulsive) form of it is being revealed.

Frame 7: **Yetzer ha-ra** sees an open doorway radiating light (the essence of **yetzer ha-tov**). **Yetzer ha-ra** speeds towards the light, wanting to challenge and engage in yet another illusion that will continue its purpose.

Frame 8: **Yetzer ha-tov** expels **yetzer ha-ra** out of this gate. Inside this doorway (symbolically) lies our power from within our awareness to confront our **yetzer ha-**

ra and reveal its true ugliness. The way to deal with the forces of *yetzer ha-ra* is to use "the fence" of our inner strength, belief/spiritual comfort and shut this door to it, locking it out and excluding its destructive influence. In other words, to allow the G-dly presence (*yetzer ha-tov*) to rule. The Hebrew letter *Yud* dominates the painting, illuminated from the crown upon the letter. *Yud* is the first letter in the Tetragrammaton of G-d's name (*Yud Key Vav Key*) and stands for His presence – the ultimate *yetzer ha-tov*! It represents the potential in all of us. Thus the *yetzer ha-tov* prevails over the *yetzer ha-ra*.

10: Numbers

(acrylic on canvas 76 x 56.5 cm) 2008. [Science or Religion]

Numbers and plus signs i.e. 6 + 1 + 3 float on water/sea, like islands. Ron's image is sitting on one of them, looking into the distance. Each of us (at times) feels as if we are alone, isolated and living on an island, upon a slightly turbulent sea surrounding us. The aerial view allows the viewer to observe that each number and plus sign is actually a piece of a (living) hedge. The symbolism here is that there is a purpose to it all (life) but a bit out of our reach. We can only understand the island we live on (hang onto). Is this another fence? In this case, the numbers signify the 613 *mitzvot* (commandments) written in the Torah. The addition of 6 + 1 + 3 = 10 is a reference to the ten G-dly utterances at Mt Sinai – the Ten Commandments. Man (sitting on a worldly level) cannot see the complete significance of these *mitzvot*. Only G-d (and the viewer) can see the complete "picture".

11: Kedoshim

(Watercolour on paper 71.5 x 56 cm) [Introduction]

Leviticus 19:1 *"You must be Holy since I am G-d and I am Holy"*. This quote is depicted along the bottom of the painting. This *parsha* (weekly portion) *Kedoshim* is the centre of the Torah and the above quote is central to the Torah and to Judaism. The *parsha* seems to paraphrase the Ten Commandments, therefore I painted them as if on the two tablets, in their "original" (first) incarnation where the letters were written by G-d and suspended miraculously where one could see through and around them.

Over the top of these tablets is depicted the Kabbalistic "Tree of Life" (*Sefirot*), the G-dly attributes through which G-d functions. Each *Sefirah* is represented by a droplet of water, the symbol of Torah.

12: Hula Valley from Ramot Naftali

(Acrylic on canvas 137 x 152 cm) 2007. [Ageing]

Hula Valley is the breadbasket of Israel; one of the most fertile regions. I am painting the Valley from an elevated viewing area outside the Moshav Ramot Naftali. The depiction of myself in the act of painting reinforces the artifice of art.

13: Images of Tanya, Gate of Unity and Belief, Chapter 12

(Silk screen print on paper 67 x 47 cm) 2001. [Belief and Bureaucracy]

This is the final image of ten prints dealing with the idea of the Unity of G-d and Creation as elucidated by Rabbi Schneur Zalman of Liadi in his famous work *Tanya*.

G-d creates through the "garment" of Hebrew letters, G-d's mystical speech. Within the letters that make up the "garment" are contained all references to creation: land, vegetation, animals, birds and fish. The creation of Man is implied by the coat garment that seems to hover over a mystical seascape. The spiritual is embedded within the physical.

14: Painting Me Painting

(Acrylic on canvas 91.5 x 76 cm) 2007. [Continuity]

I depicted myself as I paint on location, this time in Israel. I am painting an imaginary Hebrew letter *Alef* which, together with the other Hebrew letters in the painting, spells out the word Adam as reference to the first biblical man. In this case these gigantic letters that dominate the scene are sprouting from the landscape like cultivated hedges or natural sculptures. Culture + nature + the act of painting.

15: Ki Teitzei

(Watercolour on paper 71.5 x 56 cm) 2008. [Behaviour]

This painting deals with the *parsha* of that name in the Torah (Deuteronomy 21.10-25.19). The image depicts what is considered to be the easiest *mitzvah* (commandment) in the whole Torah. *If one happens to come upon a bird's nest in the wild and desires to take the eggs or the chicks, one must first shoo away the mother bird* (Deuteronomy 22.6-7). The reward for doing this mitzvah is long life.

The image superimposed over the narrative is of *tzitzit* (a fringed garment) commanded to be worn.

16: A Planted Garden

(Acrylic on canvas 183 x 168 cm) 2007. [Water, Life and Numbers]

In this fictional garden or park, hidden among the trees are growing hedge-like Hebrew letters. The world continues to be created by the speech of G-d through the holy language of Hebrew.

17: Lights

(Acrylic on canvas 196 x 166 cm) 1994. [Happiness]

An outline of a naked male figure (the quintessential Adam) hovers erect yet vulnerable over an archetypal Australian landscape. Light bulbs (symbols of unrealised potential/ideas) surround him like an aura of light. They seem to provide the light in the painting. Instead of the sun, an open flower displaces it.

18. The Book is Everywhere

(Acrylic on canvas 122 x 122 cm) 1998. [Religion and Science]

In a mystical desert (perhaps the Negev in Israel) in a desolate landscape of stones is a gigantic open book carved out the stone like a monument. What kind of book is it? A book of laws? Of fiction? Of stone? This book is capable of being filled with "anything" and "everything". It is already filled with the land, with nature and culture even though it is only a transient mirage. However, the book is in the process of "conversing" with the land.

The male figure, dwarfed by the book, seems insignificant in this setting. We seek the spiritual but often end up with stones.

Victor Majzner © 2009

Ron Goldschlager is Managing Director of Hermal Mortim Group, a diversified investor and manager of businesses and property. He holds an honours degree in Chemical Engineering from Monash University and was Chairman of Leibler Yavneh College from 1990–93. Ron has a passion for helping to ensure a better future for the next generation and beyond. Philanthropy is a high priority, with a focus on sustainability and partnership. These days, Ron's primary motivation in business is to mentor his great team of very capable young people. Ron and his wife Dina share the same vision of family and community values; they have four children and ten grandchildren who all love both Australia and Israel.

Rabbi Adin Steinsaltz who lives in Jerusalem is internationally regarded as one of the leading scholars and rabbis of this century. His monumental project of translating and reinterpreting the classic Jewish text of the Oral Law, the Babylonian Talmud, has been acclaimed as the most important Judaic publication of the century.

Rabbi Steinsaltz has written over 60 books which have been translated into more than 15 languages and numerous articles on a great variety of topics. He has lectured at major universities and research institutions in the US and Europe. A profound spiritual leader, scholar and philosopher, he received Israel's highest honour, the Israel Prize, in 1988.

Victor Majzner is an artist who has held over 50 solo exhibitions in Australia and New Zealand, participated in many group exhibitions and has been awarded numerous prizes for his artwork.

Earth to Sky, the art of Victor Majzner by Leigh Astbury was a Macmillan publication (2002) about his art. His limited edition publications *The Australian Haggadah* (1993) and *Painting the Torah* (2008) are an original combination of Jewish Biblical texts with his artwork, and were inspired by his commitment to the development of a Jewish Art, relevant to a contemporary context.

Lightning Source UK Ltd.
Milton Keynes UK
UKHW031232200319
339513UK00005B/546/P